The Peace Corps

an annotated bibliography

The Peace Corps

an annotated bibliography

ROBERT B. MARKS RIDINGER

G.K.HALL &CO.

70 LINCOLN STREET, BOSTON, MASS.

HC
60.5
R53
1989

Library of Congress Cataloging-in-Publication Data

Ridinger, Robert B. Marks, 1951-
    The Peace Corps, 1961-1986.

    Includes index.
    1. Peace Corps (U.S.)--Bibliography. I. Title.
Z7164.P3R53 1989 [HC60.5] 016.3612'6'06073 88-32801
ISBN 0-8161-8912-9

This publication is printed on permanent/durable acid-free paper
MANUFACTURED IN THE UNITED STATES OF AMERICA

Contents

The Author

Robert Marks Ridinger, assistant professor in the University Libraries at Northern Illinois University, is a subject librarian for many fields of the social sciences, among them anthropology, sociology and foreign languages. He holds an M.A. in anthropology from Case Western Reserve University and co-authored Anthropological Fieldwork: An Annotated Bibliography (1988) and served on the editorial board of the Library-Anthropology Resources Group (LARG) publication Biographical Directory of Anthropologists Born Before 1920 (1988). Professor Ridinger has held an internship in the Geography and Map Division of the Library of Congress. From 1976 to 1980, he served as assistant Librarian at the National University of Lesotho as a member of the United States Peace Corps.

Preface

In 1961, so history records, President John F. Kennedy created an agency to provide mid-level technical assistance to developing nations in the persons of American volunteers. Twenty-five years after the famous "first Volunteers" of Peace Corps/Ghana I stepped down onto the soil of Accra and sang the Ghanaian national anthem in Twi, a huge literature had been brought into existence, both through the publications issued by the agency itself (including memoirs by returned Peace Corps Volunteers (PCVs) and coverage in the popular and scientific presses. While the sheer volume and variety of these materials prohibits the compilation of a comprehensive bibliography on the Peace Corps, researchers wishing to use the information require a representative sampling of the major genres to better orient their investigations. The present bibliography is intended to provide that overview for the period 1961 to 1986.

Materials within the bibliography have been arranged to cover the three phases of Peace Corps life: the creation and development of the agency and its programmatic emphases, individual country programs (including the treaties and agreements which created them) and the active roles for change and influence played by returned Peace Corps Volunteers (RPCVs) following their completions of service. Types of materials included are government documents, Peace Corps documents and publications, books, dissertations, research monographs, memoirs, periodical articles and videotapes. Commercial films such as the South African e Lollipop which have a PCV as a main character have been omitted.

In the course of any project, certain individuals contribute to the overall success of the work without realizing it. I wish here to express my gratitude to Professors Felix Eme Unaeze, Laura Schroyer, and Elaine Blowers of the University Libraries, Northern Illinois University for listening to progress reports with good humor, and Dr. Clark Neher, Department of Political Science, Northern Illinois University and RPCV/Thailand, for constructive criticism. Special thanks and kudos to Victoria Reich and Marian Francois of the Peace Corps Information Services Library, Washington, D.C. for aid in tracking down elusive Nigerian treaties and generous hospitality.

vii

Having answered a host nation request and had the privilege of serving as assistant librarian at an African university for three memorable years, this work is dedicated to the person who made that request, H.E. Ma'Lineo Nana Tau, University Librarian, National University of Lesotho.   <u>Kea leboha</u>.

Robert B. Marks Ridinger
Subject Librarian,
Sociology/Anthropology/
Geography
RPCV/Lesotho
Northern Illinois University
DeKalb, Illinois

August, 1988

History of Peace Corps

1   "Academy of Science Studies Peace Corps". AA1.13:2/8
    InterACTION, 2, n.8 (May 1974): 1-2.
        The Peace Corps Advisory Committee, a body established under
    a contract between the agency and the National Academy of Science,
    conducted a six-month investigation of the projected needs of
    developing nations for the next decade and made recommendations as
    to changes in Peace Corps policies. Membership and structural
    information on the committee is included.

2   ACTION. 1972 Annual Report. AA1.1:972. Washington, D.C.:
    ACTION, 1972.
        This is the first report of the newly-created agency
    intended by President Richard Nixon to bring all federally-
    connected programs of voluntary service under one unit of adminis-
    tration, while taking into account the autonomy and different
    needs of each. Within six months of the creation of ACTION,
    general cuts in Congressional funding threatened to force the
    cancellation of many Peace Corps programs and early termination
    for hundreds of volunteers. Strong support from returned volun-
    teers and the American public as a whole led to the restoration of
    funds by both Congress and the President. The first fifty-five
    pages of the report are devoted to the progress and changes which
    occurred in the Peace Corps between July, 1971 and June, 1972.
    Among them were the negotiations for the entry of volunteers into
    the Central African Republic, attainment of an equilibrium between
    generalists and technically skilled volunteers in the field, the
    consolidation of two regions of Corps service into the NANEAP
    (North African, the Near East, Asia and the Pacific) so as to
    create three approximately equal divisions of the field agency,
    African regional program improvement in the training of those
    personnel intended for Francophone Africa, a major readjustment
    due to the India-Pakistan war, and the designing of the parliament
    building of Western Samoa by a volunteer architect. Detailed
    country summaries of objectives, numbers of personnel and any
    distinctive problems regarding Corps work are provided for all
    host nations with volunteers currently resident.

3   ACTION. Annual Report 1973. AA1.1:973. Washington, D.C.
        This report covers the activities of Peace Corps during its
second year of incorporation under ACTION. With an increase to
7,354 volunteers (from a previous high of 6,984) and entry to six
additional host nations (Oman, Bahrein, Yemen, Gabon, the
Seychelles and the Gilbert and Ellice Islands). Corps development
continued to display energy and diversity. Over 85% of training
was conducted in-country. Emphasis on bi-national involvement was
reflected in growing numbers of host nationals placed on program
staffs, and nearly one quarter of all volunteers were engaged in
work in the agricultural sector. Regional coverage of Francophone
and Anglophone Africa, Southern Africa, the NANEAP countries
(North Africa, the Near East, Asia and the Pacific), Latin America
and the Caribbean completes the Corps section of this report.

4   ACTION. Annual Report 1974. AA1.1:974. Washington, D.C.:
     ACTION, 1974.
        The final sixteen pages of this annual report cover Peace
Corps history for the 1974 fiscal year. Placed under the heading
"international operations", fourteen pages cover a wide variety of
activities from earthquakes in Nicaragua and Peru to the
involvement of volunteers in mitigating the effects of the seven-
year drought in the Sahel through well construction and building
of fishponds. Regional coverage high-lights overall trends in
programming, with notable efforts being urban development and
public works in southern Africa, continuing emphasis on food
production in Latin America (with 31% of volunteers posted to
that region participating), education and public health in the
countries of the NANEAP region and the re-entry of Corps personnel
to the West African nation of Gabon following a five-year gap and
prior expulsion. A final section on the role played by Peace
Corps men and women in multinational aid efforts such as the
United Nations Volunteer Program complete the work.

5   ACTION. Annual Report, 1975. AA1.1:975. Washington, D.C.,
     ACTION, 1975.
        In this ACTION annual survey, Peace Corps history for the
period of the 1975 fiscal year is included in a nine page section
entitled "international Operations." The brevity of the section
does not admit of great detail in the information presented-
although other sections of the Report contain valuable data as
well. The Introduction by ACTION Director Michael Balzano notes
that this year saw the signing of an agreement with the government
of Rwanda to inaugurate a Corps program there, while in three
other countries--Peru, Iran and Ethiopia--programs were ended due
to the decisions of the host nations to utilize their own
personnel or due to political reasons of security and instability.
The general survey for the fourteenth year of Peace Corps is
presented according to the region of service, with general trends
given from member nations. A short section detailing the progress
and problems of the Peace Corps School Partnership program
completes the contents.

6   ACTION. 1977 Annual Report. AA1.1:977. Washington, D.C.:
     ACTION, 1977.
         In FY1977, Peace Corps training philosophy returned to the
     practice of skill training "generalist" volunteers for technical
     assignments. This change was part of a re-examination of Corps
     programming, in consultation with host governments, to assure that
     volunteers were being placed to meet the basic human needs of the
     poorest segments of the populations. As a result of this process,
     increased emphasis began to be placed upon assigning personnel to
     projects involving food supply, water supplies, health, housing
     and education. A new stress upon providing assistance to the
     women of the developing world was adopted. The section of text
     dealing with Corps in this report is arranged by region of
     service: Africa, Latin America, NANEAP, with brief summaries by
     country as to the number of volunteers in service, their posting
     and the plans for future placement.

7   ACTION. Annual Report, 1978. AA1.1:978. Washington, D.C.:
     ACTION, 1978.
         One of the most important developments in the history of the
     Peace Corps occurred on August 2, 1978, with the signing by Presi-
     dent Carter of an amendment to the Peach Corps Act recognizing the
     importance of women in development. Over 300,000 Americans wrote
     inquiring about service, and a general shift from specialized
     efforts towards the meeting of basic human needs--clean water,
     nutrition, health and food production--was continued. Coverage of
     the Peace Corps regions is highly detailed, with country-by-
     country data given on numbers of volunteers in service and the
     projects upon which they are engaged. Several bar charts are
     included presenting an illustration of the distribution of basic
     human needs and volunteer efforts by field as well as budget
     information. Photographs illustrating local program volunteers at
     work are included.

8   ACTION. Annual Report 1979. AA1.1:979. Washington, D.C.:
     ACTION, 1979.
         Peace Corps developments in 1979 are surveyed in this annual
     overview of ACTION. Following a brief examination of the ways in
     which orientations of programs have altered since the inception of
     Corps in the early 1960's, shifting from a teachers and
     generalists group to a specialists field, three developments which
     occurred in 1979 are presented as illustrating future trends of
     Corps work. These were the signing of an agreement between the
     Peace Corps, the United Nations High Commission on Refugees, and
     the U.N. Volunteer Programme, an attempt to increase the
     reciprocal aspects of Corps efforts through assisting host nations
     in creating their own versions of Corps services, and an emphasis
     on appropriate technology.
         Early in 1978, the Office of Programming and Training Coor-
     dination was created to provide an in-house source of information
     on technical matters and to adapt training and programming needs
     to host nation requests. Special projects underway in 1979
     through this office included the introduction of Centers for

Assessment and Training (CAST) as a method of preliminary
selection and beginning training, programs in alternative energy,
a focus on women in development, creation of language materials
for six new host nations and the design of workshops for Corps
field staff. The Information and Collection Exchange (ICE)
continued its function of collating volunteer experiences and
issuing that experience in the form of manuals available to all
host nations. With the new emphasis in the Peace Corps Act on
women in development, projects underway in Lesotho, Thailand, the
Philippines and El Salvador are profiled. Regional coverage is
provided for all host areas, with data presented by country.
Statistical tables on each region are also included.

9   ACTION. 1980 Annual Report. AA1.1:980. Washington, D.C.:
      ACTION, 1980.
          This annual report covers the first year in which the Peace
Corps functioned with a restored degree of autonomy within the
larger structure following legislation to that effect. Major
program developments in the period were the drafting of a core set
of training goals and materials intended to augment volunteer
effectiveness throughout the time of service, beginning plans to
use the twentieth anniversary of the Peace Corps in 1981 as an
occasion for both educating the public about the continued existence of Corps as well as the creation of an organization to
reinvolve veterans in development activities, and the creation of
new relationships with United Nations agencies permitting personnel to assist in refugee relief work and increased collaboration
with the Agency for International Development. Country highlights
are given for programs in Upper Volta, Sierra Leone, the Dominican
Republic, Costa Rica, Nepal, and the Philippines. Discussions of
changes in programming emphases and training center on health,
water and sanitation, energy, fisheries, agriculture and forestry.
A special section covers the involvement of Corps with the Women
in Development focus. Training changes emphasize the use of the
CAST (Center for Assessment and Training) method of selection and
advantages of utilizing data from the Information Collection and
Exchange (ICE) office of Corps in the training plans.

10   ACTION. 1981 Annual Report. AA1.1:981. Washington, D.C.:
      Actions, 1981.
          This report's coverage of the work and development of the
Peace Corps in 1981 is prefaced by an introduction written by
Loret Miller Ruppe, Corps Director, in which the departure of
personnel from Colombia, Ivory Cost, Brazil, South Korea and
Nicaragua is noted. Diversification of Corps programming
continued, with the multiplicity of assignments listed. Country
programs summarized are Kenya, Togo, Jamaica, Honduras, Morocco
and Thailand.

11   "ACTION Agency Nominee Survives Foes in Senate". Christian
      Science Monitor, (8 May 1981): 2.
         A news report on the confirmation by voice vote in the U.S.
      Senate of the nomination of Loret Ruppe and Thomas Pauken as heads
      of the Peace Corps and ACTION. Concern with possible use of
      volunteers as intelligence agents or the rise of that perception
      due to Pauken's appointment are voiced.

12   "ACTION Director Visits Peace Corps Volunteers". AA1.13:3/3.
      InterACTION, 3, n.3 (December 1974): 12.
         ACTION Director Michael Balzano undertook a series of on-
      site inspection trips to the host nations of Jamaica, Venezuela,
      Colombia, Korea, Malaysia, Iran and Thailand during 1974. Details
      of the trip are provided.

13   "ACTION's Fully Equipped Library Stand Ready to Serve
      Volunteers". AA1.13:1/8. InterACTION, 1, n.8 (May 1973): 3.
         An interview with Rita Warpeha, librarian of the head-
      quarters library of ACTION in Washington, detailing the resources-
      -such as technology handbooks, pamphlets and posters-- which are
      available upon requests from volunteers.

14   ADAMS, VELMA. The Peace Corps in Action. New York: Follett,
      1968.
         In the summer of 1962, Velma Adams sent a four-page
      questionnaire to 250 volunteers scattered through the twelve host
      nations of the time. The replies from those early volunteers, as
      well as extensive reporting based upon more than two years of
      travelling to host nations and interviewing staff, counterparts
      and host officials as well as volunteers form the core of this
      book. It provides an in-depth look at the first two years of the
      Peace Corps, complete with frank admissions of problems and ill-
      designed planning. Two appendixes discuss factors prospective
      applicants should consider and present sample questions from the
      Peace Corps Placement Test. This latter is especially important
      for comparing the shift in criteria over time.

15   ADHIKARY, POORNA KANTA. Instructional Effect on Question
      Asking Behavior of Prospective Peace Corps Science and
      Mathematics Volunteer Teachers. Ed.D. dissertation. Indiana
      University, 1972.
         This dissertation focuses on the issue of skill training for
      teachers and the degree to which it can be defined and improved.
      Beginning with the agreement that effective questioning is one of
      the most valuable verbal skills a teacher can possess, an examina-
      tion of an experiment done on a group of thirty volunteers in
      training at the University of California-Davis for service in
      Nepal is reviewed. The postings intended for these volunteers
      were as science and mathematics instructors in the Nepal school
      system, itself undergoing attempts at modernization at this time.
      The core of the study was to determine to what measurable extent a
      programmed text centered on question asking could improve
      trainees' skills in this area, as well as how modern techniques
      could be introduced to Nepali schools most effectively. Adhikary

began with four basic questions of study, figuring in as a
variable the limited facility the volunteers possessed in Nepali
at the time. The experiment began on the first day of a period of
peer teaching evaluation targeted for two weeks and lasted seven
days. Volunteers were divided into an experimental and a control
group. Instruction was provided to the experimental group while
the others received only the standard Peace Corps briefing for the
time. Results indicated a significant improvement in the variety
and types of written questions designed for use by the volunteers.
Question asking behavior is also seen as amenable to change
through use of question sessions used as part of language instruction in host country tongues and dialects. The results of this
experiment were viewed as applicable to all Peace Corps training
programs. Two appendixes contain a complete bibliography of cited
references and the full text (in both English and Nepali) of the
experimental text used for the Nepal group.

16   "Africa Conference Discusses Goals". AA1.13:2/3. InterACTION,
      2, n.3 (December 1973): 4.
         Peace Corps Directors from 21 African countries and staff
from the Washington headquarters offices met in Monrovia, Liberia
in September, 1973, for the Ninth Annual Conference of Peace Corps
Directors in Africa. Four specific recommendations emerged from
the meetings in the areas of bi-national co-operation, co-ordina-
tion of Peace Corps work with the U.N. Economic Commission for
Africa, maintenance of the Francophone training office in Dakar,
Senegal and formation of a task force to plan future African
programs.

17   "The Ag Sector--Support and Service". Peace Corps Times,
      (January/February 1986): 15-17
         A survey article of the support offered to volunteers
serving on agricultural projects through the Office of Training
and Program Support. Following interviews with two sector
specialists in OTAPS, details of inservice training and the
African Food Systems Initiative are presented.

18   "Age Is An Asset, Says Peace Corps, Now Seeking More Senior
      Volunteers". Aging, 204 (October 1971): 9.
         A brief news item covering the role that senior citizens can
and have played in Peace Corps service, and details of the methods
of recruitment. A specific booklet on the subject has been
produced by the agency.

19   "Age Still An Asset In the Peace Corps". AA1.13:4/12.
      InterACTION, 4, n.12 (16 September 1976): 9.
         The roles played by senior volunteers in various host
nations are explored. A common theme is the respect accorded the
elder person in many societies for their knowledge and experience,
in contrast to the dominant attitude in American culture. Host
countries used as an example are Honduras, Ghana and El Salvador.

20   "Agriculturalists Needed in PC". AA1.13:1/6. InterACTION, 1,
     n.6 (March 1973): 5.
         The need of the Peace Corps for volunteers willing to serve
     in agricultural programs, which comprise one-quarter of all
     assignments, is becoming more crucial. In 47 nations, their work
     ranges from increasing food and livestock production, building
     irrigation systems and stocking fisheries to veterinary medicine
     and agronomy. One problem noted is that many older individuals
     from farm backgrounds have the impression that the Peace Corps is
     only for the young and thus consider themselves unqualified.

21   "Agriculture in the Peace Corps". Foreign Agriculture, 1,
     (28 January 1963): 8-9.
         A brief overview of the need for and involvement of agricul-
     tural specialists in the first two years of the Peace Corps. The
     bulk of the article is composed of photographs illustrating
     assignments in Pakistan, Brazil, and St. Lucia. As of 1963, some
     2,000 more agricultural volunteers could be used. Most of the
     personnel are retrained generalists or general farmers with
     specialities such as beekeeping or irrigation systems.

22   ALBERTSON, MAURICE L., ANDREW E. RICE and PAULINE E. BIRKY.
     New Frontiers for American Youth: Perspective on the Peace
     Corps. Washington, D.C.: Public Affairs Press, 1961.
         In late 1960, Colorado State University was requested to
     perform a research study to ascertain whether the idea of a "Peace
     Corps" was viable and, if so, how its objectives, fundamental
     organizational features, training, conditions of service and
     programs could be set up. The bulk of this volume is composed of
     that text, with additional materials from later publications and
     sources issued after the passage of the Peace Corps Act on
     September 22, 1961. Appendixes include the full text of the Peace
     Corps Act, a list of country Representatives in Ghana, Chile,
     Colombia, Malaya, the Philippines, Tanganyika and West Africa, and
     a bibliography on historical antecedents of the Peace Corps such
     as the Point 4 program. This study provides both the academic
     assessment of the Peace Corps idea and the popular flavor of
     debate at a time when the very suggestion was under serious
     question. Several newspaper cartoons are also included,
     depicting--and, in some cases, lampooning--the Peace Corpsman off
     to "save the world."

23   "Altruistic Energy". Christian Science Monitor, (17 January
     1985): 19.
         An editorial expressing approval of the massive response to
     the Peace Corps' request for agricultural workers to fill the
     needs of a projected African program. This is seen as an expres-
     sion of a larger pool of energy which could be profitably tapped
     for domestic changes as well.

24   "And Away They Go!". Time, 77 (8 September 1961):   22-23.
      The departure of the first Peace Corps contingents for
service in Ghana and Tanganyika is related, with the Rose Garden
ceremony hosted by President Kennedy noted. Items of advice on
overseas life drawn from a guidebook entitled "Working Effectively
Overseas" are used to illustrate the genre of problems volunteers
may face. The reception of the Ghana group seems to augur well
for the future.

25   ANDERSON, PEGGY. "Recruiting: A Team Effort". Peace Corps
      Volunteer, 4, n.2 (December 1965): 4-7. S19.11/2:4/2.
      The author, an Peace Corps veteran of Togo, describes the
effort and stresses--as well as rewards--of being a recruiter for
the Corps on college campuses. This offers an interesting view of
the problems of recruitment from the inside, and preserves the
tactics being used in the mid-1960's.

26   ARNOLD, CHARLES B.   "Culture Shock and A Peace Corps Field
      Mental Health Program". Community Mental Health Journal, 3,
      1967:   53-60.
      Using field data from Peace Corps/Bolivia, this article
reports upon psychiatric investigations of the phenomenon known as
"culture shock." First defined by Kalervo Oberg on the basis of a
set of symptoms in 1955, it is viewed as a mental illness, and one
which Peace Corps training and selection, as well as in-country
medical and psychiatric staff, must deal with. In the host
country, it is the Peace Corps staff physician, often, who must
cope with these problems. After reviewing the professional
efforts advanced to cope with this issue, Arnold presents a field
mental health regimen he developed for Peace Corps/Bolivia. This
took the form of group therapy-type sessions at in-country orientation for newly-arrived volunteers prior to posting to their
assigned sites. During the period of service, assignment of
volunteers in pairs and encouragement of mutual support groupings
in the volunteer population were found to be effective. Group
atmosphere was effective based upon seven factors which are specified. The return rate of volunteers from Bolivia was less than
twenty-five percent of that for the Latin American region as a
whole. While useful, the author cautions that there is not enough
data to really evaluate the system.

27   ASHABRANNER, BRENT. "From the Peace Corps, A New Kind of
      Teacher". National Elementary Principal, 47 (April 1968):   38-
      42.
      The actions taken by returned volunteers are many and
varied, but for the volunteer with overseas teaching experience,
the schools of urban America represent a new and familiar challenge at the same time. Their applications of skills developed in
other cultures, in schools with as little or fewer resources than
inner city America has proven effective. The perception of the
American educational community that Peace Corps teaching was
somehow lacking began to erode in 1965. In that year, the Commission on Teacher Education and Professional Standards urged school

districts to hire the pool of returning volunteers with educational experience. Examples of such hiring are then given from New
Jersey, Washington, D.C.'s Cardozo Project, Cleveland and Phila-
delphia. Problems encountered by volunteers include lack of
professional distance, inability to maintain classroom discipline,
and the inapplicability of the "person-to-person" approach in
certain settings. Despite these difficulties, Ashabranner
believes that "if the former volunteers can see their way through
the first months of adjustment, they promise to make an invaluable
contribution."

28   ASHABRANNER, BRENT. <u>A Moment in History: The First Ten Years</u>
    <u>of the Peace Corps</u>. Garden City, New York: Doubleday, 1971.
       This is an account of the growth and development of the
Peace Corps from its beginnings up to 1971 as seen by an insider.
Ashabranner began his involvement with Corps as the liaison of AID
to Sargent Shriver's efforts to establish Peace Corps in Nigeria.
After Shriver's departure, Ashabranner found himself in charge of
setting up the in-country program, concluding negotiations with
various ministries, and preparing for the first group of volunteers to be trained at Ibadan. It was this latter group which
gave birth to the famous "post card incident". Historical information as to the growth and development of Peace Corps programs in
Nigeria and India, in particular the teaching and agricultural
sectors, is given in some depth. Changes in programming, training
techniques, and the vagaries of Peace Corps as a part of American
domestic politics up to the beginning of the Viet Nam War make
this an absorbing account of some of the shakiest moments in the
agency's history.

29   BABBITT, SAMUEL F. "The Peace Corps and Science Teachers".
    <u>Science Teacher</u>, 29 (May 1962): 30-31.
       A general overview of the participation of science teachers
in Peace Corps programs, and the benefits which such service can
have for subsequent career advancement in the American school
systems. Two-volunteers teaching in Ghana are profiled in photographs accompanying the article.

30   BALK, ALFRED. "Western Man at His Best". <u>Saturday Review</u>, 49
    (23 April 1966): 15.
       A brief overview summarizing the accomplishments and tasks
of the Peace Corps in its first five years of existence. In 1966,
some 12,000 volunteers were at work in forty-six nations, with the
largest regional contingent in Latin America. Service effects on
the character of the individual volunteers is represented by
quotations from Malaysia, the Philippines and Ethiopia. Among the
benefits accrued from the creation of Corps noted is the creation
of a vast amount of material for the teaching of languages which
had few or no such curricular texts prior to that time. The title
of the article is drawn from a quotation by historian Arnold
Toynbee referring to the caliber of the volunteers.

31   BALLENDORF, DIRK ANTHONY. The Development of a Regional Plan
      for the North Africa, Near East Asia and Pacific Region of the
      Peace Corps. Ph.D. dissertation. Harvard, 1973.
          The activity reported on by this dissertation occurred
      between October, 1971 and September, 1973 in the academic world,
      at the Peace Corps itself, and in the United State Congress. A
      memo from the Director of the Peace Corps on September 30, 1971,
      noted that the budget reduction of the continuing appropriation
      was from $88 million to $82 million, and emphasized the need for
      both regional directors and in-country staff to develop coherent
      plans for the future. A second funding cut to $77.2 million
      exacerbated the need for planning. The author of this disserta-
      tion reports on his involvement with NANEAP restructuring as
      assistant chief of program and training, chairing a task force
      responsible for creating a three-year plan for allocation of
      regional resources. The development of this document is consid-
      ered against the background of relating Peace Corps work to a
      theoretical framework of underdevelopment research. As the NANEAP
      analysis was the first to be completed and served as the model for
      a Peace Corps-wide effort ordered by the Director, Kevin
      O'Donnell, on March 29, 1972, Ballendorf's account of this project
      is extremely valuable. Information is also provided on the
      revisions of individual in-country plans and their component
      requests and Congressional policies affecting the agency in its
      firs years as a part of ACTION. Appendixes contain the full texts
      of O'Donnell's memo of 1972 and suggested revisions sent out for
      country directors. Ballendorf served as one of the first volun-
      teers in the Philippines from 1961 to 1963 and later as staff in
      Micronesia.

32   "Balzano Calls For Agency Unity". AA1.13:1/10. InterACTION,
      1, n.10 (July 1973):   5.
          A statement by Michael Balzano, Director of ACTION, as to
      his views for the goals of the agency. This provides a framework
      for Peace Corps programs of the period of the early 1970's.

33   "Balzano Named ACTION Head". AA1.13:1/6. InterACTION, 1, n.6
      (March 1973): 1.
          A news report covering the appointment of Michael Balzano, a
      former staff assistant to the President, as the new Director of
      ACTION. A brief summary of his qualifications and background is
      provided.

34   "Balzano Places Community First". AA1.13:1/7. InterACTION, 1,
      n.7 (April 1973): 1.
          A statement by Director-designate Michael Balzano outlining
      his philosophy of service, which places the people served at the
      center of consideration and sees the volunteers as a primary
      importance, with staff taking a strictly support role. It offers
      a clear view of the opinions of ACTION's future under the Nixon
      administration.

35 BANTA, JAMES E. "Health Problems Encountered By the Peace
     Corps Overseas". <u>American Journal of Public Health</u>, 56, n.12
     (December 1966): 2121-2125.
          The formation of the Peace Corps medical staff and the
     issues facing an in-country doctor are reviewed together with
     specific health questions worldwide. Field medical officers
     typically divide their time among four activities: preventive
     medicine, preventive psychiatry, consultant for in-country health
     programming, and personal involvement in volunteer work in a
     health project. An examination of Peace Corps field data on
     health care must be based upon the monthly reports submitted by
     these physicians. Two visible trends are the increase in
     emotional disorders--viewed as a function of more accurate
     reporting--and a decline in the incidence of infectious hepatitis.
     The latter is viewed as a response to the usage of gamma globulin
     injections as prophylaxis. Rabies and dental problems remain
     widespread among Corps personnel. "Exotic and tropical diseases",
     while present in varying degrees, have not approached early
     predictions. The profile of the volunteer is seen to be much the
     same as for a control group of similar age in the United States.
     Factors influencing this are seen to be the high degree of
     selection employed in choosing personnel and health training as
     part of field preparation.

36 BARLOW, LISA. "On Peace Corps". <u>Christian Science Monitor</u>,
     (19 November 1981): 23.
          A letter from a returned volunteer with three years service
     in West Africa objecting to the "return of the missionary spirt"
     as expressed by Matthew Cossolotto in his article in the <u>Monitor</u>
     of September 2, 1981. Barlow stresses "the unfairness of
     inflicting our changing ideals and goals on developing countries".

37 BAROWIEC, ANDREW. "Africa Can't Dig the Peace Corps".
     <u>Cleveland Plain Dealer</u>, (3 January 1965): 7.
          "Despite several years of effort, most Africans are
     basically puzzled by the Peace Corps". To illustrate this
     statement, the author notes that volunteers in Africa have been
     accused of everything from espionage to arrogance, but that,
     overall, the reception after the first three years has been warm.
     Countries represented in the sample of reactions are Ghana, Gabon
     and Tunisia.

38 DANIEL, BARRY. "Brainwashing the Peace Corps". <u>Nation</u>, 236
     (7 May 1983): 572-573.
          In the original Peace Corps legislation, an amendment was
     introduced by Senator Jack Miller of Iowa, requiring that trainees
     "be instructed in the philosophy, strategy, tactics and menace of
     communism" (p.572.). Although present, this provision was little
     used under the successors of Sargent Shriver until the Reagan
     administration. In 1981, Section 8 (c) was resurrected through
     the efforts of rightist organizations. To approach the subject in
     a more current fashion, an audio-visual presentation entitled
     "Americans Abroad" was created for showing to volunteers in
     training. This article discusses the reaction to this sort of

training of a pilot group of volunteers bound for service in
Guatemala. Overall reaction was negative, with complaints being
that the presentation insulted their intelligence, it was too
simplistic, addressed only the Soviet form of Communist society,
and was seen to be a form of loyalty test. Pointing out the
possible political motives for such training, the author concludes
by saying that, "when in the field, clear distinctions between
good and evil will not be as easy to make as the creators of the
film believe".

39   BAYLEY, EDWIN R. "The View from Inside the Peace Corps".
     Progressive, (September 1961): 27-30.
          Composed by the publicity director for the Peace Corps, this
     article offers a mirror reflecting attitudes towards the agency
     during the very first months of its existence, including doubts as
     to whether the requisite legislation making it a permanent organi-
     zation would ever make it to the floor of Congress for debate.
     Covering topics ranging from early fears regarding manpower avail-
     ability to profiles of the first country programs, this is a
     window into the time when Corps was a new and somewhat uncertain
     idea.

40   BENJAMIN, THEODORE DAVID. A Program for the Training of
     Teachers of Physics and Chemistry for Science in the Peace
     Corps in the Secondary Schools of English Speaking Africa.
     Ed.D. dissertation. Columbia University, 1968.
          For the Peace Corps, the training of volunteers as teachers
     within the short span of time available has always presented
     difficulties, the more so as many trainees have little or no
     formal training in the field of education. The study reported on
     by this dissertation originated in the work of the author with the
     Nairobi Science Teaching Centre between 1961 and 1964, involving
     teacher upgrading in the physical sciences for a geographical area
     encompassing Kenya, Uganda, Tanzania and Rhodesia. Prior to this
     time, Benjamin had worked as a faculty member at Columbia from
     1940-1957, specializing in the training of science instructors.
     In 1965, the Teachers for East Africa program sponsored by
     Columbia was taken over by the Peace Corps: Benjamin served as
     trainer for twelve groups of volunteers bound for service in East
     Africa, Ghana, Nigeria, Somalia and West Cameroon.
          The dissertation consists of three sections--an introductory
     briefing focusing on the problems of adequate technical instruc-
     tion, ten sections detailing approaches to specific issues "so
     that the trainee experiences exactly what the student experiences
     as he learns" (p.19) and an evaluation of the effectiveness of the
     program, using the summer 1967 group of trainees bound for Ghana
     as illustration. As one of the few technical analyses of a
     specific Peace Corps training program by an educator with
     substantial expertise in the field, this document offers both a
     rare insight into teacher training challenges and a model for use
     by other agencies faced with similar situations.

41   BENNETT, MERIDAN. "Evaluation and the Question of Change".
     Annals of the American Academy of Political and Social Science,
     365, (May 1966): 119-128.
        The Peace Corps Division of Evaluation and its various roles
     and functions as related to staff, volunteers and agency program-
     ming is reviewed. Limited by the types of volunteers requested
     and the available pool of actual persons available, programming
     has always been somewhat dependent on accurate field data. An
     historical consideration of the origins and growth of the evalua-
     tive machinery from 1961 to 1965 is presented. Problems facing
     the evaluators include lack of proper placement of volunteers,
     ineffective training plans and programs, and agency staff suspi-
     cion as to the role and function of the field visitor. Changes
     introduced as a result of such reporting are also noted. The
     procedure for the collection and compilation of a typical evalua-
     tion is then illustrated. Future recommendations are for a closer
     co-operation between field evaluation and research as "the reflec-
     tive arm of the Peace Corps" (p.127).

42   BERLEW, F. KINGSTON. "A Volunteer Must Use the Language".
     S19.11/2. Peace Corps Volunteer, 3, n.8-9 (June-July 1965):
     2, 23.
        Written in reply to claims that the volunteer can function
     effectively in his post without a substantial knowledge of the
     local language, this article stresses the advantages of full
     cultural participation and notes the retreat into obsessive work
     of those who fail to develop linguistic ease.

43   BLACTCHFORD, JOSEPH. "The Peace Corps: Making It in the
     Seventies". Foreign Affairs, 49, n.1 (1970): 122-135.
        In this essay, Joseph Blatchford, third Director of the
     Peace Corps, sets out his views as to the direction the agency
     will follow in the 1970's. These "New Directions" involve several
     specific points of programming change: increased recruiting of
     personnel with special skills, closer co-ordination with private
     agencies of standing within the host nations, placement of volun-
     teers as a part of multinational projects where feasible, shifing
     of Corps personnel to the high priorities of host nations as
     stated by themselves, with increased long-range planning:
     increased minority recruitment and better utilization of the
     talents, skills and experiences of the returned volunteers upon
     problems in the United States. This article can be seen as a
     capsule manifesto expressing the basic shift in Peace Corps
     policies which occasioned massive debate both within and outside
     the agency during the Nixon administration.

44   BOLLING, LANDRUM R. "The Peace Corps: Making Friends for
      America". Saturday Evening Post, 254 (September 1982): 66-7,
      84.
           A brief historical look at Peace Corps, its activities and
      approaches to problem-solving in the 1980's. Noting the wide-
      spread lack of awareness of the Corps' continued existence and
      function, supporters as varied as "Miss Lillian" Carter, the King
      of Tonga, Fr. Theodore Hesburgh of Notre Dame and Senator Paul
      Tsongas are used as examples of involvement.

45   BONKER, DON. "For A Go-Get'm Peace Corps". Christian Science
      Monitor (15 June 1979): 23.
           A review by a member of the House of Representatives of the
      history of the Peace Corps since its merger with other agencies to
      form ACTION in 1971. In March, 1979, the Foreign Affairs
      Committee of the House voted to remove Corps from ACTION, with
      requisite legislation passing the full House in late April. Since
      1977, Rep. Bonker has advocated a restored independence for Peace
      Corps.

46   BORDERS, WILLIAM. "Decade-Old Peace Corps Charting a New
      Course". New York Times (30 November 1970): 1,12.
           A conference of Peace Corps officials and representatives of
      24 African nations was held in the city of Niamey, Niger for a
      period of five days in November, 1970. Recognizing that there had
      been a decline in the popularity of serving in Corps among
      American citizens and that the priority needs of the host
      countries were changing as well, certain decisions were taken
      regarding policy. The "numbers game"--measuring the success of a
      country program by the total figure of volunteers posted there--
      was abandoned. Married couples with children would now be
      considered as volunteers, and closer consultation with host
      governments was planned. A review of the shift from generalist to
      experienced specialists as preferred volunteers--chiefly due to
      host country requests--completes the article.

47   "Boston Hold Peace Corps Fair". AA1.16:2/1. Reconnection, 2,
      n.1 (May 1979): 14.
           On February 13, 1979, the returned volunteer organization of
      the Boston area sponsored that city's first fair to publicize the
      opportunities of Peace Corps service. Speaker and guest of honor
      was Senator Paul Tsongas, of Massachusetts, RPCV-Ethiopia.
      Questions from the floor centered on the future of Corps and the
      atmosphere in Congress towards it.

48   BRAESTRUP, PETER. "Peace Corps to Use Puerto Rican Camp".
      New York Times (6 April 1961): 1,15.
           A site for Peace Corps training in physical conditioning,
      first aid, tropical sanitation and "spartan living" has been
      located twelve miles south of the port of Arecibo, Puerto Rico.
      Volunteers will spend twenty-six days at the two camps--which will
      be segregated by sex--following a projected three to six months
      training at mainland universities. Advantages of the Puerto Rican
      site include immersion in a bilingual environment, exposure to

Latin culture, and observation of Puerto Rico's own program of rural community development. Corps has completed and begun distribution of a guidebook to its operations and functions. Training programs would be geared to specific overseas assignments as soon as agreements were reached with host nations.

49 Bringing The World Back Home: The 25th Anniversary Of The Peace Corps. Stoneham, Massachusetts: Color Film Corporation, 1986. Produced by the National Council of Returned Peace Corps Volunteers.

This videotape was made as a recording of the 25th reunion conference of the Peace Corps, held in a great white tent on the Mall in Washington from September 18-22, 1986. Beginning with a view of the march to Arlington Cemetery on the final day of the conference, all major speeches and social events are covered. Speakers included Sargent Shriver, Loret Miller Ruppe, Senator Chris Dodd, Her Excellency Madame Corazon Aquino, and representatives of many aid organizations. Details of the Congressional Reception, the memorial service for fallen members of Peace Corps, and the festival of Third World cultures held as a celebration of a common heritage are also included.

50 BROWN, JUDITH. "The Peace Corps and the Development of Foreign Language Instructional Materials". Linguistic Reporter, 11, n.5 (October 1969): 1-3.

By 1968, the Peace Corps had provided classes to volunteers in 150 "neglected" languages, languages for which classroom materials were not easily available. For over 100 of them, Corps itself was obliged to produce these materials. Three approaches were taken to creating linguistic sources: training contracts, materials development contracts, and co-operation with other agencies within the federal government. Details of each are included. As part of its tenth anniversary, the Center for Applied Linguistics in Washington, D.C. issued a study of all language materials prepared by Peace Corps between 1961 and 1968. The final bibliography contains 238 entries, covering basic courses, intermediate and supplementary texts, lexical materials and instructor's manuals. Types of materials created are seen to reflect changing emphases in Corps programming. A list of the languages is then given.

51 BROWN, THOMAS J. "The Peace Corps and the Military". New Republic, 154, n.24 (11 June 1966): 29-30.

A letter to the New Republic replying to the suggestion by Secretary Robert McNamara that Peace Corps be an alternative to military service. The writer objects that such a move would deprive Corps of its unique voluntary nature, prevent qualified women from serving, lower the general quality of volunteers and badly damage the non-political image the Peace Corps has worked so hard to achieve and maintain.

52   "The Bruce Murray Case".   S19.11/2:8/3-4.   <u>Volunteer</u>, 8,
      nos.3-4 (March-April 1970):   10-12.
           A survey of the first legal test of the Peace Corps policy
      governing the freedom of volunteer expression overseas. The case
      involved a member of Peace Corps/Chile who signed a petition pro-
      testing American bombing of North Vietnam and was subsequently
      brought home and reclassified 1-A by his local draft board.   On
      Christmas Eve, 1969 Judge Raymond Pettine of the U. S. District
      Court in Rhode Island found in favor of Murray.

53.   BUSH, GERALD WILLIAM.   <u>The Peace Corps, 1961-1965:   A Study In
      Open Organization</u>.   Ph.D., dissertation, Northern Illinois
      University, 1969.
           Written by a candidate in the field of political science,
      this dissertation places the bureaucratic organization of the
      Peace Corps within the framework of organization theory and
      politics.   Drawing upon the writings of scholars in the sociology
      of organizations such as Max Weber and Victor Thompson, seven
      characteristics of bureaucracies are given: technical specializa-
      tion by units, delegation to each unit based upon functional
      criteria, an appointment and promotion system based upon merit,
      abstract rules intended to be applied in all cases, hierarchy,
      primacy of the official occupation, and impersonality in the
      application of rules and regulations. The first years of Peace
      Corps organization failed to exhibit these distinguishing marks,
      leaving Bush to characterize Corps as "a non-bureaucratic organi-
      zation by design" (p.2).   In sharp contrast to the theoretical
      principles of the professional literatures, Peace Corps exhibited
      purposeful turnover of staff every five years, an almost total
      absence of functional hierarchy and flexible rules applied on an
      individual basis.   This phenomenon is then offered as a model for
      possible re-examination of the classical theory of bureaucracy.

54   BUTLER, LEWIS H.   "The Overseas Staff".   <u>Annals of the American
      Academy of Political and Social Science</u>, 365 (May 1966):   83-
      92.
           The rationale for the existence of an overseas staff
      supporting the work of the volunteers is set out, with a
      hypothetical day in the life of an in-country Director offered as
      example.   Noting that the prohibition on staff members remaining
      longer than five years has recently been made part of the Peace
      Corps Act by amendment, such constant turnover is viewed as a
      strength, returning trained and proven people to the United States
      and drawing staff from the same source as the volunteers they
      serve with.   Language facility was not a notable feature in any
      but a few of the early country Directors, although with the
      increased recruitment of volunteers to staff positions this has
      begun to change.   Admitting that "despite many individual
      successes, the process of selecting and training staff for
      overseas service has . . . suffered by comparison to that of the
      volunteers" (p.91), greater emphasis is to be laid upon improve-
      ment of the staff.   Given the nature of Corps life and service,
      some failures are viewed as inevitable.   The author was country
      director in Malaysia from 1963-1964.

55   CALVERT, LAURA D. "Notes on the Peace Corps Language Training
      Program". Modern Language Journal, 47, n.7 (November 1963):
      319-323.
          In this article, Laura Calvert, director of the the instruc-
      tion program in Spanish run by the Peace Corps at the University
      of New Mexico, details the format of this crucial portion of
      training. Following a course outline and structure of both class-
      room and informal sessions, such as using only the language at
      mealtimes, questions of language teaching are dealt with.
      Admitting that, "since at best we can teach only the most
      important things in our limited time, we try to select material
      that has not only linguistic, but also cultural and informational
      value", her analysis and presentation give an in-depth view not
      only of actual training but of the philosophical issues underlying
      it.

56   CALVERT, ROBERT. "Peace Corps Service and Career Choice".
      Vocational Guidance Quarterly, 14, n.4 (Summer 1966): 236-
      240.
          Looking over the first six years of the Peace Corps'
      existence, the Director of the Career Information Service examines
      the observed changes in both career orientation and professional
      choice made by members of this group. Items noted include a
      preference for overseas service when possible, choice of social
      work as an option, and an increase in the number interested in
      pursuing work in medicine or government. The Career Information
      Service itself was deleted from the original legislation creating
      Corps, and only in 1963, under a Carnegie Corporation grant, did
      it appear. It was not until 1964 that the agency itself was
      authorized to assume this responsibility. The outline of career
      information and preparation for life post-Peace Corps as presently
      offered to volunteers is given. Calvert concludes that
      "individual volunteers recognize that they must work as hard to
      serve our society as they worked overseas" (p.240).

57   CAMPBELL, G. RICARDO. "The Peace Corps: An Ideal Endures".
      L2.70/4:19/1. Occupational Outlook Quarterly, 19, n.4 (Winter
      1975): 3-9.
          Written by a returned veteran of Peace Corps/Brazil, this is
      a general overview of the progress and idealism of Peace Corps.
      Director Michael Balzano's comments as to the survival of the
      "essence of voluntarism" are also included as a rebuttal to the
      idea that Corps has outlived its usefulness. Qualifications for
      volunteers and methods of applications are sketched. The article
      is lavishly illustrated with photographs of volunteers in varied
      settings from Tonga to Sierra Leone and quotations from their own
      letters and diaries.

58   CAREY, ROBERT G. The Peace Corps. New York: Prager, 1970.
           This volume was written at a time when the basic directions
      and planning of Peace Corps were undergoing revision according to
      the "New Directions" emphasis of Director Joseph Blatchford. The
      five points which comprised this program are woven through the
      text. The first eight years of Peace Corps experiences in
      training, recruitment and support of volunteers, overseas
      obstacles to effective functioning, language teaching and program
      development are reviewed. Regional chapters on Latin America,
      Africa, the North Africa, Near East and South Asian group of host
      nations, and East Asia and the Pacific focus on overall program
      emphases as well as profiling individual country programs. In
      Latin America, the stress is on community development; in Africa,
      upon education; agricultural assistance in North Africa, and
      technical expertise in health care and related areas in the
      Pacific. The value of these summaries lies in their compression
      of years of programming into a form where changes are readily
      visible. Chapters on the relationship of Peace Corps to Congress,
      activities of the returned volunteers, and a brief outline of the
      "New Directions" scheme complete the work. Appendixes contain the
      text of the Peace Corps Act and a summary of volunteers serving as
      of May 1, 1969, by country and program. Charts are also provided
      giving statistical data on the number of volunteers by country
      since the inception of the agency.

59   CARTER, GEORGE E. "The Beginnings of Peace Corps Programming".
      Annals of the American Academy of Political and Social Science,
      365 (May 1966): 46-54.
           Basic problems of Peace Corps programming stem from two
      factors: all personnel are volunteers, which produces a mixture
      of talents, and these personnel may serve only in host country
      settings for which they have been specifically requested. As the
      Peace Corps developed, by 1963 it was evident that the majority of
      volunteers would be generalists. This necessitated creation of
      five models: placement as teachers of specific academic subjects,
      teachers of English as a foreign language, community development
      workers, "co-teachers" assisting host country educators, and
      technical assistance in concentrated groups. This last is best
      exemplified by the first group of surveyors and geologists to
      serve in Tanganyika. Generalists are seen to have the advantages
      of flexibility in adapting to host country situations, a good
      broad-based education relative to the host country, an analytical
      approach to problem solving, and a high degree of receptivity to
      Peace Corps training methods. In an effort to stretch the limited
      supply of specialists, pyramid programming has been tried, with
      one technical expert advising a group of generalists. Each of the
      five models is then analyzed for strengths and weakness, with the
      co-teaching, community development and TEFL programs seen as
      either vague in conception or frustrating to both host country
      personnel and volunteers. The author was the first Director of
      Peace Corps/Ghana.

60   CASSELBERRY, DIANE. "Peace Corps". <u>Christian Science Monitor</u>
     (11 October 1974): 9.
         "Because the words 'Peace Corps' and 'volunteer' cannot be
     easily translated in many languages, few people understand what
     you are doing there or why you may be one of them." With this wry
     observation, a returned volunteer recounts what persons entering
     Corps service may expect in actual on-site living. This item
     appears as part of a general presentation of lifestyles choices
     available to young people in the 1970's.

61   "Celebrations Marks Peace Corps' Tenth Anniversary".
     S19.11/2:9/3-4. <u>Volunteer</u>, 9, nos.3-4 (March-April 1971): 15-
     16.
         The first celebrations of the tenth anniversary of the Peace
     Corps began in the Kingdom of Tonga, with the Crown Prince
     Tupouto'u in attendance, and continued on the far side of the
     world with a gala reception in Washington, D.C. at ACTION
     headquarters. The latter was attended by such notables as Senator
     Hubert Humphrey and former Peace Corps Director Jack Vaughn.

62   "Celeste Named Peace Corps Director". AA1.16:2/1.
     <u>Reconnection</u>, 2, n.1 (May 1979): 5.
         President Carter announced the appointment of Richard F.
     Celeste, former lieutenant governor of Ohio, as Director of the
     Peace Corps. In 1963, he served as a Peace Corps consultant and
     later worked for four years on a special agriculture development
     project in India.

63   "Central America: Volunteers Work in Six Lands Much Alike in
     Problems, Past". S19.11/2:3/8-9. <u>Peace Corps Volunteer</u>, 3,
     n.8-9 (June-July 1965): 11-28.
         A group of thirteen articles written by both country volun-
     teers and staff covering Corps work in Guatemala, El Salvador,
     Honduras, Nicaragua, Costa Rica, British Honduras and Panama as of
     1965.

64   "Charges Against PC Refuted By Director". AA1.13:3/5.
     <u>InterACTION</u>, 3, n.5 (February 1975): 1, 8.
         The full text of a statement issued by ACTION Director
     Michael Balzano on December 5, 1974 following publicity on the
     expulsion of Peace Corps workers from Peru. The Peruivian govern-
     ment charged volunteers with working as agents of the CIA. In
     this statement, Balzano reviews the history of Corps policy on
     espionage and its relationship with the intelligence agencies of
     the federal government.

65   CHERNUSH, KAY. "The AID/Peace Corps Relationship Grows".
      Front Lines (22 May 1980):   2-3.
          An article drawn from the journal of AID, this item
      discusses the evolution and changes which have entered the
      relationship of the Peace Corps and the Agency for International
      Development. From the earliest days of Peace Corps, when AID
      personnel were regarded as "the enemy" to an AID filled with
      returned volunteers, the alterations in both groups have been
      gradual and dynamic.

66   CLEVELAND, HARLAN. The Future of the Peace Corps. Palo Alto,
      California: Aspen Institute for Humanistic Studies, 1977.
          In the summer of 1976, the Aspen Institute was requested by
      ACTION to conduct an independent analysis and evaluation on the
      possible futures of the Peace Corps and to make recommendations on
      specific points. Questions involved were the type of world
      Americans would be obliged to confront in the next decades of the
      twentieth century, how volunteer service programs would address
      the felt needs and motivations of Americans responding to global
      problems, and what changes were necessary for the Peace Corps to
      remain a viable vehicle for combining the two. Interviews
      included some seventy former volunteers attending employment
      counseling, as well as former staff and outside observers.
      Referring to the Peace Corps as "alive but invisible", this report
      clearly explores the rising perception that "basic human needs"
      must be met. Revival for the Peace Corps is seen as possible
      through several steps, the first of which is its separation from
      ACTION and the re-appointment of a director able to lead. This
      study suggests the transformation of Peace Corps into a public
      corporation on the lines of National Public Radio, thus making it
      more accessible to all and expanding the avenues for joint efforts
      with other international agencies.

67   CLEVELAND, HARLAN. "Internationalizing the Concept of the
      Peace Corps". Department of State Bulletin, 44 (April-June
      1961):   551-552.
          In this address, given before the Washington Council of the
      Experiment in International Living on March 28, 1961, a call was
      made for the use of volunteers from the proposed Peace Corps in an
      international aid effort drawing upon resources of existing United
      Nations bodies and affiliated organizations. Proposals of assign-
      ments ranged from the archaeological salvage of the monuments of
      Nubia to UNESCO's education programs in Africa. This text is of
      particular interest in light of the later treaties between the
      United States and two of the bodies mentioned, the Food and
      Agriculture Organization of the United Nations and the Inter-
      national Labor Organization, for the participation of volunteers
      in their ongoing work in various host countries.

68   COLEMAN, TERENCE DEAN. Peace Corps Volunteers in the
      Developing World: A Quantitative Study. M.A. thesis,
      American University, 1980.
          In February, 1979 a worldwide survey of Peace Corps volun-
      teers was conducted which requested them to describe the quality
      of life of the recipients of their services, who were classed as
      either students or trainees, co-workers and counterparts or direct
      service recipients such as hospital patients. Volunteers were
      asked to rate their host groups on six variables: literacy level,
      command of simple arithmetic, access to safe water supplies and
      adequacy of protein and caloric intake to prevent chronic mal-
      nutrition. The results of this survey were then matched with the
      ratings assigned to the same nations on the Physical Quality of
      Life Index (PQLI) developed by the Overseas Development Council.
      The research reported here had three objectives: "1.) to
      determine what relationships exist between what the volunteers
      perceive as the quality of life of their recipients and country
      level data assembled from outside sources that attempt to describe
      the overall quality of life in a country and 2.) "to test the
      hypothesis that a very low level of development in a country will
      adversely effect the efforts of the Peace Corps to serve the poor"
      (pp.2-3). The latter question addressed itself to the level of
      infrastructure needed before Peace Corps programs could reach the
      poorest segments of a community. The third objective was to
      determine how the results of such a comparison could be applied to
      Peace Corps programming in specific and development activities in
      general. Comparisons of the two data sets indicated that PQLI
      indicators of literacy were the only category directly applicable
      to volunteer data. The hypothesis is advanced that Peace Corps
      personnel in the poorest nations may be contributing most to
      development through education and that host governments may be
      using Peace Corps volunteers to build the infrastructure for
      future projects. Researchers should note that it was shortly
      after the survey was done that a shift in overall Corps program-
      ming to an emphasis on "basic human needs" was announced: thus,
      this dissertation provides a view of some of the factors which may
      have contributed to this decision. Two appendixes contain the
      graphs illustrating set comparisons, the full text of the
      questionnaire used, and a bibliography which is chiefly
      statistical materials.

69   COLMEN, JOSEPH G. "A Discovery Of Commitment". <u>Annals of the</u>
      <u>American Academy of Political and Social Science</u>, 365 (May
      1966): 12-20.
           In attempting to explore the reasons used as rationales for
      volunteering to serve in the Peace Corps, three studies done in
      1962, 1963, and 1964 are profiled and their results presented.
      Notable findings included parental influence as a deciding factor
      in declining invitations to training and the relative unimportance
      of barriers to Corps service as opposed to its advantages. Faced
      with the multiplicity of factors, the author concludes that "it
      may be that we will never have a perfect fix on why people do
      something as complex as join the Peace Corps" (p.20). At the time
      of writing, Colmen was the Corps Associate Director for Planning,
      Evaluation and Research.

70   "Colombia Volunteer Leader Dies of Accident Injuries".
      S91.11/2:2/1. <u>Peace Corps Volunteer</u>, 2, n.1 (November 1963):
      3.
           An obituary notice for a member of Peace Corps/Colombia
      killed in a jeep accident. Profile of the first seven volunteers
      to die overseas are included for historical information.

71   "Commending the Peace Corps on Its 25th Anniversary".
      <u>Congressional Record</u>, 132, n.125 (22 September 1986):
      .H7880-84.
           The full text of House Resolution 546, congratulating the
      Peace Corps on 25 years of service to both host nations and the
      United States. Comments by Congressman Fascell, one of the
      original co-sponsors of the Peace Corps Act, and the texts of
      proclamations by the cities of Coral Gables and Miami and the
      Board of County Commissioners of Dade County, Florida, are also
      included. Remarks by Congressman Broomfield of Michigan,
      Congressman Lagomarsino of California and several other members of
      the House are appended. Note is taken of the upcoming awarding of
      the Sargent Shriver Awards, with brief biographies of the 1986
      recipients inserted into the <u>Record</u>.

72   "Concurrent Resolution of Hawaii Legislature Relating To Peace
      Corps". <u>Congressional Record</u>, 107, Part 4, 1961: 4849.
           Upon the request of Senator Long of Hawaii, the full text of
      a resolution passed by that state's legislators supporting the
      idea of a Peace Corps and offering the resources of Hawaii as a
      "staging center for recruitment and training" was read into the
      record. Among the assets of Hawaii noted is an heritage of lead-
      ership "in matters of racial understanding and harmony."

73   "Confidentiality and the Peace Corps". <u>American Journal of</u>
      <u>Psychiatry</u>, 122, n.10 (1966): 1191.
          This is a letter replying to references made in an earlier
      article to the "tenuous" grounds upon which a psychiatrist may
      refuse to release data on a patient to the Peace Corps. The
      author takes strong issue with such a view, referring to the
      opinion of the General Counsel for the Peace Corps to illustrate
      the matter. In such a situation, the psychiatrist is under no
      obligation to testify, as would be the case in a legal proceeding.
      The issue of confidentiality is viewed as paramount, as there is
      no guarantee as to how such information would be used.

74   <u>The Peace Corps</u>. Congress U. S. House of Representative.
      Hearing Before The Committee On Foreign Affairs, House Of
      Representatives, Eighty-Seventh Congress, First Session On H.R.
      7500, A Bill To Provide For A Peace Corps To Help The Peoples
      Of Interested Countries And Areas In Meeting Their Needs For
      Skilled Manpower (August 11 and 15, 1961): Washington, U. S.
      Government Printing Office, 1961. Y4.F76/1:P31/5.
          This document is the complete transcription of the hearing
      held in the House of Representatives before the Committee on
      Foreign Affairs on the proposed act to create the Peace Corps.
      The bulk of the document is comprised of memoranda and statements
      submitted for inclusion in the permanent record by individuals and
      the Peace Corps itself on various points ranging from volunteer
      health care to objections raised against the bill by the Daughters
      of the American Revolution. Persons testifying before the
      committee include the Honorable Henry Reuss of Wisconsin, who
      proposed a similar program to the government under the Point Four
      plan, Andrew J. Biemiller, director of the legislation department
      of the AFL-CIO, and R. Sargent Shriver, Director of the Peace
      Corps. The massive number of appended papers present graphically
      the perceived benefits and danger thought to be inherent in the
      creation and operation of such an agency.

75   <u>The Peace Corps</u>. Congress U. S. House of Representatives.
      Hearing Before the Committee On Foreign Relations, United State
      Senate, Eighty-Seventh Congress, First Session on S.2000 (A
      Bill To Provide For A Peace Corps To Help The Peoples Of
      Interested Countries And Areas In Meeting Their Needs For
      Skilled Manpower) June 22 and 23, 1961. Washington, D.C., U.
      S. Government Printing Office, 1961. Y4:F76/2:P31/2.
          This document is a complete transcription of the hearing
      held in the United Senate upon the bill which would later become
      the Peace Corps Act. The bulk of the document is composed of the
      statements made to the Foreign Relations Committee by various
      persons addressing the worth of the proposed act. Included in the
      list of persons are such figures as the executive director of the
      National 4-H Club Foundation of America, representatives of the

American Friends Service Committee, officials of CARE and the
Mennonite Central Committee, and R. Sargent Shriver. Three
appendixes contain cost principles for Peace Corps grants, general
provisions for contracts between the Peace Corps and non-profit
institutions such as universities, a letter from the national
commander of the American Legion, and articles drawn from the
Washington Post and the New York Times.

76   Congress. House of Representatives. Committee On
      International Relations. The Peace Corps in West Africa, 1975:
      Report Of A Staff Survey Team. Washington, D.C.: Government
      Printing Office 1976. Y4.In8/16:Af8/2/975.
         This report is the findings of a survey team sent to West
Africa to determine the effectiveness and problems of five Peace
Corps programs between November 28 and December 18, 1975. Issues
addressed were the need for specific programs, qualifications of
individual volunteers by project, the level of coordination in
existence between Corps personnel and officials of the host nation
and the value of the Peace Corps contribution to each country's
plan of development. Countries visited were Sierra Leone, the
Ivory Coast, Upper Volta, Ghana and Senegal. Following an
introductory section which summarizes the main findings of the
teams five distinct parts of the document examine management and
administration of Peace Corps programs in the five nations, health
care for volunteers in this region as of 1975, selection and
training procedures--and their worth--as reflected in the
personnel comprising these programs, country effort planning, and
a special report on the state of Peace Corps/Nigeria (at this time
reduced to only three volunteers). Problems noted include a high
instability rate for country directors and staff support,
insufficient health care facilities and staff for the huge
geographic areas involved, the addition of screening inappropriate
volunteers to local country staff responsibilities, and a need for
more agricultural volunteers in all countries of the region. In
terms of the overall objective--determining the field implementation of Director Joseph Blatchford's "New Directions" program--
the conclusion is that these five points are "essentially
inoperative in West Africa" (p.6). Few regional volunteers have
technical training, there are few or no volunteer families and
most personnel are "generalists". Comparisons with Asian Peace
Corps programs are made and recommendations made for the region as
a whole. In the case of Nigeria, background of the effect of
internal political struggles on the demise of the Corps is
presented in detail.

77   Peace Corps: Purpose And Perspective. First Session U. S.
      Congress House of Representatives. Committee On International
      Relations. Subcommittee On International Development Hearings,
      September 8.20, and 29, 1977 Y4.In8/16:P31/4.
         Following the election of President Carter in 1976, there
was intense interest in revitalizing the Peace Corps, but great
difference of opinion as to the way in which this should be
carried out. Accordingly, a series of hearings was held to obtain
advice from all concerned parties. This document contains a full

transcript of those hearings held in September, 1977. Testimony
was given by Sam Brown, Director of ACTION, Thomas Scanlon,
president of Benchmarks, Inc., and one of the first volunteers to
serve in Chile, Harlan Cleveland, and authors C. Payne Lucas and
Kevin Lowther. Statements were also received from the Hon.
Christopher Dodd, of Connecticut, Donald Bonker of Washington and
the Rev. Theodore Hesburgh of Notre Dame University. The general
consensus was that changes were needed and that an optimum
solution would be to re-establish the Peace Corps as an independent organization. Appendixes contain the full text of "The
Future Of The Peace Corps, a report prepared for ACTION by Harlan
Cleveland, supporting statements by several outside bodies, and
the text of H.R. 9774. The last item was introduced into the
House of Representatives on October 27, 1977 by Senator Tsongas,
Rep. Bonker and several other co-sponsors, and is entitled "A Bill
to Restate the Purpose of the Peace Corps." This bill was the
beginning of the effort which culminated in 1981 with the removal
of Peace Corps from ACTION and its re-emergence on the national
scene.

78   U. S. Congress. House Of Representatives Report no. 95-1049.
      95-2H.rp.1049. Peace Corps Act Amendments Of 1978.
      In this bill to make certain changes in the Peace Corps
basic legislation, dated April 11, 1978, in addition to fiscal
matters and opposing views, the following addition is made to
section 2 of the Act: "It is the policy of the United States . .
. to make available to interested countries and areas . . . men
and women qualified for service abroad . . . to help the peoples
of such area in meeting their needs for trained manpower,
particularly in meting the basic needs of those living in the
poorest areas of such countries." It was this piece of
legislation which formally made the concept of "basic human needs"
a part of the framework of the Peace Corps after nearly two
decades of volunteer service which addressed portions of it in
various ways.

79   Congress U. S. House of Representatives. Public Law 87-293.
      An Act To Provide For A Peace Corps To Help the Peoples of
      Interested Countries and Areas In Meeting Their Needs For
      Skilled Manpower. H.R. 7500. United States Statutes At Large,
      87th Congress 1st Session, 1961, .75: .612-625. GS4.111:74.
      This is the complete text of what quickly became referred to
as "the Peace Corps Act", the basic legislation defining the
purposes, administrations, functions, limits and participants in
the carrying out of President Kennedy's planned Corps. Full
details are provided requisite to setting up the agency, adminis-
tering training, inclusion of foreign nationals in the program,
funding and such details as the adoption of a distinctive insignia
for the literature issued by the Peace Corps. A specific
provision makes all participants in the Corps remain eligible for
the draft, and foreign language proficiency is written in as well.

80   Congress U. S. House of Representatives. Public Law 95-331--
      August 2, 1978. <u>An Act . . . To Make Certain Changes In the</u>
      <u>Peace Corps Act</u>. United States Statutes At Large, v.92, Part
      1, 95th Congress, Second Session, 1978: .414-16.
      GS4.111:92/pt.1.
            This act, signed into law by President Jimmy Carter in the
      autumn of 1978, besides making appropriate fiscal arrangements for
      continuing Corps projects, also added the following paragraph to
      Section 3 of the original Peace Corps Act: "In recognition of the
      fact that women in developing countries play a significant role in
      economic production, family support, and the overall development
      process, the Peace Corps shall be administered so as to give
      particular attention to those programs, projects, and activities
      which tend to integrate women into the national economics of
      developing countries, thus improving their status and assisting
      the total development effort." This reflected the rising
      consciousness of the United Nations Decade for Development and its
      emphasis on women of the Third World. Researchers interested in
      further data on the effects of Corps programming in this area
      should also consult Perdita Huston's <u>Third World Women Speak Out</u>
      (   ).

81   U. S. Congress. U. S. House of Representatives. Select
      Committee On Hunger. <u>The Peace Corps: 25 Years Of Alleviating</u>
      <u>Hunger</u>. Washington, D.C., Government Printing Office, 1986.
      Y4.H89:P31.
            This report was part of an evaluation by the Select
      Committee on Hunger of the contributions and roles played by
      United States programs and agencies in addressing the component
      problems of world hunger, malnutrition, agriculture and health
      care. After a brief historical sketch of Peace Corps' origin, the
      focus shifts to the history of its involvement with questions of
      "basic human needs"--areas of income generation, and community
      development. An amendment to the original Peace Corps Act in 1978
      stressed the role of women in development. A summary of the
      activities of Peace Corps in these areas in 1986 is then provided,
      with examples from Asia, Latin America and Africa. In particular,
      the importance of the African Food Systems Initiative is stressed.
      This latter is a program which will "assist local communities to
      develop and implement their own technologies for improvement in
      food systems" (p.4). Other problems being addressed by Corps
      workers include desertification, agriculture extension, fish
      management, water and sanitation, and food conservation. A short
      outline of the Peace Corps Partnership program is then given. The
      Committee supports the continuation of Corps activities against
      hunger (while recommending that the number of volunteers be
      substantially increased): that the African Food Systems
      Initiative be expanded beyond its original target countries of
      Zaire, Lesotho, and Mali: and that the focus on women as
      contributors to development continue to be made a significant part
      of Corps planning.

82   Congress. U. S. House of Representatives. Subcommittee On
      Inter-American Affairs of the Committee On Foreign Affairs.
      Eighty-Ninth Congress First Session Hearing. Peace Corps
      Activities In Latin America And The Caribbean. (6 October
      1965). Y4.F76:P31.
          This document is a complete transcript of testimony given
      before the Committee on Inter-American Affairs by Frank
      Mankiewicz, Regional Director of the Peace Corps for Latin
      America: Gretchen Handwerger, Deputy Director for Latin
      America: Paul Bell, Acting Officer for the West Coast Division, and Michael
      Edwards, Acting Officer for the Central America-Wet Indies
      Division. The format of their presentation is a country-by-
      country survey and review of the successes, problems and details
      of programming of Peace Corps efforts in the region. Congressman
      Henry Gross of Iowa was among the more pointed questioners.
      Issues raised involved cost effectiveness, the presence of Corps
      in some nations where other similar agencies of foreign govern-
      ments were at work, qualifications of Peace Corps teaching
      personnel, changes from university to field training methods, and
      political considerations of possible Corps involvement against
      Cuban or Soviet aid. Countries for which profiles are provided
      are Bolivia, Guatemala, El Salvador, Honduras, Jamaica, Panama,
      Uruguay, Venezuela, Brazil, Peru, Chile, Ecuador, Colombia, the
      Dominican Republic, Costa Rica, British Honduras, Barbados, and
      St. Lucia. As an account of the origins of these country programs
      and their history and status as of 1965, this report is
      invaluable.

83   CONSIDINE, JOHN M. "Two Ways to Aid the Latins". Sign, 42
      (19 May 1963): 12-13.
          This interview with Fr. John Considine focuses on the
      similarities and differences between the United States Peace Corps
      and the Papal Volunteers, the latter created by Pope Paul several
      months prior to the announcement of the Peace Corps. In 1963, 175
      members were serving in twelve countries of Latin America. Living
      conditions and orientation are contrasted, with the wide publicity
      given the Peace Corps viewed as having helped other voluntary
      service groups.

84   COSSOLOTTO, MATTHEW. "How About Adopting A Village?"
      Christian Science Monitor (16 July 1982): 23.
          Written by a volunteer serving in West Africa, this article
      proposes an increased use of volunteers by research institutions
      in the United States as well as co-ordinators of aid on a
      community-to community basis, which the author terms "sister
      villages". This approach is seen as much cheaper and more
      effective than other types of existing foreign aid plans.

85   COSSOLOTTO, MATTHEW. "Leaving Washington for the Path of
     Service". Christian Science Monitor (2 September 1981):   23.
     Reflections on the United States' role in foreign assistance
by a legal aide in the House of Representatives who had just
accepted an invitation to train as a volunteer. Cossolotto urges
a national debate on the value of voluntary service and warns
potential volunteers not to be swayed by relatives, traditional
patterns of career development and education and their own
weaknesses. Revitalization of the Corps is called for via
increased budget allocations.

86. COSSOLOTTO, MATTHEW. "Peace Corps Is Back." Christian Science
     Monitor (February 7, 1985):   16.
     An editorial on the sudden revival of interest in the Peace
Corps through the public appeal for volunteers to serve in an
African food system initiative. As part of further efforts to
improve and rebuild the agency, the Returned Peace Corps
Volunteers of Washington, D.C. have issued a report. Entitled
"Peace Corps 1985: Meeting the Challenge", it contains five
recommendations: restoration of field volunteers to a minimum of
10,000; establishment of Goal 3 of the Peace Corps Act--education
of American regarding the realities of the Third World--as an
agency priority; removal of the appointment of country directors
from the political patronage process; appointment of a qualified
returned volunteer as the next Director of Peace Corps, and
creation of a special advisory body composed of returned volunteers to recommend future changes to the agency with regard to
programming and planning. Cossolottto warns the Yuppie philosophy
of "me first" is still to be dealt with, but the attitude is not
seen as a serious threat to the revival of Corps in the public
mind.

87   COSTANZO, RICHARD. Cross-cultural Adjustment Among Peace Corps
     Volunteers. Ph.D. dissertation, University of Chicago, 1981.
     The data upon which this dissertation is based were obtained
in four surveys of the complete body of Peace Corps volunteers in
service in 1975, 1976, 1978 and 1979, although the bulk of the
information is drawn from the 1976 responses. The objective of
the research was to examine the phenomenon of culture shock within
the framework of cognitive attitude theory, specifically utilizing
the concept of cognitive inconsistency. Based on the theories of
Oberg and others a U-shaped distribution in the incidences of
culture shock was forecast. Constanzo attempted to ascertain
whether or not such a distribution did in fact exist, using the
Peace Corps as his experimental population. Both affective and
attitudinal measure were employed. Analysis of the data indicated
a moderate U-curve was present, with the variation noted as due in
part to the presence of many uncontrolled variables in the
environment of the study. Culture shock was measured through the
application of three guidelines: work satisfaction, intensity of
friendship with host country nationals and psychological well-
being as perceived by the volunteer. Variables seen as
uncontrolled were too many to list individually although three of
the most significant are noted: geographical region of service,

number of hours worked per week, and fluency in the host country tongue. Constanzo defined critical moderating variables as those which affected the degree to which individuals were able to correctly anticipate future events in the culture entered.

88   COTTON, JOHN W. Par For the Corps: A Review of the Literature
      On Selection, Training and Performance of Peace Corps
      Volunteers. Santa Barbara, California: 1973. 3 vols.
          This three-volume bibliography and essay provides a frame-
      work for the analytical and research literature produces by and
      for the Peace Corps up to 1975. Useful both as a reference work
      on the information-gathering process and as an actual
      bibliography. Researchers should also be aware that this document
      is available on the ERIC database as document 110672.

89   "Country Directors Focus on Furthering Peace Corps Goals."
      AA1.13:5/1. InterACTION, 5, n.1 (October 1976): 11.
          A conference of country directors of Peace Corps programs
      from more than fifty nations was held in Columbia, Maryland on
      August 16-20, 1976. This gathering, the first such meeting since
      1969, focused upon ways of improving volunteer placement to
      increase effectiveness. Reports of task forces centering on
      programming systems, use of skill-trained volunteers vs
      generalists and the part voluntarism can and should play in inter-
      national development are summarized.

90   COVINGTON, PHILIP. "Energy and the Peace Corps." AA1.16:2/3.
      Reconnection 2, n.3 (December 1979): 2, 20.
          This article reports on the involvement of Peace Corps
      volunteers in coping with the energy crisis in their host nations.
      Under a grant from the al-Dir'iyyah foundation, the Peace Corps is
      conducting an energy survey of patterns of energy usage and
      possible alternatives in Senegal, the Philippines and Micronesia.
      With placement at the level of the people, volunteers are well
      situated to obtain such information. Other possible roles of
      volunteers in promoting energy management are also discussed.

91   "CREST Center for Reassessment and Training." Peace Corps
      Times (July-August 1985): 6-9.
          Two methods of staging for trainees are available for
      selection by country directors, the (CAST) Center for Assessment
      and Training (an eight day event held about five weeks prior to
      departure for in-country assignments) and CREST. The latter is
      held for those who have been accepted into Corps and is held five
      days prior to departure. It consists of the first stages of
      training itself, including orientation to the Peace Corps, infor-
      mation on the host nation, immunizations and transition data
      relating to personal psychological adjustments for service. A
      CREST held in Miami for a group of trainees bound for Ecuador is
      described in detail as an example.

92   "Dandy Dan in Africa." New Yorker Magazine 42 (30 April
      1966): 38-9.
            An article and interview with Dan Daniel, a New York radio
      announcer covering his three-week trip to Tunisia, Niger, and the
      Ivory Coast to interview members of the Peace Corps. The
      resulting tapes would be distributed free by the Peace Corps and
      host station WMCA to fifteen hundred radio stations nationwide, as
      part of a campaign to publicize the fifth anniversary of the Peace
      Corps. Daniel's reactions to the volunteers are also presented,
      being compounded of amazement, admiration and sheer stubbornness.
      Forty volunteers in the three host nations were interviewed.

93   DAY, RICHARD R. and ALBERT B. SARAKA. An Introduction to
      Spoken Baoule. Preliminary Text. Washington, D.C.: Center
      For Applied Linguistics, 1968.
            This manual was created under sponsorship of the Peace Corps
      for programs teaching the Baoule language, an Akan language of the
      Niger-Congo group of African languages. Utilizing the "microwave"
      approach, 184 "cycles" "of lessons cover vocabulary, structure and
      grammatical patterns, with accompanying glosses in both French and
      English. Linguistic materials were selected "using basic patterns
      in contexts based on phases of life most likely to be encountered
      by Peace Corps Volunteers". Researchers should be aware that this
      document has been entered in the ERIC system under the entry ED
      048591.

94   DEPASSE, DERREL B. "The Peace Corps and the Third World
      Forestry Crisis." American Forests and Forest Life 91, n.7
      (July 1985): 22-4, 53-4.
            The involvement of Peace Corps personnel in forestry
      projects in host countries is profiled, using examples from
      Guatemala, the Philippines, Dominica and Ecuador. Historical
      background on Corps response to requests is given and host country
      problems outlined. The latter include establishment of three
      nurseries, environmental education, modification of traditional
      agricultural and fuel consumption patterns and erosion control.

95   DEUTCHMAN, ARNOLD. "Volunteers In the Field: Teaching."
      Annals of the American Academy of Political and Social Science
      365 (May 1966): 72-82.
            "The Peace Corps teacher role has posed problems of a
      peculiar sort" (p.73). Beginning with this statement, the
      differing perceptions of the volunteer, his host country
      colleagues and students and Peace Corps Washington are presented.
      Issues facing the volunteer working in a teaching setting include
      classroom discipline, a syllabus which may be highly colonial in
      nature and unrelated to host country life, an external system of
      examinations and rote learning. Advantages of such a situation
      are that the expectations of the teacher's behaviors will not be
      as precisely defined as might otherwise be so, permitting greater
      flexibility in classroom approaches. Such change in traditional
      methods may create friction between school staffs and the
      volunteers unless common sense is used. Volunteer teachers feel a
      need to know they are fulfilling a real need in their country: in

some situations, such as the experiment in "co-teaching" in the Philippines, this has not been the case. Community roles which can be taken on by the teacher are also examined, with personnel taking part in everything from road building and well digging to holding adult literacy classes and inoculating their neighbors against tuberculosis. Four points for all volunteers in education are presented, stressing the place of the school within its cultural matrix and its role in fostering a need for achievement as part of development. Admitting that there are as many obstacles as there are volunteers, teachers "must of necessity accept imperfect solutions" (p.82).

96 DOBYNS, HENRY F., PAUL L. DOUGHTY and ALLAN B. HOLMBERG. Peace Corps Impact in the Peruvian Andes: Final Report. Cornell University: Department of Anthropology, 1966.

In late 1962, the Department of Anthropology at Cornell University initiated a research contract to study the impact on host communities of members of Peru III, all of whom had trained on campus in Ithaca. With a research and academic involvement in Peruvian anthropological studies reaching back to 1948, Cornell's anthropologists had been asked to prepare volunteers who would be participating in the PNIPA (Plan Nacional de Integracion de la Poblacion Aborigen). Using a comparative method of analysis PNIPA Volunteers in Indian communities in the Departments of Ancash, Ayacucho, Cuzco and Puno-Tambopata were selected as the experimental population. Baseline information on the fifteen host communities and regions had been compiled through earlier work by Cornell staff centering upon the settlement of Vicos. Following an introductory discussion of research design and modification, detailed descriptions of each community and Peace Corps program by Department are provided. The project results indicated that Peace Corps volunteer impact upon host communities could be quantified and measured according to objective criteria, with volunteer placements accelerating the process of development. This study ranks as one of the earliest attempts by a training university with a history of regional expertise to assess in-country contributions of Peace Corps personnel and to then fit that contribution into an overall matrix of national development research. The document text is illustrated with selected photographs showing the varieties of tasks engaged in by Peru III members. A lengthy bibliography is also provided.

97 Doing Business With The Peace Corps: A Guide For Contractors. Washington, D.C., Peace Corps, Office of Financial Management, 1985. PE1.8:B96.

A short publication for private organizations and firms interested in bidding on contracts for supplies of various goods and services to the Peace Corps. Contracts are offered in four areas: volunteer recruitment (primarily audiovisual in nature): training services (language, skill and cross-cultural training):

development of program materials (for example, appropriate technology, forestry and health) and logistical support for the volunteers in the field. Details of the Corps procurement system and information for bidders are provided. An appendix lists the types of services usually put out for bid.

98   "Draft May Defer Peace Corpsmen." New York Times (7 March 1961): 1,29.
       At a news conference in Washington, D.C., several days after the issuing of the executive order which created the temporary Peace Corps, Sargent Shriver stated that his organization "would take the world by surprise". He also disclosed that Major General Lewis Hershey, Director of the Selective Service System, had remarked that returning Peace Corps veterans eligible for the draft would probably receive "further deferment." This meant that persons completing 2 years of Corps service would not automatically be drafted upon their return to the United States. Shriver also noted the creation of a career planning board for the advising of returning volunteers. Several countries in Asia and Africa had already expressed interest in having Peace Corps work in various capacities.

99   DUHL, LENONARD J., ROBERT L. LEOPOLD and JOSEPH T. ENGLISH. "A Mental Health Program for the Peace Corps." Human Organization 23 (Summer 1964): 131-6.
       An outline of the mental health support systems and training roles which psychiatrists have assumed in the Peace Corps, this article was composed by three professionals who had served or were currently serving as staff members. Psychiatric needs are seen to lie in three specific areas of Corps: selection and placement, training, and in-country support. Each of these phases of applied psychiatry is explored in detail. Emphasis is placed upon the uses found for techniques developed in other fields as well as the difficulties which the relatively unstructured situation may pose for those psychiatrists more familiar with the traditional format of the office consultation. Volunteer data from the field was insufficient to address the problems of re-entry and the degree to which Corps was prepared to assist returning volunteers in coping with them. This article was originally given as a presented paper at the 119th Annual Meeting of the American Psychiatric Association in St. Louis, Missouri on May 9, 1963.

100   DUSHANE, GRAHAM. "Idealism for Export." Science, 133 (31 March 1961): 977.
       An opinion piece by the editor of Science on the idea and future of the Peace Corps. Note is taken of the participation of experienced personnel in the social sciences and education as members of the planning staffs. Written one month after President Kennedy established the Corps by an executive order, this offers a look at the early reception accorded the notion by the intellectual community of the United States.

101   EDWARDS, MIKE. "Teachers in the Peace Corps." Saturday Review
      (30 July 1963): 42-4, 59-60.
           In mid-1963, the first group of Peace Corps teachers
      returned to the United States. This article by a Corps press
      officer examines the types of volunteers who become teachers--many
      of whom were not in teaching prior to their service--the
      classroom situations encountered, and their relation to education
      in America. A map is included locating all teaching volunteers as
      of March 31, 1963, showing the number assigned to the various host
      countries. Examples of volunteer life are included from the
      Philippines, British Honduras, Ghana and Nigeria. Problems
      encountered in-country included mismatching of volunteers to
      schools, language learning and coping with differing systems of
      education. The volunteer view of their work is best expressed in
      this quote from a member of Peace Corps/Philippines: "The
      important thing that we are doing is not that which can be
      measured with a camera. People in other projects can photograph a
      bridge they've designed, a road they've helped build or a toilet
      they've constructed. But who can photograph the mind of a child"
      (pp.44, 59)?

102   EGAN, LEO. "Eisenhower, At Rally Here, Derides Kennedy
      Policies". New York Times (25, October, 1961): 1.
           Former President Dwight Eisenhower spoke at a political
      rally in New York City in support of Republican candidates on
      October 25, 1961. The tone of his speech was heavily critical of
      actions and policies of the new Kennedy administration. The Peace
      Corps came in for severe attack, being dismissed as "a juvenile
      experiment" Eisenhower also suggested that it be sent to the moon,
      since that was also "an undeveloped country." Reference was made
      to an incident involving a member of Peace Corps Nigeria, Margery
      Michelmore, which proved that Corpsmen "did not even know what an
      undeveloped country was."

103   "Eight Volunteer Views: The Down-To-Earth Problems of Central
      American Agriculture". AA1.13:3/9. InterACTION, 3, n.9 (June
      1975): 6-7.
           Accounts by volunteers serving in the nations of El
      Salvador, Costa Rica and Ecuador in the agricultural sectors
      describing their projects and the difficulties facing these
      countries. Programs mentioned include improving methods of forage
      preparation and feeding, extension work with small gardens to
      improve local diets and introduce new potential cash crops and
      livestock management efforts.

104   ENGLUND, DAVID L. "Peace Corps Training and the American
      University". International Review of Education, 11, n.2
      (1965): 209-17.
           Problems encountered in designing a training curriculum and
      environment for volunteers within traditional American higher
      education are reviewed, using the experiences of the first three
      years' training groups as a base. Stating that "many universities
      have done a less than adequate job of training for Peace Corps
      service" (p.209) the article explores the conflicts involved in

the collision of two such different systems as the environments of
Corps and the American academia, "between the speculative orientation of the academician and the experiential and political prowess
required in an action oriented program such as the Peace Corps"
(p.210). Viewing the real issue as how best to utilize available
resources of the universities to address formulations of project
descriptions is next examined. Thirteen principles which were
used by the University of Hawaii at Hilo to guide the training of
more than 1000 volunteers for Southeast Asian nations are then set
forth as an example. Among them are emphases on program
flexibility, a preference for isolating the training site as much
as possible, stressing of performance, and questions of rapport
and commitment. The Hawaiian matrix can be summarized in the
statement, "the more nearly training approaches actual overseas
conditions the more relevant it will be" (p.214). Researchers
should note that this article was originally given as a paper at
the American Psychological Association Convention, Los Angeles,
September 4-7, 1964.

105   An Evaluation Model for Assessing the Effects of Peace Corps
      Programs in Health and Agriculture. Washington, D.C.:
      Practical Concepts Incorporated (PCY), 1977.
          This research report was prepared at the conclusion of a
      contract with Peace Corps whose objective was the development of
      practical methods of evaluating impact, effectiveness and
      efficiency of programs in agriculture and health. Evaluation
      goals were to describe both the contexts within which Peace Corps
      projects in these spheres were operating and the system of
      resource allocation. Seven research questions based upon these
      objectives are posed and evaluation models evolved and documented.
      The staff which carried out this study included one member from
      the evaluation division of ACTION and four psychology faculty from
      Northwestern University.

106   "Executive Order 10924: Establishment and Administration of
      the Peace Corps in the Department of State". Code of Federal
      regulations, 1959-1963 Compilation, pp. 447-8. GS4.108 959-
      1963.
          With this order, issued on March 1, 1961, President John F.
      Kennedy brought the Peace Corps into existence. The four
      provisions of this order define that the agency shall be created
      by the secretary of state, how it shall be financed, and state its
      functions. These are to "be responsible for the training and
      service abroad of men and women of the United States in new
      programs of assistance to nations and areas of the world."

107   "Executive Order 11103: Providing for the Appointment of
      Former Peace Corps Volunteers to the Civilian Career Services".
      Federal Register (1963): 3571. GS1.107:28 1963.
          The complete text of the order by which President Kennedy
      made volunteers who had completed successful service eligible for
      service in other branches under a recognized status. Certificates
      of service were to be issued to all persons who fulfilled two
      years of service, with provision made for exceptional cases.

108   "Experiment in International Living to Train PCVs".
       AAl.13:5/6. InterACTION, 5, n.6 (March 1977): 7.
          An agreement has been signed between ACTION and the Experi-
       ment in International Living in Brattleboro, Vermont to train 160
       Peace Corps volunteers for assignments in Cameroon, Senegal, Upper
       Volta, Mali, Niger, Gabon, Mauritania and Chad. Training sessions
       will last eight weeks and center on the subject specialties of
       rural development, livestock breeding, health care, printing and
       vocational education. Staff members represent both the American
       professional community and expatriates with service in the host
       nations.

109   "Experiment, Peace Corps Work for Same Goals". Peace Corps
       Volunteer, 3, n.7 (May 1965): 7-11. S19.11/2:3/7.
          A profile of the Experiment in International Living, which
       has administered several Peace Corps projects as well as providing
       its Vermont facilities as training grounds for numerous groups of
       volunteers.

110   EZEKIEL, RAPHAEL-SAFRA. Differentiation, Demand and Agency In
       Projections of the Personal Future: A Predictive Study of the
       Performance of Peace Corps Teachers. Ph.D. dissertation,
       University of California-Berkeley, 1964.
          This dissertation in social psychology is significant for
       two reasons: it focuses on the very first group of Peace Corps
       volunteers to serve anywhere, the teachers of Ghana I, and it
       utilizes a novel concept of personality development analysis
       through projective autobiography. This technique makes the inner
       experiences of an individual part of the research process and
       amenable to quantification to some degree. Following an introduc-
       tion describing the place of the study in relation to other social
       psychological studies on the need to achieve and personal time
       perspective, a profile of the members of Ghana I and their assign-
       ments is presented. During on-campus training at Berkeley in
       1961, each volunteer was asked to compose three autobiographical
       essays, covering the planned life course should the application
       for Corps service not be accepted, one after five years recounting
       post-Peace Corps life, and one in the applicant's fortieth year.
       These essays were then related to actual performance on site as
       reflected in the first and second year evaluations conducted in
       Ghana. Findings are then offered and conclusions for the overall
       field of social psychology and Peace Corps training stated. The
       data this work contains on the forty-two people who began the work
       of Peace Corps is unique and invaluable.

111   Fairfield, Roy P. "Peace Corps Training at Ohio University".
       School and Society, 92 (14 November 1964): 339-41.
          American universities have played a significant role in the
       training of the Peace Corps, both through the provision of train-
       ing sites and faculty and staff members as resources. This
       article examines both the general program outline of training as
       to contents and the follow-up structure utilized by Ohio
       University to support and improve their work for Peace

Corps/Cameroon. Written by the campus coordinator for three
groups of trainees, this provides an excellent look at the
difficulties of setting up training and the possible solutions to
them.

112   "FARM Project Sends 11 Texans to Liberia". AA1.13:1/9.
       InterACTION, 1, n.9 (June 1973): 6.
           An informal arrangement between the Peace Corps and several
       American universities, known as FARM (Future Agricultural Research
       Manpower) is supplying volunteers for the agricultural sector in
       many host nations. This article notes the departure of eleven
       trainees as part of this effort for service in Liberia. Feedback
       to schools of agriculture is provided through the visits of
       professors to countries where volunteers are presently serving.
       As of 1973, eight host nations had been visited: Brazil, Ecuador,
       Peru, Columbia, Zaire, Togo, the Ivory Coast and Liberia. With
       such background information, students may apply for a specific
       host country project.

113   FERRIGNO, JAMES M. "Peace Corps Projects At the University of
       Massachusetts". Modern Language Journal, 47 (November 1963):
       323-7.
           A report on the linguistic training given at Massachusetts
       for two different groups of volunteers bound for the Ivory Coast,
       Senegal and Niger. Insufficient data regarding trainee aptitude
       for foreign languages, although available, was not made use of
       until nearly the start of the program through bureaucratic
       troubles. Lack of adequate time for the design of a program,
       selection of staff and curriculum planning were laid at the door
       of Peace Corps Washington, with the warning that host institutions
       must not be put" in a time squeeze." While supporting the ideals
       and plans of Peace Corps service, Dr. Ferrigno stresses that
       improved language training will hasten the time when volunteers
       can begin to adequately cope with the local languages and thus be
       more effective in their assignments.

114   "15,000 Respond to Peace Corps Plea for Farmers". Successful
       Farming, 83 (April 1985): 11.
           On January 10, 1985, the Peace Corps issued a special call
       for persons with agricultural experience and background to come
       forward as volunteers. Four months later, some 15,000 persons had
       responded, many of them with twenty and thirty years of practical
       farming behind them. Officials of the Corps expressed amazement
       and stated that they would be able to fully answer requests from
       host countries for workers in this field for the first time. The
       usual percentage of agricultural requests filled is between fifty
       and sixty percent. Many of the new volunteers will be assigned to
       the African Food Systems Initiative, a program using a team
       approach, as opposed to individual placements as in the past.

115   "First Black Peace Corps Head Forced to Resign Her Post". Jet,
       55 (14 December 1978): 6.
            Dr. Carolyn Payton, appointed by President Jimmy Carter as
       the director of Peace Corps during its time under ACTION, resigned
       after several weeks of dispute with Sam Brown, head of the latter
       agency. Unresolvable differences over the running of the Peace
       Corps and its place in ACTION were said to be behind the
       dismissal. The article notes that over the two decades since the
       Eisenhower administration, many black appointees have been obliged
       to leave their positions. Brown had put forth the suggestion that
       the Peace Corps would function better as a smaller agency with
       better-trained personnel.

116   The First 120 Days of ACTION: November 1, 1971. AA1.2Ac8.
       Washington, D.C.: ACTION, 1971.
            The first three months of the existence of the umbrella
       agency ACTION and its effect on the seven voluntary service
       programs comprising it is given in detail. On July 1, 1971,
       Director Blatchford sent letters to all volunteers in the field,
       explaining the new agency and its functions. He traveled to five
       African host nations of the Peace Corps to further extend under-
       standing, while Kevin O'Donnell, acting Associate Director of
       Corps, visited Peru, Chile, Brazil, Paraguay and Venezuela.
       Members of the Peace Corps National Advisory Council toured host
       nations of East Asia as well as Kenya, Ghana, and Ethiopia. Nine
       objectives for ACTION are stated based upon consultation among
       member agencies. Peace Corps changes are noted in a shift from
       training within the United States to training in the host country,
       with 80% of all training taking place overseas. By 1973, it is
       planned that all training will follow this format. Training
       models from Ghana, India, Western Samoa and Ethiopia are noted.
       General future plans and goals for the agency, as far as can be
       stated at the time, compose the remaining portion of the document.
       For researchers wishing to understand the changes within and about
       Peace Corps, following its incorporation within ACTION, this
       source provides valuable background data as well as the develop-
       ments of Corps itself in 1971.

117   FITZGERALD, MERLE INGRASSIA. The Peace Corps Today. New York:
       Dodd, Mead and Company, 1986.
            A children's book written upon the occasion of the 25th
       anniversary year of the agency, this volume presents the history
       of Corps work and offers a readable look at its contributions in
       terms comprehensible to contemporary young people. Photographs of
       volunteers and Third World school children illustrate the volume.

118   "Fisheries Sector: Past Experience Paves the Way for New
       Efforts". Peace Corps Times (September/October/November 1985):
       16-8.
            A brief overview of the history of Peace Corps involvement
       in fisheries projects, and their advantages as sources of protein
       to unbalanced diets. Examples of such efforts are given from
       Zaire.

119   "Flow of Books on Peace Corps Passes 11:   2 More Are Coming".
       Peace Corps Volunteer, 2, n.11 (September 1964):   5.
       S19.11/2:2/11.
           A review of the books published on the Peace Corps between
       its foundation in 1961 and mid-1964. Each title is briefly
       examined and full publication information given. Items listed
       here have been entered under their authors and titles elsewhere in
       the present work.

120   "Focus--National Volunteer Week". Peace Corps Times (May/June
       1985):   6-9.
           A profile of Kathy Gilchrist, Phil Heilman and Lynn
       Blaylock, the three persons chosen as the 1985 Volunteers of the
       Year and honored by President Reagan. Details of their assign-
       ments and projects in Burkina Faso, Micronesia, and Barbados are
       included.

121   FORBES, MALCOLM S. "The Moral Equivalent of War". Forbes, 88
       (1 July 1961):   7-8.
           In this editorial comment, the publisher of Forbes considers
       the Peace Corps to be a fulfillment of William James' concept of
       a moral equivalent of warfare, with participants gaining all the
       experience and developing all the virtues which James pointed out
       warfare engendered in its survivors. Benefits for American
       foreign policy and business are seen to be substantial. The
       request of Sargent Shriver that businesses grant leaves of absence
       to trained personnel who wish to serve is favorably viewed, with
       American Telephone and Telegraph already having done so.

122   "Free Peace Corps Ads Cut". Christian Science Monitor
       (2 January 1970):   14.
           The advertising firm of Young and Rubicam, New York, reports
       that the Advertising Council, Inc., has decided to replace Peace
       Corps public service announcements with environmental groups. The
       latter are viewed as requiring more help in achieving a place in
       the public mind. Folders containing news of the Corps will be
       sent out several times a year in place of the promotional spots.

123   "French-Speaking West Africa: Volunteers Encounter 'La
       Civilization Francaise' In Former Colonies". Peace Corps
       Volunteer, 3, n.8-9 (August 1965):   7-23. S19.11/2:3/8-9.
           A collection of thirteen articles composed by staff and
       volunteers in the African host nations of the Ivory Coast, Niger,
       Guinea, Senegal and Togo. Researchers should note that some of
       these items have been entered under the country sections elsewhere
       in this bibliography.

124   FREUNDLICH, PAUL. "The Peace Corps on Film". Peace Corps
       Volunteer, 5, n.11 (September 1967):   17-21. S19.11/2:5/11.
           Film maker Paul Freundlich created seven films about the
       Peace Corps for agency use. This article is a series of interview
       questions on the changes in filming the Peace Corps world. To
       him, "there is really only one problem: The reality of the volun-
       teer in the field and the problem of doing justice to that

reality" (p.17). Films reviewed here are A Choice I Made, This Land and One Step At A Time. At the time this piece appeared, forty-two promotional films had been produced for Corps use, chiefly in recruiting programs.

125   FRIEDMAN, FREDERICA. "Peace Corps Forestry: There's a Forest in Your Future". American Forests and Forest Life, 71, (February 1965): 20-1, 56-8.
      Involvement of Peace Corps volunteers in forestry activity in host countries is illustrated with case studies from Ecuador, Nepal, Chile, East Pakistan and Nigeria. Volunteers are seen as bridges permitting the local forestry personnel to gain knowledge of updated techniques and to, in part, set forestry policy for their host nations through their contributions of time and effort. Details of Peace Corps admission standards are then provided.

126   FRIEDMAN, FREDERICA. "The Peace Corps in Art: A Report". American Artist, 29 (June 1965): 80, 97-101.
      A survey article covering the activities of volunteers in the area of arts and crafts work. Examples range from art education in Guayaquil, Ecuador, formation of crafts marketing cooperatives for regional weaving in Colombia, ceramic workshops in Ayacucho, Peru, use of cartoons in public health work in Ecuador, and establishment of a School of Graphic Arts in Kabul, Afghanistan. Language barriers and cultural resistance are noted as factors which may impede such projects.

127   FULLER, WILLIAM A. "A View of the Peace Corps". Educational Forum, 30 (November 1965): 95-101.
      Written by a former representative for a joint Near East-Foundation-Peace Corps effort in Iran (1962-1964), this article offers some scathing criticism of both the Peace Corps organization and personal shortcomings of volunteers. Volunteers are seen to be wanting in an awareness of the implications of adopting host country dress, possessing insufficient command of the local language prior to their arrival on site, unaware of the fact that his or her actions will be seen by host country people not as individual idiosyncrasies but as national traits, and described as "often gruff, unpolished, inconsiderate, insulting, patronizing and downright childish" (p. 97). Little evidence for these charges is adduced other than personal communications to the author and one report of a language instructor. Fuller also states that the media receive little or no bad publicity from the agency itself and none from overseas due to the fact that all press releases must be cleared by the Peace Corps if coming from a host country. Improvement in all these areas is seen to be necessary if the Peace Corps is to function in the manner originally envisaged. Researchers should note that at the time this was written, several thousand volunteers had already completed service and returned to the United States, and that Peace Corps/Iran continued to function successfully.

128   "Fund Lack Forces Peace Corps Cut". <u>Christian Science Monitor</u>
       (7 February 1972): 3.
            Prior to adjournment on December 17, 1971, Congress passed a
       continuing resolution for a Peace Corps budget of $77.2 million.
       Due to Senate inaction on the $68 million appropriated by the
       House of Representatives, Corps Director Blatchford has frozen
       applications and plans to reduce the 8,000 volunteers in the field
       by half and possibly cancel programs in as many as fifteen
       countries.

129   GARBARINI, M. "Michigan Influence Felt in the Peace Corps".
       <u>Michigan Education Journal</u>, 40 (November 1962): 254-55.
            A survey article detailing the participation of the
       universities and citizens of the state of Michigan in the growth
       and training of the Peace Corps. Both the University of Michigan
       and Michigan State University have served as training sites for
       groups of volunteers intended for service in Thailand and Nigeria
       respectively. Joseph Kaufman, speaking as the Peace Corps
       representative at the conference of the Michigan Association of
       School Administrators in the autumn of 1962, asked for the
       assistance of the Michigan educators in locating qualified
       candidates. Photographs included illustrated scenes from the
       training of the Thailand group, including language instruction and
       learning <u>takraw</u>, a popular sport.

130   "Go Everywhere, Young Man". <u>Time</u>, 77 (24 February 1961): 59.
            This brief article examines the origin of the Peace Corps,
       the types of personnel envisaged for it and the training they
       should receive--focussing on skills needed in the host country.
       After a comparison with the only other organization sufficiently
       similar then in existence--the British Volunteers In Service
       Overseas (VSO) Program--examples of field situations are given
       from Botswana, Sarawak, British Guiana and the Solomon Islands.

131   "Gold Medal To Sargent Shriver". <u>Congressional Record</u>, 132,
       n.40 (27 March 1986): S3762-63.
            The consideration of S.1756, a bill which authorized the
       Senate to agree to the creation of a special gold medal for the
       honoring of R. Sargent Shriver, first Director of the United
       States Peace Corps. The medal was to be struck to commemorate the
       twenty-fifth anniversary of the founding of the Peace Corps in
       1961. Its design was to bear the symbol of the Peace Corps on one
       side with an image of Sargent Shriver, and on the other a listing
       of all the names of Directors of Peace Corps up to 1986. The
       chief presenter, Senator Chris Dodd, paid tribute to Shriver and
       recalled his own service as a volunteer in the Dominican Republic
       from 1966 to 1968. The bill was read for a third time and passed.

132 GORMAN, JOHN. "Leaner Peace Corps is Thriving". Congressional
Record, 130, n.59 (9 May 1984): S5494.
This article is a concise overview of the changes which the
agency has experienced since its inception in 1961, focusing
specifically on the political changes and the elimination of many
programmatic features found unworkable in the mid-1970's.
Interviews with Loret Miller Ruppe, ministry officials from Nepal,
and former in-country directors are included. One notable feature
is the explanation of the catalyst for Peace Corps becoming a
separate entity again in 1981, the nomination by President Reagan
of a former military intelligence officer as the head of ACTION.

133 GRANDE, PETER P. "Use of Self and Peer Ratings in a Peace
Corps Training Program". Vocational Guidance Quarterly, 14,
n.4 (Summer 1966): 244-46.
This article reports on a study done upon a group of volunteers in training in an effort to ascertain whether any relationship existed between their self-images and the ratings given them
by their peers. These latter were most often of the nature of "Do
you believe this person will be a successful Volunteer?" A
significant correlation was noted between lower ratings by volunteers and subjects judged ineffective by Peace Corps evaluation
board. "This suggests that the trainees themselves are in an
advantaged position to make . . . valid judgments regarding the
future success or failure of fellow trainees" (p. 245).

134 GREENING, THOMAS C. "When a Group Rejects Its Leader". Small
Group Behavior, 4, n.2 (May 1973): 245-48.
The experiences of a group leader in a Peace Corps training
program of sensitivity training are related, with a view towards
helping other group therapists use the experience of being
constantly challenged as a way of improving their skills. This is
a shortened version of a paper given at the meeting of the Group
Psychotherapy Association of Southern California on January 17,
1965.

135 GROTHE, PETER. "Peace Corps and the American High School".
Journal of Secondary Education, 37 (March 1962): 162-65.
Written by a consultant to the Peace Corps, this short piece
reviews the ways in which high schools can assist the Peace Corps
through informing students of its plans and purposes, and ways in
which students who may wish to enter Corps subsequent to graduation can plan their studies.

136 "Growing Stronger...Growing Better: A Message from ACTION
Director Mike Balzano". AA1.13:2/10. InterACTION, 2, n.10
(July 1974): 1, 4.
A summary statement issued by Michael Balzano following the
completion of his first full year as head of ACTION. While almost
exclusively devoted to domestic programs in the United States,
Balzano's text does note the deployment of $4.5 million in aid to
the drought-stricken nations of the Sahel, much of it done with
advice from the Peace Corps. Plans for reprogramming returning
volunteers are also mentioned.

137   GUZMAN, JOHN EDWARD. <u>Major Administrative Problems of the</u>
       <u>Teacher Corps/Peace Corps Program and Their Priorities</u>. Ph.D.
       dissertation, Washington State University, 1976.
           This dissertation reports on the results of a survey
       questionnaire sent to forty-two project directors, interns,
       instructors, field administrators and host country personnel at
       three universities involved in the preparation of volunteers for
       overseas service. Direct observation and interviews supplemented
       the questionnaire data. The three universities differed substan-
       tially in their experience with training for overseas posting,
       with Texas Southern University having a long relationship with
       training for Ghana, the State University College at Buffalo a
       close involvement in Afghanistan, and Washington State the least
       experience training for Spanish-speaking host nations, with the
       direct link to Venezuela. Among the results of the survey were
       the opinions that achieving language facility ought to be a major
       objective of training, closer collaboration in all stages of
       planning was called for between host country ministries and the
       American university holding the training contract, and that a more
       systematic method of evaluating training effectiveness was
       required. The negotiation of a long-term agreement with a
       university to provide a particular skill needed in the host
       country was viewed as the optimum situation. The full text of the
       questionnaire is supplied in an appendix.

138   HANDY, DEIRDRE CATHLEEN PATRICK. <u>The Relationship of</u>
       <u>Hierarchical Need Level to Success of Peace Corps Trainees</u>.
       Ph.D. dissertation, University of Texas, 1966.
           This dissertation reports on psychological research done
       using a model based upon Abraham Maslow's theory of an "hierarchy
       of needs" (physiological, safety, belongingness and love, esteem,
       etc.) with motivations of deficit and growth. In a 1954
       application of his hierarchy to a group of young adults, Maslow
       found only one in 3,000 who satisfied his definition of "growth-
       motivated", leading him to conclude that "self actualization of
       the sort I had found in my older subjects was not possible in our
       society for young developing people" (p. 11). Handy proposed to
       use a sample of young adults--in this case, 191 members of six
       Peace Corps training programs carried out at the University of
       Texas between June, 1965 and May, 1966--hypothesizing that
       Maslow's model of need order and scores on the ACL (Adjective
       Checklist Manual) would be related to selection board decisions on
       each trainee. Statistically relationships were established for
       the fifteen listed needs making up the ACL scale. Especially
       important were needs for achievement, endurance, order, dominance
       and nurture as related to success in training. The six programs
       from which the sample population was drawn represent the full
       gamut of early training orientations, including community

development, laboratory technology, secondary school language
teaching, nursing and university instruction. Host nations for
these groups are not specified. The ACL is recommended as
applicable to other similar situations. This study represents a
clear example of the many ways in which Peace Corps attempted to
set up a system of evaluation in training and the problems it
confronted in doing so.

139   HANFF, HELENE. Good Neighbors: The Peace Corps in Latin
      America. New York: Grosset and Dunlap, 1966.
      Intended as supplementary reading for elementary school
students in social studies courses, this book provides a brief
history of the Peace Corps goals and programs in Brazil, Bolivia,
Honduras, Colombia and Peru.

140   HAPGOOD, DAVID and MERIDAN BENNETT. Agents of Change: A Close
      Look at the Peace Corps. Boston: Little, Brown and Co.,
      1968.
      The history, evolution, problems and successes of the Peace
Corps for the period from 1961 to 1967 are analyzed and evaluated
in this volume. "How or what is the Peace Corps doing? The
question is more easily asked than answered" (p. 18). In their
attempt to do so, the authors examine the institutions into which
volunteers are sometimes projected, the colonial heritage which
they may often support (and which interferes with true development), Corps teachers and their various contributions, rural
action programs (including school-to-school projects) public
health and birth control, and community development. While all
Corps efforts are criticized it is community development which is
most severely hit. Training plans and their alteration since 1961
also are noted. The final chapter presents the authors' concept
of the volunteer as an "agent of change". Such persons usually
work along several lines: "to adapt and apply improved productive
technology, to understand the local culture, to explain the
intruding world culture, to increase the options and the power of
his hosts while deliberately limiting his own" (pp. 206-11).
Corps is seen against the turmoil of Vietnam and domestic protests
as "one of the faces that America presents to the world. . . .
Today that face is eclipsed by the mask of power" (p. 238). It is
through service as agents of graceful change that Corps will make
its most lasting contributions.

141   HARRIS, JESSE G. "A Science of the South Pacific: Analysis of
      the Character Structure of the Peace Corps Volunteer".
      American Psychologist, 28, n.3 (March 1973): 232-47.
      Until the summer of 1970, psychological assessment of volun-
teers was undertaken by outside consultants serving as chairmen of
selection boards. At this time, such formal assessments were
eliminated as untenable though useful, and the author does not
attempt to evaluate the merits of this change. Rather, his
orientation is towards exploring, based on a research report,
aspects of field evaluation of volunteers and what this could
contribute to the development of psychology as a relevant part of

federal programs. While acknowledging that, for the decade 1961-
1971, worldwide attrition rates for volunteers appear to have
increased, Harris admits that "to specify the attributes which are
of importance and to demonstrate the generality of such requirements for all Peace Corps assignments is a research task that has
never been conducted to completion" (P. 234). With some seventy-
five percent of all training programs taking place in the host
countries, it seemed possible to test the adequacy of trainee
psychological defenses and coping mechanisms under the moderate
stress conditions presented by such programs. It was felt that
only such observations could assist in the creation of a more
accurate and rational system of evaluation for effective service.
Prerequisites for and functions of an overall evaluation procedure
are stated. Peace Corps Tongah was chosen as the field situation
due to the author's previous connection with that program as a
field selection officer. Drawing upon a series of open interviews
with fifty-three volunteers, Tongan educational staff and Peace
Corps personnel, field rating forms were developed. These took
the form of a list of thirty-two items covering performance,
personal and interpersonal attributes. Data are analyzed through
factor analysis and discriminate analysis. Two successful groups
of volunteers, Tonga III and TongaV, were included in the sample.
Character traits were found to be the most important single
category distinguishing successful volunteers from early
terminees, and equally important with performance variables. The
final section of the paper examines the implications of this
research for the profession of psychology, criticizing the old
selection board structure and positing reasons for its failure.
Harris notes that "it is possible that psychology relinquished
involuntarily its significant role in the Peace Corps . . . in
part . . . because psychology had not established a beachhead of
organized research on which to defend itself" (p. 246).

142   HARRIS, MARK. <u>Twenty-One Twice: A Journal</u>. Boston: Little,
       Brown & Co., 1966.
              In this personal account of his life for a period of months
in the mid-1960's, one of the evaluators hired by the Peace Corps
for objective reporting on country programs describes his recruitment by Sargent Shriver, the lengthy--and sometimes ludicrous--
security background checking done by the FBI, and finally his two
weeks roving and observing in a West African host nation to which
he give the name of Kongohno, and which is not Ghana or Liberia.
This rambling work is useful for the look it provides at a part of
Peace Corps work whose reports were in many cases not declassified
until several years later.

143   HARRISON, ROGER and RICHARD L. HOPKINS. "The Design of Cross-
       Cultural Training: An Alternative to the University Model".
       Journal of Applied Behavioral Sciences, 3, n.4 (1967):
       431-68.
       The application of a traditional university model of
curriculum construction to solving problems of designing an effective training program for the Peace Corps has not proven to be
successful. In this paper, the weaknesses of the model are
analyzed, with the chief flaw seen in the areas of overseas living
requiring knowledge of interpersonal relations. The goals of
university education and overseas education are contrasted, with
significant divergences in overall goals noted. An alternative
model employed by the authors during the summer and fall of 1965
at the Peace Corps Training Center at Arecibo, Puerto Rico is
outlined. Projects involved were the Ecuador/RCA Colonization
Project and the regional arts and crafts project for Ecuador,
Chile and Bolivia. Usage of returned volunteers as part of the
training staffs is suggested. The characteristics of the alternative model include structure of the training by the trainees
themselves--exclusive of language training--as a spur to
individual initiative and an emphasis on the environment of training. The basic units were problem-solving projects of various
types, analogous to situations volunteers would encounter on site.
Examples of these are raising chickens and pigs, mutual instruction in welding, arts and crafts and accounting, and physical
fitness tests. Staff members are seen as guides and facilitators
of projects. The core of the alternative model emphasized self-
sufficiency as much as possible and the ideal sources of the
skills needed for trainees are the returned volunteers themselves,
who have already learned how to learn and innovate. The traditional models are viewed as useful for abstract data but useless
for practical survival skills.

144   "Have Ideals, Will Travel". Economist, 199 (10 June 1961):
       1112-14.
       "A desire to go abroad to serve humanity is not sufficient
qualifications for membership in President Kennedy's Peace Corps."
With this blunt statement a brief examination of Peace Corps
preliminary testing is begun and a profile of projects already
approved in 1961 provided. Testing focuses on trainees' abilities
in verbal matters, their knowledge of American history, and
specialized knowledge of English, agriculture, mechanics and so
forth through a host of other special crafts. Noting that, at
present, no training in anti-Communist propaganda is included in
Peace Corps preparation, the author speculates whether Congress
might insist on this as a condition of funding Corps on a permanent basis, and notes that many feel that such work should be left
to established missionary and educational groups.

145   "Health Projects in Peace Corps Programs". <u>Auxiliary Leader</u>,
      3, (July 1962):   12.
          As part of the overall expansion of Peace Corps programs, a
      sharp increase in volunteers in the health sciences is noted. As
      of June 1962, 51 such volunteers were in the field, with another
      125 in training. In the latter group were the first physicians to
      go abroad as volunteers, the bulk of whom will be assigned to the
      Federation of Malaya. Other specialists recruited include
      licensed practical nurses, public health nurses, laboratory tech-
      nicians and dentists. No requests for hospital administrators had
      been received as yet, but Corps officials expected that such would
      be forthcoming. The changes in Peace Corps in the first year of
      operation are noted, such as the presence of some volunteers in
      their sixties.

146   "Healthy Yearling". <u>America</u>, 106 (24 March 1962):   809.
          An editorial opinion reviewing the achievements of Peace
      Corps in its first year of existence, expressing strong support
      for expansion of the agency. Success is noted by the "fact that
      the Soviets have stolen the idea lock stock and barrel."

147   "Help A Friend Build A Future". AA1.10:2/3. <u>Transition</u>, 2,
      n.3 (March 1973):   23-5.
          A promotional overview of the School Partnership Program of
      the Peace Corps, in which American schools are paired with commu-
      nities wishing to construct their own facilities in assistance and
      cross-cultural exchange. This is presented as one way in which
      returned volunteers can continue to contribute.

148   HENRY, EDWIN R. "Selection of Volunteers". <u>Annals of the</u>
      <u>American Academy of Political and Social Science</u>, 365 (May
      1966):   21-8.
          The objectives and procedures for the selection of a Peace
      Corps Volunteer are set forth in detail, beginning with the
      initial application and testing and following through the psycho-
      logical screening during the training period itself. Researchers
      should bear in mind that Peace Corps training has undergone sub-
      stantial changes since this article was written. As an historical
      record of the care given to the choosing of the first groups of
      volunteers it is invaluable.

149   HENRY, EDWIN R. "What Business Can Learn from Peace Corps
      Selection and Training". <u>Personnel</u>, 42, n.4 (1965):   17-25.
          Written by the former director of selection for the Peace
      Corps (1963-1964), this article explores both the selection
      structure and process used by the organization, and some of the
      aspects of the training curriculum. Grounds for disqualification
      include self-selection, medical reasons, and inability to show
      necessary linguistic proficiency. Recommendations for the
      business community are to develop a pool of qualified people in

their own spheres, to better manage a group of trainees by
extending and intensifying their training programs, and, above
all, to utilize the proven expertise of Peace Corps volunteers
upon their return. Union contracts covering benefits for
employees who decide to serve in the Peace Corps are seen as an
indication that business is beginning to make the necessary
adaptations

150   HESS, DONALD K. "ACTION/Year One: International Operations--
      the Peace Corps". AA1.10:1/6,7. Transition (July/August
      1972): 5-7.
          This article is an examination of the "state of the Peace
      Corps" by then-Director Donald Hess, assessing the agency's prog-
      ress and future as of mid-1972. Possible changes in training,
      program orientation, placement of volunteers and degree of host
      country participation in both staffing and funding are discussed.

151   HESS, DONALD. "PC Director Replies to Criticism". AA1.13:1/4.
      InterACTION, 1, n.4 (January 1973): 6.
          In this article Donald Hess, Director of the Peace Corps,
      answers statements made in the September 8, 1972 piece in Life
      Magazine entitled "Whatever Happened to the Peace Corps?", specif-
      ically that the agency is growing middle-aged and stodgy, that
      "the lovers and developers no longer battle over the soul of the
      agency: the lovers have left and the developers have won", and
      that many volunteers are of middle-age or older. Hess points out
      that the bi-national nature of Corps service has been completely
      ignored by the Life piece, as well as exploding the stereotypes
      presented in the item. The article appeared upon the occasion of
      debate in the Congress over U.S. foreign aid programs and their
      reassessment.

152   HENZEL, FRANCIS. "Peace Corps Volunteer or Missionary--Does It
      Really Make Any Difference?". Catholic World, 208 (February
      1969): 205-7.
          The strongly similar roles of Peace Corps volunteers and
      missionaries in Third World nations are explored in this essay.
      It is the allegiance of each--the one to the concern of the
      American people, the other to God--which "gives a peculiar defini-
      tion to his service" (p. 207). Members of the missionary group
      are called upon not to let their concerns with bricks and schools
      and wheat fields blind them to their underlying purpose.

153   HILLIARD, ASA C. "Cross-Cultural Teaching". Journal of
      Teacher Education, 18 (Spring, 1967): 32-5.
          Writing out of two years' experience as educational advisor
      to Peace Corps teachers in Liberia, the author examines problems
      facing any teacher who moves from one culture to another and
      wishes to function adequately. The chief questions are ones of
      communication and the various means by which it can be impeded or
      augmented. Issues addressed include dialects of a common

language, differences in preferred styles of speech and
incongruities of value systems. The teacher--faced with such
conflicts as situations where familiar practices seem totally
ineffective--"need not become a different person in his new
culture. His values need not be hidden from view; he need only
avoid forcing them on his pupils" (p. 34). Examples are given
from a study done with the Kpelle of Liberia and reflect
accurately the problems Peace Corps teachers encounter in both
training and field situations.

154   HIMELSTEIN, PHILIP. "Worldminded Attitudes and Expressed
       Interest in the Peace Corps". Journal of Social Psychology,
       78, Part 1 (1969): 151-52.
       The WMS (World-Mindedness Scale) was originally developed to
identify "the individual . . . whose reference group is mankind".
A test on a group of subjects drawn from undergraduate classes in
psychology examined the correlation of scores on the WMS with
reactions to four questions regarding service, real or future, in
the Peace Corps. Scores on the WMS clearly decreased as attitudes
towards Corps became increasingly unfavorable. The finding
supported the use of the WMS as a valid research tool and "the
notion that students interested in the PC tend to be idealistic
unselfish individuals concerned with service to developing
nations" (p. 152).

155   HOBBS, NICHOLAS. "A Psychologist in the Peace Corps".
       American Psychologist, 18 (January 1963): 47-55.
       Writing when, as the author admits, "the Peace Corps has
been in operation for less that 18 months", this article is both a
consideration of the psychological questions raised by the
creation of an institution such as Peace Corps at all, and the
problems involved in determining valid psychological criteria for
the selection and elimination of prospective volunteers during
training. Factors mentioned include demographic information on
the average volunteer, regional distribution of the requests for
different types of volunteers, the applicability of certain
standardized psychological tests, and the issue of idealism. One
interesting admission is that the Peace Corps Placement Test,
described as "elaborate and time consuming " (p. 51) is not seen
to have a significant correlation with either the opinions of
final selection boards or in-country representatives as to the
successful performance of the volunteer. Hobbs poses the question
that, given all the available evidence, how durable will the
institution be? Stating that "the volunteer has himself to
offer--and that's it. Is this enough?" (p. 53), a field visit to
volunteers is necessary. In this instance, the field sites were
at Legaspi, in Bicol Province of the Philippines and Tanganyika.
Based upon these visits, Hobbs is optimistic for the future. An
interesting view of the earliest days of Peace Corps and the role
psychology was asked to play in it.

156   HOOPES, ROY. The Complete Peace Corps Guide. New York: Dial
      Press, 1961.
         This work is one of the earliest pieces of literature on the
      Peace Corps not issued by the agency itself or written by a member
      of the staff. The author's preface states its purpose: "in spite
      of all the opinions which have been expressed about the Peace
      Corps, and all the newspaper and magazine articles which have been
      written, it is surprising how much misinformation exists about the
      Peace Corps . . . how it originated and what it is designed to
      achieve" (p. viii). Among the more interesting features of this
      history are detailed outlines of the projects in Tanganyika,
      Colombia, the Philippines, Chile, St. Lucia, Ghana, India,
      Nigeria, Pakistan, Sierra Leone, Malaya and Thailand. The tests
      administered to prospective volunteers are discussed and sample
      questions are provided as illustration. Training is covered
      briefly and some of the rules and regulations are stated. The
      final chapter is devoted to "the Peace Corps and the Draft", with
      a postscript on the challenge and response offered to the youth of
      the United States. In view of the many changes and alterations
      which the Peace Corps experienced during its existence in the
      first years of life, it is instructive to have this volume
      preserving the image of the agency and its initial reception among
      the American people as well as overseas.

157   HOOPES, ROY. The Peace Corps Experience. New York: Clarkson
      N. Potter, 1968.
         This photographic work is devoted not so much to a chrono-
      logical history of the Peace Corps, as was the 1965 volume The
      Peace Corps: A Pictorial History, as to relating the flavor of
      the total experience of serving in the Peace Corps, whether in
      Washington on on-site in a host nation. Opening with a foreword
      by then-Vice President Hubert Humphrey, chapters cover training,
      teaching, community development, agriculture, public health,
      miscellaneous assignments (which range from restoration of the
      Grand Mosque in the Tunisian city of Kairouan to designing a
      system of feeder roads in India) and re-entry to American city
      life. Individual countries profiled begin with a chapter entitled
      "Two Young Ladies in Niger" focusing on public health work being
      done in the town of Illela, Niger and include most of the nations
      in which Corps personnel were working in 1968. The great majority
      of photographs comprising the book were taken by a team of three
      Corps staff photographers, with some contributions by volunteers.
      All photographs are in black and white. Some accounts of volun-
      teer service are drawn from longer accounts which have been
      separately published, although the bulk of the texts are written
      specifically for this work. Researchers will find the variety of
      a subjects covered especially interesting in view of later
      programming changes in Corps approaches to host nations and their
      needs.

158   "Hoover Declines Peace Corps Post". New York Times (11 March
        1961): 8.
            Former President Herbert Hoover declined an invitation from
        President Kennedy to serve as chair of a citizen's advisory
        committee for the Peace Corps, citing age and prior commitments.
        Progress in the organization of the new agency and plans for
        teachers training are noted.

159   HORN, MIRIAM. "'Kennedy's Children' Come Of Age". U. S. News
        and World Report, 101, n.13 (29 September 1986): 78.
            A short historical summary of high points in Peace Corps
        history. The shift from A.B. generalists to technical expertise
        and a reduction in numbers--along with a budget "less than the
        budget for military marching bands"--in noted. Despite this, Horn
        observes "what the Peace Corps has lost in dollars and manpower,
        it makes up in imagination."

160   "House GOP Joins Support for Reagan Foreign Aid Bill".
        Christian Science Monitor (11 December 1981): 2.
            Republican members of the House of Representatives joined
        their Democratic colleagues to support President Reagan's $12
        million foreign aid bill. One of the amendments to this bill re-
        established the Peace Corps as an independent agency.

161   "Human Skills In the Decade of Development: Summary Report of
        the Conference on Middle Level Manpower, San Juan, Puerto Rico,
        October 10-12, 1962". S1.2.4710-12. Department of State
        Bulletin, 47 (October/December 1972): 853-59.
            The International Conference On Middle Level Manpower held
        in 1962 at San Juan, Puerto Rico was sponsored by the U. S. Peace
        Corps. Representatives from forty-one nations met to consider
        ways in which human skills could be most effectively applied for
        the proposed decade of development. Four major problems dominated
        the proceedings of the Conference: Peace Corps experiences were
        judged from both American and host country perspectives and found
        to be effective: other nations (among them Norway, Colombia,
        Honduras, Germany, Chile, Belgium and the Philippines) are in the
        process of organizing similar programs with the Peace Corps as a
        model: private training by industry was seen as an effective
        option insufficiently explored, and special procedures for the
        dissemination of training in fields of skill such as medicine and
        community development. With the aim of the conference "to bring
        into sharp focus certain practical next steps, against the back-
        ground of underlying agreement" three main themes emerged from the
        discussions. These were that, first , modernization requires a
        sense of individual involvement in the effort; second, that the
        values of development can be as great for the donor nations as
        well as the recipients, and third, that "no aspect of the joint
        development effort is likely to build this sense of communal
        purpose . . . more than the face-to-face requirements of creating
        and diffusing human skills" (p. 858). The continuing arrangements
        set up at the conference are set out in an annex of the main
        report.

162   HUSTON, PERDITA, ed. <u>Third World Women Speak Out: Interviews in Six Countries on Change, Development and Basic Needs</u>. New York: Praeger, 1979.
      Written by a freelance journalist appointed as regional director of the NANEAP countries (North Africa, Near East, Asia and the Pacific) of the Peace Corps, this volume expresses the hopes, desires, needs and the problems of the women of six developing nations. The information contained in this book is the result of a massive campaign of personal interviews carried out by the author in Kenya, Egypt, Sudan, Sri Lanka, Mexico and Tunisia. Huston notes the congruence of their statements with the priorities expressed in the documentation of the United Nations International Women's Year and the World Plan of Action for the 1976-1985 Decade for Women. Interview selections are arranged in order under specific chapters on positive and negative perceptions of social changes and the factors that drive them, the roles of women within the family, social constraints upon women's activities and possibilities in light of traditional customs and beliefs, issues of nutrition, health and family planning, access to education (and discussion of its nature) and political participation. Appendixes contain content analysis of the interviews, economic and social indicators of development for the six nations in tabular form, and background on the author and contributing organizations. Although written just prior to Huston's appointment to the NANEAP directorship, this volume touches Peace Corps in two important ways: it portrays graphically the situation which the Peace Corps program emphasis on "women in development" attempts to address, and also provides background information on three host nations of the Corps, Tunisia, Kenya and Sri Lanka. Researchers wishing further data on this program should consult the text of the 1978 amendment to the Peace Corps Act which added this emphasis to Corps programming.

163   "Immediate Opportunities for Mathematics Teachers In the Peace Corps". <u>Mathematics Teacher</u>, 55 (April 1962): 237.
      This news item reviews the requests from Thailand, Ecuador, North Borneo/Sarawak, Venezuela, Nigeria and the Ivory Coast for mathematics and science teachers. Details of training and overseas support are also included.

164   INGWERSEN, MARSHALL. "Peace Corps Adapts to GOP Rule With 'Up By the Bootstraps' Theme". <u>Christian Science Monitor</u> (21 April 1981): 5.
      An interview with Loret Ruppe and Thomas Pauken, new directors of the Peace Corps and ACTION respectively. The chief concern is whether Peace Corps can survive and function well in an atmosphere of increasing political conservatism. Ruppe stresses aspects of Corps which, in her view, make it fit a conservative mind-set. Pauken addresses fears that his background in Army intelligence could compromise the neutrality historically earned by volunteers.

165   "Inside the Peace Corps". <u>Seventeen</u>, v.23 (May 1963): 152-53,
        194.
            Interviews with three members of the Peace Corps, reviewing
        their decisions to enter, their training experiences and the
        challenges of their sites. Countries represented are Colombia,
        Ecuador and Sarawak.

166   <u>InterACTION</u>. AA1.13. Washington, D.C.: ACTION, 1972-1977.
            This publication served as the chief vehicle for communica-
        tion among the various branches of ACTION and, after August 1973,
        included information for former volunteers which had been previ-
        ously published in the defunct journal <u>Transition</u>. Researchers
        seeking information on the roles played in these years by Peace
        Corps volunteers within the framework of ACTION should consult
        this source.

167   "It is Almost As Good As Its Intentions". <u>Time</u>, 82 (5 July
        1963): 18-22.
            A survey article examining the progress, problems and accom-
        plishments of the Corps in its first two years of existence. A
        lengthy profile of R. Sargent Shriver, first director of the
        agency, is included. Examples of volunteers in the field are
        given from India, North Borneo, Brazil, St. Lucia, Venezuela and
        Ethiopia. Among the responses to Corps activity has been the
        action of twelve nations to create similar programs of their own
        to complement the effort. Noting that "because it has been rough,
        the reality is more meaningful than that unflawed popular image"
        (p. 18).

168   IVERSEN, ROBERT W. "The Peace Corps: A New Learning
        Situation". <u>Modern Language Journal</u>, 47 (November 1963): 301-
        304.
            Written by the Deputy Director of Training, this article
        examines the total Peace Corps experience as a learning situation.
        Beginning with the second and third provisions of the Peace Corps
        Act, which specify that the agency "should provide an opportunity
        for Americans to learn about other peoples and for other people to
        learn about Americans" (p. 301), the roles of universities in the
        training process is outlined. The training course preparing
        volunteers for Indonesia at the University of Iowa is presented as
        an example of intensive training created for a total environmental
        simulation of the host country. Benefits for the hosting
        institution are the creation of courses in languages which may not
        have had formal programs of instruction and the flexibility of
        being stretched to their limits in possibilities of adaptation to
        new challenges. The key to successful Peace Corps training is
        that "an immense amount is learned because the trainees are
        convinced of its relevance" (p. 304).

169   JAMES, JOSEPHINE. <u>Peace Corps Nurse</u>. New York: Golden Books,
        1965.
            A work of juvenile fiction describing a young woman's entry
        to the Peace Corps and her growth during training.

170   JENKINS, LORIN B. S19.11/2:4/3. "The Peace Corps and CARE".
       Peace Corps Volunteer, 4, n.3 (January 1966):   25-7.
       The joint participation of CARE workers and Peace Corps
personnel in aid projects across the world is examined. A case
study is offered of a coastal village in Sierra Leone.

171   JOHANSSEN, BEETRAM B. "Peace Corps Gets New Slant from Its
       Energetic Director". Christian Science Monitor (4 April 1970):
       2.
       An interview with Joseph H. Blatchford, Director of the
Peace Corps, after his first year in office. Program shifts which
have been initiated include an emphasis on the recruiting of
trained specialists and technicians, removal of the rule banning
families from serving, and discussion of a Peace Corps development
fund.

172   JOHNSON, LYNDON B., President. "President Johnson Pays Tribute
       to Peace Corps Volunteers". Department of State Bulletin, 55
       (October-December, 1966): 496-99.
       This is the complete text of remarks made by President
Johnson at a ceremony at Georgetown University on September 13,
1966 at which S.3418, An Act to Amend the Peace Corps Act, was
signed into law. In these remarks, he referred to the vision of
Corps service and noted that the Peace Corps school-to-school
program had been discussed in Congress. Stating that "to hunger
for use, and to go unused is the worst hunger of all", Johnson
called upon the young people of both the United States and the
world to consider what they might learn from the example set by
Peace Corps volunteers.

173   JOHNSON, LYNDON B. "President Transmits Fifth Annual Report of
       Peace Corps to Congress". Department of State Bulletin, 56
       (January-March 1967):   529.
       The complete text of the letter sent to the Congress of the
United States by President Lyndon Johnson accompanying the fifth
annual report of the Peace Corps on March 6, 1967. In the letter,
plans for the action of Corps in 1968 are set out, and the progress made through its efforts in the first five years of its
existence duly noted. Eighteen other nations had established
their own versions of Peace Corps by this date using the American
example as a guideline.

174   JOHNSON, LYNDON B. "Remarks on the Fifth Anniversary of the
       Peace Corps at the Swearing in of Jack Hood Vaughn as
       Director". Public Papers of the Presidents: Lyndon B.
       Johnson. 1966 I, Document 93, pp. 232-35. GS4.113:966.
       Washington, D.C., Government Printing Office, 1967.
       Speaking in the East Room of the White House on March 1,
1966 upon the swearing-in of the second Director of the Peace
Corps, Jack Vaughn, President Johnson acknowledged the accomplishments of Corps workers and of Sargent Shriver. He referred

several times to the war in Viet Nam and hoped that, when peace
had been restored, volunteers could be sent to that nation as
well. Vice President Humphrey then administered the oath of
office to Mr. Vaughn. Researchers should be aware that this
document is also available in the Department of State Bulletin,
v.54, January-March, 1966.

175   JOHNSON, LYNDON B., President. "Report on the Peace Corps:
      Statement by the President on the School-To-School Program,
      with Fact Sheets on That Program and the Exchange Peace Corps".
      GS4.114:2/26-52. Weekly Compilation of Presidential Documents
      (25 July 1966): 949-51.
            A summary of the school-to-school program worked out through
      the U. S. Peace Corps, with full fact sheets about that program
      and the proposed Exchange Peace Corps. These items were released
      following a personal briefing of the President by Jack Vaughn,
      Director of the Peace Corps. Details of fund-raising projects are
      included. Initial discussions on the exchange idea have been held
      with Israel, Mexico, the Philippines, Argentina and Ethiopia.

176   JOHNSON, LYNDON B. "Remarks Upon Announcing Appointments in
      the Peace Corps and in the Department of Housing and Urban
      Development". Public Papers of the Presidents: Lyndon B.
      Johnson. 1966 I, Document 12, January 17, 1966, pp. 24-5.
      GS4.113:966. Washington, D.C., Government Printing Office,
      1967.
            In the Fish Room of the White House at a news briefing on
      January 17, 1966, President Johnson announced the appointment of
      Jack Hood Vaughn, then Assistant Secretary of State, as the second
      Director of the Peace Corps. Sargent Shriver, the first Director,
      would be taking administrative control of the War on Poverty
      program. A brief outline of Mr. Vaughn's career in government is
      provided.

177   JOHNSON, LYNDON B., President. "Statement By the President on
      the Peace Corps' School-To-School Program, July 18, 1966".
      Public Papers of the Presidents: Lyndon B. Johnson. 1966 II,
      Document 352, p. 734. GS4.113:966.
            The text of a statement released by the White House as part
      of a group of documents relating to Peace Corps activity and to
      the effectiveness of the school partnership program. As of that
      date, 150 schools had been constructed in 24 counties via aid
      channeled through local Peace Corps personnel.

178   JOHNSON, THOMAS A. "Peace Corps or Africa: Who Benefits
      More?" AA1.13:2/7. InterACTION, 2, n.7 (April 1974): 3, 11.
            The title question of the distribution of benefits between
      African host nations and the U. S. from PCV talents is explored.
      Comments from counterparts, while noting that many volunteers are
      accepted by ministries to avoid the political squabbles of placing
      a national in their positions, acknowledge the value of their

work. The lack of training counterparts in some cases is also
noted as a flaw in Corps service. The Peace Corps viewpoint is
given through interviews with three volunteers serving in Mali,
Liberia and Senegal. This article originally appeared in the New
York Times.

179 JONES, CHARLE CLYDE. The Peace Corps. An Analysis of the
Development Problems Preliminary Evaluation and Future. Ph.D.
dissertation, West Virginia University, 1967.
The first five years of organization programming and
problems experienced by the Peace Corps are the subject of this
dissertation in political science. The agency is regarded as
being at a critical point in its development with this study seen
as providing "data and opinions which might serve as a groundwork
for needed discussion" (p. iv). Corps development is viewed as
the secularization of the volunteer tradition present in American
culture. Following an introductory analysis of the development of
this idea through the political process, successive chapters
address Corps structure, problems and possible futures. The
author examines the withdrawals of volunteers from Cyprus, Ceylon
and Indonesia as well as ongoing issues relating to in-country
programs in the Dominican Republic, Ghana and Panama. General
recommendations for the agency's development are stated.
Researchers will find this work a compact summation of available
data on the Peace Corps for the period 1961-1966 although the
treatment of individual topics is cursory. Useful tables include
the career status of the first 5,395 returned volunteers and
opinions of college students who did not join Corps. For greater
detail on issues raised in this dissertation, the Annual Reports
of Peace Corps for the indicated years should be consulted as well
as the proceedings of the first conference of returned volunteers
published under the title Citizen in a Time of Change.

180 JUAREZ, LEO J. Role Strain, Culture Shock and Performance:
Toward the Operationalization of a Theory of Role Strain.
University of Kentucky Center for Development Change,
Development Paper Number 8, March, 1973.
This research paper reports on the results of an analysis of
data obtained in the fall of 1970 and spring of 1971 from a group
of volunteers being trained under the "New Directions" program.
Following a general discussion of cultural shock and training
shock, both are viewed as manifestations of one phenomenon, role
strain. This latter is defined as "the difficulty that an individual feels or expresses in attempting to care out his role
obligations (p. 2). Sources of strain and coping strategies are
then set forth, with hypotheses as to the relationship between
reported levels of strain and field performance listed. Results
of data obtained in training and the field indicated that training
programs should include the knowledge of role strain, its symptoms
and effective means of coping with them. An interesting view
expressed in this paper is that training is an intermediate testing ground for volunteers to accustom themselves to new and different tensions similar to those they will later encounter in
their host nations.

181   KAGHAN, BENJY.   "Peace Corps Seen in Future African Continent
       Development". AA1.13:4/5. InterACTION, 4, n.5 (February
       1976): 3,9.
            In September, 1975, the University of Ibadan hosted a four-
       day International Symposium on Wildlife Management, focusing
       attention on the untapped wildlife potentials of West and Central
       Africa. In attendance were eleven Peace Corpsmen representing
       five host nations. Example of park development and wildlife
       research are offered from Niger and Nigeria itself. Conference
       conclusions are briefly summarized.

182   KARNEY, REX.   "Peace Corps A Farce, Says Editor of Illinois
       Newspaper". S19.11/2:1/2. Peace Corps Volunteer, 1, n.2
       (December 1962): 2.
            A reprinted editorial from the Rockford, Illinois Morning
       Star of August 19, 1962, attacking Peace Corps as "the most over-
       rated, over-publicized and over-sold travel club in the
       world . . . as silly a bit of political boondoggling as any
       American politician has ever devised."

183   KAUFFMAN, JOSEPH F.   "A Report on the Peace Corps: Training
       for Overseas Service". Journal of Higher Education, 33
       (October 1962): 361-65.
            Written by the then-director of training at the end of the
       first year and a half of the existence of the Peace Corps, this
       article explores the contributions made by these first volunteers,
       as well as covering the history of the foundation of Corps and
       reactions overseas. Emphasis is laid upon the creation and struc-
       turing of training programs and the role played by American
       universities in this effort. Their contributions have taken the
       form of participation by both faculty and resident host-country
       nationals in the areas of cross-cultural experiences and factual
       briefings. Problems encountered in training noted are the tradi-
       tional American approach to higher education, which is viewed as
       too rigid to accommodate the desired type of curriculum, teaching
       foreign languages for which instructional materials are not
       readily available, constructing a flexible training format able to
       respond to the wide variety in trainee background, and
       difficulties in locating institutions with the requisite area
       studies programs and resources. Benefits for host institutions
       are then detailed. The program of Peace Corps/Nigeria is used as
       an example of volunteer placement.

184   KAUFFMAN, JOSEPH F.   "United State Peace Corps". Year Book of
       Education, 1964: 380-84.
            Written by the Corps Director of Training, this capsule
       summary begins with those precursor organizations of the Peace
       Corps such as the American Friends Service Committee and the
       Thomasites of the early twentieth century. A basic outline of the
       goals and objectives of the educational processes used by trainers
       is then presented, with detailed coverage of country programs in
       Ethiopia, Malawi, Liberia, and Nigeria.

185   KENNEDY, JOHN FITZGERALD, <u>President</u>. "Letter to the President
       of the Senate and the Speaker of the House Transmitting A Bill
       to Continue and Expand the Peace Corps". <u>Public Papers of the
       Presidents: John F. Kennedy</u>. 1962, Document 64, February 26,
       1962, pp. 164-65. GS4.113:962. Washington, D.C.: Government
       Printing Office, 1963.
           The full text of a letter sent upon the first anniversary of
       the executive order which created the Peace Corps, requesting an
       increased appropriation to permit Corps expansion from 2,400
       volunteers, to maximum possible under the original legislation and
       funding, to 6,700 by June 30, 1963. Foreign reception of Corps is
       seen as very favorable, as witnessed by the requests for more
       personnel from established host countries and inquiries from
       others. A profile of the population of 2,700 presently serving is
       also given.

186   KENNEDY, JOHN FITZGERALD, <u>President</u>. "Letter to the President
       of the Senate and to the Speaker of the House Transmitting Bill
       to Strengthen the Peace Corps, July 4, 1963". <u>Public Papers of
       the Presidents: John F. Kennedy 1963</u>, Document 294, pp. 555-
       57. GS4.113:963. Washington, D.C.: Government Printing
       Office, 1964.
           The full text of a letter of transmittal sent by President
       Kennedy to Congress accompanying a bill requesting funding for the
       expansion of Peace Corps from 9,000 to 13,000 volunteers by
       September, 1964. The additional volunteers had been requested by
       Latin American and African nations. Kennedy noted the return of
       the first groups of veterans and praised their contributions, as
       evidenced by statements in a variety of host country presses and
       official statements from Jamaica to Ethiopia.

187   KENNEDY, JOHN FITZGERALD. "Peace Corps. Message From the
       President of the United State. March 1, 1961". House
       Documents, 87th Congress, n.98 <u>House of Representatives
       Journal, 87th Congress</u>, 1 March, 1961, pp. 275-77. XJH87-1.
           This is the complete text of the presidential message to
       Congress from President Kennedy recommending the establishment on
       a permanent basis of the Peace Corps. Given on the same day as
       Executive Order 10924, which created the Corps on a temporary
       pilot basis, it views the interim structure as a source of data on
       building a more effective permanent institution. Development is
       seen to be not just an American problem. Volunteers will go only
       where they are invited, and work only in those programs which have
       been expressed clearly by a host nation. After listing the
       sources of possible personnel, membership qualifications and the
       distinctive characteristics, the President goes on to point out
       the benefits which will accrue to America from the returning
       members of Peace Corps. The message was referred to the House
       Committee On Foreign Affairs.

188   KENNEDY, JOHN F., President. "Remarks to a Group of Peace
        Corps Trainees, August 9, 1962". Public Papers of the
        Presidents: John F. Kennedy, 1962, Document 325, pp. 608-609.
        GS4.113:962. Washington, D.C.: Government Printing Office,
        1963.
            A brief address given on the South Lawn of the White House
        to a highly diverse group of 613 volunteers. Countries for which
        they were bound were Ethiopia, Nepal, Turkey, Ecuador, Venezuela,
        British Honduras, Cyprus, Togo, Niger, Senegal and Sierra Leone.
        It was this group of volunteers which doubled the number of avail-
        able teachers in Ethiopia's schools simply by landing at Addis
        Ababa.

189   KENNEDY, JOHN FITZGERALD, President. "Remarks to a Group of
        Peace Corps Volunteers, August 30, 1962". Public Papers of the
        Presidents: John F. Kennedy, 1962, Document 354, p. 657.
        GS4.113:962. Washington, D.C.: Government Printing Office,
        1963.
            A short speech given to a group of twelve Peace Corps volun-
        teers in the Fish Room of the White House prior to their departure
        for overseas service. The President noted that one volunteer was
        over seventy and still willing to go and serve, and hoped that
        other older Americans would also realize that they could make many
        further contributions to the cause of peace. Among the countries
        of destination were Pakistan, Ethiopia, Brazil, Malaya, India and
        Peru.

190   KENNEDY, JOHN FITZGERALD, President. "Remarks to the National
        Advisory Council for the Peace Corps, May 22, 1961". Public
        Papers of the Presidents: John F. Kennedy, 1961, Document 199,
        pp. 391-92. GS4.113:961.
            In this speech to the group of prominent Americans who had
        been selected as the advisory council on the creation of the Peace
        Corps, President Kennedy announced "the third Peace Corps project,
        which will be to send 300 teaching assistants to the
        Philippines," and expressed his pleasure at the rate at which the
        American people were responding to the challenge of Corps service.
        He noted that on May 27, the first qualification tests for the
        Peace Corps would be administered across the country.

191   KENNEDY, JOHN FITZGERALD, President. "Remarks Upon Signing the
        Peace Corps Bill". Public Papers of the Presidents: John F.
        Kennedy, 1961, Document 380, September 22, 1961, pp. 614-15.
        GS4.113:961. Washington, D.C., Government Printing Office,
        1962.
            In these remarks given upon the signing of the basic piece
        of legislation creating the Peace Corps as a formal government
        agency, President Kennedy noted the bipartisan effort which had
        gone into the drafting and passage of this bill and the large
        number of capable personnel who had offered themselves for service
        in host nations. Referring to plans by other nations to institute
        similar programs, the President stated that "the sure sign of a
        good idea is that you can follow it."

192   "Kennedy For Study of U. N. Peace Corps". New York Times
      (9 March 1961): 18.
         At a news conference in Washington on March 8, 1961,
      President Kennedy suggested that the idea of an international
      Peace Corps under United Nations auspices might be profitably
      considered by that body. This statement came in response to a
      reporter's question as to whether Americans might be welcome in
      some nations as volunteers. The President further stated that
      Peace Corps would go only where it was "warmly welcome."

193   KENRICK, CHRISTINA. "New Attempt to Reorganize Peace Corps".
      Christian Science Monitor (12 March 1979): 4.
         Under a mandate from President Carter, efforts are underway
      to examine Peace Corps and ACTION to determine their futures.
      Rep. Don Bonker of Washington has announced he will reintroduce
      his 1977 bill calling for the removal of Peace Corps from ACTION.
      In his view, ACTION Director Sam Brown has been imposing his own
      philosophies at the expense of the original purpose of Corps
      programming. An advocate of the "basic human needs" approach,
      Brown has stressed the importance of global interdependence while
      leaving little room for policy debate. The forced resignation of
      Peace Corps Director Carolyn Payton is offered as an example.

194   "Kentuckians in the Peace Corps". Kentucky School Journal, 42
      (October 1963): 30-31, 34, -41.
         Biographies of twelve citizens of Kentucky currently serving
      as volunteers. Countries of service represented include Nigeria,
      Pakistan, the Philippines, Somalia, Liberia, Thailand, Ethiopia
      and Nepal.

195   KING, MARY E. "The Role of the Skill-Trained Volunteer in
      International Public Health: Peace Corps' Health Programming
      and Health Policy in Developing Countries." American Journal
      of Public Health, 71, n.4 (1981): 408-9.
         At its 1978 conference in Alma Ata, the World Health Organi-
      zation adopted two goals: immunization of every child in the
      world against the six basic childhood diseases by 1990, and
      attainment of an adequate level of primary health care for all the
      world's citizens by the year 2000. This represents a significant
      shift in the policies of many nations: to achieve this, national
      health plans must be geared to the provision of "the foundations
      for a healthy life: clean water supplies . . . understandable
      nutrition education, and culturally acceptable protein." This can
      be done most effectively through the actions of community health
      workers. Third World governments are taking increasing note of the
      strategies evolved and created by volunteers as motivators and
      trainers in local health care fields. Recent efforts at providing
      all volunteers with the basic knowledge necessary for community
      health work further support the conference goals. Through such
      training and activity, "the volunteers essentially strengthen the
      ability of ordinary people to care for themselves and for each
      other" (p. 409), the basic aim of all community work in health-
      related areas.

196   KOPKIND, ANDREW. "How Fares the Peace Corps?" New Statesman,
       71 (11 February 1966): 184-85.
            This view from the British press notes that the central
       concern of the Corps has changed to community development from
       more general assistance ideas, and speculates on the role and
       impact returning volunteers will have on American society and
       politics. Noting that "the very idea of different agencies of the
       same government consciously exploring opposite approaches in
       foreign affairs at the same time is worth the whole Peace Corps
       business" (p. 185).

197   KOPKIND, ANDREW. "Peace Corps' Daring New Look". New
       Republic, 154, n.6 (5 February 1966): 15-20.
            The "new look" of the article title is the matrix of
       programming, political squabbling and political outside pressures
       engendered by the Corps situation in 1966 under its second
       director, Jack Vaughn. The bulk of the article focuses on the
       "community development" programs in vogue at the time in Latin
       America, seeing them as part of the revolutionary changes being
       sought at home by groups such as policy positions is also
       examined. Kopkind sums up the Peace Corps as "the last remaining,
       isolated and beleaguered outpost of the New Frontier."

198   KULAKOW, ALAN. Foreign Language Training in the United States
       peace Corps. Washington, D.C.: Peace Corps, 1967.
            Written by the Director of the Division of Language Training
       of the Peace Corps, this document surveys the languages taught by
       the agency between 1961 and 1967, describes the format of instruc-
       tion (including evaluating the contribution of Foreign Service
       Institute language proficiency exams) and raises issues to be
       considered by co-ordinators of language programs. Sixty-three
       host nations are represented. The full text is entered on the
       ERIC database as document ED 152 114.

199   LAKLAN, CARLI. Serving in the Peace Corps: True Stories of
       Three Girls in Africa and the Philippines. Garden City, New
       York: Doubleday, 1970.
            Serving In The Peace Corps contains popularized treatments
       of the experiences of three Peace Corps women who worked in
       Malawi, the Philippines, and Nigeria. Two of them, Kathleen
       Catapano and Yvette Polcyn, found their husbands in their group of
       volunteers. An interesting look both at their lives and at the
       image presented to the youth of America as to what it meant to
       serve in the Peace Corps during the 1960's.

200   LANDRUM, ROGER. "The English Language and the Peace Corps".
       English Journal, 53 (March 1964): 180, 185-90.
       The creation of cultural unity and internationalization of
the English language is viewed from the perspectives of the classroom, with specific problems encountered by instructors listed.
Among these are the not infrequent usage of pidgin English,
transference of speech patterns from a non-Western language into
the English grammatical setting and the growing regional varia-
tions in slang. The Peace Corps volunteers teaching English are
seen to have a unique contribution to make in the field. Examples
used are drawn from the author's service in Peace Corps/Nigeria.

201   LAVINE, DAVID and IRA MANDELBAUM. What Does a Peace Corps
       Volunteer Do? New York: Dodd, Mead and Company, 1964.
       A popular work for juvenile readers centering upon Peace
Corps history, programs and the problems faced by volunteers in
the field. The lavish use of photographs of both training and
volunteers on-site make this a distinctive volume.

202   "Lawyers in the Peace Corps". Student Lawyer, 13 (May 1985):
       7-8.
       Of the 15,000 persons answering Loret Ruppe's call for
assistance to famine-stricken Africa, forty lawyers offered themselves. An inquiry to the Peace Corps Public Affairs Department
reveals that, of the 5,200 volunteers presently serving overseas,
eight are lawyers. Four legal specialists are working in the
Solomon Islands, with the remainder in Jamaica, Thailand, the
Central African Republic, and Papua New Guinea. It is unclear as
to the usage, if any, being made of their legal training in
assignment to host countries.

203   LEISZ, NADINE M. "Peace Corps". Journal of Forestry, 83,
       (December 1985): 740.
       A brief examination of the types of forestry work being done
by volunteers. Examples given are the construction of seedling
nurseries, community conservation projects, agroforestry and
promotion of forest lands as an economic reserve. The writer
makes the point that forestry cannot be separated from the basic
needs of the society. "Enhancing natural resources while
fostering self-reliance within communities . . . it is here that
the social forester and the Peace Corps volunteer become one."

204   LEOPOLD, ROBERT L. and LEONARD J. DUHL. "New Frontiers in
       Psychiatry: the Peace Corps". Psychiatric Studies and
       Projects, 2 (January 1962): 1-9.
       Beginning with a brief history of the psychiatric aspects of
volunteer selection and evaluation, this article views Corps as an
unparalleled opportunity for psychiatrists wishing to explore new
preventive techniques. Most aspects of Corps psychiatry are tied
to the bases of crisis theory, anticipatory guidance and interaction within social systems. Conceptual problems are often seen

in the conditions of induced stress effected during training, and
counseling can lead to more effective management of volunteer
reactions to new cultural stimuli. Support from fellow volunteers
and staff is seen to be vital to continuing success in field
situations. The overall success of the agency as a whole is
viewed as in part due to effective psychiatric advice, but the
data are as yet too scanty to permit a more definitive analysis.

205   LEOPOLD, ROBERT L. and LEONARD J. DUHL. "The Peace Corps: A
       Historical Note on a New Challenge to Psychiatry". Journal of
       Nervous and Mental Disease, 137, n.1 (July, 1963).
            An historical presentation of the ways in which the involve-
       ment of the discipline of psychiatry has grown and changed in the
       first years of the agency's existence. The areas of selection,
       training and staffing are addressed.

206   LERNER, MICHAEL A. "Peace Corps Imperiled". New Republic, 185
       (25 November 1981): 6-8.
            The ideological impact of domestic American political
       maneuvering upon the Peace Corps under the Nixon, Ford and Carter
       administrations is reviewed. Moving from the original position of
       a well-funded and publicized agency with a coherent approach to
       host country requests, during the Nixon years it was described by
       Sam Brown, Director of ACTION, as suffering from "cultural
       imperialism". Objections to Peace Corps programs of teaching
       English were succinctly rebutted in a survey done in 1979. Under
       the leadership of Richard Celeste, the balance began to be re-
       dressed in favor of the original goal of meeting "basic human
       needs". The writer calls for the Reagan administration to remove
       Peace Corps from ACTION and re-establish it as a viable indepen-
       dent agency so that it can regain its effectiveness.

207   LEVITON, DAN. "The Peace Corps and Professional Preparation".
       Journal of Health, Physical Education and Recreation, 38 (March
       1967): 77-8.
            Beginning with the origins of Peace Corps training programs,
       the orientations of both Corps and the American universities doing
       training are presented. The relationship between the two organi-
       zations is seen as vital and constantly evolving. Implications of
       the continuing challenge of Corps service to the training and
       development of physical educators, such as the necessity of
       inclusive new curricula covering anthropology and sociology, are
       presented and discussed. As an example of the changing environ-
       ment facing trainers of professionals in many areas, the views of
       Fr. Theodore Hesburgh of Notre Dame are given.

208   LISTON, ROBERT A. Sargent Shriver: A Candid Portrait. New
       York: Farrar, Straus and Company, 1964.
            A biography of Sargent Shriver, covering his life and
       government career up to his appointment as head of the War On
       Poverty. Material on the Peace Corps is included in chapters
       eight, nine and ten.

209   LIVINGSTON, ELLEN. "Peace Corps at 25 Recovers Its Vigor".
       Congressional Record, 131, n.174 (16 December 1985): E5641-
       42.
          An insertion in the Congressional Record of an article
       originally appearing in the Miami Herald covering a symposium at
       the University of Miami honoring the 25th anniversary of the Peace
       Corps. Director Loret Ruppe spoke on this occasion and noted that
       Florida was a good place for recruiting due to the wide ethnic and
       chronological mixture of its population. Three returned volun-
       teers from the Miami area were also interviewed.

210   LOBSENZ, NORMAN M. The Peace Corps. New York: Franklin
       Watts, 1968.
          A general discussion of the purposes and challenges of the
       Peace Corps intended for a juvenile audience. Limited illustra-
       tions of volunteers on-site are included.

211   "A Look At Peace Corps--Present and Future". AA1.13:2/4.
       InterACTION, 2, n.4 (January 1974): 3, 12.
          This article is an interview with the newly appointed
       Associate Director of ACTION's International Operations, Nicholas
       Craw. Craw's background with Project HOPE and VISTA is set forth,
       as well as his views on certain aspects of Peace Corps program-
       ming. Outspoken feedback from volunteers is welcomed, and the
       observation is made that Corps has no specific criteria to use in
       deciding whether to withdraw from a host nation.

212   LUCE, IRIS, ed. Letters From The Peace Corps. Washington,
       D.C.: Robert B. Luce, Inc., 1964.
          This is a collection of letters written home by volunteers
       to Peace Corps staff in Washington, friends and relatives which
       discusses a wide variety of subjects. Among these are reasons for
       wanting to serve overseas, evaluation of training programs in
       light of latter experiences in the host country, descriptions of
       the methods of training between 1961 and 1964, living conditions
       in a varied array of geographical and climatic settings, and
       recommendations to prospective Corps members. Countries repre-
       sented in this volume include Malaya, Nepal, Ethiopia, Chile,
       Colombia, the Philippines, Nigeria, Sierra Leone, Ghana, Bolivia,
       and Tanganyika.

213   LOWTHER, KEVIN and C. PAYNE LUCAS. Keeping Kennedy's Promise:
       the Peace Corps--Unmet Hope of the New Frontier. Boulder,
       Colo.: Westview Press, 1978.
          "This book is intended as catharsis for all who believe--as
       we do--that the Peace Corps has not lived up to its promise, but
       that it can" (p. xi). With this statement, the authors begin a
       critical examination of the agency, finding fault at many points.
       Data presented here are based upon four sources which together
       span the period from the Corps' creation in 1961 to the middle
       years of the Carter administration, when the chief question was
       how to restore the agency to prominence. These are the Corps' own

evaluations of country programs, internal documents bearing on
agency policies, interviews with former volunteers and the
authors' own participation in the life of Peace Corps for a total
of eighteen years. Following criticism of the "numbers game' of
the early years, inconsistency in leadership strengths, programming deficiencies and in particular community development projects, the authors state five areas where skilled volunteers (those
having received proper training or with the necessary background
experience) can truly assist the Third World. These are education, health, energy, food production and jobs. A call is issued
for the restoration of the independence of Peace Corps from ACTION
and the improvement of training. In light of the subsequent
emphases in Corps programming on "basic human needs", this work
stands as an articulation of changes to come.

214   LUNSTRUM, JOHN. "The Mystique of the Peace Corps: A Dilemma".
       Phi Delta Kappan 48 (November 1966): 98-102.
       The author served as an advisor to a Peace Corps educational
project in Sierra Leone. In this article, he explores two problems noted by representatives of higher education who have worked
with Corps, relating to the mystique of toughness and competence
and the preoccupation with building a favorable image. The first
is related to amateurism which tends to disregard tested methods
of evaluation and involves in-country staff in periods of almost
continual disruption with little sense of history or a record of
previous project successes to measure current efforts against.
While accepting the romanticizing of the Corps as a publicity
effort, Lunstrum notes that "the volunteers themselves rebel
against image building" (p. 100). Using examples from his time in
Sierra Leone, the "gung-ho" approach to service is seen to backfire in terms of local cultural norms being minimized or dis-
regarded in favor of policy made in Washington. The emphasis on
local area projects arranged by volunteers in their vacation time
is particularly heavily castigated. Judging the whole scheme of
evaluation and assessment in terms of the future of a healthy
Peace Corps, Lunstrum notes that "if there is to be an enduring
and productive partnership between American education and the
Peace Corps, it must be based on the proposition that universities, colleges and schools have an equal voice in the design,
administration and evaluation of educational projects" (p. 100).
This article provoked a rebuttal from Frank Mankiewicz entitled
"Peace Corps Without Tears."

215   LUTZKE, JIM. "Learning--The Extension Way". Extension Service

       Review, 47 (January 1976): 18-19.
       Training of Peace Corps interns in the Michigan State
University College of Agriculture and Natural Resources program is
illustrated by following a typical day of visiting local extension
workers. Stops including a rabbit-raising operation, goat breeding stations, and a commercial fish farm. Interns in this group
were scheduled for service in Thailand and the Philippines.

216 LYDEN, FREMONT J. "Success in the Peace Corps".
    Administration Review, 26, n.4 (1966): 354.
    After noting that, for the Peace Corps to become a consis-
tent success, it would be necessary to be aware of the characteristics of the successful volunteer, Lyden reports on Paul Hare's
work in evaluating personnel in the Philippines. Predictions made
on the basis of experience, psychological characteristics and
personal behaviors were all found to be in error when matched
against actual field performance. Lyden indicates a possible
danger to Corps in continuing to use such measures as criteria,
"when we have no assurance that they have any relevance to the
environmental context of the job under consideration."

217 MCCLOSKEY, PAUL W. "Person to Person Peace". Today, 15
    (February 1961): 6-8.
    Written prior to the establishment of the Peace Corps by
John F. Kennedy's executive order in March of 1961, this article
examines the history of the idea of a "youth corps" for overseas
service. Five characteristics of the proposed organization are
listed as desirable: a small scale beginning, with a maximum
enrollment of 10,000; complete freedom from any connection with
military aid; careful screening to obtain volunteers who sincerely
believe in the goals of the agency, not in perpetuating images
such as those advanced in The Ugly American; a period of service
of two or three years; co-operation with private agencies: entry
to foreign countries only at the invitation of the host
government, and transportation paid by the United States, with a
basic wage still to be determined. Political opinions regarding
the idea are then reviewed.

218 MC DONOUGH, JAMES. "Notes of a Peace Corps Reject". Esquire,
    65 (January 1966): 90, 122-23.
    A trainee from the pool for Costa Rica III at Saint Louis
University relates the experiences within training and the wrench
upon being "deselected". This is one of the few accounts of Peace
Corps training from the 1960's which discusses the constant
evaluation from the recipient's point of view.

219 MACFARLANE, RUTH. The Community College and the Peace Corps.
    Ph.D. dissertation, Claremont College, 1965.
    This dissertation explores the question of the ability of
the community colleges of the United States to serve effectively
as training grounds for Peace Corps volunteers. Noting that "the
community college has been ignored in research on the role of
higher education in world affairs" (p. 7), Macfarlane develops a
training model in which the pasadena City College would train one
hundred volunteers for service in the callampas (urban slums) of
Chile. Factors included in the design of the model range from the
structure of Peace Corps itself, types of training programs which
a community college cold support and the structure of a community
college as well. Peace Corps/Chile was selected as the focus of
this model as it was the first training group to be carried out
under contract with an American university or group of universities and hence the first available example of Peace Corps training

done through higher education. The absence of the community colleges from Peace Corps training as of 1965 is blamed on a lack of vision by college administrators and what Macfarlane terms "myopia in Washington." This research is especially valuable in the context of the history of Peace Corps training and the paths it chose and approaches used over some twenty-five years.

220   MCGREW, THOMAS J. "For The Peace Corps, A Worthy Gamble".
        Congressional Record, 130, n.29 (13 March 1984): E964.
        Reprinted from the Los Angeles Times of March 6, 1984, this article was written by the chairman of the Returned Volunteer Committee on the Budget. Its focus was the call by the Kissinger Commission Report for an expanded volunteer effort in Central America as part of the Reagan Administration's foreign policy toward that region. While endorsing the idea of renewing Peace Corps involvement in Latin America at a time when it has all but vanished, McGrew takes exception to the limitation of this service to those nations where the United States has a political problem. Cloaked in the guise of a program to combat illiteracy through an influx of teachers to "the states with a high illiteracy problem, which happen to be our friends Honduras, Guatemala and El Salvador", the article raises the specter of Corps used as a political tool. McGrew states that he would accept the proposal of an increased Latin American Peace Corps because the ideas and contributions made by the volunteers in the rural areas targeted for help will not be under the control of politicians in either America or the host nation.

221   MCGRORY, MARY. "Seminarians to the Peace Corps?" America, 114
        (29 January 1966): 167.
        On November 15, 1965, Sargent Shriver unveiled a new sugges-tion for obtaining manpower for the Peace Corps--that seminarians of all faiths be granted what was termed a "citizen sabbatical" to participate in Corps efforts overseas. Dr. Joseph English pres-ented the idea to the National Vocational Directors Conference in Pittsburgh and, after receiving their enthusiastic endorsement, traveled to Rome for discussions with heads of orders. A copy of the plan was also left for the consideration of Pope Paul. Reaction at the Vatican was decidedly mixed.

222   MCHAM, DAVID. "The Peace Corps". Adult Leadership, 11
        (November 1962): 141-142.
        Focusing specifically on adult education efforts of the Peace Corps, this article explores programs underway in Brazil and Colombia as examples of community education at work. Other host countries which have adult education programs are Sierra Leone, the Dominican Republic, and Guatemala. A general overview of the objectives of such programs is then presented.

223   MCNASPY, CLEMENT JAMES, S.J. "Whatever Happened to the Peace
      Corps?" America, 148 (15 January 1983): 29-31.
          Written by a staff member of America who surveyed a group of
      people in 1961 to determine their reactions to the new-born Peace
      Corps, this article looks at the intervening decades to determine
      the validity of early concerns. These latter included wondering
      about such things as whether Americans were tough enough to stand
      the projected life of a volunteer, harmful effects on development
      efforts, and influence of local governments. Feeling in 1983 that
      some of the concerns "were either idle or scattered to the winds"
      (p. 29), a brief history of recruitment is given, from the
      generalists of the 1960's to the specialist requests of the 1970's
      and 1980's. Final careers of volunteers are also examined. ·
      Examples are given from the viewpoint of the author's service in
      Paraguay and the volunteers with whom he came in contact. While
      approving, the writer notes that "on the whole, Peace Corps
      service is notably unglamorous, even imperceptible in immediate
      results" (p. 30).

224   MANIAGO, JO ANNE BARKER. The First Peace Corps: The Work of
      the American Teachers in the Philippines, 1900-1930. Ph.D.
      dissertation, Boston University, 1971.
          Under Act 74, signed by President McKinley on January 21,
      1901, a Department of Public Education was sent up for the newly-
      acquired Philippine Islands. The general superintendent of this
      system was given "authority . . . to obtain from the United States
      one thousand trained teachers" (p. 289). These thousand teachers
      were, in effect, forerunners of the Kennedy ideal of Peace Corps
      service as it was formulated in the 1960's. Maniago analyses the
      historical, political and cultural milieu of the Philippines in
      the early twentieth century and includes applications from partic-
      ipants, accounts of their life (and frustrations) and evaluates
      their role in view of conditions in the islands met by the
      "second" Peace Corps. As a comparative historical treatment of
      the idea of voluntary service and changing U. S. foreign policy
      over seventy years, it presents invaluable background to the Peace
      Corps philosophy.

225   MANKIEWICZ, FRANK. "The Peace Corps Without Tears". Phi Delta
      Kappan, 48, n.3 (1966): 103-04.
          Replying to the criticisms leveled against the role of
      educational institutions as advisors to Peace Corps in John
      Lunstrum's article "The Mystique of the Peace Corps: A Dilemma",
      the author rebuts the charges of amateurism and its drawbacks by
      saying "Charges and countercharges are wispy and hard to catch"
      (p. 104). Depriving volunteers of such tools as jeeps and forcing
      them closer to the life lived by their host country counterparts
      is seen as necessary to combat a tendency on the part of volunteer
      teachers to remain close to their school compounds and not to
      penetrate into the local community. Evaluations of success rates
      are offered from sources other than the ones listed by Lunstrum.

226   "March Under Peace Banner". S19.11/2:7/12. Peace Corps
       Volunteer, 7, n.12 (November 1969): 28-9.
          On October 15, 1969, 155 staff members of Peace Corps
       Washington, following a red banner reading "Peace Corps For Peace"
       protested in the nation's capital as part of the Vietnam
       Moratorium. Other opposition events are also profiled.

227   MARCKWARDT, ALBERT H. "Training the Peace Corps for English
       Teaching Abroad". Modern Language Journal, 47, n.7 (November
       1963): 310-14.
          The role of teachers of English as a special type of educa-
       tional assistance to developing nations, and the Peace Corps'
       contribution to it, are reviewed in this article. With approxi-
       mately one-quarter of all volunteers in service in February, 1963,
       either engaged in or preparing for such instruction, the types of
       training necessary to fitting out a volunteer to perform success-
       fully in this task are examined. Twenty-one American universities
       had trained TEFL instructors for the Peace Corps, with five compo-
       nents of information briefly outlined. Application of TEFL skills
       by returning volunteers are seen as a way of reducing a critical
       need in this field of American education.

228   MARQUARDT, WILLIAM F. "The Training of Teachers of English As
       a Second Language in the Peace Corps". Language Learning, 12,
       N.2 (1962): 103-14.
          Beginning with the premise that knowing a host country
       language will doubtless insure "the sort of communication that
       must take place if the Corpsman and the people are to understand
       each other" (p. 103), a case is also made for much of the communi-
       cation being in the volunteer's language. Among reasons for the
       usage of English are its prestige value, utility in the introduc-
       tion of concepts for which the host tongue may not possess equiva-
       lencies and as a key to published research on technical subjects.
       Training in host languages possesses four advantages: it permits
       the volunteer to deal directly with his co-workers without having
       to resort to translators, gives the volunteer an entroit into a
       foreign culture through evidence of respect, provides the
       opportunity for insights to alternative methods of conceptualizing
       the world, and, most basic, the language will illustrate cultural
       differences more graphically than any other feature quickly
       available to the volunteer. Specialists in TESL (Teaching of
       English as a Second Language) are seldom a part of Peace Corps
       unless specifically requested: nonetheless, many volunteers find
       themselves holding impromptu classes in English. Marquardt recom-
       mends that "the very first contingents of Corpsmen" be trained to
       some degree with the basics of such instruction. A list of needed
       skills and concepts is then set forth. Researchers should bear in
       mind that this article was written when the Peace Corps was only a
       year old and field input on language learning had not achieved the
       dimensions of later years.

229   "The Married Corps".   S19.11/2:3/1. Peace Corps Volunteer, 3,
       n.1 (November 1964):   5.
       A history of the volunteers who have met their spouses
through the Peace Corps up to the fall of 1964, including
marriages to host country nationals.

230   MARSHALL, MARILYN. "The Peace Corps: Alive and Well, and
       Looking For Blacks". Ebony, 39 (October 1984): 48-54.
       Addressing the question often asked by Third World peoples
whom Peace Corps serves of "where are the Black Americans?", this
article reviews participation of black America in Corps programs
and staffing. Reasons given for the relatively low number of
blacks in Corps are the history of local community volunteerism in
black America being limited to one's own area, the priority of
finding a position immediately after graduation, and the "assump-
tion that the Peace Corps is geared toward young Whites" (p.
52). Notable members of Corps such as Carolyn Payton, Director,
and staff members are illustrated to make the point that Corps
service can be an excellent means of growing both personally and
professionally.

231   MARTIN, DONALD O. The Organization and Operations of the U. S.
       Peace Corps Public Information Division. Ph.D. dissertation,
       American University, 1966.
       Written by a sociologist as "a discussion in some depth of
the structure, responsibilities and operations of the public
information unit of a Federal agency unique in the history of this
or any other nation" (p. ii), this thesis is intended to benefit
public information officials both within and outside government.
The mission and tasks of the Public Information Division are
specified in detail, ranging from preparing informational copy for
the Congressional Record and documenting the annual Peace Corps
Report to compiling weekly status briefings on the agency for the
President. Personnel requirements are examined separately, while
the duties of each major component of the Division--college and
hometown news, radio and television, photography, resources and
research, recruiting and general assignments--are outlined.
Division work also extends overseas to encompass informational
needs which may arise from local situations, examples being the
death of a volunteer or a political upheaval such as the Dominican
Republic crisis of 1965. The author's evaluation of the performance of the Division is "excellent . . . particularly when one
considers the potential for disaster represented by the thousands
of healthy, vigorous Peace Corps volunteers serving in all corners
of the globe" (p. 93). Suggestions for the future improvement of
the Division are made. Martin's thesis provides a detailed look
at one of the most crucial sectors of Peace Corps operations at
the height of Corps popularity in the 1960's.

232   MENNINGER, W. WALTER and JOSEPH T. ENGLISH. "Psychiatric
        Casualties From Overseas Peace Corps Service". Bulletin of the
        Menninger Clinic, 29, n.3 (1965): 148-58.
            At the inception of Peace Corps service, early estimates
        were that from 20 to 50 percent of all volunteers might be
        returned as unable to complete their assignment. The psychiatric
        profession was called upon to construct selection mechanisms which
        would diminish the chances of unfit persons being sent into the
        field. The present paper examines the reasons for return of the
        54 volunteers who had been returned for psychiatric reasons as of
        April 30, 1964. They represent 0.5 percent of all volunteers in
        the field. Characteristics of returnees are reviewed and their
        symptoms listed. Upon return, most are seen by a Peace Corps
        psychiatrist, with some hospitalization occurring. The role of
        psychiatric assessment in the training program and its relation to
        persons later seen as unstable is also explored. Five case
        studies are then presented illustrating the range of problems
        possible in this situation. A dearth of information from agencies
        similar to the Peace Corps makes it difficult to evaluate the
        significance of both the selection system and the psychiatrists'
        performance within it. The authors recommend that the psychiatric
        interview continue to be used in training but on a selective basis
        only.

233   Michigan. University. Information Services. Transcript of
        Remarks Made by John F. Kennedy, 2 A.M., October 14, 1960.
            This document is the full text of the extemporaneous remarks
        made by then-candidate Kennedy to a huge group of students at Ann
        Arbor who had waited up for his arrival. It was here that the
        first suggestion of a new organization was given, through the
        rhetorical questions "How many of you who are going to be doctors
        are willing to spend your days in Ghana? . . . willing to spend
        your lives traveling around the world? On your willingness to do
        that . . . to contribute part of your life to this country will
        depend the answer to whether a free society can compete." The
        transcript was taken from a local new agency's recording of the
        speech.

234   MILMOE, MEG. "Pennsylvania's Peace Corps Teachers".
        Pennsylvania Journal, 112 (September 1963): 10-12, 33.
            This article looks at the role teachers from Pennsylvania
        are actively taking in the Peace Corps, focusing on volunteers
        serving in Ghana, Turkey, Ethiopia and Nigeria. Photographs
        illustrate additional workers in Thailand and El Salvador.
        Benefits of teaching experience in Corps are outlined and
        recruiting standards stated.

235   "Minority Activity in the Peace Corps". Congressional Record,
        117, Part 18 (6 July 1971): 23541-42.
            This item of the Congressional Record consists of an article
        from the Richmond News Leader of June 25, 1971, commenting upon a
        recruiting letter sent to black Americans by a returned volunteer
        working at headquarters in Washington. In that letter, Peace
        Corps service is described as a way to "go where your talents can

be used, where Black and Brown people make the decisions that affect their lives" (p. 23542). The decidedly racist tone of statements made in the letter outraged several members of Congress and stimulated calls for a closer look at the Peace Corps. Headquarters staff admitted that "portions of the text could have a negative interpretation" and said no further mailings were planned.

236   "Mr. Shriver Visits Guinea as President's Representative".
       Department of State Bulletin, 45 (July-September 1961): 24.
       Sargent Shriver, Director of the Peace Corps, was the representative sent to meet with President Sekou Tore of Guinea from June 14-15, 1961, at the latter's invitation. During that visit President Toure had indicated that he would discuss possible Peace Corps activities in Guinea. Mr. Shriver was accompanied by George Carter, who would subsequently become country director for Ghana.

237   MITCHELL, BARBARA. Let's Go to the Peace Corps. New York: Putnam, 1968.
       A descriptive book for juvenile readers based upon the Peace Corps program in the Philippines.

238   "MLAT". S19.11/2:8/3-4. Volunteer, 8, nos. 3-4 (March-April 1970): 20-21.
       The Modern Language Aptitude Test, used as a screening mechanism for eight years of Peace Corps Language training. Its format was to present prospective volunteers with an unknown language and take them through a series of grammar and vocabulary exercises.

239   "Mondale Has Plans for Peace Corps". Christian Science Monitor (13 September 1976): 2.
       Charging that officials of the Nixon administration had "beat the life out of Peace Corps . . . because it had this idealistic tone . . . they found offensive", Senator Walter Mondale said that, if elected, he and Governor Carter of Georgia would work to revitalize the agency.

240   "More for More". Time, 90 (27 October 1967): 32.
       In a fiscal year where many government programs have had their budgets massively slashed, Director Jack Vaughn's request for an increase in the funding for Peace Corps--and its subsequent approval by Congress with only a 3% cut--stands out as an exceptional success. Increased funding will be used to put some 17,750 volunteers into fifty-eight countries. An outline of language training and types of jobs held by volunteers is also included. As Vaughn states, "the range of work seems limited only by the Peace Corps collective imagination."

241   MORHNER, IRA. "The Peace Corps: Revolutions Without Blood".
      Look, 30 (14 June 1966): 40-46.
         The senior editor of Look magazine considers the progress
      made by the Peace Corps in its first five years of existence and
      notes the new emphasis on community development which was they
      current. Interviews with Jack Vaughn, Director and other senior
      Peace Corps officials are included, as are examples of community
      development successes and failures, mainly from the nations of
      Latin America.

242   MOUAT, LUCIA. "Community Groups Join With Peace Corps to Build
      Schools". Christian Science Monitor (29 December 1981): 5.
         A news item explaining the mechanics of the Peace Corps
      Partnership program which supplies funds for school construction
      and community projects in host nations. The history of the idea
      over the last eighteen years is described.

243   MOUAT, LUCIA. "Single U. S. Volunteer Corps Held Most Likely
      to Succeed". Christian Science Monitor (16 February 1971): 2.
         President Richard Nixon, in a speech at the University of
      Nebraska, suggested that VISTA, the Peace Corps, and other
      agencies involved with voluntary manpower be merged into one unit.
      Joseph Blatchford, Director of the Peace Corps, has been tapped as
      head of the new agency. His proposed changes in Corps policy,
      such as increased recruitment of skilled professionals, and
      problems of consolidation are explored.

244   "Munoz Offers Training". New York Times (11 March 1961): 8.
         Luis Munoz Marin, Governor of Puerto Rico, stated that his
      island's contribution to the Peace Corps would be to serve as a
      training area for "mainlanders" invited to Latin American nations.
      Recruitment of Puerto Rican nationals was not seen as viable at
      that time.

245   "Musical Based on Peace Corps Opens in Capital". S19.11/2:1/4.
      Peace Corps Volunteer, 1, n.4 (February 1963): 4.
         Hot Spot, a musical comedy allegedly treating life in the
      Peace Corps opened in Washington, D.C. on February 5, 1963. Its
      cast starred Judy Holliday as the feckless nurse Dulcy Hopwinder,
      posted to the nation of D'Hum "where nothing ever happens."
      Critical reception was cool.

246   "Nairobi Women's Forum". Peace Corps Times
      (September/October/November 1985): 8-9.
         A meeting lasting ten days termed "Forum '85" was held in
      Nairobi, Kenya, to mark the end of the United Nations' Decade for
      Women. This article examines the contributions made by Peace
      Corps through its "Women in Development" programs and the papers
      given by Peace Corps members attending as representatives of their
      host nations. Specific information related to the Women in Devel-
      opment effort was supplied from a booth outside the exhibit hall
      where the conference took place.

247   NEEDLE, JUNE. "Peace Corps Librarians in the Developing
      World". Special Libraries, 68, nos. 5-6 (May-June 1977):
      206-10.
         Librarians serving in Colombia, Chile and Kenya are profiled
      and their working challenges and problems discussed in detail.
      These range from the creation of a preservation program for rare
      items and incunabulae to the organization of a specialist library
      in oceanography to children's librarianship and medical library
      development. The writer notes that, in addition to the volunteers
      mentioned here, others have recently departed for a variety of
      assignments in Fiji, the eastern Caribbean, Honduras, and the
      Kingdom of Lesotho.

248   NEEDLE, JUNE. "Peace Corps Planning in the World's Parks".
      Parks and Recreation, 12 (August 1977): 16-21, 54.
         An overview article presenting the variety of jobs being
      performed by the Peace Corps in the areas of national park devel-
      opment and planning. These include drawing up legislation for a
      national park system, managing a local park and educating the
      surrounding communities about its importance, creating visitors'
      centers and libraries, range management, environmental education
      and wildlife biology. A shift has occurred since the earliest
      period of Peace Corps history, with host nations now requesting
      environmental specialists with some degree of training and profes-
      sional experience. Through joint programs with the Smithsonian
      Institution and the National Park Service, personnel are being
      encouraged to join Corps, with additional training being provided
      for the specific site where possible. Examples of actual service
      used as illustration represent the Philippines, Costa Rica,
      Lesotho, Fiji, and Upper Volta.

249   NELSON, RICHARD H. "Herdsmen and Shepherdesses in the Peace
      Corps". Breeder's Gazette, (December 1962): 5-7.
         This is a brief report on the Peace Corps involvement in the
      fields of animal husbandry. Projects cited include work on
      parasite control in Malaya, breeding improvement in East Pakistan,
      and detailed outline of a current effort underway on St. Lucia.

250   "New Center in Virgin Islands". S19.11/2:3/7. Peace Corps
      Volunteer, 3, n.7 (May 1965): 6.
         A six-acre site on the island of St. Croix has been leased
      by Peace Corps as a training camp, becoming the third facility
      available to prepare volunteers for service. The first groups to
      use its equipment and buildings will serve in Gabon and Nigeria.

251   "A New Debate: Activists As PCVs". S19.11/2:4/2. Peace Corps
      Volunteer, 4, n.2 (December 1965): 8-10.
         The role of students activists as potential volunteers is
      examined, and a place seen for them in service, provide that they
      "come aboard on Peace Corps terms." All sides of this tangled
      question are raised, from the possible compromising of the
      apolitical nature of Corps to the damage that could be wrought by
      enthusiastic young politicos.

252   "New Hosts: Libya and Paraguay". S19.11/2:4/12. Peace Corps
      Volunteers, 4, n.12 (October 1966): 2.
           Volunteers will arrive in the new host nations of Libya and
      Paraguay in September and December, 1966 respectively. The Libyan
      contingent of eighteen teachers will work in secondary schools and
      institutions of higher education, while the Paraguayan volunteers
      will serve as agricultural workers, home economists and university
      lecturers.

253   "New Initiative Focuses on Central America". Peace Corps Times
      (March/April 1985): 18.
           With the passage of the Central American Democracy, Peace
      and Development Initiative Act of 1984, new imperatives for
      assistance were mandated for Peace Corps. In response to the
      recommendations of the Kissinger Commission reports upon which the
      Act was based, Peace Corps formulated the Initiative for Central
      America (IFCA) for the host nations of Costa Rica, Belize,
      Honduras and Guatemala. Focussing on the period 1985-1989
      emphasis will be placed on self-help, rural housing, health and
      nutrition, small enterprise development, functional and specific
      literacy and teacher education. Funds from the IFCA will enable
      the regional programs to answer requests for more volunteers, with
      a target rate of 375 per year to be added to the host nations
      gradually. All volunteers will receive training in the skills of
      adult education to increase their effectiveness within both formal
      and nonformal educational settings.

254   "Peace Corps Education: New Support for an Old Program".
      Peace Corps Times (March/April 1985): 16-17.
           A review of the program support offered by the Office of
      Training and Program Support (OTAPS). These range from in-country
      seminars for volunteers teaching in various settings, monitoring
      and improving training given to education volunteers prior to
      their departure for postings, and to provide support information
      to the country staff. The latter includes disseminating the
      manuals and other compiled date from the Information Collection
      Exchange section of Corps to appropriate volunteers. Examples of
      situations involving OTAPS support are given from Lesotho,
      Honduras and Kenya.

255   "New Trends In Peace Corps Print". S19.11/2:6/1. Peace Corps
      Volunteer, 6, n.1 (November 1967): 12-14.
           A sampling of cover art and news coverage from in-country
      newsletters from some of the Corps host nations. Representative
      issues of Colombia's Porvenir, the Peace Corps India Digest,
      Sierra Leone's Kriopolitan, the Klong of PC/Thailand, Aliyejitolea
      of Tanzania, Ang Boluntaryo of the Philippines and JumpUp from
      Venezuela.

256   "Newsletters, 'Semi' and 'Non'".   S19.11/2:3/4.   Peace Corps
       Volunteer, 3, n.4 (February 1965):   5.
           In twenty of the forty-six nations which act as hosts to the
       Peace Corps, volunteer newsletters are issued to provide outlets
       and commentary.   This article reviews their names and considers
       what place they have in the life of the Corps.

257   "Nigeria Greets Peace Corps".   New York Times (8 May 1961):
       6.
           The Minister of Information for the Eastern Region of
       Nigeria, Mr. B. C. Okwu, has offered the Peace Corps the use of
       facilities of a school in that area as a training center for
       volunteers.   The announcement of this offer to the American
       Secretary of State for African Affairs was made at a news
       conference in Lagos on May 7, 1961.

258   "1967: Year of the Linguist".   S19.11/2:5/5.   Peace Corps
       Volunteer, 5, n.5 (March 1967):   5-6.
           A review of Peace Corps language training difficulties and
       proposed solutions, including the requirement of minimum language
       competency for all volunteers prior to overseas service.

259   "Nnamdi Azikiwe Hails Peace Corps Idea".   New York Times (9
       March 1961):   18.
           Speaking at a news conference in Lagos, Dr. Nnami d Azikiwe,
       Governor-General of Nigeria, hailed President Kennedy's idea for a
       Peace Corps.   In his view, it was "a bold and imaginative attempt
       to grapple realistically with the thorny problems . . . of
       developing countries of the world."

260   NOLTING, BARBARA.   "Librarians in the Peace Corps".
       Southeastern Librarian, 13 (Winter 1963):   211-16.
           Barbara Nolting, a volunteer stationed at the Institute of
       Jamaica, describes her own work and that of other librarians
       serving the Peace Corps in the early 1960's.   Countries reporting
       are East Pakistan, Costa Rica, Malaya, Venezuela, Sierra Leone and
       Turkey.   Projects range from setting up school libraries and
       cataloging manuscript collections to creating working collections
       for government ministries.

261   "Nomination of Loret M. Ruppe to be Director of the Peace Corps
       February 13, 1981".   Public Papers of the Presidents: Ronald
       Reagan (1981):   99.   GS4.113:981.   Washington, D.C.:   Government
       Printing Office, 1982.
           A news release announcing the intention of President Reagan
       to nominate Loret Ruppe as the new Director of the Peace Corps.
       Her background and qualifications are summarized.

262   NORMAN, HENRY R. "Peace and the Peace Corps". <u>Nation</u>, 206,
       n.12 (1968): 362, 378.
         This is a letter from Henry Norman, the first and only in-
       country director of Peace Corps/Guinea, as a rebuttal to the
       charges that its expulsion was related to United States
       involvement in Vietnam. Other cases of Peace Corps expulsion by a
       host nation are placed in context: "in Turkey, it was the Cyprus
       question: in Mauritania, it was the Middle East war: in
       Pakistan, it was our relationship with India; and in Gabon it was
       the strings from Paris manipulated by a leader determined to rid
       Africa of any American presence." Acknowledging the fact that
       host nations may choose to use Peace Corps as a convenient target
       for expressing their displeasure with American foreign policy,
       Norman argues that each case should be examined factually and not
       be seen immediately as an objection to Vietnam. The charges upon
       which this letter is based were made by Gerald Berreman in his
       article "The Peace Corps: A Dream Betrayed", <u>Nation</u>, v. 206,
       February 26, 1968.

263   NORMAN, PHILIPA. "Peace Corps Internship". <u>Black Collegian</u>,
       11 (April-May): 104-05.
         A brief account of a typical Peace Corps internship
       experience by a medical student who spent the summer of 1980
       working in the Office of Programming and Training developing
       health information for volunteers. Other aspects of this program
       included research on minority recruitment to the Peace Corps and
       studies of civil and welfare rights, foreign policy and problems
       of development.

264   "Now, Language Tests". S19.11/2:3/1. <u>Peace Corps Volunteer</u>,
       3, n.1 (November 1964): 4.
         Language proficiency tests administered by the Foreign
       Service Institute will be given both at the end of service and the
       end of training, as well as at various points during a tour of
       duty. The goal is the overall assessment and improvement of
       language instruction.

265   NUSSBAUM, BRUCE. "Did Christ Have a Crewcut?" <u>Far Eastern
       Economic Review</u>, 65, n.39 (25 September 1969): 771-74.
         A sharply critical article by a former volunteer examining
       the political impact Corps service has on both the host countries
       and the United States. Corps is seen as a reinforcer of
       conservative colonialist trends, as a deflector of needed
       criticism both at home and abroad, and as a minor, if highly
       visible, arm of the American propaganda machine. The program in
       the Philippines and the use of returned volunteers by such
       agencies as AID in Viet Nam are offered as illustration.

266   OBI, ENUENWEMBA. Peace-Corpsism, New York: Pageant Press,
       1962.
       Written by a Nigerian professor of philosophy, this volume
treats the Peace Corps as less a political or technical program
than as an instrument for the execution of a vision of moral
philosophy. Terming that philosophy "Peace-Corpsism", Obi
explores the benefits and barriers to achieving world peace via
this method of service. This is one of the few volumes which
places the moral ideas underlying the Corps in a broader frame of
the history of ideas and reflects well the atmosphere of the early
1960's when the Peace Corps was a new and intriguing phenomenon.

267   O'GARA, JAMES. "Daughters of the American What?" Commonweal,
       74 (19 May 1961): 198.
       The opposition of the Daughters of the American Revolution
to President Kennedy's proposed Peace Corps--by a vote of 2,082 to
1--is noted and decried. Pointing out that "the world will not
indefinitely survive two-thirds hungry and on-third fed", the
author supports the idea strongly. The image of the "ugly
American" and similar arguments used against the idea of a Peace
Corps are also mentioned.

268   O'GARA, JAMES. "Innocence Abroad". Commonweal, 75 (13
       November 1961): 142.
       Beginning with the Michelmore affair in Nigeria, the writer
points out that, because the members of the Peace Corps are
recruited predominantly from the middle and upper classes of
American society, collisions with the truths of poverty are
inevitable and emotionally shocking. Advocating a better degree
of preparation before going overseas, O'Gara suggests that
volunteers travel to such areas as the coal country of West
Virginia or the slums of New York City to lessen their naivete and
acquaint themselves with the issues of poverty firsthand.

269   "Old Style Training Camps Close". S19.11/2:7/9. Peace Corps
       Volunteer, 7, n.9 (August 1969): 18-19.
       The two Peace Corps training camps, Radley and Crozier, near
Arecibo, Puerto Rico, are being phased out in favor of a new
center in Ponce. A brief history of the camps and photographs of
two of the training techniques used in them is given.

270   "Older Corps is Urged". New York Times (30 July 1961): 52.
       The president of the National Council on the Aging, G.
Warfield Hobb, in a letter to Sargent Shriver, urged that the
Peace Corps accept qualified candidates over 65 years of age. In
his opinion "this would give the Peace Corps 170,000 top-notch
experienced people." While there is no upper age limit to
service, recruiting had been concentrating on those between 18 and
32 years of age.

271   "Omega Brothers 'Make the Difference' in the Peace Corps".
       Oracle, 70, n.1 (Winter 1986-1987): 8.
           Written on the occasion of the celebration of the twenty-
       fifth anniversary of the Peace Corps, this article chronicles the
       contributions made by volunteers who were members of the Omega Psi
       Phi fraternity from the earliest days in Ghana to the present.
       Alumni mentioned include C. Payne Lucas, former country director
       of Peace Corps/Togo and founder of Africare, Gregory Newton, M.D.,
       creator of the Peace Corps College Relations Program, and Michael
       Smith, a recently returned member of Peace Corps/Zaire. Lucas and
       Smith relate their views on the value of Corps service, and the
       role of black volunteers in Africa.

272   "On Global Living". Christian Science Monitor (19 June 1980):
       22.
           A letter to the Monitor from Richard Celeste, Director of
       the Peace Corps, addressing issues raused in a commentary in an
       earlier issue. Stating that "survival demands cooperation, and
       cooperation requires communication", he points to the 80,000
       returned volunteers as a resource for the United States
       educational system. Language training in particular is
       emphasized, as "any education for the 1980's which is not global
       is a cruel hoax."

273   "188 Families Join Peace Corps". AA1.13:1/2. InterACTION, 1,
       n.2 (November 1972): 4.
           As of November, 1972, 188 families were serving in various
       capacities within Peace Corps host nations. Family volunteers are
       seen to be more experienced and to show another side of the
       American society to host nationals. Problems relating to this
       types of service are placement, housing and degree of interaction
       with the community. Placement of married volunteers with families
       was introduced as part of ACTION Director Joseph Blatchford's "New
       Directions" program. A further 100 families are scheduled to
       depart for their sites in 1973 and 1974.

274   OSBORN, JOHN. "Dissent: Peace Corps on the Line".
       S19.11/2:8/3-4. Volunteer, 8, n.3-4 (March-April 1970): 7-9,
       22.
           On January 6, 1970, shortly before the visit of Vice
       President Agnew to Kabul, seven volunteers and two staff members
       of Peace Corps/Afghanistan presented a statement to the American
       Embassy criticizing the official U.S. involvement in Vietnam. In
       February, eight members of Peace Corps/Tunisia turned their backs
       on Secretary of State William Rogers during an address to the
       American community in that nation. This article explores the
       vulnerability of Peace Corps to political protests by active
       volunteers and questions "how can a volunteer express disagreement
       with the foreign policy of his government without violating his
       role as an apolitical worker in another country?" (p.6). A letter

from Director Joseph Blatchford stressed that, while the basic
freedoms of every volunteer would be respected, it was up to the
individual country directors to ascertain what constituted
political involvement and appropriate forms of protest within a
specific situation. A sample of the comments of the press is also
included.

275   OBORN, JOHN. "There Will Be One Billion People Living In
       Cities of the Developing World By 1980". S19.11/2:8/9-10.
       Volunteer, 8, n.9-10 (September-October 1970): 6-10.
       The explosive growth of Third World cities and the problems
this poses for development were examined at a conference sponsored
in July, 1970 by the Peace Corps. Attending were volunteers with
urban experience as well as several foreign specialists. The two-
day meeting debated the merits of urban community development
projects and needed qualities of personnel who will serve in such
a setting. At the time of the conference, some 400 volunteers
were assigned to urban posts. Examples of programs underway in
Venezuela, Malaysia and Guinea are offered as illustrations of the
possibilities.

276   OSBORN, JOHN. "Volunteer Interview: Joseph Blatchford".
       S19.11/2:8/5. Volunteer, 8, n.5 (May-June 1980): 5-13.
       An extended interview with Joseph Blatchford, Director of
the Peace Corps, given in 1970, following his first full year of
service in that post. Topics covered include the philosophy of
the "New Directions" espoused by Blatchford, the place of
generalists in Corps work and the ongoing debate as to the level
of skills required to answer increasingly sophisticated host
nation requests.

277   OSTERLUND, PETER. "Peace Corps at 25: "We've Traveled Quite a
       Ways". Christian Science Monitor (25 October 1985): 1,6.
       An historical review of the changes which have occurred in
Peace Corps programming, recruitment, evaluation and selection
over the first twenty-five years of the agency's existence.
Factors such as public revulsion over Vietnam and political use of
the agency under ACTION are viewed as having diminished the
effectiveness and damaged the public image generally held by
American. Interviews with Loret Ruppe, Sargent Shriver and Bruce
Cohen, Corps director of recruiting, are also included.

278   "Palm Reflects on Five Years as Fisheries Specialist". Peace
       Corps Times (September/October/November 1985): 19.
       An interview with Roger Palm, Fisheries Sector Specialist in
the Peace Corps Office of Training and Program Support. For the
first four years of its developed programming (1977-1981),
emphasis was placed on duplicating successful aquaculture projects
in developing countries. The period 1981-1985 saw a new direction
towards inland capture fisheries and marine community fisheries,
as well as re-evaluation of established projects.

279   PARMER, J. NORMAN. "Foreword". Annals of the American Academy
       of Political and Social Science, 365 (May 1966):   ix-x.
          A brief preface to a volume of the Annals devoted
       specifically to the origins, both political and historical, of the
       Peace Corps and its first five years of existence. The essays in
       that volume are included in this bibliography under their own
       entries. Parmer was the first Representative of the Peace Corps
       in Malaya.

280   PARMER, J. NORMAN. "The Peace Corps and the Conduct of United
       States Foreign Affairs". In International Dimensions In the
       Social Studies. National Council for the Social Studies
       Yearbook 38 (1968):   38-53.
          Regarding the Peace Corps as one arm of the United States
       foreign policy, the author views its role as "modernization . . .
       of attitudes, values and institutions . . . The Peace Corps is
       the only significant foreign policy instrument of the United
       States . . . engaged in . . . changing attitudes" (p. 39). Corps
       activity is viewed as a continuation of the American liberal
       spirit. Specific spheres of volunteer placement examined are
       community development and teaching. A clear understanding of the
       goals of Peace Corps is seen as essential for effectiveness in the
       field. Stressing that the goal of Corps is to alter host country
       attitudes, constant redefinition for both volunteers and the
       American public is called for. Problems preventing such work from
       being effective in the field include deficiencies in control of
       the local languages, the view that the value system of the host
       country requires little or no changes, and identificaton with the
       host culture. Contact with the affluent members of a host society
       is seen as possible if the precise goals of Corps service are
       unclear. For the production of "a world of politically
       independent and socially and economically viable states" (p. 53).
       Parmer regards the Peace Corps as the most effective arm of the
       U.S. Foreign policy system. The author served as the first
       Director of Peace Corps/Malaya from 1962-1963.

281   PARSONS, CYNTHIA. "Madam Ambassador Makes Mark". Christian
       Science Monitor (11 May 1968):   13.
          An interview with Carol C. Laine, United States Ambassador
       to the Kingdom of Nepal. She reviews the work being done by
       members of Peace Corps in that country, noting particualarly an
       effective program of science teaching, using locally available
       materials to build problem-solving experiments.

282   PATRIC, JAMES H. "Peace Corps in Tropical Forestry". Journal
       of Forestry, 78, n.11 (November 1980):   700-02, 705.
          Participation of Peace Corps workers in the effort to stem
       massive deforestation and erosion problems of environmental
       degradation in the developing world are profiled in this review
       essay. Beginning with statements made by then-President Carter in
       his environmental speech of August 2, 1979, the problem of demand
       for firewood is used as an example. The Peace Corps has been
       involved in forestry-related projects almost from its inception,
       with most volunteers working in one of four areas: reforestation,

village woodlots, agroforestry, and wood-conserving technology. A joint redirection of policies by both Peace Corps and the Agency for International Development promises more success in this area. Actual examples of volunteer services used are a seedlings project on Luzon in the Philippines, forestry instruction in a professional setting in the Dominican Republic and the establishment of a village nursery in twenty-one communities of Upper Volta. The community-based approach to developing increased awareness and strategies to cope with the swiftly altering biosphere is seen as the most effective, and one in which Peace Corps can play a significant role.

283   "PC and Sports: More Than Fun & Games". AA1.13.:3/5.
       InterACTION, 3, n.5 (February 1975): 1-3.
       A short review article covering the physical education and sports activities of volunteers serving their host nations as coaches, trainers and teachers. The philosophy of sports as teaching endurance, stamina and fortitude is also explored as a contributor to developing nations.

284   "PC Craft Programs". AA1.13:2/9. InterACTION, 2, n.9 (June, 1974): 8.
       A survey of countries using Peace Corps members in handicraft industries as of 1974. Countries included are Honduras, El Salvador, Iran, Jamaica, Upper Volta and Sierra Leone.

285   "PC Partnership Program Launches Speakers' Bureau".
       AA1.13:5/5. InterACTION, 5, n.5 (February, 1977): 1,8.
       The Peace Corps Partnership Program has established a bureau to supply returned volunteers to speak to groups requesting input on building schools, wells, health units and other joint projects. The community education gained for the Corps and its effect on the American awareness of the Third World in general are also assessed.

286   "PC/Smithsonian--Six Years Together". AA1.13:5/3.
       InterACTION, 5, n.3 (December 1976): 1.
       A profile of the status of the joint Peace Corps-Smithsonian Institution program placing volunteers in scientific and technical fields in environmental and natural science research projects. A photograph of a member of Peace Corps/Chile engaged in mariculture research is used as illustration. More than 500 such volunteers have so far been placed.

287   "PCV Mementoes Called for by Archive Group". AA1.13:4/4.
       InterACTION, 4, n.4 (January 1976): 6.
       The National Anthropological Archives Division of the Smithsonian Institution has invited returned volunteers to contribute any materials collected or written during their service. As of January, 1976, forty-three veterans had responded with diaries, photographs, tapes, letters and personal journals. Examples are given from Senegal and Upper Volta.

288   "PCVs Relish 'Tomato Man'".   AA1.13:4/12.   InterACTION, 4, n.2
       (September, 1976):   1,3.
          A profile of Dr. Bernard Pollack, professor of horticulture
       at Rutgers University, who is a participant in the Peace Corps'
       FARM (Future Agricultural Research Manpower) project. As part of
       his work at recruiting volunteers and assisting those already on
       site, Pollack has made several trips to West Africa, distributing
       seeds, advice and equipment to volunteers in countries as diverse
       as the Gambia, Niger, Upper Volta and Senegal. His efforts at
       educating the student body at Rutgers University about the Peace
       Corps are also noted.

289   "PCVs Organize Tech. Info. Group".   AA1.13:4/1.   InterACTION,
       4, n.1 (October 1975):   15.
          In the Nicaraguan capital of Managua, the Clearinghouse of
       Peace Corps Intermediate Technology (COPCIT) has been set up for
       those volunteers who may require information on appropriate tech-
       nology from projects already underway.

290   "PCVS Surveyed Show High Morale, Motivation, Concern".
       AA1.13:4/5.   InterACTION, 4, n.5 (February, 1976):   1.
          In mid-July, 1975, a questionnaire was sent to all volun-
       teers currently serving in Peace Corps by the National Voluntary
       Service Advisory Council. The purpose was to obtain information
       to supplement the Council members' observations of Corps activi-
       ties in both Washington, D.C. and in host nations. Over 66 per
       cent of all personnel responded, many including personal letters
       to augment their answers. Results (analyzed in this article)
       indicate a high level of morale with regard to Corps service and
       personal growth, divided opinions on types of assignment and
       training effectiveness and questions on levels of support being
       provided.

291   "PCVs Tackle Third World Environmental Ills".   AA1.13:4/2-3.
       InterACTION, 4 (November-December 1975):   8.
          Early in 1975, InterACTION sent out a survey to members of
       the Peace Corps involved with environmental programs, requesting
       their opinions on reasons for governments to take an interest in
       ecological and natural resource problems, as well as their views
       on the ways in which their own service had affected personal views
       on the United States' ecological issues. Returns from that survey
       form the basis of this article. Examples are provided from
       Malaysia, Fiji and Nepal.

292   U.S. Department of State. 1st Annual Peace Corps Report. (30
       June 1962) Washington, D.C.:   Peace Corps.
          This is the most historic of all the reports to be issued by
       the Peace Corps, mirroring as it does the first frantic year of
       growth and activity. Its eighty pages open with a brief history
       of the idea of a Peace Corps and proceed to consider decisions
       involved in creating standards for selection and training pro-
       grams. The eleven programs in place by June, 1962--Chile,
       Colombia, Ghana, Nigeria, the Philippines, East Pakistan, West
       Pakistan, St. Lucia, Sierra Leone, Tanganyika and Thailand--are

described through excerpts from letters written by volunteers serving in these countries. Statistical information, bureaucratic tangles and reactions to the Peace Corps by the American press, the overseas press (chiefly host nations) and the Communist press are frankly and honestly exhibited. An appendix details the search begun in April, 1961 to recruit talent for the headquarters staff in Washington.

293   U.S. Department of State. Peace Corps. Second Annual Report. S19.1:963. Washington, D.C.: Government Printing Office, 1963.

This second annual report of the Peace Corps covers a period of growth, diversification and expansion from seventeen host nations to forty-six. Each continent is covered in detail, with full statistics by country for volunteers in service or in training. Examples of volunteer life are given from El Salvador, Ghana, the Philippines, Togo, Nepal, Tanganyika, North Borneo/Sarawak and Colombia. Peace Corps operations (recruitment, staffing, selection, training, and cooperation with the private sector) are reviewed. Of particular interest is the section on new program directions and expansion of existing plans. In this listing are such new projects as an educational television network in Colombia, graduate lawyers to serve as instructors and researchers in African law schools and ministries, counterpart training in the United States, a school construction project in Gabon, orientation and involvement for staff wives, the usefulness of regular volunteer conferences and the role returning volunteers are playing regarding the agency in general. Criticism and praise (both foreign and domestic) is presented from points as distant as Panama, Ecuador, Ethiopia, Nigeria, Malaya, the Philippines, Tunisia, Nyasaland, and Venezuela. A case study of Janet Hanneman, a volunteer in mental health in Lahore, Pakistan, closes the report. Photographs depicting sections of volunteer life provide profuse illustration.

294   U. S. Department of State. Peace Corps. Third Annual Report. S19.1:964. Washington, D.C.: Peace Corps, 1964.

By the end of June, 1964, more than 2,000 volunteers had completed tours of service and returned to the United States, some of them to staff positions within Corps itself. At that time, there were 10,078 volunteers in the field or in training. Notable events of the year included the awarding of an honorary degree to Sargent Shriver, Director of Peace Corps, by Chulalongkorn University in Bangkok. Regional charts showing country-by-country statistics are followed by accounts from volunteers serving in Peru, the Ivory Coast, Nepal, Pakistan, Bolivia and Thailand. These are matched by contributions drawn from letters sent to volunteers since their return. The effects of political crises in host nations on Peace Corps are highlighted, particularly the Dominican Republic, Bolivia, Panama, Cyprus and Tanganyika. New approaches in Corps activities are an expanded number of vacation projects by volunteers, ranging from a day camp for children in Nigeria to inventorying storehouses of textbooks in Ethiopia, the inauguration of the Advanced Training Program, in-house training

at two camps in the hills of Puerto Rico near Arecibo, a successfully begun educational television training scheme in Colombia and
the use of volunteer secretaries in Corps positions. A review of
the "other nations' Peace Corps" covers the work by citizens of
the Netherlands, Germany, El Salvador and Zambia. A budgetary
overview is followed by a section on Peace Corps nurses. An
expanded section covers the work being done in American institutions by returned volunteers. Projects such as the Cardozo inner
city schools effort in Washington, D.C. are highlighted.

295   U. S. Department of State. Peace Corps. Fourth Annual Report.
       S19.1:965. Washington, D.C.: Peace Corps, 1965.
            The fourth year of Peace Corps was in many ways a coming of
       age as an agency and was one of crisis as well as development.
       The latter was most evident in the first Conference of Returned
       Volunteers held at the State Department in March, 1965. At this
       unique forum, a key issue was the definition of the special expe-
       rience of the volunteer. The rise of campus revolt in the United
       States and the crisis in the Dominican Republic posed new
       challenges to Corps personnel and tested their ideals. As of June
       30, 1965, 8,624 volunteers were assigned to 46 host nations, with
       4,604 in training. The Peace Corps program in Afghanistan is
       presented as an example of what may face a typical program in view
       of cultural resistance to acceptance for both individuals and the
       institution in general. New overall developments in Corps plan-
       ning and structure in the period were a renewed emphasis on the
       recruitment and assignment of physicians to attack "grass roots"
       health conditions, the arrival of the first members of an Exchange
       Peace Corps in the United States from India, the expansion of
       volunteer service programs in other countries, adoption of new
       techniques of language instruction (including the "immersion
       method") and the foundation of a new training center on St. Croix
       in the Virgin Islands. Following a capsule overview of Corps
       activity in Sabah, a lengthy section examines the aforementioned
       Conference and the contributions (and problems) facing the
       returned volunteer. The Report ends with a detailed discussion of
       the history of Peace Corps in the Dominican Republic, the back-
       ground to the 1965 political upheaval, and the actions taken by
       the individual volunteers during the fighting. A noteworthy
       feature of this report is the acceptance of both sides of Peace
       Corps personnel as neutral, permitting them to act as go-betweens
       in negotiations of prisoner exchanges and to aid in distributing
       food and clothing and working as nurses to wounded of all
       political factions.

296   U. S. Department of State. Peace Corps. Fifth Annual Report.
       S19.1:966. Washington, D.C.: Peace Corps, 1966.
            "The Peace Corps is a victim of its own innovations." With
       this startling statement, the annual report of the fifth year of
       Peace Corps takes up the evolution of the idea of the agency and
       its own--as well as host country--expectations of its success.
       The new countries which volunteers entered in 1966 are reviewed,
       with earlier research on Corps activity in Peru appearing as a
       report from Cornell University. The study found that communities

which had hosted a volunteer "developed nearly three times as fast as those without" (p. 14). Sections on training, recruiting-- including a poster which states boldly "Peace Corps Goes to Paradise"--and long-term planning complete the background informa- tion. The Corps program in the nation of Niger is presented in detail, with the work of public health nurses in the town of Illela and community workers in Madaoua profiled. A lengthy pictorial essay covers the history of Peace Corps from John Kennedy's initial speech at the University of Michigan to the fifth anniversary celebration in 1966. Charts detailing present Corps assignments and a section interviewing returned volunteers complete the volume.

297   U. S. Department of State. Peace Corps. Sixth Annual Report.
      S19.1:967. Washington, D.C.: Peace Corps, 1967.
      The sixth annual report records the year in which, for the first time, the number of returned volunteers exceeded the number on site. The year in which the 30,000th volunteer went overseas, and the year in which Peace Corps became caught in world political squabbling and was expelled from the Republic of Guinea in West Africa. Beginning with sections on the continuing evolution of the philosophy of Peace Corps and new directs in recruiting and training, a detailed examination is given to Corps activity in the Trust Territory of Micronesia. The Guinean event is followed from background to the landing of the expelled volunteers in Senegal. Of particular interest is the section entitled "Six Years Later", which summarizes five research studies done on volunteers in Colombia, Malawi, the Philippines and Peru. Field evaluation of the co-operatives idea in Latin America and the impact of the infusion of several hundred teachers into the Ethiopian school system is also listed. Summary statistical tables by continent and country are followed by a special survey of returned volun- teers, using the members of Sierra Leone I as the example. Four members of this group are then interviewed to gain their perspec- tives on the value of Corps service.

298   U. S. Department of State. Peace Corps. Seventh Annual
      Report. S19.1:968. Washington, D.C.: Peace Corps, 1968.
      The seventh year of Peace Corps history is presented in concise detail. New countries added to the group of host nations in this year were the Kingdom of Lesotho, Dahomey, Fiji, the Gambia, Tonga, Upper Volta and Western Samoa. Programming changes included a greater involvement of host country personnel in the planning and choice of volunteer assignments, increasing use of native speakers in language training in the United States (and mutual planning to maximize its benefits), growing demands from the American educational community for returning volunteers, and placement of six former volunteers as country directors. In Colombia, the Peace Corps was awarded the nation's highest honor, the Francisco De Paula Santander Medal. The country profile in this report focuses on the Kingdom of Nepal, where volunteers are working in the fields of agriculture, construction, and education, the latter including designing a mathematics and science curricu- lum. Training methods have shifted towards emphasizing actual

experiences over classroom instruction, although linkages with
some universities have continued since the inception of Corps.
New centers for training were set up in the Virgin Islands,
Micronesia, and at Escondido, California. A statistical summary
of Corps activity and expenses is given, with the "Impact"
section focusing on volunteers in the fields of health care and
community prevention in Bolivia, Malawi (the latter for a tuberculosis campaign) and Afghanistan. Six returned volunteers relate
their reflections and experiences of re-entry to complete the
report.

299   U. S. Department of State. Peace Corps. <u>Tenth Annual Report</u>.
       S19.1:971. Washington, D.C.: Peace Corps, 1971.
       This is the last report issued by the Peace Corps as an
independent agency prior to its incorporation under ACTION by
order of President Nixon on July 1, 1971. It begins with a
preface by Neil Armstrong, chair of the Peace Corps National
Advisory Council and Joseph Blatchford, Director of the Peace
Corps. The general tenor of the report addresses the degree to
which the planned "New Directions" program has been effective in
providing host countries with technically skilled personnel.
Programs were opened in the Solomon Islands, Mali and the
Democratic Republic of the Congo, while withdrawal became necessary for various reasons from Nigeria, Bolivia, Ceylon, Panama and
Guyana. Regional reports on Africa, Latin America, East Asia and
the Pacific and the North Africa/Near East/South Asia and budget
figures make up the bulk of the text. An increasing view of
volunteers as "theirs as well as ours" and the outlook for 1972
under the proposed ACTION agency completes the programming
coverage.

300   U. S. Department of State. Peace Corps. <u>Annual Report 1984</u>.
       Washington, D.C.: Peace Corps, 1984.
       In FY1984, the Peace Corps began planning for its twenty-
fifth anniversary, to be celebrated in October, 1985. As part of
this, three new initiatives in programming were adopted for the
Caribbean Basin, Central America and Africa. The last, the
African Food Systems Initiative, is "a long term effort building
upon Peace Corps' present program in Africa to assist up to 12
African nations to reverse a 20-year downward trend in food
production . . . to help small scale farmers improve food production and develop locally appropriate systems for the delivery of
food to those who need it" (pp. 2-3). Other events of note in
this period include the re-entry of Corps to Grenada and the
completion of phase-out in Malaysia. Country overviews are given
for Papua New Guinea, Yemen, the Eastern Caribbean (comprising
some 9 island nations) Honduras, Swaziland and Kenya.

301   MADOW, PAULINE, ed. <u>The Peace Corps</u>. New York: H. W. Wilson,
       1964.
       This volume is a collection of selected articles on the
first three years of the existence of the Peace Corps, on "its
origins, its operations, and its accomplishments, set forth by
government officials, observers of world opinion and others" (p.
4). The "others" are the volunteers themselves, speaking from
their service sites in Togo, Pakistan, Colombia and other host
nations. Many of the articles included in this work have been
entered in this bibliography under their individual titles.
Researchers will find this a handy overview of both domestic
relations and world opinion during the years when Peace Corps was
establishing itself.

302   "Peace Corps". <u>Christian Science Monitor</u> (10 March 1986):
       21.
       A letter objecting to the assertion in an editorial in the
<u>Monitor</u> on March 4, 1986 that Peace Corps' best days were past.
The author notes that the educational level of those invited to
training is higher, training is more comprehensive and emphasizing
a greater level of technical skills. Underexposure to the press
and Congress is decried as contributing to the absence of a
positive public image.

303   "Peace Corps Ads Called Politicking". <u>Christian Science
       Monitor</u> (18 May 1971): 5.
       Representative Wayne Hays of Ohio (Dem.) has demanded the
removal of some Peace Corps radio and television advertisements
presently airing in seventeen states, charging them to be "cynical
political exploitation of the efforts overseas of hardworking
young Americans." Hays charges that the states where the ads in
question are being made public are also those where Republican
senators will stand for re-election in 1972. Hays is the chair of
the House subcommittee which oversees the activities of the Peace
Corps.

304   "Peace Corps Adventure For Not-So-Young M.D.s". <u>Today's
       Health</u>, 47 (November 1969)): 17.
       A news item announcing openings for physicians to serve as
country medical officers for Peace Corps programs. Prior to 1967,
officers of the Public Health Service fulfilled this need, partly
under the benefit of draft deferments. With the elimination of
that provision in 1967, the private sector of the medical
community has been taking up the slack. Thirty-eight doctors went
overseas in 1969, and others have been recruited for 1970. Examples are given from Nepal and Swaziland.

305   "Peace Corps and AID Agree to Support Small Businesses in
       Developing Countries". Business America, 6 (2 May 1983):   16.
           A joint project of the Peace Corps and the Agency for Inter-
       national Development (AID), called the Small Project Assistance
       Program, has been created. AID will set aside $40,000 for each of
       the forty-one nations where both agencies operate. Projects will
       be approved by in-country Directors of Peace Corps programs and
       managed by volunteers. The maximum allotment for one project in
       $10,000. Areas targeted for funding include energy conservation,
       food production, agricultural technology demonstration centers and
       business co-operatives. A parallel program will provide technical
       guidance for volunteers working in the S.P.A. fields. It should
       be noted that Peter McPherson, the Director of AID who signed the
       agreement, is himself a former member of Peace Corps.

306   "Peace Corps and Churches". America, 105 (1 July 1961):   477.
           Speaking to critics of the Peace Corps who believe that the
       organization should not take advantage of the established network
       of contacts and facilities built by American private voluntary
       agencies, this opinion column decries such a view as indefensible.
       Pointing out that the Peace Corps intends to assist such groups
       through aid in filling gaps in previously formed institutions such
       as hospitals and agricultural cooperatives, use of the argument
       that this violates the separation of Church and State is seen as
       an unnecessary waste of resources. Note is also take of the
       formation of a Peace Corps desk by the National Catholic Welfare
       Conference to aid in locating suitable candidates for volunteers
       from Church membership.

307   "Peace Corps and Churches". America, 107 (1 December 1962):
       1167.
           An editorial comment upon a recent article in Christian
       Century cautiously endorsing the aid of churches in assisting
       Peace Corps in the recruiting of suitable candidates for service.
       The article appeared on November 14, 1962.

308   "The Peace Corps and ETV". S19.11/2:4/9. Peace Corps
       Volunteer, 4, n.9 (July 1966): 8-17.
           A group of five articles covering the involvement of the
       Peace Corps with educational television projects. Examples are
       drawn from the Colombian effort.

309   "Peace Corps and ORT". Peace Corps Times (January/February
       1986): 17-18, 24.
           A survey article defining the purpose and methods of oral
       rehydration therapy (ORT) as a preventive health measure and the
       roles being played by health volunteers in its utilization. A
       protocol signed between the Peace Corps and the Agency for Inter-
       national Development in 1984 mandates Corp participation in ORT
       activities. Countries where Corps is already involved with intro-
       ducing or maintaining ORT theory as public health work are the

Dominican Republic, Mauritania, Liberia, Zaire, Swaziland, Nepal, Gabon, Senegal and the Philippines. A manual for volunteer use has been compiled. An outline of the ORT training program offered as in-service assets by the Office of Training and Program Support is also included.

310   "Peace Corps Around the World". Saturday Review, 49 (23 April 1966): 16-17.
       This is a photoessay illustrating the variety of positions and activities engaged in by volunteers. Countries included are Colombia, El Salvador, Costa Rica, Bolivia, Tunisia, Jamaica, Sierra Leone, and Afghanistan.

311   "Peace Corps Asked for Math Trainees". Christian Science Monitor (23 May 1968): 4.
       Thirteen host nations have asked for volunteers with mathematics backgrounds to begin training in the summer of 1968. Placement will be at elementary, secondary and university levels and in teacher training programs.

312   "Peace Corps Asks Cooperation". Extension Services Review, 41, n.7 (July 1970): 2.
       An announcement that the Peace Corps is intensifying its efforts to recruit trained agriculture specialists. The changes from exclusively single persons to families is noted. Secretary of Agriculture Hardin has endorsed this effort and urged the land-grant institutions to assist the agency in locating qualified candidates. Through an agreement between Corps and fifteen schools, some 200 agriculture graduates will enter training after graduation. Older experienced people with years of farming experience are of particular value. This latest effort represents a shift from utilizing non-agriculturalists with only limited training in this sphere. Peace Corps work is seen as a logical part of extension activity.

313   "Peace Corps Asks for Physical Educators". Journal of Health Physical Education and Recreation, 33 (April 1962): 4.
       A recruiting notice of possibilities available to specialists in physical education in Peace Corps service. Details of projects in the Ivory Coast, Ceylon, Tunisia, Iran and Thailand are given.

314   "Peace Corps-Battle Stations". Economist, 274 (10 February 1979): 51.
       The "state of the Peace Corps" in 1979 is briefly reviewed. The agency is described as "being torn apart by internal quarrels over the direction in which it should be moving". President Carter's appointment of Sam Brown as director of ACTION and his conflicts with Carolyn Payton, Director of Peace Corps, are outlined. Some of Brown's ideas were seen as a bit radical, such as

using Corps personnel in an effort to improve relations with
radical nations such as Vietnam.   Investigators for the House
Appropriations Committee have also charged Brown with fiscal
mismanagement and recommended that ACTION itself be dissolved.
The latter move is seen as a good possibility for the survival of
Peace Corps.

315   "Peace Corps Bids Farewell to Sarge".   S19.11/2:4/6.   Peace
       Corps Volunteer, 4, n.6 (April 1966):   12-13.
            An illustrated account of the celebration held on February 1
       27, 1966, upon the termination of Sargent Shriver's service as
       Peace Corps Director.   The full text of the document presented
       to him at the time is reprinted.

316   "Peace Corps Budget Approved".   Higher Education, 18 (May
       1962):   16.
            A news report on the granting of the Peace Corps budget for
       fiscal year 1963 by Congress.   Approximately 10,000 volunteers in
       32 countries will be supported by these funds.   Details of Peace
       Corps programming as it was in 1963 are provided in statistical
       form, with both types of assignment and geographic regional data
       presented.

317   "Peace Corps Calls for 1,500 Volunteers".   American Teacher,
       10, n.3 (January 1964):   7.
            Sargent Shriver, Director of the Peace Corps, announced the
       largest spring training program in the agency's history for 1964,
       in response to an increased volume of requests for volunteers from
       African, Asian and Latin American nations.   Elementary, secondary
       and university level teaching personnel were required, with
       specialists in English, mathematics and science emphasized.
       Countries listed as destinations for this group of volunteers are
       Somalia, Malaysia, Nigeria, Ecuador, Nepal, Thailand, India,
       Jamaica, Togo, Colombia, Panama, Iran, Bolivia, Brazil, Chile,
       Venezuela, Tanganyika and the Dominican Republic.

318   "Peace Corps Campaign to Recruit Farmers".   Christian Science
       Monitor (21 April 1970):   15.
            Frank Pixley, chief of the Peace Corps agricultural desk, is
       heading an intensive recruiting campaign aimed at obtaining 550
       new volunteers in this area by September 1, 1970.   Demand is
       increasing in host countries for experts in seeds, animal breed-
       ing, fertilizer and mechanization.   Older personnel are viewed as
       a way of balancing out the college image of Corps and of taking
       the Peace Corps mission one step further, beyond education into a
       basic area.

319   "Peace Corps Catches Fire In Colleges". Life, 50 (17 March
       1961): 34-41.
          A photo essay recording the reaction of America's college
       students to the challenge of the Peace Corps. Much skepticism is
       evident. Debate includes the question of why there had to be a
       new agency simply to fulfill a campaign promise and why existing
       forms of foreign aid are insufficient. A statement by Sargent
       Shriver on the types of personnel desired and examples of other
       American projects already functioning are included.

320   "Peace Corps Celebrates 25th Anniversary". Congressional
       Record, 132, n.123 (18 September 1986): H7075-7076.
          The text of a message delivered in the House of Representa-
       tives by Rep. Henry of Michigan, congratulating the Peace Corps on
       its twenty-five years of service to its host nations and the
       enriching effect it has exerted on the American people. The
       reunion conference scheduled for Washington, D.C., for September
       18-22, 1986 is welcomed, and an invitation issued to members of
       Congress to attend the reception honoring volunteers to take place
       that evening. Rep. Henry was a volunteer in Liberia and Ethiopia
       from 1963 to 1965.

321   "The Peace Corps Comes to NIU". Illinois Education, 50, n.4
       (December 1961): 152-53.
          A brief outline of the training program set up at Northern
       Illinois University in DeKalb to prepare the first group to serve
       in the Federation of Malaya. The location was chosen because of
       Northern's links with that country, both through faculty and
       library collections. Thirty-nine trainees, ranging in age from 22
       to 49, will work in the fields of health care, economics, and
       technical assistance. Subjects included in the training course
       are first aid, physical conditioning, southeast Asian history and
       culture, American studies, language training in Malay, Tamil and
       Chinese and Peace Corps orientation. Upon arrival in Malaya in
       early 1962, further language training will take place before the
       volunteers are posted out.

322   "Peace Corps Disappointment". America, 106 (13 January 1962):
       456.
          An editorial comment expressing regret over the announcement
       by Sargent Shriver on December 15, 1961, that church agencies
       would not be co-sponsored organizations of the Peace Corps. The
       feeling of the author is that these agencies have much to offer
       the Peace Corps in the way of experience and facilities, and that
       this announcement is a direct contradiction of a previous text.
       In a guidebook issued in April, 1961, it was stated that projects
       meeting Peace Corps standards would not be barred from receiving
       support "because it is sponsored by a religious or sectarian
       group." Despite Shriver's action, the chair of the American
       Council of Voluntary Agencies, Bishop Edward Swanstrom, has
       pledged continued support of Corps. It is hoped that the position
       of Corps on this point will change in time.

323   "The Peace Corps: Down and Almost Out?" <u>Christian Century</u>, 89
       (19 January 1972):   57.
            This editorial comment deplores the proposed reduction in
       numbers of volunteers from 8,000 to 4,000 and the merging of Peace
       Corps with ACTION. Failure on the part of Congress to appropriate
       sufficient funding for a continued high level of activity, the
       occupation of the Dominican Republic and the war in Viet Nam are
       all seen as taking their toll on volunteer morale. Readers are
       asked to call their legislators so that this "illustration of
       national demoralization and scrambled priorities" can be
       reversed.

324   "Peace Corps Enters 5 Nations Since 1970". AA1.13:1/2.
       <u>InterACTION</u>, 1, n.2, (November 1972):   6.
            This historical article provides details on the entry of the
       Peace Corps to five new host nations between 1970 and 1972, to-
       gether with an overview of their assignments. Nations which
       invited the Peace Corps in this period include Mali, where twenty-
       four volunteers are working in agriculture: Mauritius, with
       volunteers involved with sugar cane research and preparing pro-
       grams for the national education television network: the Central
       African Republic (which welcomed its first contingent of seven
       volunteers with an airport reception): Zaire (where a public
       works project involves the training of Zairois mechanics) and
       Mauritania.

325   "Peace Corps Expands". <u>Christian Science Monitor</u> (12 June
       1973):   4.
            An expansion of Peace Corps service through invitations from
       the governments of North Yemen, Oman and Bahrein will bring to
       sixty-one the total number of host nations. Forty new volunteers
       in these initial postings will include nurses, agricultural exten-
       sion workers, well diggers, financial analysts, engineers and an
       air-conditioning and refrigeration specialist.

326   "Peace Corps Exports Idealists". <u>Congressional Record</u>, 132,
       n.14 (18 February 1986): E309-10.
            An article originally published in the <u>Bergen Record</u> and
       inserted for the perusal of the members of the House by Rep. Jim
       Courter, himself an RPCV from Venezuela. The focus of discussion
       is on whether the volunteer of the 1980's is a new and perhaps
       better breed than his predecessors, a view espoused by Director of
       Corps Loret Ruppe. The author decided to test this claim through
       an examination of materials in the Peace Corps Archives at the
       Smithsonian Institution and by interviewing returned volunteers.
       The consensus was that, despite external political pressures such
       as Viet Nam and the assassination of John Kennedy, "the idealism
       has endured."

327   "Peace Corps: Eye of the Storm".   Newsweek (4 September 1961):
       20.
       A brief news report on the controversy surrounding the
actions of Charles Kamen, at the time in training for the Philippines. As a past leader of the student council at Brandeis, his
protests and objections to the showing at the Miami, Florida
Rotary Club of a film entitled "Operation Abolition", purporting
to show that student demonstrations against the House Committee on
Un-American Activities were Communist-inspired are reviewed. Upon
learning of Kamen's selection as a Peace Corps trainee, the club
launched a wave of protests trying to have him removed. Sargent
Shriver, Director of the Peace Corps, refused, saying that Kamen
would qualify for service on the basis of his training performance, not for past political involvements. The atmosphere of this
event is best expressed by the comment of conservative Rep.
William Jennings Bryan Dorn of South Carolina, who remarked "the
impression we get is that the Peace Corps is going to be staffed
by beatniks."

328   "Peace Corps--A Family Affair".   AA1.13:3/8.   InterACTION, 3,
       n.8 (May 1975):   5.
       The story of how three generations of an Oregon ranching
family have served as agriculture and livestock volunteers in
Ecuador and Colombia.

329   "The Peace Corps Future".   Christian Science Monitor (4 March
       1986):   17.
       An editorial reflecting on the possible development of the
Peace Corps on its 25th anniversary year. The idealism and
pragmatism which blend to create Corps are lauded although federal
support is seen to have been lacking in the past with Loret
Ruppe's observation that the current budget of $124 million is
less than the Pentagon spends on newspaper and magazine subscrip-
tions in a year. Private support for the Corps is seen as more
viable.

330   "Peace Corps Gets Request".   Christian Science Monitor (29 May
       1968):   6.
       Sixteen host nations have requested volunteers with physical
science backgrounds to begin training in the summer of 1968. A
sample program in Central America calls for chemists and chemical
engineers to be trained as fish processing technologists for
Honduras, El Salvador and Panama. Their assignments will be to
set up salting and drying yards.

331   The Peace Corps Handbook.   AA3.11:4200.7/2.   Washington, D.C.:
       Printing Office, 1978.
           This is the manual of rules, regulations and expectations
       issued to each volunteer at the beginning of training and which
       each person was expected to retain throughout their service as a
       guideline for procedures and policies. Coverage is comprehensive,
       reaching from initial application and the medical requirements to
       appropriate ways of handling local politics overseas. The book is
       illustrated with photographs showing volunteers from Africa, Asia
       and Latin America on-site to further show the prospective volun-
       teer what to expect.

332   "Peace Corps Head Resigns". Los Angeles Times (29 March 1972):
       8.
           Kevin O'Donnell, Director of the Peace Corps, announced his
       intention to resign the post effective April 30, 1972 and return
       to private industry. Reasons cited were the five-year personnel
       policy of Peace Corps and the current budget crisis of the
       agency.

333   Peace Corps Impressions. San Francisco: Northern California
       Council of Returned Peace Corps Volunteers, 1986.
           This videotape is a selection of slides taken by members of
       the NorCal RPCV group illustrating their living conditions, the
       natural environments of host nations, and the people among whom
       they lived. Voice-overs address the problems of reentry shock,
       the need for educating America about the realities of the Third
       World, continued involvement, and the human face of poverty and
       frustration. Running time is thirteen minutes.

334   "The Peace Corps in the City". S19.11/2:4/11. Peace Corps
       Volunteer, 4, n.11 (September 1966): 5-38.
           A collection of articles examining the success and viability
       of the urban volunteer. Among the cities represented in the
       articles are Kabul, Afghanistan; Maracaibo, Venezuela; Ekisehir,
       Turkey; Nairobi, Kenya; Guatemala City, Guatamala; Bangkok,
       Thailand; and Caxias, Brazil.

335   "The Peace Corps: An Interview with Robert Taylor". Black
       Collegian, (May-June 1979): 12-14.
           An interview with Robert Taylor, a recruiter and former
       volunteer who is trying to bring more minorities into the Peace
       Corps. While in Guinea, his assignment was as an English
       instructor. Reflecting on his experiences with minority recruit-
       ment, he notes that "in many cases, countries are asking why don't
       we have more minorities." The present level of such representa-
       tion in Corps stands at two per cent, while Taylor sees a goal of
       twenty per cent or higher as desirable. Incentives for black
       college students to join, such as subsequent value for employment,
       are then presented.

336   "Peace Corps is Looking for 2,700 Special People". AA1.13:5/7.
       InterACTION, 5, n.7 (April, 1977): 13.
            A review of the summer call for volunteers in 1977 from the
       sixty-four host nations. Openings range from a watershed manager
       for Nepal, metalwork instructors for Tunisia, a dentist for Swazi-
       land and English teachers for Chad.

337   "The Peace Corps: JFK's Bold Legacy". Look (14 June 1966):
       34-39.
            A series of paintings by Norman Rockwell, celebrating the
       Peace Corps spirit and illustrating volunteers in the field in
       Ethiopia, India and Colombia.

338   "Peace Corps Kept Part of ACTION". AA1.16:2/2. Reconnection,
       2, n.2 (September 1979): 7.
            On June 23, 1979, House and Senate members voted to keep the
       Peace Corps within the framework of ACTION. In the spring of
       1979, the House of Representatives voted to remove the Peace Corps
       from ACTION and place it under the International Development
       Cooperation Administration, with the proviso that, should IDCA not
       be established, the Peace Corps would then become independent
       again. President Carter then issued an executive order giving the
       Peace Corps increased autonomy within ACTION including budgetary
       matters.

339   "Peace Corps Launches Search for Technical Info". AA1.13:4/5.
       InterACTION, 4, n.5 (March 1976): 1,6.
            To facilitate the exchange of useful information on effec-
       tive solutions to development problems, the Peace Corps is
       requesting materials created by volunteers be collected for dis-
       semination both within the agency and to other groups working in
       the international field. One co-ordinator is to be responsible
       for gathering technical data for each host nation and forwarding
       copies of documents to Washington.

340   "Peace Corps Legislation Signed Into Law by President Kennedy".
       Department of State Bulletin, 45 (July-September, 1961): 603.
            This entry is the full text of the press release dated
       September 22, 1961, issued upon the signing into law of the Peace
       Corps Act. Kennedy expressed his pleasure at the speed and
       numbers of the response to the idea of a Peace Corps and noted
       that "the sure sign of a good idea is that you can follow it."

341   "Peace Corps Makeup Under Fire". Christian Science Monitor
       (1 January 1978): 2.
            In a paper prepared for the American Enterprise Institute,
       former ACTION Director Michael Balzano charges that Third World
       nations need trained specialists rather than the generalists
       favored by Peace Corps officials. Sam Brown, the present Director
       of ACTION, views people as more vital than skills, with
       generalists as younger, more flexible and easier to recruit.
       Balzano warns that Corps must adjust to the new realities or face
       the end of its usefulness.

342   "Peace Corps Marks 15 Years of Services". AA1.13:4/12.
       InterACTION, 4, n.2 (September 1976): 1,8.10.
           An historical consideration of the progress made in program-
       ming volunteers to specific needs and problems since 1961. Among
       these are the increasing number of older volunteers, the questions
       of complementarity between skilled workers and generalists, expan-
       sion of veterans in the international arena and educational
       changes wrought in the United States by the returned volunteers
       who have gone into American colleges and school systems.

343   "Peace Corps Needs Trainers". American Forests and Forest
       Life, 92 (March 1986): 18.
           A call for training proposals in the areas of forestry and
       conservation, beekeeping, vegetable and crop production, small
       animal husbandry, secondary math and science education and water
       and sanitation technology. The desired proposals would create a
       village-based atmosphere in a location in the United States in
       preparation for service in Africa. Host countries for these
       volunteers are not specified.

344   "Peace Corps: Negroes Play Vital Role in United States Quest
       for Friends Abroad". Ebony, 17 (November 1961): 38-40.
           This article focuses on the efforts of the then-new Peace
       Corps to recruit black Americans for both field and staff posi-
       tions. A brief outline of Corps training and service is provided.
       Photographs include vignettes of both training for Ghana and
       several of the individual black volunteers.

345   "Peace Corps' Newly Launched Information Collection and
       Exchange Seeks Support From Many Sources". AA.13:4/7.
       InterACTION, 4, n.7 (April 1976): 13, 16.
           The Peace Corps ICE (Information Collection and Exchange)
       system is profiled, with emphasis on the contributions its litera-
       ture and accumulated experience can make to the international
       development community. Eight manuals in the fields of construc-
       tion, forestry and conservation, grain storage, well excavation,
       inland fisheries, health education, and volunteer education and
       training are summarized. Future contributions are outlined and
       applications suggested.

346   Peace Corps News, Washington, D.C.: Peace Corps, June 1961 --
       November, 1962.
           This was the first news publication issued by the Peace
       Corps during the first eighteen months of its existence. It
       combined with Volunteer in November, 1962, to form Peace Corps
       Volunteer, which title continued until the amalgamation of Corps
       with other agencies to form ACTION in 1971.

347   "Peace Corps: 1976". S19.11/2:4/5. Peace Corps Volunteer, 4,
       n.5 (March 1966): 7-26.
            A collection of fourteen articles speculating on the next
       ten years of the development of the Peace Corps. Authors for the
       specially solicited section included Vice President Hubert
       Humphrey, the Ambassador of Liberia, and several returned
       volunteers.

348   "Peace Corps Nurses". Nursing Outlook, 16 (November 1968):
       40-41.
            A photo essay showing volunteer nurses at work in Malaya,
       Bolivia and Tunisia. A brief text notes that of the 14,500
       personnel in the field at that time, over two hundred were
       registered nurses. Problems and challenges of the nursing situa-
       tions are also shared by a volunteer from Niger.

349   "Peace Corps Oath Changed". S19.11/2:8/9-10. Volunteer, 8,
       nos.9-10 (September-October 1970): 24.
            A line in the Peace Corps Oath of Service requiring all
       volunteers to affirm they are not a member of "an organization
       which advocates the overthrow of our constitutional form of
       government" has been dropped from the text. This action was taken
       in response to the 1969 Supreme Court decision that requiring such
       a loyalty oath was unconstitutional. New text which is more
       general in nature has been written to replace the statement.

350   "Peace Corps Opens Research Lab". S19.11/2:4/7. Peace Corps
       Volunteer, 4, n.7 (May 1966): 18-19.
            The foundation and duties of the Peace Corps Orientation and
       Information Center are set out. Examples of problems facing both
       in-country staff and volunteers are offered as rationales for the
       establishment of the center.

351   The Peace Corps Partnership Program. AA1.11.:4200.30.
       Washington, D.C.: ACTION 1978.
            A promotional brochure explaining the Peace Corps Partner-
       ship program to United States citizens who may wish to provide
       assistance. Partnership projects are designed by the people of a
       host community and co-ordinated by a volunteer. Sample proposals
       may be obtained from the Peace Corps headquarters in Washington,
       D.C. A noteworthy feature of this publication is the large number
       of excerpts from letters written by volunteers to stateside
       partners, illustrating the range of Partnership enterprises.

352   "Peace Corps Partnership: What It Is and How It Works, Who
       Helps and Why They Do". AA1.13:4/9-10. InterACTION, 4, nos.9-
       10 (June-July 1976): 14, 17.
            A two-section article reviewing the structure of the
       financial assistance rendered to host country communities through
       projects designed by volunteers, and the types of cross-cultural
       learning which donor groups and organizations have experienced.

353   The Peace Corps: A Pictorial History. New York: Hill and
       Wang, 1965.
           The only attempt made at compiling a photographic history of
       Peace Corps from its inception through the full expansion of in-
       country programs as they existed in 1965. Beginning with a
       section covering the varieties of training methods used--including
       such things as "the only working water buffalo in the United
       States" and a complete Asian village built in Hawaii's Waipio
       Valley (along with language training and Outward Bound courses)--
       the volume then examines each of the main regional programs in
       detail, providing summary data as to how Corps services were being
       used in the host nation and what changes, if any, had been intro-
       duced in application of volunteers. Photographs are lavished on
       every subject from school teaching on the Peruvian coast to
       nursing in Thailand. Host nations covered are Bolivia, Peru,
       Chile, Ecuador, Venezuela, Brazil, El Salvador, the Dominican
       Republic, British Honduras, Colombia, Cyprus (the only nation from
       which Peace Corps has withdrawn due to danger to its volunteers
       from civil war), Turkey, Afghanistan, Pakistan, Nepal, Thailand,
       Malaysia, Morocco, Tunisia, Guinea, Ghana, Ethiopia, Cameroon,
       Liberia, Sierra Leone, Nigeria, Tanzania and Togo. An
       introduction entitled "The Road To Peace" by Sargent Shriver, then
       Director of the Peace Corps, provides philosophical background to
       the stories of individual volunteer action which comprises each
       section.

354   "The Peace Corps Plan". Commonweal, 73 (17 March 1961): 625.
           Describing the idea of a Peace Corps as "presenting an
       inspiring challenge all the way", this editorial stresses the
       importance of suitable training for the volunteers in the first
       groups. Language facility, a realistic knowledge of local
       problems and issues, and avoidance of political subjects are
       viewed as vital. Volunteers should conduct themselves as
       "implicit witnesses" to American culture and values.

355   "Peace Corps Plan". Christian Science Monitor (1 September
       1977): 2.
           Speaking in Nairobi, Kenya, an official of the United States
       announced that 1,000 Peace Corps volunteers would be requested for
       tree planting and natural resources conservation work. The
       occasion was an international conference on the spread of desert
       areas around the world. No specific host nations are mentioned.

356   "Peace Corps Portfolio". S19.11/2:4/12. Peace Corps
       Volunteer, 4, n.12 (October 1966): 5-29.
           A photographic portfolio illustrating facets of the various
       host nations of the Peace Corps, taken by volunteers.

357   "Peace Corps Programs Lauded". AA1.13:2/3. InterACTION, 2,
       n.3 (December 1973): 4.
          This article is comprised of excerpts from a speech given by
       Robert Gardiner, executive secretary of the U.N. Economic Commis-
       sion for Africa at the Ninth Annual Conference of Peace Corps
       Directors in Africa in Monrovia, Liberia in September, 1973.
       Areas singled out for special mention were agriculture, health and
       rural development.

358   "Peace Corps Reaction: Shriver, Ending Tour, Reports Response
       Is Favorable". New York Times (14 May 1961): 48.
          Speaking in Bangkok, Thailand after visiting six African and
       Asian nations for discussions regarding Peace Corps services,
       Sargent Shriver reported a generally positive reception of the
       idea. He announced an agreement with the government of Tanganyika
       to supply twenty highway surveyors, four civil engineers and four
       geologists. This group would enter training on June 1, 1961 and
       receive two additional months of training in country. Nations
       visited by Shriver were Ghana, Nigeria, India, Pakistan, Burma,
       Malaya and Thailand. The Philippines were to be the final
       possible host nation with which discussions would be held.

359   The Peace Corps Reader. Washington, D.C.: Peace Corps Office
       of Public Affairs, 1969.
          This is a volume of letters, excerpts from books by former
       volunteers, criticisms, and essays that looks at virtually every
       aspect of Corps life from language training to coping with
       cultural frustrations. Many of these items have been annotated
       under the host nation where the volunteers served.

360   "Peace Corps Recruiting Farm Workers for Africa". Christian
       Science Monitor (11 January 1985): 2.
          On January 10, 1985, the Peace Corps asked for applications
       from 10,000 agricultural workers to fill the request of African
       nations affected by famine and drought for 600 workers immedi-
       ately. In the long view, these applications will be used to staff
       a projected ten-year effort at improving African food supply and
       distribution systems.

361   "Peace Corps Recruiting in Industry". Industry Week, 168 (1
       March 1971): 20-21.
          Plans by the Peace Corps to actively recruit older more
       experienced specialists from industry are outlined. The chief
       source of these people is seen as being "victims of layoffs,
       relocations or job obsolence." A co-operative effort with company
       personnel offices to identify potential volunteers is seen as most
       effective.

362   "Peace Corps Report". America, 106 (2 December 1961): 318.
          On November 18, 1961, Sargent Shriver returned from an
       inspection tour of twenty-five days to Peace Corps programs in
       Latin America and held a press conference at the Sheraton East
       Hotel in New York. Stating that "there is a wave of anti-poverty,
       anti-hunger and anti-tyranny" now abroad in Latin America through

Corps activity, Shriver pronounced himself well pleased with the
performance of these initial contingents in Chile and Colombia.
The latter has requested twice the present complement of volunteers, while Chile has asked for more workers for both rural and
urban projects. In addition, Peru, Bolivia, Brazil and Venezuela
have requested Corpsmen. Stressing that Latin America could
absorb all of the 3,000 volunteers presently in the field, Shriver
proposed to field a total of five hundred volunteers for the six
host countries by June of 1962.

363   "Peace Corps Role in Cultivation of Fisheries Production
       Discussed". AA1.13:5/1. InterACTION, 5, n.1 (October 1976):
       7.
           During a conference of country directors of the Peace Corps
       held in Columbia, Maryland, August 16-20, 1976, Dr. Tapan
       Banerjee, program manager in the Philippines, presented informa-
       tion on the participation of volunteers in current and future
       fisheries-related activities. Fifteen host nations were involved
       with fish culture as an alternative food source and industry as of
       1976. The first nation to do so was Togo. This article summa-
       rizes the key points of Banerjee's address.

364   "Peace Corps Seeks Architects, Engineers". Architectural
       Record, 157 (January 1975): 41.
           The joint program of environmental management and natural
       resources planning of the Smithsonian Institution and the Peace
       Corps offers architectural and engineering personnel a chance to
       serve in both administrative and field capacities. Types of
       projects listed include the rebuilding of the city of Managua,
       Nicaragua following an earthquake, teaching architecture and
       related courses in the University of Kabul, Afghanistan, and
       harbor design for Western Samoa. Other national projects profiled
       are those of Venezuela, Ethiopia, Philippines, Botswana, Barbados,
       Fiji, Sarawak, Honduras and Thailand.

365   "Peace Corps Seeks Retired Teachers". Chicago Schools Journal,
       44 (December 1962): 142.
           A call for 1,000 retired or recently retired teachers to
       consider service in the Peace Corps. Details and benefits
       provided to volunteers are cited. Some seventy projects in forty
       host countries required personnel.

366   "Peace Corps Seeks Skilled Tradesmen". AA1.13:1/8.
       InterACTION, 1, n.8 (May 1973): 6.
           Using Abner Andrew, a volunteer serving as a teacher of
       automotive mechanics in the Philippines, as an example, this
       article points up the need for skilled tradespeople in Peace Corps
       and the difficulties of recruiting them. Andrew's workshop is
       examined in some detail.

367   "Peace Corps Shapes Up". <u>America</u>, 104 (11 March 1961): 746.
      Commenting on President Kennedy's original announcement of a
proposed Peace Corps, the effort is seen to be a serious one. The
appointment of R. Sargent Shriver as Director and his efforts at
creating the agency are noted, as is a research study done at
Colorado State University, stressing the value of person-to-person
work done by personnel living under local conditions. The report
also stressed the value of working through private agencies,
rather than creating a new organization. As an historical view of
Peace Corps in its infancy, the final caveat that "the agency
should content itself with giving grants to private groups already
equipped to train personnel to meet the specific requests of the
needy lands" is most instructive.

368   "Peace Corps Song". AA1.13:2/7. <u>InterACTION</u>, 2, n.7 (April
      1974): 8.
      As part of the celebration of the 15th anniversary of the
founding of the Peace Corps, the Peace Corps song is being made
available to bands across the United States. It was originally
written by Graham Overgard, entertainment director for the Detroit
Lions football team, and performed on Thanksgiving Day, 1963, five
days after the death of John F. Kennedy. At that time, a half-
time show with placards spelling out PEACE CORPS and flags of all
nations with resident volunteers was given. The text is available
from a music publisher in San Diego.

369   "The Peace Corps Takes the Field". <u>Life</u> (15 September 1961):
      63-66.
      A photo essay examining various episodes in the training of
volunteers, including physical fitness and survival training. At
the time of writing, eighty volunteers were serving in Ghana and
Tanganyika, eighteen on St. Lucia, and sixty-two in Colombia.

370   <u>The Peace Corps TIMES</u>. PE1.9:978. Washington, D.C.: Peace
      Corps, 1978 to date.
      This periodical forms the major information exchange for
volunteers in the field, and fills the gap left by the former
<u>VOLUNTEER</u> magazine's dissolution. Contents include news stories
from host nations, country profiles of programs and summaries of
staffing changes, and articles on information available or
required for completion of projects. Publications held in the
Peace Corps' Information Collection and Exchange sector are
regularly listed. Selected articles from the <u>Times</u> have been
included in the appropriate headings of this bibliography.

371   "Peace Corps to Dedicate Puerto Rico Camps Today". <u>New York
      Times</u> (17 July 1962): 4.
      The formal dedication of two Peace Corps training camps near
Arecibo, Puerto Rico was held on July 17, 1962. At the ceremony,
the installations were renamed Camp Crozier and Camp Radley, to
honor the first volunteers killed on duty. Sargent Shriver,
Director of Peace Corps, the parents of the deceased, and the
complement of trainees at the camps attended.

372   "Peace Corps to Launch Aid Invasion of Famined Africa". <u>Jet</u>,
       67 (28 January 1985): 8.
            A news report of the crash recruiting program announced by
       Loret Ruppe, Director of the Peace Corps, to locate 10,000 agri-
       culture specialists for African nations threatened with famine.
       The 24 nations affected need the services of soil scientists,
       foresters, farmers, animal raising experts and veterinarians.

373   "Peace Corps Training at Howard". <u>Ebony</u>, 18 (November 1962):
       69-70.
            An examination of the training program for the Peace Corps
       conducted at Howard University in Washington, D.C. Howard was
       chosen due to its strong program of African studies and because of
       its predominantly black student body, which it was hoped would
       give the trainees experiences in cross-cultural situations prior
       to their leaving the United States. Among the trainees were the
       first group of physicians and fishermen ever to serve in Corps;
       Host countries to receive these personnel were Cyprus
       (agricultural programming and geological mapping), Togo (fisher-
       men), Niger, Senegal, and Sierra Leone. Areas other than those
       indicated in the group were food production, health and athletic
       training. The accompanying photos show the physical training
       given the volunteers, language classes and cultural briefings
       conducted by the Howard faculty and invited consultants.

374   "Peace Corps Unrest". <u>New Republic</u>, 161 (27 September 1969):
       31.
            A letter from Joseph Blatchford, Director of the Peace
       Corps, addressing certain points raised in a story by Paula Stren
       in the August 23-30 issue of <u>New Republic</u> regarding dissatisfac-
       tion. The earlier story is rebutted on several key points and
       shown to be based on false or, at best, incomplete information.
       Topics included are the withdrawal of volunteer lawyers from the
       Trust Territory of Micronesia, high staff turnover, and the
       "unpopularity" of the five "new directions" introduced by
       Blatchford with the approval of President Nixon.

375   "Peace Corps Volunteer". <u>Occupational Health Nursing</u>, 22
       (April 1974): 32.
            An interview with Nancy Jo Columbus, a volunteer nurse
       stationed in the town of Danli, Honduras. Details of local health
       problems--including coping with machete wounds and most births--
       and the joys of adapting to Honduran culture are related. General
       information on Peace Corps Honduras is also included.

376   <u>The Peace Corps Volunteer: 10th Anniversary Issue</u>, 9, nos. 5-6
       (Summer 1971).   S19.11/2:9/6-5-6.
            An extended presentation in text and pictures of the accom-
       plishments, changes and problems of the first ten years of the
       Peace Corps. Many of the text sections are written by volunteers
       recalling their assignments or officials and heads of state of
       host nations describing the manner in which Corps has impacted
       their peoples. Geographical areas included are Africa, Latin
       America, North Africa, the Near East, Southwest Asia, East Asia

and the Pacific. Among the contributors are President Hamani
Diori of Niger, Nene Mate Kole of Ghana, and Margaret Mead. A
striking feature of this edition of the Volunteer is the photographs submitted as part of an anniversary contest.

377   "Peace Corps Volunteers Read Saroyan and Spock". Library
       Journal, 87 (15 November 1962): 4157.
       Peace Corps headquarters in Washington, D.C. has inaugurated
a program of supplying volunteers with lockers of paperback books.
Items chosen for inclusion cover American life and culture, its
political, social and economic programs and its literary past.
Each locker has approximately 175 books ranging from Dr. Benjamin
Spock's Baby and Child Care (in Urdu, Malay or Persian depending
on the country) to works by Mark Twain, James Fenimore Cooper,
Earle Stanley Gardener and Alexis De Tocqueville. Simpler
materials are also included for classroom use and literacy programs. Volunteers are encouraged to leave their collections
behind upon completion of service.

378   "Peace Corps Volunteers Serve the Cause of Conservation".
       AA1.13:5/7. InterACTION, 5, n.7 (April 1977): 8-10.
       A general overview of the participation of Peace Corps
personnel in the worldwide efforts at conserving and developing
natural resources. This has taken the form of popular education
in Costa Rica and the Philippines, drafting plans for nine
national parks in Malawi, wildlife censuses in Thailand and Zaire
and writing policy documents for many host nations. A history of
Corps involvement with the environmental program in the Third
World is included, as are interviews with several of the volunteers whose projects are described. Of particular note is the
charting of a completely subterranean park in the Philippines.
Photographs illustrating types of service are provided.

379   "Peace Corps Volunteers Train at L.A. Hospital". Modern
       Hospital, 105 (October 1965): 196.
       A news note reporting that thirty volunteers intended for
work in Chile are being trained at the Los Angeles County General
Hospital. The group includes community health workers, registered
nurses, laboratory, dental and x-ray technicians. Simulation of
an intercultural environment has been achieved through work with
American Indian students.

380   "Peace Corps Volunteers Work Hard to Combat Malnutrition in the
       Third World". AA1.13:4/9-10. InterACTION, 4, nos.9-10 (June-
       July 1976): 11, 16.
       The problems of child malnourishment, introducing new
sources of protein to local diets, raising nutritional standards
and gradually altering traditional customs which affect the child
are all challenges facing Peace Corps members working in health
care. This article offers examples of volunteer projects from
Niger, Liberia, Costa Rica and the Philippines.

381   "Peace, Politics, and Blatchford". S19.11/2:8/5. Volunteer,
       8, n.5 (May-June 1970): 17-19.9.
            A survey article examining the pressures brought to bear on
       the Peace Corps and Director Joseph Blatchford in May and June of
       1970 by opponents of the Viet Nam War and members of the Congress
       and the Committee of Returned Volunteers. Details of protests
       held outside Corps offices in Washington and public statements
       made by Blatchford are included.

382   PENNIMAN, HOWARD. "Peace Corps Requirements". America, 104
       (25 March 1961): 808.
            Focusing on the problem of how much and of what nature Peace
       Corps training should be, the author advocates a longer period of
       training skills other than languages, cultural factors and tech-
       nology. Stating that "our colleges and universities do not
       graduate youngsters sophisticated enough to hold their own in the
       endless arguments into which they will be drawn by local or
       itinerant Iron Curtain Communists", Penniman calls for the
       rudiments of Communism to be included in training as a type of
       ideological immunization.

383   PERRY JAMES M. "Critics Say Ex-Radical Acts Slowly As Chief of
       Agency: Brown, 'But I Need Time'". Congressional Record, 123,
       Part 30, (15 December 1977): 39649-39651.
            A reprinted article from the Wall Street Journal of December
       12, 1977, profiling Sam Brown, newly-appointed Director of ACTION.
       Peace Corps was listed as ACTION's highest priority program at
       this time, and many alumni--both staff and volunteers--were disap-
       pointed in Brown's refusal to separate Corps from ACTION and his
       inability to restore the spirit which had been so evident in the
       earlier days under Sargent Shriver and Jack Vaughn. Through the
       appointment of Carolyn Payton, Brown is trying to increase
       minority representation in Peace Corps, and has traveled to many
       of the host countries for a first-hand look. A switch is the
       renewed emphasis on "generalist" volunteers versus the trained
       specialists being sent prior to Brown's appointment. Change in
       recruiting procedures was also being discussed.

384   PETER, WALTER G. "Peace Corps Seeks Biologists". Bioscience,
       21, n.8 (15 April 1978): 379-381.
            The possibilities of participation in the joint Peace Corps-
       Smithsonian Institution program of providing skilled scientists in
       specific environmental and ecological fields to developing nations
       are outlined for biologists. A short history of the agency and
       advantages of service are presented. For the scientists, these
       latter include working for two years on research in a field set-
       ting, opportunities to move ahead rapidly in one's career, and the
       chance of both financial and travel support at a time when
       research funding from conventional sources is limited. Examples
       of current projects are included from Uganda, Chile, Western
       Samoa, Tonga, Iran, and the Philippines.

385   PETER, WALTER G. "Smithsonian-Peace Corps Program Scrapped".
       Bioscience, 28 (October 1978): 665-666.
            The joint Peace Corps-Smithsonian program which had provided
       host countries with some one thousand biologists, conservation-
       ists, limnologists, forestry experts, agronomists, soil scientists
       and wildlife management personnel since its inception in 1970 was
       allowed to lapse in 1978. The reasons for this were partly fiscal
       but chiefly a shift in Peace Corps priorities towards meeting
       "basic human needs". An effort such as the Smithsonian's was
       viewed as too sophisticated and expensive. Generalists would be
       recruited to fill positions left vacant by the absence of
       professionals and would receive training in the specialty prior to
       overseas service. The author notes that "the Peace Corps
       hierarchy is not eager to discuss why the program lost favor" (p.
       666), citing Director Carolyn Payton's refusal to respond to
       inquiries of the Wildlife Society as an example of this.

386   PETERS, CHARLES. "The Relevance of the Peace Corps". The
       Peace Corps Reader. Washington, D.C., Office of Public
       Affairs, Peace Corps, 1969: 148-52.
            The question of the relevance of the Peace Corps in the era
       of the Viet Nam War is answered through an examination of the
       goals of the organization. Charges of cultural imperialism are
       rebutted by noting that the world's cultures are already blending
       and it is necessary to insure that the best values of each are
       preserved.

387   "Pilgrims of Peace". Senior Scholastic, 86 (11 March 1965):
       16-17.
            A contrasting article of the services rendered to the host
       nations by missionaries and members of the Peace Corps. While the
       churches are changing their approaches to missionary activities,
       the Peace Corps has the advantage of not having an historic asso-
       ciation with colonialism. The example of a member of Peace
       Corps/Peru working in a barriada is offered as illustration of the
       nature of this service.

388   "Place of PCV's in Third World Health Care System Examined".
       AA1.13:5/1. InterACTION, 5, n.1 (October 1976): 7.
            At the international meeting of Peace Corps country direc-
       tors in Columbia, Maryland, August 16-20, 1976, Dr. Jarrett
       Clinton, a former staff physician of Peace Corps/India, delivered
       an address on Third World health conditions and the present and
       future roles volunteers can play in alleviating them. This
       article summarizes the chief points of that speech.

389   "Plaque Marks PC Birthplace". S19.11/2:2/8. Peace Corps
       Volunteer, 2, n.8 (June 1964): 5.
            A bronze memorial plaque has been set into the steps of the
       University of Michigan Student Union to commemorate the spot
       where, at 2:00 A.M. on October 14, 1960, President Kennedy first
       issued the challenge later expanded into his famed speech at the
       Cow Palace.

390   "Poor Peace Corps". New Republic, 166, n.8 (19 February 1972):
       7-8.
            Eight months into the fiscal year of 1972, the Peace Corps
       had still not received an approved budget. The continuing resolu-
       tion ensuring the agency's existence supplied only $72 million per
       annum: a situation which if not corrected would force the recall
       of up to one half of the 8000 volunteers then on site and with-
       drawal from 15 of the 55 nations serving as host countries. Rep
       Otto Passman, a longtime enemy of Corps and chair of the House
       Appropriations Subcommittee on Foreign Affairs, is the chief
       obstacle to passage of the funding. His views can best be seen in
       this quote: "if I had to meet my Maker in three minutes . . . the
       last decision . . . would be to abolish the Peace Corps." A joint
       House-Senate conference committee is scheduled to discuss a final
       budget proposal.

391   POWELL, RICHARD. Don Quixote, U.S.A., New York: Scribners,
       1966.
            An hilariously sincere volunteer with the unlikely name of
       Arthur Peabody Goodpasture arrives in the host nation of San
       Marcos and by a series of improbable events winds up as the head
       of state.

392   "Pravda Scowls" Christian Science Monitor (6 January 1971):
       4.
            A news report from Moscow quoting Pravda, the official party
       newspaper's description of the Peace Corps as "a tool for
       spreading the notorious American way of life." Connections of the
       agency with the CIA are also hinted.

393   "President Issues Executive Order On Administration of Peace
       Corps". Department of State Bulletin, 47 (July-September
       1962): 329-30.
            This is the full text of Executive Order 11041, issued
       August 6, 1962, to regularize the administration of the Peace
       Corps. Executive Order 10924, Kennedy's original order creating
       the Peace Corps, was superseded by this text. Topics addressed
       include powers reserved to the President under the Peace Corps Act
       of 1961, allocation of funds and security requirements.

394   "President Johnson Establishes New Personnel System for Peace
       Corps". Department of State Bulletin, 53 (October-December
       1965): 765.
            Pursuant to the passage of Public Law 89-134 on August 24,
       1965, a new personnel system was created for the Peace Corps,
       limiting employment of senior staff to five years. This placed
       them on a similar basis with the volunteers they administered.
       The present announcement is the full text of Executive Order
       11250, giving the Secretary of State authority to shift Peace
       Corps personnel into the new system. Said authority was then
       delegated by the Secretary to Sargent Shriver, Director of the
       agency, for actual implementation.

395   "President Kennedy Names Members of Peace Corps Advisory
      Council". <u>Department of State Bulletin</u>, 44 (April-June 1961):
      583.
         On March 30, 1961, John F. Kennedy announced the appointment
of a group of prominent Americans to form the Peace Corps Advisory
Council. The stated purpose of the Council, "representing a cross
section of American life and thought . . . to give guidance and
counsel in the development of the activities of the Peace Corps"
is also included. Members of the group were active and interested
in world affairs, and numbered such people as Harry Belafonte,
Rev. William Sloan Coffin, Justice William O. Douglas of the
Supreme Court and David Lilienthal among them.

396   "President Proposes Legislation for Establishing Peace Corps".
      <u>Department of State Bulletin</u>, 44, (April-June 1961): 980.
         The complete text of a letter from President John F. Kennedy
to the Hon. Sam Rayburn, Speaker of the House of Representatives
and to Lyndon Johnson dated May 31, 1961. This letter accompanied
the proposed legislation which later was signed into law as the
Peace Corps Act. The thoughts of Kennedy and his view of Corps as
"a special and timely opportunity" are preserved here.

397   "President Recommends Expansion of Peace Corps". <u>Department of
      State Bulletin</u>, 46 (January-June): 521.
         In this letter to Lyndon B. Johnson, President of the
Senate, President John Kennedy urged an increase in appropriations
to permit the expansion of Peace Corps from the then maximum of
2,400 volunteers to some 6,700 by June 30, 1963. This expansion
was seen to be necessary in view of the great interest taken by
host countries in receiving massive numbers of new volunteers.
Nigeria, one of the earliest countries to receive a contingent,
had requested an additional 400 teachers. Expansion of Corps
would also create a larger pool of Americans with valuable overseas experience which could then be applied in other ways for the
benefit of this country, such as membership and service in the
Foreign Service.

398   "President Transmits Fourth Annual Report of Peace Corps to
      Congress". <u>Department of State Bulletin</u>, 54 (April-June 1966):
      635-36.
         The full text of a letter sent by President Lyndon Johnson
to accompany the fourth annual Peace Corps report. Signs of
progress listed include the expansion of the number of personnel
stationed in Afghanistan, an increased in the total number of
volunteers while the average cost of support has declined, and the
fact that "the Peace Corps is the largest producer and consumer of
language materials in the world." The President then discusses
where the returned volunteers--4,545 in number as of June 30,
1965--are working.

399   "President Transmits Sixth Annual Report of Peace Corps to
        Congress". S1.3:558/1501-13. Department of State Bulletin
        (April-June 1968): 505-06.
            This entry is the full text of the letter sent by President
        Lyndon Johnson to Congress accompanying the annual report for the
        Peace Corps in 1968. Details of the work being done by the 12,000
        Corpsmen serving are given. For the first time in the agency's
        history, the number of returned volunteers surpassed the number
        presently in the field.

400   "Protect the Peace Corps". Christian Science Monitor (2 May
        1979): 24.
            An editorial objecting to the vote of the House of Represen-
        tatives to make the Peace Corps part of an as-yet-uncreated
        "International Development Cooperation Agency." Reviewing the
        problems the Corps has faced since its placement under ACTION in
        1971 by President Nixon, strong support is voiced for keeping the
        agency free of any affiliations with official United States
        foreign policy. The opposition of returned volunteers to the
        proposed mergers is also noted.

401   "Proud to Make a Difference. Peace Corps At 25". Peace Corps
        Times (December 1985): 6-8.
            A report on the commemorative activities held at the
        University of Michigan, Ann Arbor, of John Kennedy's speech at
        2:00 A.M., on October 14, 1960, issuing the first challenge to
        American youth to create the Peace Corps. Detailed coverage of
        the symposium held under the theme "America's Role in Africa's
        Development: Past And Future" are also included, with excerpts
        from addresses delivered by Loret Ruppe and Sargent Shriver.

402   "Program Zeroes In On Scarce Skills". AA1.13:2/6.
        InterACTION, 2, n.6 (March 1974): 5.
            To obtain an increased number of volunteers with specific
        professional skills, such as architects, city planners, civil
        engineers and vocational education teachers, the Peace Corps in
        1969 set up an internship program. This article details the
        structure and scope of that program as it existed in 1974.

403   "Programming: Matching Peace Corps' Resources to the Needs of
        Host Countries". Peace Corps Times (July/August 1985): 15-18,
        24.
            The basic issues of contemporary programming decisions and
        matching volunteers with host country requests are explored in
        interviews with Peter Kresge, Director of the Program Support
        Division, Office of Training and Program Support, and several
        assistant country directors for programming. Need for an increas-
        ingly integrated method of program design and development is being
        addressed through the construction of a three volume series
        entitled the "Integrated Programming System". This set is intend-
        ed to supplement materials from the sector guidelines to assist
        staff responsible in obtaining a balanced program between host
        country requests and available Peace Corps resources.

404 RAFTERY, S. FRANK. "Skilled Workers in the Peace Corps".
     <u>American Federationist</u>, 77 (November 1970): 9-13.
          Written by the president of the Painters' Union, this
     article examines the various tasks skilled tradesmen have per-
     formed in the Peace Corps. A useful feature of the essay is its
     chronicle of the ways in which the need for skilled personnel has
     changed over the first ten years of the existence of Corps.
     Joseph Blatchford, third Director of the Peace Corps, expressed
     his desire to point the agency in more relevant directions to meet
     the needs of the 1970's. American labor leaders were in agreement
     that their membership could make a significant contribution to the
     developing world. As a member of the National Advisory Council of
     the Peace Corps, the author visited the island of Ponape in
     Micronesia in the summer of 1970. A detailed report on a road-
     building project and the formation of a construction company to
     carry it out illustrate the activity of volunteers. Examples are
     also given from Guinea and Iran.

405 "Recruiting the Activists". <u>Newsweek</u>, 66 (8 November 1965):
     66.
          In an effort to reach the activists on America's college
     scampish and attempt to channel some of their energy into the
     Peace Corps, Warren Wiggins, deputy director of the agency, has
     planned a series of meetings with groups ranging from the radical
     SDS to the more conservative Young Americans For Freedom. The
     lure is the emphasis in Corps programs on community development
     action and its potentialities. Admitting that the line between
     community organizing and advancing specific political solutions is
     a fine one, Wiggins believes that Corps personnel have generally
     followed the mandate to stay out of local politics. The case of
     the Dominican Republic, where volunteers treated the wounded on
     both sides of the conflict, is offered in support of this state-
     ment. Draft deferments for Corps participants are also a factor
     for activists to consider.

406 REDMON, COATES. <u>Come As You Are: the Peace Corps Story</u>. New
     York: Harcourt Brace Jovanovich, 1986.
          An engaging look at the formation and first years of the
     Peace Corps by a former senior writer of the agency. Beginning
     with the speech by John F. Kennedy at the Michigan campus in which
     the Peace Corps was first mentioned, its development and adven-
     tures during the administration of R. Sargent Shriver are covered
     in detail. Personal interviews with staff alumni of that period
     such as Bill Moyers, Warren Wiggins, Jack Vaughn and the first in-
     country representatives illuminate a side of the Peace Corps which
     was not accessible to the popular media.

407   "Remarks at the Presentation Ceremony for the Peace Corps
       Awards April 18, 1983". Public Papers of the Presidents:
       Ronald Reagan 1983, Volume I, pp. 551. Washington, D.C.:
       Government Printing Office, 1984.
            Speaking in the Rose Garden of the White House at the begin-
       ning of National Volunteer Week, President Reagan honored six
       members of the Peace Corps who had made outstanding contributions
       "to the noble cause of peace". The volunteers were all awarded
       citations in absentia except for Sister Madeleine Chorman of Peace
       Corps/Ghana. Other nations represented included an architect in
       Yemen, a fish culture worker in Guatemala, an environmental worker
       in Paraguay, an epidemiologist in Zaire and a speech therapist in
       Malaysia. Director Ruppe of the Corps was present and read the
       citations.

408   "Remarks of President Ronald Reagan At Peace Corps Africa Sent-
       Off". Peace Corps Times (May/June 1985): 3.
            The full text of remarks made by President Reagan at a
       ceremony on the second day of National Volunteer Week honoring
       three members of Corps as Volunteers of the Year--Kathy Gilchrist
       (Peace Corps/Micronesia), Lynn Blaylock (Peace Corps/Barbados) and
       Phil Heilman (Peace Corps/Burkina Faso). The African food crisis
       agricultural needs, and the response of Americans to the Peace
       Corps request for participants is seen as an expression of a
       sensibility of giving. Frequent reference is made to the song "We
       Are the World" and other efforts at famine relief.

409   Report of the National Bipartisan Commission on Central
       America, January, 1984. Pr.40.8:B52/C33.
            The Bipartisan Commission was established by order of
       President Ronald Reagan to determine appropriate elements of a
       long-term United States policy towards Central America. Recog-
       nizing that both long- and short-term needs were required to be
       met, various areas were examined, among them history of the
       region, economic issues, security problems and human development.
       In the latter area, the topic of literacy expansion is addressed,
       with the following recommendation: "We recommend that the Peace
       Corps expand its recruitment of front line teachers to serve in a
       new Literacy Corps. A Literacy Corps of qualified volunteers
       would be created to engage in direct teaching and also to train
       Central Americans to teach their compatriots. The Peace Corps has
       had long experience in this function. We urge a dramatic expan-
       sion of volunteers in the region from the current 600 to a figure
       five or six times as great, largely in eduction. Emphasis in
       recruitment should be on mature persons who speak Spanish . . .
       We recommend that Peace Corps activities be expanded at the prima-
       ry, secondary and technical levels in part by establishing a
       Central American Teacher Corps, recruited from the Spanish-
       speaking population of the United States" (pp. 70-71). This
       reflects the resurgence of Corps as a separate agency, although
       the rate of expansion urged is somewhat unrealistic.

410 "Report on the Peace Corps. Highlights of a Report to the President by Jack Hood Vaughn, Director, July 18, 1966". GS4.114:2;26-52. <u>Weekly Compilation of Presidential Documents</u> (25 July 1966): 948-49.

A brief statistical report on the "state of Peace Corps" as of July 18, 1966. Items of interest are the departure of the 20,000th volunteer for overseas duty, entry of Corps to Chad, Botswana, Micronesia, South Korea, Mauritania and Guyana, and expansion of projects in India and Micronesia in the fields of agriculture and law. Researchers' wishing fuller details of Corps at this moment in time should consult the fourth and fifth annual reports of Peace Corps.

411 REUSS, HENRY S. "Youth for Peace". <u>Progressive</u> (February 1961): 16-18.

An article proposing the establishment of A "Point Four Youth Corps" by an early advocate of the idea of such service. Representative Reuss's proposal was drawn up in 1959, with Congressional legislation authorizing a feasibility study given in June, 1960. This article gives the details of the proposed Youth Corps as to purpose, qualifications for membership, size and draft status of Corps enlistees. It was against the background of proposals such as these that President Kennedy made the original decision to create the Peace Corps, and thus perpetuate ideas such as those advanced by Reuss and others. An interesting feature of this article is Reuss' story of how his witnessing four American teachers setting up schools in the jungles of Cambodia inspired the Youth Corps idea.

412 RICE, GERARD T. <u>The Bold Experiment: JFK's Peace Corps</u>. South Bend, Indiana: University of Notre Dame Press, 1985.

This is the most recent of general works covering the history and changes within the Peace Corps.. Emphasis is placed upon the early Kennedy period of the agency's existence and on data drawn from the evaluators' reports, many of which have never been made public. Among the contributions Rice makes in this work are a survey of the manner in which the American and foreign media portrayed the Corps during its formative years and the effects this had upon volunteer effectiveness in the field. Researchers using this volume will find an extensive collection of documented footnotes useful in locating information on particular points. For a useful comparison, Rice's earlier work, <u>Peace Corps In The 1980's</u> (414) should also be consulted.

413 RICE, GERARD T. <u>Peace Corps in the 80's</u>. PE1.2:P31/2. Washington, D.C.: Peace Corps, 1986.

This historical and contemporary consideration of the goals and collective experiences of Peace Corps volunteers was written as part of the celebration of the twenty-fifth anniversary of the agency in 1986. Its emphasis is upon the Peace Corps as it has diversified since the 1980's period, with such programs as the African Food Systems Initiative, the Caribbean Basin Initiative, the Initiative for Central America and other new programs set out in detail. The second section of the text is devoted to the

manner in which the three stated goals of Corps are being
achieved, and where such achievement will carry future planning.
The final chapter is entitled "Voices of Peace Corps", and consists of excerpts from letters written by volunteers, statements
and addresses made by host nations officials, as well as local
families and counterparts, and reflections on their service by
returned volunteers. Researchers will find this work a useful
capsule overview of Peace Corps as it entered and adapted to the
changing needs of the 1980's. For a more historical treatment,
consult the author's Twenty Years of Peace Corps and The Bold
Experiment.

414   RICE, GERARD T. Twenty Years of Peace Corps. AA4:.2:P31/6.
       Washington, D.C.: Peace Corps, 1981.
       Written upon the occasion of the twentieth anniversary year
of Peace Corps in 1981, this historical summary evaluates the
progress of Corps volunteers and programming in terms of the three
goals of the Peace Corps Act. Beginning with the origins of the
Corps in the times when volunteers were known as "Kennedy's
Children", the first section discusses the vast number of changes
in both priorities and details of programming which the needs and
altering environments of the Third World have obliged the agency
to make. Considerations of the recognition in the late 1970's of
the "women in development" and "basic human needs" factors of
world development are presented in careful outline. The second
section focuses on the actual text of the Peace Corps Act and
measures the history of the agency against its dream and goals,
with a fair amount of success. Illustrations are provided by
photographs of volunteers at work in countries ranging from Niger,
Bolivia, Malaysia, Sierra Leone, Senegal, Kenya, Ghana and
Nicaragua to scenes of its earliest history during the Kennedy
era.

415   ROBERTS, WALLACE. "R.I.P.: Peace Corps and VISTA". Saturday
       Review, 55 (1 April 1972): 38-40.
       A satirical piece attacking the shifting of Peace Corps and
VISTA under the organizational rubric of ACTION by President
Nixon. The two groups are seen to have died from "lack of
support". While the tone is deliberately wry, it conveys the
flavor of this period of Corps history quite well.

416   "The Role of the Volunteer As Trainer". AA1.13:3/9.
       InterACTION, 3, n.9 (June 1975): 3.
       An examination of the roles in which volunteers may
contribute most effectively to training sessions held in-country.
Conclusions stated in this discussion were reached at a training
meeting held in May, 1975 in Quito, Ecuador for the Latin American
Region of Corps. Seven specific roles were seen for volunteers,
although due caution is also demanded regarding availability and
length of service of those chosen to assist.

417   ROTH, LESTER J. "Piqued By Peace Corps". Phi Delta Kappan,
       48, n.5 (1967): 255.
       A letter from a faculty member in Fresno, California,
       endorsing the views set out in John Lanstrum's article of
       November, 1966 in the Phi Delta Kappan. The latter stressed that
       the educational establishment should be recognized as having an
       equal voice in designing and administering educational projects.
       Roth notes that his own protest on the same issue elicited a sharp
       retort that he misunderstood the nature of Peace Corps, and com-
       ments "the Peace Corps would do well to peek over its Ivy League
       shoulder."

418   RUBBA, PETER A. and MARC J. ROSENBERG. "Videotape in Short,
       Intensive Instructor Training". Technological Horizons in
       Education, 7, n.1 (February 1980): 39-40.
       A brief summary of the use of videotape cameras as feedback
       devices in the training program run at Southern Illinois
       University for volunteers assigned to Tonga and Western Samoa.
       Originally intended as an evaluative mechanism which would be
       effective quickly, the videos became essentially a trainee project
       as well, making them more visually oriented and enabling the
       training staff to provide more individualized instruction. An
       increased sense of participation in the program was also noted as
       a result of the control of each individual of their own taped
       teaching practicums.

419   RUPPE, LORET MILLER. "Famine and Drought: There Are No Easy
       Solutions on the Road to Peace". Congressional Record, 131,
       n.159 (19 November 1985): S15753-56.
       The complete text of a speech delivered by the Director of
       the Peace Corps, Loret Ruppe, at ceremonies at the University of
       Michigan on October 14, 1985. The purpose of these ceremonies was
       to mark the twenty-fifth anniversary of the night when then-candi-
       date John F. Kennedy stood on the steps of the Student Union and
       challenged the listening crowd to serve overseas in what would
       become the Peace Corps. Her focus was on the "greatest obstacle
       to peace-hunger." The Michigan symposium and others like it were
       hoped to serve as forums for the discussion of effective means of
       coping with the African food crisis, as well as for world hunger
       issues in general. The focus of Peace Corps programs on "women in
       development" was formally acknowledged by an amendment to the
       Peace Corps Act in 1979. A new program for bringing the "green
       revolution" to Africa, entitled the African Food Systems Initia-
       tive, is explained in detail, with teams of volunteers already
       working in Lesotho, Botswana, and Niger. The second component in
       fighting hunger, Ruppe believes, is maximizing research and devel-
       opment, while the third is for solutions which can be implemented
       at local levels for drought and famine. Through the efforts and
       examples of returned Peace Corps volunteers, the experience of
       famine is being brought home to Americans, and it is the genera-
       tion of the 1980's which must now act until "Africa is no longer a
       hostage to drought and famine" (p. S15756).

420   RUPPE, LORET MILLER. "The Peace Corps: One Facet of the U.S.
       Role in Building World Community". Lutheran Theological
       Seminary Bulletin, 64, n.3 (Summer 1984): 36-47.
            The complete text of a speech given by Loret Ruppe, Director
       of the Peace Corps in Washington, D.C., reviewing the place of
       Corps work in the overall field of development projects. Topics
       addressed include the Caribbean Basin Initiative, women in devel-
       opment, the need to recruit more older Americans and members from
       minority groups as volunteers, and areas needing further aid.
       Questions from the audience and Director Rupp's responses follow.
       Her most trenchant statement in summary was "There's nothing
       simple about the Peace Corps."

421   RUPPE, LORET MILLER. "A Wise Investment in Peace". Christian
       Science Monitor (October 22, 1981): 23.
            A selection drawn from the text of a speech given by Loret
       Ruppe, Director of the Peace Corps, to members of the Commonwealth
       Club in San Francisco. The practical benefits of Peace Corps
       service are spelled out--including the role Third World nations
       play as both markets and suppliers of the United State economy. A
       call is issued for more volunteers and an increased awareness of
       Corps activity.

422   SCHOENKOPF, SARAH. "Overseas Ohioans". Ohio Schools, 41
       (April 1963): 14-15.
            A survey article highlighting the contributions begin made
       by volunters from the state of Ohio currently serving in host
       nations. Countries represented include Ceylon and the Cameroons.
       Information on applying is also included.

423   SCOTT, THOMAS D. "The Peace Corps and the Private Sector: the
       Failure of a Partnership". Annals of the American Academy of
       Political and Social Science. 365 (May 1966): 93-104.
            This article discusses the history of the work done in
       logistics, programming and support in the early years of Corps
       existence by established private institutions such as CARE, the
       Experiment in International Living and the United States
       universities. Beginning with the creation of Peace Corps by a
       group of Kennedy "New Frontiersmen", independent programming was
       established and certain private sector groups excluded, chiefly
       the church-related bodies. While this was justified under the
       doctrine of the separation of church and state, it deprived Corps
       of many long-standing networks of contact and supply.
       Universities failed to fill the gap left by this decision for
       several reasons, among them reluctance to commit to long-term
       programs overseas and quick surfeit with the flood of contracts.
       Peace Corps' first contract project was with CARE in Colombia, and
       later with the Near East Foundation in Iran. Problems of selec-
       tion, training and field support through local representatives are
       also discussed. The major factor in the dissolution of a promis-
       ing alliance seems to have been the rapid, somewhat chaotic growth
       of the Peace Corps in its early years, although internal staff
       opposition to outside contractors was also present. A call is
       made for long-range planning by Peace Corps and a re-evaluation of

the contributions which can be made by the private sector. From 1962 to 1965, the author served the Peace Corps as Director of the Division of Private and International Organizations.

424　SAIKOWSKI, CHARLOTTE.　"On A Leaner Peace Corps".　Christian Science Monitor (22 March 1973):　1,4.
　　　An interview with Donald K. Hess, Director of the Peace Corps, examining the more professional image which the agency has acquired. With 6,800 personnel (down from a former high of 15,000) and an emphasis on skilled professionals, and greater sensitivity to local mores and customs in matters of hair length and dress, Corps faces the future with optimism. The new director of ACTION, Michael Balzano, is known to insist on programs which produce, a plan agreeable to Corps staff and volunteers. Increasingly clear definition of assignments is also noted.

425　SALACUSE, JESWALD W.　"Lawyers Have a Volunteer Role".　S19.11/2:5/9.　Peace Corps Volunteer, 5, n.9 (July 1967):　12-14.
　　　A veteran of Peace Corps/Nigeria who taught law at Ahmadu Bello University discusses the utility of legal skills in a developing nation and the ways in which Corps personnel can attempt to meet some of these needs.

426　SALAS, GLENDA CORDES.　The Peace Corps Impact.　M.A. thesis, California State University:　Fullerton, 1982.
　　　This thesis from the discipline of anthropology takes as its purpose the examination of "the ways in which deep involvement in another culture may affect the lives of the individuals concerned and to what extent new attitudes can result from such an experience" (p. 14). Data were obtained from questionnaires sent to returned volunters in 1981 and 1982, consisting of seven open-ended queries designed to elicit responses regarding attitudes and cultural influences, personal understanding before and after Peace Corps, and Corps influence on their career plans. A brief precis of the history of Corps is followed by a discussion of methodology and twenty-three profiles of individual volunteers based on questionnaires returned. In the section entitled "Analysis of Findings and Discussion", each of the seven survey questions is taken in order, with responses as received. The "Peace Corps impact" of the title is seen in both personal and professional terms, the latter ranging from continuing involvement with foreign service agencies such as CARE to "getting political" in the promotion of needed change in the United States. Researchers will find the summary of perceptions of Corps impact on volunteers drawn from other writings on the agency highly useful. Appendixes give the text of correspondence with Peace Corps and raw data from six of the questionnaires.

427   SANTON, HENRY J.   "The U. S. Peace Corps: A Living Memorial to
      President Kennedy".   Eastern World, 18, n.8 (August 1964):   15-
      16.
           In this review article, the history and accomplishments of
      Peace Corps are noted.   The text of Kennedy's executive order is
      mentioned, and the "ideal volunteer" is defined.   Acting as the
      heirs of the Kennedy vision, the goals of the lamented administra-
      tion "may yet be completed by this loosely ruled, highly motivated
      group of individualists scattered through jungle, slum and moun-
      tain peaks" (p. 16).

428   "Sargent Shriver on the Need for an Independent Peace Corps".
      Congressional Record, 124, Part 9 (24 April 1978):   11254-56.
           This entry is the statement of testimony given by Robert
      Sargent Shriver, first Director of the Peace Corps, to the House
      of Representatives International Relations Subcommittee supporting
      passage of the Peace Corps Reform Act.   The Act would have made
      Peace Corps a separate government agency, removing it from its
      subsidiary position under ACTION.   The revitalization of Corps, in
      his view, must come from several sources: reorganization so as to
      appeal to "that special breed of people who volunteer"; elimina-
      tion of bureaucratic concerns in the planning and execution of
      Peace Corps policy decisions, willingness to take risks, and
      restoration of the philosophy that it is the individual who
      matters in American society.   An understanding of the role volun-
      teers play in exemplifying our system of government and societal
      beliefs is seen as vital to the freedom of the Peace Corps.
      Examples of Corps service mentioned are the Dominican Republic and
      Shriver's refusal to send the volunteers to Viet Nam.

429   SAYRES, WILLIAM.   Do Good.   New York: Holt, Rinehart and
      Winston, 1966.
           A work of fiction, narrated by an anthropologist, of the
      colorful and pungent reception accorded a volunteer upon his
      arrival in a Latin American host nation.

430   SEAMAN, PAT.   "Africa Food Systems Takes First Steps".   Peace
      Corps Times (March/April 1985):   8.
           In late February, 1985, the first assessment team for a host
      nation of the African Food System Initiative returned from Mali.
      In their report, several suggestions were made as to placement of
      volunteers in country, concentrating upon three geographic areas.
      A second team departed for Zaire on February 28th.   The basic
      premise of the AFSI is the concentration of multiskilled volun-
      teers in one area over a period of years so as to address causes
      of hunger and drought long-term.   Reception by the Malian govern-
      ment was extremely positive.

431   "Service in the Peace Corps". National Elementary Principal,
       41 (April 10962): 62.
       Stating that "a narrow provincialism may be a teacher's
greatest handicap", this article reviews the advantages accruing
to participation in Peace Corps service for educators. Experi-
encing another culture from inside, and gaining flexibility in
approaching professional problems are seen to be invaluable contributions in the evolution of an effective teacher.

432   SHAFFER, ROBERT H. "Peace Corps: Antidote for Provincialism".
       School and Society, 95 (15 April 1967): 261-63.
       American college students and their demands for relevant
experiences of personal maturation, challenge and responsibility
are considered in the overall context of changing higher education. While no significant change in the institutional structure
of American higher education is seen, answers to these student
demands are viewed as both crucial and proper. International
experiences are seen to be the best way for such hopes to be
realized, and "Peace Corps or similar service for those who can
qualify would seem to be one of the best avenues for such experience" (p. 262).

433   SHEA, DONALD R. "The Peace Corps and Foreign Language
       Education--A Foreword". Modern Language Journal, 47, n.7
       (November 1963): 299-300.
       Recognizing that the Peace Corps has made and continues to
make significant improvements in the area of foreign language
instruction, such preparation is viewed as part of the overall
effort to make volunteers effective in their field assignments.
Stating that "approximately forty percent of a Peace Corps training program is now devoted to language instruction" (p. 299) this
statistic is used to measure the state of foreign language
instruction in the United States and the contribution returning
volunteers will make, both in the classrooms and through a heightened perspective on the issue.

434   SHEA, DONALD R. "The Preparation of Peace Corps Volunteers for
       Overseas Service: Challenge and Response". Annals of the
       American Academy of Political and Social Science, 365 (May
       1966) 29-45.
       Adequate and thorough training is a key part of insuring the
success of a volunteer in the field. When the Peace Corps was
initially created, few or no facilities for such in-depth training
were available. After considering several models, most of the
early training sessions were contracted out to universities due to
their physical plants and experienced staffs. The Training Division of Corps established a basic training manual as a model for
all subsequent programs to follow as a guide to structuring their
own efforts. Stating that the single goal of training was "to
prepare the volunteer for the successful performance of his
specific assignment overseas" (p. 32), these early programs were
made up of eight basic components--technical skills, area studies,
languages, American studies, world affairs, health and medical
training, physical conditioning and Peace Corps orientation.

Looking at the training programs after the first two years, a key
factor in their success is seen to be the high quality of the
trainees and their motivation. A disagreement and conflict in
orientation between host universities as to the goals of training,
together with inadequate information provided to them by Peace
Corps sometimes resulted in massive logistical troubles. By 1965,
however, both Corps and the host schools had learned from each
other and had improved their training plans noticeably. Changes
made included lengthening the period of training, emphasizing
greater language proficiency, more detailed technical studies,
integration of curriculum materials to present a total picture of
the host country and culture, reducing the amount of stress on
volunteers, and utilizing the returned volunteers as resource
persons. On their side, the universities were supplied with
better advance information, annual training contracts, opportunities for actual research of mutual benefit and adoption of the
"transitional training" model where applicable. This later
involved the recreation of a host country environment as closely
as possible. Examples of this are the village built in the Waipio
Valley by the University of Hawaii to simulate South East Asian
conditions and programs conducted through the University of New
Mexico. Both higher education and the Peace Corps are seen to
have learned much from each other.

435   SHEAHAN, JAMES V. "Teachers Around the World". Journal of
       Secondary Education, 38 (December 1963): 109-112.
           A review article examining the experiences of the Peace
       Corps volunteers who have served as teachers in the first two
       years of the agency's existence. Early doubts as to the utility
       of the volunteers in educational settings have been dispelled.
       Volunteers are working in levels of education ranging from elemen-
       tary through university, and instructing in subjects as diverse as
       home economics, chemistry, industrial arts and science. Although
       living conditions may vary widely, most volunteers agree on the
       challenges of teaching in environments where familiar equipment is
       not available and common assumptions do not apply, spurred on by
       the eagerness of the students to learn. Other obstacles include
       the collision of the volunteers with different cultural practices
       and customs, and coping with systems which have emphasized rote
       learning as an instructional tool. Rebutting the charges that
       Peace Corps has depleted the American pool of available teachers,
       Sheahan notes that many of the volunteers encounter teaching as a
       profession in Corps and remain in that field upon their return.

436   SHEPHERD, GEORGE W. "Christian Hope for the Peace Corps:
       Peace, Freedom and Service". Social Action, 30 (January 1964):
       7-13.
           Written by a researchers with two years of experience in
       Uganda, this article considers the place of Peace Corps work and
       service within the larger framework of Christianity, and the ways
       in which Christians who wish to practice their ideals many find
       Corps a vehicle for such fulfillment. The intersection of the

two, as when Peace Corps teachers are posted to church schools, is noted. The absence of churches from the forefront of revolutionary struggles for change, and the opportunity offered for Christians to correct this image through Corps service, is a repeated theme.

437 SHERBURNE, JAMES A. "Looking For A Job? Go International". American Forests and Forest Life, 79 (September 1973): 12-13.
A brief overview of the joint environmental program being run by the Peace Corps and the Smithsonian Institution. Averting or minimizing the impact of rapid development on fragile environmental systems is viewed as crucial to the proposed changes seen as necessary by host governments. Case studies are given from Guatemala, Liberia, Chad, Brazil, Ghana, Iran and Swaziland.

438 SHIPP, RANDY. "Peace Corps: Putting It Back on the Map". Christian Science Monitor (21 August 1979): B4.
An interview with Richard Celeste, newly-appointed Director of the Peace Corps. Discussion covers the need for increased visibility and re-education of the American public as to the effectiveness of the volunteers. Celeste notes that whereas in the 1960's the initiative for placement of volunteers lay with the United States, host country ministries now have clear ideas as to where Peace Corps personnel can fit within their own development plans.

439 SHRIVER, SARGENT. "Address By the Honorable Sargent Shriver, 25th Anniversary of the Peace Corps". Congressional Record, 131, n.159 (19 November 1985): S15751-753.
The complete text of an address given by Sargent Shriver at the University of Michigan in Ann Arbor to commemorate the speech by John Kennedy at that institution in 1960 which first issued the challenge of overseas service in Corps to the young people of America. In this speech, Shriver called for a recommitment to the underlying values of Peace Corps service and for a better use of the potentials of the returned volunteers in waging peace in the United States.

440 SHRIVER, SARGENT. "Ambassadors of Good Will: the Peace Corps". National Geographic (September 1964): 297-313.
A brief introduction to a special series of articles on the Peace Corps published in National Geographic on the work being done in eight host nations. Shriver recounts personal experiences in both the creation of the agency and visits to host nations, warning that "the answer to the question 'what is the Peace Corps' is not so easy."

441 SHRIVER, SARGENT. "Driftwood, Puppets and a Better Life". Journal of Industrial Arts Education, 23 (May 1964): 12-14.
The Director of Peace Corps discusses the various ways in which industrial arts skills are being and can be applied by volunteers. These range from a project in Jamaica making lamps out of old driftwood to house construction in Gabon to repairing trucks in Afghanistan. Community development workers with such

skills and backgrounds are seen to have a distinct advantage in
gaining acceptance to a host community. This includes raising
funds for projects, which in the case of a volunteer in St. Lucia
meant designing puppets and putting on shows. Shriver notes that
"no matter what skills volunteers possess, they will come in handy
sooner or later in an overseas setting" (p. 13).

442   SHRIVER, ROBERT SARGENT. "Five Years with the Peace Corps".
       Saturday Review, 49 (23 April 1966): 14, 18, 54.
       In 1966, Sargent Shriver completed his term as the first
director of the Peace Corps, to take over administration of the
War on Poverty program. In this reflective essay, he reminisces
about the difficulties of creating both an image and a public
(domestic and overseas) receptive to the implementation of Corps
goals and objectives. Early debates included everything from
health care to whether the name should be changed. Shriver offers
a definition of the volunteer which is highly descriptive--"a new
breed of overseas American doing the world's work in the world's
farthest corners, . . . not for dollars, glory, nationalistic or
imperialistic purposes, but for man" (p. 18).

443   SHRIVER, SARGENT. "Mango for the Peace Corps Teacher". NEA
       Journal, 51 (April 1962): 48-49.
       A general essay covering the challenges and rewards of
teaching as a volunteer. Problems mentioned include readjusting
to a different structure of education and examination, languages
and conflicting interpretations of syllabus requirements. Details
of living conditions and serve in Ghana and the Philippines are
noted.

444   SHRIVER, SARGENT. "Outlook for Corpsmen: Army Could be
       Better". Life, 50 (17 March 1961): 38-39.
       An early statement by then-Director-designate Shriver as to
the sort of persons who could successfully become a volunteer and
projections as to the types of living and working situations which
they will face. At this stage in the Corps history, everything
was very much in the planning stages, and this article thus
provides a useful comparison with Corps programming as it finally
developed. Researchers should be aware that this statement
appears within a larger feature story on the Peace Corps.

445   SHRIVER, ROBERT SARGENT. "Peace Corps Lawyers--Building
       Emerging African Societies". Congressional Record, 109, Part
       29 (1 August 1963): A 1925-27.
       Comparing the history of the United States following the
Revolutionary War with the condition of many of the newly-indepen-
dent nations of Africa, Sargent Shriver addresses the issue of
their need for trained legal personnel. In the autumn of 1963,
following a tour of several West African states, projects were
drawn up for Sierra Leone, Liberia, Nigeria and Cameroon, with
Ethiopia and Malawi also seen as possible hosts for legal volunteers. After briefly outlining the British and traditional
systems of justice as they existed in Africa, Shriver reviews the
projects that the lawyers--then in training--would participate in.

These range from teaching in the University of Nigeria Law School, assisting the Attorney General of Cameroon, organizing a backlog of cases for the Sierra Leone legal system, and aiding in the development of newly-founded law schools in Malawi and Ethiopia. Liberian volunteers will assist in implementing recommended reforms for that nation's civil service administration. A call is made to the legal community of the United States to take up this challenge by granting leaves of absence for those wishing to serve.

446   SHRIVER, SARGENT. Point of the Lance. New York: Harper and
       Row, 1964.
       This volume is a collection of speeches and addresses delivered by Sargent Shriver, Director of the Peace Corps, between 1961 and 1964. Topics covered include the Peace Corps itself, the War on Poverty, civil rights issues, education and health and the spiritual heritage of the United States. Two appendixes list the members of the Peace Corps National Advisory Council for 1963-1964 and in-country representatives for the period 1961-1964 for forty-six host nations where Corps personnel were serving. The title is drawn from a remark by the Minister of National Economy of Bolivia, who saw the Peace Corps as "your punta de lanza" of the Alliance for Progress. In the section specifically on the Peace Corps, speeches listed include Shriver's address at Chulalongkorn University in Bangkok on the occasion of accepting an honorary doctorate and his thoughts given at the International Conference on Middle-Level Manpower meeting in San Juan, Puerto Rico. A uniquely valuable look at the mind of the man who made the Peace Corps dream a reality.

447   SHRIVER, SARGENT. "Shriver Reports on Far East Visit to
       Volunteers". S19.11/2:1/1. Peace Corps Volunteer, 1, n.1
       (November 1962): 6-7.
       A report of the Director of Peace Corps on the five week trip to the Philippines, Thailand and Malaysia, reviewing living conditions and host country relations to volunteers.

448   SHULDINER, HERBERT. "Wanted: Skilled Hands for the Peace
       Corps". Popular Science, 186 (June 1965): 72-75, 208.
       A general article examining the Peace Corps need for volunteers with training or background in industrial arts such as electronics, carpentry and metalworking. Examples are given from Pakistan, Tunisia, Afghanistan, Cameroon and Tanganyika. Application information is also included.

449   "Sidelight on the Peace Corps". Kentucky School Journal, 42
       (October 1963): 10-11.
       A brief summary of the activities and definition of Peace Corps in its first two years of existence.

450   SILL, MAURICE L. "The Four Stages of Transculturation".
      S19.11/2:5/4. Peace Corps Volunteer, 5, n.4 (February 1967):
      11-24.
         A sociologist serving on the staff of the Peace Corps Office
      of Training offers a model for the process of cultural adaptation
      undergone by volunteers. Four stages are outlined: discovery,
      self-alignment, participation and devolution.

451   "6 Peace Corpsmen Die in 1969". S19.11/2:8/1-2. Volunteer, 8,
      nos.1-2 (January-February 1970): 20-21.
         Obituaries for the six volunteers and one trainee who died
      in 1969. Causes of death included car accidents, meningitis,
      cancer, and heart failure. Since the inception of Corps in 1961,
      55 volunteers and five trainees have died.

452   "600,000 Books Shipped Overseas In Recent Weeks".
      S19.11/2:1/11. Peace Corps Volunteer, 1, n.11 (September
      1963): 1, 15.
         A general article discussing the provision to volunteers
      serving as teachers of book boxes containing chiefly reference and
      technical items but also fiction. The intention is both to sup-
      plement volunteer effectiveness and to provide core collections
      for possible community libraries.

453   "6,000 Tell Peace Corps They'll Sign up for Africa". Christian
      Science Monitor (16 January 1985): 2.
         In response to an appeal by Loret Ruppe, Director of Peace
      Corps, for volunteers to aid African agriculture, over 6,000
      specialists, many of them farmers from the Midwest, have applied
      to the agency. In addition to farmers, additional assignments as
      part of the program will include water systems specialists, health
      and nutrition postings and mechanics.

454   SKINNER, RALPH K. "Vaughn Promotion Pleases Panama".
      Christian Science Monitor (24 February 1965): 4.
         A review of the reaction in the Panamanian press and diplo-
      matic corps of the appointment of Jack Hood Vaughn, former
      Director of the Peace Corps, as Assistant Secretary of State for
      InterAmerican Affairs. His familiarity with the region, gained as
      a field evaluator of Peace Corps programs, is seen by many as a
      decided asset.

455   SMITH, TERENCE. "Politics Charged to a U. S. Agency: Ex-Peace
      Corpsman Cites Memo As Evidence". New York Times (8 April
      1972): 5.
         In testimony before the Senate Foreign Relations Committee,
      Thomas Scanlon, a member of the first contingent of volunteers to
      serve in Chile and presently head of a Washington, D.C. consulting
      firm, charged that ACTION had become politicized to "an
      unprecedented and shocking degree." A memo from the San Francisco
      regional office covering an investigation of the political
      affiliation of staff members was cited as evidence. Scanlon

proposed that Peace Corps be removed from ACTION and established as a private non-profit international foundation. Although the charges were denied by ACTION representatives, committee chair Senator J. W. Fulbright said he would order an examination of the matter.

456   "Smithsonian Is Seeking Peace Corps Volunteer Diaries".
       AA1.13:3/7. InterACTION, 3, n.7 (April 1975): 1.
       Hermann Viola, director of the anthropological archives of the Smithsonian Institution has requested diaries, tape record- ings, drawings and photographs which Peace Corps veterans may have created while serving. His purpose is to preserve the data on people and events of the host cultures as seen through the eyes of the men and women who lived a new culture.

457   "Smithsonian-Peace Corps Program Links Development with Environmental Quality". AA1.13:4/2-3. InterACTION, 4, nos. 2- 3 (November-December 1975): 1, 7-9.
       A general discussion of the origins and contribution made by volunteers serving in the joint program of the Peace Corps and the Smithsonian Institution in environmental preservation, conserva- tion and resources management. Interviews with James Sherburne, program director, and individuals who have served and are serving in host nations are included. Examples of such work include ecological study of the Red Sheep in the Lake Urmiah district of Iran, creating a visitor's center and library at Thailand's Khao Yai National Park and mosquito control in Lake Maracaibo, Venezuela.

458   "Southwest Proving Ground". S19.11/2:1/12. Peace Corps Volunteer, 1, n.12 (October 1963): 6-7.
       A photo essay covering the details of life in the Peace Corps training program in northern New Mexico. Following language instruction at the University of New Mexico in Albuquerque, train- ees are sent to the D.H. Lawrence Ranch near Taos, where they work in local community-development projects. The joint academic and practical program was initiated in February, 1963. By October, more than 600 trainees had participated.

459   SPARKMAN, LEE S. et.al.Dialogue Africaine Contemporain: Level I, Washington, D.C.: Peace Corps, 1972.
       Fourteen units in the French regional dialect of West Africa are given here in a manual developed for the Peace Corps at the Center for Curriculum Development in Philadelphia. Intended for beginning students, this course offers a multimedia approach. Full text is given in the ERIC system as document ED 063 827.

460   "Special Services Solve PCV Problems". AA1.13:1/3.
        InterACTION, 1, n.3 (December 1972): 1.
        A brief profile of the Special Services office of the Peace
Corps headquarters in Washington, D.C.   Its purpose is to handle
medical evacuations, emergency leaves, early terminations of
service, transfers, parental inquiries, and family notification in
case of death. One of the more notable inquiries was a mother who
wanted to mail her volunteer son a fruitcake for Christmas.

461   U. S. Congress, Senate. "Speech of Senator John F. Kennedy,
        Cow Palace, San Francisco, California, November 2, 1960".
        Committee on Commerce. Subcommittee on Communications. The
        Speeches, Remarks Press Conferences and Statements of Senator
        John F. Kennedy, August 1 Through November 7, 1960, (87th
        Congress. Senate Report 994, Part 1, 1961): 862-66.
        The full text of the first public speech at which then-
Senator Kennedy expanded upon the idea of establishing "a peace
corps of talented young men and women willing and able to serve
their country . . . well qualified through rigorous standards,
well trained in the languages, skills and customs they will need
to know." The proposed agency is contrasted with dismal examples
of existing American inability and lack of preparation in the
areas of foreign adjustment and cultural sensitivity. The absence
of language training for many members of the Foreign Service is
particularly harshly criticized.   It was this speech which many
regard as the birth of widespread discussion and debate on the
possibilities and desirability of having such a group of Americans
working overseas.

462   SPENCE, HARRY Y., JOHN W. CASHMAN and JOSEPH A. GALLAGHER.
        "Peace Corps Health Experiences Abroad". Public Health
        Reports, 78, n.10, (October 1963): 887-92.
        Based upon data collected during the first nineteen months
of Peace Corps existence and operation by overseas Peace Corps
physicians, this article examines what patterns and conclusions,
if any, can be derived from the materials. With 44 Public Health
Service Officers stationed about the world serving as resident
physicians and counselors, field data are fairly consistent. The
South Asia and Near East region leads the statistics of disease
incidence, while all areas evidence a high incidence of
gastroenteritic problems, a phenomenon common to all volunteer
efforts overseas. A lower than expected rate of amebiasis from
sub-Saharan Africa has been ascribed to the prescription of
chloroquine as a antimalarial agent. Infectious hepatitis, a
problem in the early months, has been effectively controlled
through gamma globulin injections. Volunteer health in general
seems to be most affected by a somewhat relaxed attitude towards
health maintenance as a result of cross-cultural adaptation and a
virtual absence of exposure to exotic tropical disease as a
significant health issue. The latter is expected to increase as
more volunteers serve abroad, and steps will be taken in
prophylaxis as appropriate.

463 SPENCER, SHARON. <u>Breaking the Bonds: A Novel About the Peace Corps</u>. New York: Grosset and Dunlap, 1963.
A romance novel of two young people in the Peace Corps in Nigeria. Researchers seeking similar materials should examine <u>The Zinzin Road</u> and Karla Wiley's <u>Assignment Latin America</u>.

464 SPIVAK, MARK. "Peace Corps Stamp: Nostalgia". <u>Washington Post</u> (12 February 1972): C3.
In a ceremony at the Smithsonian Museum of History and Technology in Washington, D.C., the design and first day issues of a new eight-cent stamp commemorating the tenth anniversary of the Peace Corps was unveiled. The design shows the stars on the American flag taking wing and becoming doves of peace. A media show featuring clips from the speeches of President Kennedy and Richard Nixon was also exhibited.

465 "Sports Important to Developing Nations". AA1.13:1/6.
<u>InterACTION</u>, 1, n.6 (March 1973): 7.
A survey of the work done by volunteer Kirby Nicol in his four years of service as a physical education instructor and track and field coach in the Philippines, Tunisia and Thailand between 1968 and 1972. Nicol views sports as a high priority in a developing nations as a means of building self-confidence and national pride.

466 SPRADLEY, JAMES P. and MARK PHILLIPS. "Culture and Stress: A Quantitative Analysis". <u>American Anthropologist</u>, 74, n.3 (June 1972): 518-29.
In studying and analyzing the concept of "culture shock", one of the chief difficulties for anthropologists has been the absence of clearly stated assumptions regarding this phenomenon. With such bases clearly stated, the issue of measurement of how different stressors can be rated in a situation of change in a subject's cultural environment. The present study addresses this question, using a list of 33 terms and confrontations derived from research previously completed on culture shock. Three different groups composed the sample population: United States students with no intercultural experiences, Chinese foreign students resident in the U.S., and a sample of returned Peace Corps volunteers representing twenty-five host nations. Results indicate such a matrix of situations is effective in such research and, as well, "support . . . the idea that there may be pan-human stressors arising from some universal feature of human nature" (p.525). Readjustment problems seem to be rooted in a feeling that one's new behavior is violating the norms of one's home culture.

467   "State Department, Peace Corps to Exchange Employees".
      AA1.13:2/9. InterACTION, 2, n.9 (June 1974): 3-4.
      A new agreement signed by Nicholas Craw, ACTION's Director
of International Operations and Nathaniel Davis, Director-General
of the State Department, renews an old exchange between the
agencies of senior level personnel. Under the document, foreign
service officers may be detailed to Peace Corps for specific
periods of time.

468   STORTI, CRAIG. "Is Altruism Losing Ground in the Peace Corps?"
      AA1.13:5/4. InterACTION 5, n.4 (January 1977): 3-4.
      Originally issued in the Peace Corps Program and Training
Journal in 1976, this article explores a perceived shift in orientation between the volunteers of the early years and contemporary
personnel. The chief concern is that, while it is not possible to
train altruism and dedication into recruits, the long-term conse-
quences of having numbers of volunteers with a shallow commitment
to service and self-interested to the extreme will be dire for the
survival of Corps in general. Suggestions are offered as to
methods of coping with the problem.

469   SULLIVAN, GEORGE. The Story of the Peace Corps. New York:
      Fleet Publishing Corporation, 1964.
      A general discussion of the history of Peace Corps between
1961 and 1964 intended for a popular audience. Subjects treated
in depth include selection, training and volunteer life overseas.
Country programs discussed as examples are Bolivia, Nigeria,
Colombia, Ethiopia, Pakistan, the Philippines, St. Lucia, Turkey
and Tanganyika.

470   SUTHERLAND, DOROTHY J. "Nursing in the Peace Corps". Nursing
      Outlook, v.11 (December 1963): 888-90.
      An overview article on the roles and assignments occupied by
nursing volunteers. Background is provided on the history of
health-related requests from host countries. Nurses represented
only 5 percent of volunteers serving in 1963, but as such com-
prised the second largest group after teachers. Types of projects
using these nurses included yaws and tuberculosis control teams,
instructors in teaching hospitals and community health clinics,
public health work in rural areas, and improving care at host
country mental hospitals. Countries noted where current projects
are under way include Malaya, Bolivia, Honduras, Tunisia, India,
Pakistan, Sierra Leone and Togo.

471   SWANSTON, DAVID C. "Teaching Agriculture in the Peace Corps:
      A Thin Front Line in One Battle Against Hunger". Agricultural
      Education Magazine 42, n.4 (October 1969): 94-95.
      Peace Corps involvement in the field of agricultural educa-
tion is examined from an historical perspective. Thirteen countries requests for qualified teachers were met with volunteers in
four basic areas: agriculture education graduates for classroom
instruction as teacher trainers, science graduates for agricultural programs, liberal arts graduates who were then trained in one
specific area of agriculture, and instructors for high school

level classes on agriculture and extension agents. A total of 200
volunteers were serving currently in these capacities. Examples
are given from Ecuador, Malaysia and the Philippines.

472   "Swear In Payton, Lewis As President Nominates Aggrey, Keith to
      Posts". Jet, 53 (3 November 1977): 7.
         A news item reporting appointments made by President Carter
      and sworn in at a special ceremony by Vice-President Mondale.
      Among them was Carolyn Payton, director of counselling services at
      Howard University, thus becoming the first woman to assume direc-
      torship of the Peace Corps. Her previous association with Corps
      was from 1966 and 1969 as program director for the Eastern Carib-
      bean region.

473   "Teaching in West Africa: Volunteers Sum Up Progress,
      Problems". Volunteers, 1, n.9 (September 1962): 5-9.
         An overview of the problems facing Peace Corps teachers in
      Sierra Leone, Ghana and Nigeria. Issues raised include equipment
      shortages, language obstacles and homegrown teaching materials.

474   "Tenth Anniversary of the Peace Corps". Congressional Record,
      117, Part 26 (29 September 1971): 34094-95.
         Comments made by the Hon. Frank Horton of New York in the
      House of Representatives commemorating the tenth anniversary of
      the foundation of the Peace Corps. Changes noted are the shift to
      the recruitment of specialists versus generalists, the joint
      program in environmental matters underway with the Smithsonian
      Institution, the development of foreign national parks through co-
      operation with the National Park Service as a source of personnel,
      and an increase in overall numbers of volunteers. Rep. Horton
      agrees that "the Peace Corps is the best investment of their money
      overseas" for the American people.

475   TETER, D. PARK. "Peace Corps and Smithsonian: Deploying
      Environmental Experts". Science, 172 (25 June 1971): 1317-
      18.
         Described as "the most ambitious effort in the Peace Corps'
      search for specialized skills" (p. 1317), this article provides
      background on the joint environmental program of the Smithsonian
      Institution and the Peace Corps. At the time this article was
      written, some 300 volunteers were active in projects falling into
      this category. Examples of the type of work being done include
      bilharzia control in Ghana, national park management in Colombia,
      and oceanography in Tonga. A sister program is under consider-
      ation for the National Park Service. Kenya is offered as compre-
      hensive model of the sheer variety of roles which the volunteers
      in this phase of Peace Corps life can assume.

476   TEXTOR, ROBERT B., ed. <u>Cultural Frontiers of the Peace Corps</u>.
       Cambridge: M.I.T. Press, 1966.
            This collection of essays focuses on training, country
       programs, and the "members of the Peace Corps, past, present and
       future." The development and adaptations of the program and its
       participants are reviewed as of the agency's history up to 1966.
       The articles contained here have been annotated under the specific
       host nation each describes.

477   TEXTOR, ROBERT B. "Conclusions, Problems and Prospects". in
       <u>The Cultural Frontiers of the Peace Corps</u>, Robert B. Textor,
       ed., Cambridge, M.I.T. Press, 1966: 299-344.
            This chapter was written as summation and evaluation of the
       degree of success the Peace Corps has had in implementing the
       three objectives of the Peace Corps Act up to 1966 and the prob-
       lems facing staff members who attempt to carry them out. <u>Cultural</u>
       <u>Frontiers of the Peace Corps</u> gathered together reportage on
       aspects of the programs in thirteen Peace Corps host nations and
       it is to these nations that Textor stresses his conclusions
       chiefly apply. Topics addressed include the projection of an
       improved American image overseas, rural vs urban factors in devel-
       opment, job structure, absence of evaluative data on the countries
       for these years, limiting factors introduced by the host nation
       itself (such as political instability, inappropriate assignments
       of volunteers) the five-year rule on Peace Corps staff careers,
       language training and integrating Peace Corps with later experi-
       ences. Textor concludes that "the potential of the Peace Corps
       has only begun to be realized" (p. 342).

478   THOMPSON, LISBETH SHARON. <u>A Study of the Attitudes of Afro-</u>
       <u>American Students and Former Volunteers Toward the Peace Corps</u>.
       Master's thesis, Howard University, 1979.
            "Despite the Peace Corps Act's provisions that appointments
       shall be made without regard to race, color, creed or ethnic
       origin, the number of Afro-American Peace Corps volunteers has
       been consistently unrepresentative of this segment of the popula-
       tion" (p. 1). Beginning with this premise, the author, a Peace
       Corps recruiter at Howard University and four-year veteran of
       Peace Corps/Liberia, defined three objectives for research. These
       were: 1.) to survey contemporary attitudes among black American
       students toward the Peace Corps and compare them with earlier
       studies and reports on the issue: 2.) to survey black former
       volunteers to determine their views and evaluations of their Peace
       Corps experience, and 3.) to use this data in formulating recom-
       mendations to ACTION which would assist in the recruiting of more
       black volunteers. Topics addressed in the survey questionnaires
       included the image of the "typical" Peace Corps volunteer among
       both black students and RPCV's, the scope of black student aware-
       ness of Peace Corps programs, definition of the role of the volun-
       teers in the Third World, factors affecting the investigation of
       Peace Corps service as a career option and the causes of apparent
       apathy regarding Corps among black students. Five hypotheses were
       developed and tested against data obtained from students at Howard
       University and a pool of returned black volunteers located with

the assistance of Peace Corps itself. Following a chapter outlining earlier research projects and their conclusions on this
issue, Thompson presents her research methodologies and discusses
her results. Student concerns were related to the possible
neocolonial overtones of serving and skepticism regarding possible
links between the Peace Corps and the CIA. A positive correlation
was found between level of political awareness and motivation to
serve. Since the last survey was done in 1971, Thompson notes
that "a general trend towards the development of more positive
attitudes about the Peace Corps appears to have taken place in the
eight-year interval" (p. 98). While 97.5 percent of returned
black volunteers expressed a willingness to recommend Peace Corps
to friends, based on personal and professional growth, concerns
were also voiced regarding Peace Corps images and the low level of
minorities in both the volunteer corps and the administration.

Thompson makes seven recommendations: 1.) diminishing the
confusion between Peace Corps and the domestic programs of ACTION,
2.) increased person-to-person dialogue between Peace Corps
recruiters, administrators, and potential black applicants, 3.)
explicit responses to all questions about any links between the
Peace Corps and the CIA, 4.) utilization of returned black volunteers as recruiters, 5.) recruitment strategies stressing opportunities for personal development, cross-cultural exposure and
career development, 6.) greater emphasis on the non-discriminatory
policies of the Peace Corps and 7.) including racial information
in the folders of volunteers to permit the problem to be
accurately monitored in the future. Appendixes contain the texts
of the survey forms and a bibliography of relevant publications.

479   THOMSON, CAPTANE P. and JOSEPH T. ENGLISH. "Premature Return
of Peace Corps Volunteers". Public Health Reports, 79, n.4
(1965): 1065-73.

Covering the first seventeen months of Peace Corps training
and posting of volunteers, of 3,805 placed only 116 returned home.
The authors note that reasons for return fall into four
categories: compassionate leave, failure to adjust, dissatisfaction with the job and marriage. Other factors include medical
evacuations, psychiatric considerations and three deaths in the
field. The rates of return differ markedly between regions of
host nations, with those of Latin America leading the statistics.
Analysis of the data shows that older, less well educated volunteers placed in situations which bear little relations to their
skills are most apt to return. This becomes comprehensible in
light of the massive infusion of volunteers into ill-defined
projects of "community development" in Latin countries. Effective
types of intervention which can be taken by overseas staff members
are also discussed.

480   THURBER, ALAN. "1987 Budget Cuts Stunt Revival of Peace
      Corps". Congressional Record, 132, n.137 (7 October 1986):
      S15530.
           A reprint of an article originally published in the Arizona
      Republic newspaper and inserted in the Record by Senator
      DeConcini, consisting of an interview with Loret Miller Ruppe,
      Director of the Peace Corps, and relating the writer's own travels
      to Sierra Leone, Ghana, Mali, Togo and the Dominican Republic to
      interview Arizonans serving on-site. The type of service the
      Peace Corps provides is seen to be vital to the developing world,
      but less recognized by the present administration. As Director
      Ruppe notes, the budget for Corps "is less . . . than our annual
      expenditure for military marching bands." Cuts will force the
      reduction of volunteers from 6,200 to 5,000 in the new fiscal
      year.

481   TOLLEY, HOWARD. "Five Years of the Nixon Peace Corps:
      Politics, Vietnam and A Post-War 'Generation of Peace'".
      Intellect, 103, n.2360 (October 1974): 96-98.
           An analysis of the growth and development of the Peace Corps
      from its beginnings up to 1974, with special emphasis on the
      changes introduced under the Nixon Administration. Stating that
      "politics, Vietnam and new priorities of economics development
      pose the greatest challenge to its continued survival" (p. 96),
      the author, a political scientist, evaluates the increasingly
      partisan efforts of Director Joseph Blatchford, the replacement of
      experienced personnel under the "five-year flush" rule by
      patronage appointments, effects of Congressional opposition on
      Corps, the issue of Peace Corps and political neutrality, and the
      impact of Vietnam. The details of Blatchford's "New Directions"
      policy are spelled out in detail, along with the placement of
      Peace Corps under ACTION in 1971. Noting that many host govern-
      ments sometimes have difficulty in distinguishing Peace Corps work
      from United States foreign policy in general, Tolley stresses that
      "none of the . . . objectives can be realized if the agency
      becomes a political tool" (p. 98).

482   The Toughest Job You'll Ever Love. Washington, D.C.: ACTION,
      1978.
           A promotional film on Peace Corps service and its experi-
      ences, featuring volunteers representing Colombia, Niger and Nepal
      explaining their perceptions of what has happened to them and
      through them. A shorter version of ten minutes running time has
      also been issued in addition to this twenty-five minute version.

483   "Tradesmen Essential". AA1.13:1/12. InterACTION, 1, n.12
      (September 1973): 3.
           A report on the Skilled Hands Overseas Program (SHOP)
      created by the Peace Corps in answer to the increasing request for
      basic skills such as carpentry, mechanics, masons, machinists and
      heavy equipment operators. Over forty nations are at present
      hosting such projects. A case study of an Indiana firm which has
      become the first participant in the training of SHOP volunteers is
      also included.

484 "Trainees for Latin America Study N.Y. Problem Areas".
    S19.11/2:2/1. Peace Corps Volunteer, 2, n.1 (November 1963):
    23.
        In co-operation with the New York School of Social Work at
    Columbia University, prospective Peace Corps volunteers who will
    be assigned to host nations in Latin America are receiving
    practice work in community development in the East Harlem, Chelsea
    and lower East Side neighborhoods of Manhattan. Working with
    staffs of ten agencies, their experiences have included housing,
    rehabilitation, rat control, adult education and carpentry.

485 "Training Camp Carries On PC Spirit". AA1.13:2/8.
    InterACTION, 2, n.8 (May 1974): 15.
        Camp Crozier and Camp Radley, the training facilities
    established near Arecibo, Puerto Rico in 1961 to train members of
    the Peace Corps, have since been taken over by an agency of the
    Puerto Rican government. All memorial markers and plaques set in
    place between 1961 and 1969 will be retained, and the names of the
    centers will not change.

486 "Training Rugged for Peace Corps". New York Times (27 December
    1961): 12.
        The intensive physical training undergone by Peace Corps
    volunteers at the camps at Rio Abajo, Puerto Rico is outlined. A
    typical day begins at 6 A.M. with a two mile run (including a
    plunge in a mountain stream) and may contain overnight hikes,
    descending a twelve-story mountain, and "drown-proofing". This
    latter involves trainees being tied hand and foot and required to
    stay afloat for an hour. The Puerto Rican setting offers volun-
    teers a chance to witness successful community development pro-
    jects in a different cultural environment.

487 "Training Scheduled at Overseas College for First Time".
    S19.11/2:2/10. Peace Corps Volunteer, 2, n.10 (August 1964):
    3.
        In July, 1964, a contingent of volunteers departed for
    Turkey to complete their training in-country. The involvement of
    Robert College in Istanbul marks the first time that a significant
    portion of a training program has been carried out in the host
    nation. Volunteers involved will be teaching in the Turkish
    schools and will receive training in TEFL (Teaching English As A
    Foreign Language) methods and practice teaching, as well as
    classes in Turkish.

488   Transition: A Magazine For Former ACTION Volunteers. AA1.10.
       Washington, D.C., ACTION, vols. 1 and 2, October, 1971.
       July/August, 1973.
            This journal was issued for the purpose of maintaining
       linkages with former Peace Corps and VISTA personnel, and to
       publicize the work being done by the member agencies of ACTION.
       Subsequent to the cessation of this periodical, the materials
       covered here were incorporated into an expanded edition format of
       Inter-ACTION. Researchers wishing to follow the work of Peace
       Corps in the post-1973 period should consult the numbers of the
       later title.

489   TURNER, DAVID R. Peace Corps Placement Tests: The Complete
       Guide For Scoring High. New York: Arco, 1968.
            A guide intended to assist individuals who planned to take
       the Peace Corps selection tests. The bulk of the book is practice
       questions similar to those used in the actual examination.

490   "2 Camps Named for Fallen". New York Times (19 July 1962):
       11.
            In ceremonies at Rio Abajo, Puerto Rico, two training camps
       for Peace Corps volunteers were formally dedicated to the first
       two volunteers to die while serving in a host nations. Their
       mothers unveiled bronze plaques bearing their names before a crowd
       of more than 300 people.

491   ULRIKSON, SONITA. "New Challenge in Nursing". Tomorrow's
       Nurse (December/January 1961-1962): 7-8.
            Part of Kennedy's "New Frontier" program will be the Peace
       Corps use of nurses. The information in this note was gained
       during the visit of Ohio State students to Washington, D.C. in
       1961 to obtain more data on the Peace Corps. Nurses are called
       upon who can use the natural resources of the land and people to
       further healing. Qualities of patience and maturity are called
       for in prospective candidates.

492   UNGAR, SANFORD. "New Broom". Newsweek, 73 (2 June 1969): 56-
       58.
            A profile of Joseph Blatchford, third director of the Peace
       Corps. Appointed by President Nixon, his "belief in technical
       proficiency as the essence of effective volunteer work abroad"
       was a departure from the orientation of his predecessors. Changes
       in host country attitudes such as increased nationalism and other
       factors influencing Corps alterations are also briefly dealt
       with.

493　"Unions Help Peace Corps Recruit Skilled Workers". Engineering
　　　News Record, 185 (3 December 1970): 42-3.
　　　　　S. Frank Raftery, President of the International Brotherhood
　　　of Painters and Allied Trades was selected to serve as organized
　　　labor's representative on the Peace Corps National Advisory
　　　Council. This interview summarizes the orientation of the unions
　　　toward their role in Peace Corps activities, which is to serve as
　　　a source of instructors for technical training schools. Interest
　　　has already been shown by members of the machinists, operating
　　　engineers, sheet metalworkers and carpenters'' unions.

494　"Uniqueness of Peace Corps Reaffirmed". AA1.13:3/1.
　　　InterACTION, 3, n.1 (October 1974): 4, 11.
　　　　　Following six months of deliberations and sessions for
　　　research, a panel assembled by the National Academy of Sciences
　　　issued an endorsement of the unique character of the Peace Corps,
　　　along with ten recommendations which would make the agency more
　　　effective in future development assistance. Each of those recom-
　　　mendations is listed and discussed in this article.

495　U. S. Department of State. Food and Agriculture Organization
　　　(FAO). Peace Corps Program: Use of Volunteers In FAO-
　　　Sponsored Projects. Agreement Effected By Exchange of Letters
　　　Signed At Rome March 23 and 29, 1962. A9.12:13 Part 2. United
　　　States Treaties and Other International Agreements Services, n.
　　　5101, vol. 13, p. 2, Washington, D.C.: Government Printing
　　　Office, 1962, pp. 1391-99.
　　　　　This document contains the complete text of letters
　　　exchanged between the Director-General of the Food and Agriculture
　　　Organization of the United Nations, B.R. Sen, and the American
　　　counselor of embassy for economic affairs in Rome, H. Gardner
　　　Ainsworth, opening up the possibility of participation by Peace
　　　Corps volunteers in ongoing or newly-created projects of the FAO.
　　　Organization responsibilities of the FAO and Peace Corps with
　　　respect to volunteers are clearly defined. This agreement has
　　　remained in force since its original signing.

496　U. S. Department of State. International Labour Organization.
　　　Peace Corps Program: Use of Volunteers in ILO Projects.
　　　Agreement Effected by Exchange of Notes Signed at Geneva
　　　February 21 and 22, 1963. S9.12:14 Part 2. United States
　　　Treaties and Other International Agreements Series, n. 5458,
　　　vol. 14, p. 2, Washington, D.C.: Government Printing Office,
　　　1964, pp. 3225-28.
　　　　　The complete text of notes given between the United States
　　　ambassador to the European office of the United Nations, Roger W.
　　　Tubby, and David Morse, Director-General of the International
　　　Labour Organization, discussing the participation of Corps volun-
　　　teers in projects funded by the ILO. Volunteers will be seconded
　　　on a trial basis and the ILO and host countries are invited to
　　　contribute personnel to the selection process if they so choose.

497   U. S. Department of State. Peace Corps. <u>Adapting Language</u>
       <u>Materials</u> by Earl W. Stevick. Washington, D.C.: 1970.
           A preliminary draft of a report prepared by the Peace Corps
       for the U. S. Office of Education on effective methods of Language
       instruction. The basic premise is that all language instructors
       adapt texts and materials to some degree, with guidelines offered
       for evaluation of methods. The document draws heavily upon the
       teaching experience of the Peace Corps over the previous years of
       its training programs. The full text is entered on the ERIC
       database as document ED 044 667.

498   U. S. Department of State. Peace Corps. <u>Teacher's Handbook:</u>
       <u>Peace Corps Language Handbook Series</u>. Washington, D.C.:
       1980.
           A text from the Experiment in International Living
       describing for the instructor the basic structures and formats of
       the handbooks in special skills, grammar and communication and
       culture which have been developed for eleven languages taught by
       the Peace Corps. Teaching techniques for the grammar and cultural
       handbooks are given in specific detail. The full text is entered
       on the ERIC database as document ED 203 710.

499   "U. S. As Others See It--A Peace Corps Size-Up". <u>U. S. News</u>
       <u>and World Report</u>, 96 (12 March 1984): 48-50.
           A group of interviews with six country directors of the
       Peace Corps. Each was asked to evaluate the way in which American
       society and politics were regarded in their host nation. Opinions
       were generally favorable, with Americans still viewed as caring
       little about the Third World and economic assistance seen as
       desirable. Host nations queried were Swaziland, Guatemala,
       Morocco, Ecuador, the Philippines and the Eastern Caribbean island
       nations. All the Directors interviewed stressed the importance of
       learning from the Third World and enriching the United States
       culture thereby.

500   "U. S. Sending Africa 150 Young Teachers". <u>New York Times</u> (29
       January 1961): 1, 45.
           As a pilot project of President Kennedy's proposed "Peace
       Corps", 150 teachers were to be sent to four East African territo-
       ries to serve in secondary schools. A joint plan drawn up between
       the Teacher's College of Columbia University and Makerere College
       in Kampala, Uganda, provided the framework for their assignments.
       Preliminary indoctrination and training were scheduled to take
       place at Makerere. The group will consist of three types of
       teachers: those with some professional experience, recent gradu-
       ates and liberal arts graduates. The idea for this use of Peace
       Corps personnel arose out of a conference held at Princeton
       University in December, 1960, on educational problems in East
       Africa. Countries hosting the volunteers were to be Kenya,
       Tanganyika, Zanzibar and Uganda itself.

501   VAUGHN, JACK. "A Poet and Peasant Overture". S19.11/2:4/5.
       Peace Corps Volunteer, 4, n. 5 (March 1966): 5-6.
            An adaptation of Jack Vaughn's first speech as Director of
       the Peace Corps, given at the University of Michigan on February
       28, 1966.

502   VAUGHN, JACK. "The Peace Corps: Now We Are Seven". Saturday
       Review, 51 (6 January 1968): 21-3, 91.
            Jack Vaughn, Director of the Peace Corps, reviews the
       progress of the agency since its foundation, noting solid support
       from both Congress and the American people. At the time of
       writing, 12,249 volunteers were on post in fifty-eight countries.
       Seven years of existence had provided the Corps with some case
       studies rating its effectiveness in certain individual country
       projects. However, the speed with which training programs and in-
       country facilities were altered in response to suggestions from
       volunteers and outside consultants "puts the final research study
       in the position of commenting on conditions that no longer exist"
       (p. 22). The shift in training from specialist to generalists who
       acquire specific skills prior to departure is also noted. Skills
       displayed in the accompanying tables show education as the
       majority, with health, rural community development, agriculture,
       urban community development and public works/public administration
       making up the remainder. Problems still facing Corps include a
       chronic shortage of trained people, coping with the draft and
       public opinion on Vietnam and costs rising for an increase in the
       number of volunteers. Vaughn forecasts that the 15,317 returned
       volunteers will play a significant role in the American future
       through service in the diplomatic corps and as a leaven in their
       own communities. In an especially clear attempt to define the
       goals of what the Corps strives for, he states that "peace is a
       process of bitter encounters with reality . . . It is fit work for
       rare people" (p. 91).

503   "Vice President Humphrey to Head Peace Corps Advisory Council".
       Department of State Bulletin, 52 (January-March 1965): 250-
       51.
            This is the full text of a letter from President Lyndon
       Johnson to Vice-President Hubert Humphrey, requesting him to
       assume the chairmancy of the National Advisory Council of the
       Peace Corps, a position which Johnson had held for some three and
       one-half years. The letter contains four recommendations: first,
       that the Council convene a conference of Returned Peace Corps
       Volunteers as closely as possible to March 1, the fourth anniver-
       sary of the foundation of the Peace Corps: second, to publicize
       as widely as possible the opportunities offered to American
       citizens through Corps service: third, that veterans of Peace
       Corps be utilized in some fashion to assist the 25,000 foreign
       students resident in the United States, and lastly that the

Council make recommendations for the full use of the potentials
represented by the returning volunteers for the benefit of America
itself. Johnson notes Humphrey's involvement with the idea of a
Peace Corps for many years, and comments "a Great Society requires
Great Citizens, and the Peace Corps is a world-wide training
ground for Great Citizens".

504   "VITA Provides Timely Technical Aid to Peace Corps Volunteers".
        AA1.13:5/3. InterACTION, 5, n.3 (December 1976):   5, 11.
           In addition to the Peace Corps' own library and the ICE
(Information and Exchange System) within the agency, volunteers in
need of the technical information may turn to a third source VITA
(Volunteers in Technical Assistance) is a private concern in Mt.
Ranier, Maryland. Its structure and programs of aid are
detailed.

505   "Volunteer, 71, Extends Service for Sixth Year". AA1.13:2/4.
        InterACTION, 2, n.4 (January 1974): 14.
           An interview with Odilon Long, veteran of Peace Corps
assignments in Sierra Leone, Gabon, Togo. He relates how he came
to be attracted to Corps service and give his opinions on both
cross-cultural adjustment and the younger volunteers.

506   "Volunteers and Environment: A Peace Corps Sampler".
        AA1.13:4/2-3. InterACTION, 4, nos. 2-3 (November-December
        1975): 10-11.
           Fifteen current Peace Corps projects in the environmental
field are summarized. Host nations represented are Ecuador, Iran,
Colombia, Brazil, the Philippines, Senegal, Malawi, Nepal, Niger,
Chile and Kenya.

507   "Volunteers Serving in Asia Receive Magsaysay Award".
        S19.11/2:1/11. Peace Corps Volunteer, 1, n.11 (September
        1963):   3.
           On August 31, 1963, the Ramon Magsaysay Award, equivalent in
Asia to the Nobel Prize, was bestowed upon the members of the
Peace Corps serving in Asia. Sargent Shriver, Director of the
Corps, flew to Manila to accept the ceremony on behalf of his
personnel. Background on the award is also provided.

508   WALSH, JOHN. "Peace Corps: Agency Flourishes as Congress
        Smiles, Numbers Grow, but Full Results Are Not Yet In".
        Science, 140, (26 April 1963): 371-72.
           A consideration of the phenomenon of Peace Corps in its
second year of existence, and analysis of technical competencies
in both possible placements and volunteer candidates. Recruiting
the technically trained is not a specific goal of Corps, and while
many volunteers become involved in technical projects via short-
term intensive training, their role is not primarily limited to
this sphere. Focusing on "middle manpower", science and
mathematics teachers serving in Ghana are noted. Most volunteers

are prepared to expect circumstances requiring innovation. The pattern of volunteer placements in Latin America is contrasted with that of Africa. Noting that "the performance of the Peace Corps to date seems to have allayed the early apprehensions", the columnist reserves judgement until the return of the first groups from host nations.

509   WALSH, MARY. "Wanted: Volunteers: Graduates of Two-Year Colleges Are Valuable to the Peace Corps". Junior College Journal, 33 (May 1963): 14-16.
      Students from junior colleges make valuable volunteers for two reasons: first, most courses at such institutions result in graduates with an immediately applicable specialty, and also most of the skills are oriented toward a spectrum of local community needs. Examples of graduates from a variety of such colleges serving in the Peace Corps are then presented.

510   WALTER, MICHAEL. "Why Not a Two-Way Peace Corps?" AA1.10:1/11. Transition, 1, n.11 (December 1972): 25-7.
      Originally written while the author was serving in the Peace Corps in the Ivory Coast, this article advances the idea of a reverse Peace Corps, in which qualified citizens of foreign nations would serve in the United States. Advantages are seen to an expansion of the awareness of Americans to world problems, linguistic benefits to the Hispanic population in American schools, and a sense of equality for the donor nations with America. No specific proposals for implementing the idea are given.

511   WARPEHA, RITA C. A Bibliography of Peace Corps-related Materials: TEFL, TESL and Other English Teaching. Washington, D.C.: ACTION, 1972.
      An unannotated listing of country evaluations and language teaching items and handbooks used in Peace Corps training compiled by the then-chief librarian of the ACTION Headquarters Library in Washington.

512   "The Water/Sanitation Sector: Water For All". Peace Corps Times (May/June 1985): 17-20, 22-3.
      The involvement of Peace Corps personnel in the provision of services related to water management, sanitation, public health and similar areas is profiled in this article. Technical types of assistance provided to the volunteer by the sector specialists in the Office of Training and Support Programs are explored, with examples of projects included from Lesotho, Burkina Faso, and Nepal.

513   "Well, Can She?" Newsweek, 71 (15 January 1968): 23.
      Recruiting efforts at attracting students and interested persons to Peace Corps service seemed to be becoming less effective in the late 1960's. A conference was called by Jack Vaughn, Director of Corps, at the Bellevue Hotel in San Francisco to discuss the problems and seek ways to remedy the situation. Factors involved were the draft resistance and the Viet Nam war,

with many students viewing Corps work as an hypocrisy perpetuated
by a government unwilling to admit its duplicity. Effects of this
resistance showed up in a Harris poll indicating that some 20 per
cent of all college seniors believed they would lose their freedom
of speech if they joined the Peace Corps. Director Vaughn planned
no overhaul of the traditional messages of the reasons for Peace
Corps service. The article title comes from a slogan of the time,
which stated "Can a young girl college graduate from the Middle
West find happiness in the Peace Corps?"

514   WETZEL, CHARLES. "The Peace Corps in our Past". Annals of the
       American Academy of Political and Social Science, 365 (May
       1966): 1-11.
           Beginning with the Spanish Franciscan missionaries of the
       fifteenth century, the heritage of the Peace Corps as a "people-to
       -people" program is reviewed. Among the philosophies and groups
       noted as precursors of Corps are the traditional pacificist
       beliefs of the Quakers, the American peace movements of the nine-
       teenth and early twentieth centuries, the Experiment in Interna-
       tional Living, the Civilian Conservation Corps, the Point Four
       Plan of the Truman administration, and Operation Crossroads
       Africa. The legislative history of proposals such as those raised
       by Representative Henry Reuss and Senator Hubert Humphrey is also
       included.

515   "What Ever Happened to the Peace Corps?" Good Housekeeping,
       196 (May 1983): 253.
           Admitting that "the Peace Corps, now 23 years old, doesn't
       get the kind of attention it used to when John F. Kennedy was
       president", this news item examines in very general terms where
       Corps members are serving and in what capacities. Information on
       applying and wages is also included.

516   "Where Are You Going?": Some Problems Faced By Peace Corps
       Teachers. A Case Study of Teaching in Thailand. International
       Research Institute of the American Institutes for Research,
       January, 1966.
           This manual was prepared under a contract with the Peace
       Corps, and is based upon the collective experiences of volunteer
       teachers in Thailand up to 1966. The format presents fourteen
       problems of cultural adaptation followed by discussion questions.
       The volume was intended to be used as part of sensitivity
       training.

517   WHITTLESAY, SUSAN. U. S. Peace Corps: The Challenge of Good
       Will. New York: Coward-McCann, 1963.
           This volume is a survey of the work and functions, life and
       accomplishments of Peace Corps volunteers intended for an audience
       of junior high school age. Lavishly illustrated with photographs
       showing projects initiated between 1961 and 1963. Several volun-
       teers relate their experiences in host nations as disparate as
       Ethiopia, Ghana, St. Lucia and Chile. The final section is inter-
       esting from an historical viewpoint, as it is concerned with ways
       in which school students can prepare themselves for Corps service

and support the efforts of volunteers through partnership programs, thus providing a window into the domestic information campaigns of the Peace Corps's early years.

518   The Whole ICE Catalog. Washington, D.C.: Peace Corps
       Information Collection and Exchange, 1980 to date.
           This is an annual publication listing training guides,
       lesson plans, project reports, manuals and similar materials added
       to the collection of the ICE office of the Peace Corps. Contents
       are arranged by appropriate technology in general and by sectors--
       agriculture, AT/energy, community development, construction and
       housing, education, fisheries, health, natural resources and
       forestry, small enterprise development, water and sanitation and
       women in development. All entries are annotated.

519   "Why I'm Leaving, Why I'm Staying". S19.11/2:8/1-2.
       Volunteer, 8, nos. 1-2 (January-February 1970): 2-10.
           Interviews with volunteers who have opted for early termina-
       tion of service and those who have chosen to remain an extra third
       year, exploring their motivations and philosophies. Host nations
       represented are Nepal, Iran, Korea, Ecuador, Thailand, Panama and
       Ghana.

520   WILCK, DAVID. "Congress Gives Struggling Peace Corps Another
       Chance". Christian Science Monitor (22 December 1981): 14.
           The restoration of Peace Corps autonomy by Congress is seen
       as vital to reversing the trend of declining agency morale and
       public ignorance and disinterest. The Reagan administration urges
       increased infusion of private sector aid through increasing the
       number of returned volunteers entering the private sector, company
       leaves of absence for corporate personnel wishing to serve, and
       distinctive ways of joint ventures with private agencies. Several
       Corps officials are interviewed, among them Edward Alvarez, Corps
       deputy director.

521   WILSON, GEORGE W. "Peace Corps Director Quits". Washington
       Post (31 July 1974): A29.
           Nicholas W. Craw, 37, Director of the Peace Corps, has
       announced his resignation after less than one year in the
       position. Craw has served ACTION in varying capacities and states
       that he feels it time to move on. A letter of resignation sent to
       President Nixon has not yet been acknowledged.

522   WINDMILLER, MARSHALL. "Agents of the New Empire". Nation, 212
       (10 May 1971): 592-96.
           The author of The Peace Corps and Pax Americana places the
       general work of the agency in the context of international
       relations and foreign policy, viewing it as an extension of the
       poverty industry on an international scale. The links between
       George Lilienthals's Development and Resources Corporation, a
       principal subcontractor of Corps training programs and the
       political orientation introduced into Peace Corps by Nixon's
       appointee director Joseph Blatchford are noted. The chief context
       of debate is the ethics of economic development and the role Corps

is and should be playing in it. Increased living allowances for
volunteers and greater savings benefits, the foundation of
Transcentury Corporation to utilize returned personnel and their
knowledge of the Third World and the image of the volunteers are
all examined and found morally suspect. Stating that "it may be
that the price of development in the non-Communist world is the
creation of a new form of empire" and that "under Blatchford, the
primary focus of concern is the volunteer, not the problem for
which he presumable volunteered" (p. 595). Windmiller agrees with
the call by the radical Committee of Returned Volunteers for the
abolition of the agency. He terms it "a breeding ground for a
profound cynicism that is dangerous to our democracy" (p. 596).

523   WINDMILLER, MARSHALL. The Peace Corps and Pax Americana.
      Washington, D.C.: Public Affairs Press, 1970.
          This book is the result of disillusion with the work of the
Peace Corps by a professor formerly part of the training staff of
Ghana I. From period 1965 to 1967, his opposition to United
States involvement in Vietnam grew, while he continued to except
the Peace Corps from blanket condemnation as a federal agency.
The analysis takes as its premise that the work being done by
volunteers in various parts of the world is conducive to creation
or maintenance of existing dependencies and strictures of benefits
to an expansionist and imperialist America. The historical
periods covered reach from the Corps' formation under President
Kennedy to the initiation of the "New Directions" programming
under Joseph Blatchford, a Nixon appointee. While offering
extensive textual evidence of economic manipulation of Third World
governments and industries by American firms, the Peace Corps as
"a new CIA" is heavily criticized. The author concludes by
calling for either massive revision of the Corps or its
dissolution. The text is instructive as a mirror of the emotional
matrix which Corps had to survive in the 1960's.

524   WINGENBACH, CHARLES E. The Peace Corps: Who, How and Where.
      New York: John Day, 1961.
          This is one of the earliest publications of book length to
promote the idea of a Peace Corps, written in 1961 when no volunteers except the first groups had been selected for training.
Beginning with the history of the idea, the program for Peace
Corps/Tanganyika is examined in detail: eight weeks at Texas
Western College, twenty-six days at the Puerto Rican training
camps near Arecibo, and seven weeks in-country at the National
Resources School at Tengeru, at the foot of Kilimanjaro. Examples
of extant similar overseas efforts are then listed--the International Voluntary Services work in Indochina, an eye clinic run by
the Catholic Relief Services at Honai, South Vietnam, and a
composite diary from the Crossroads 1960 work in western Nigeria.
General issues of selection of candidates and the possibility of
an international Peace Corps are also debated. This is a valuable
example of the popular mindset in the earliest days of Corps
existence.

525   WOFFORD, HARRIS. "The Future of the Peace Corps". Annals of
      the American Academy of Political and Social Science, 365 (May
      1966): 129-46.
           Written by the then-Associate Director of Peace Corps, this
      essay is an attempt to review the progress made by the agency in
      its first five years of existence and to speculate upon what
      changes must be made to insure a viable future of growth. Noting
      that "the Children of Kennedy 'have lost both of their founding
      fathers, Kennedy and Shriver" (p. 132). Wofford views the major
      problem facing Corps between 1966 and 1970 as the definition of
      context for service. Options of development include either a
      massive expansion or a consolidation of goals. Wofford inveighs
      against the latter. using the fate of President Truman's Point
      Four Plan as illustration. While requests for volunteers continue
      to come in, a shift towards more highly trained, experienced
      workers with critical skills is noted. Long-ranged planning is
      viewed as essential if the new Peace Corps is to emerge and cope
      with the changing world it is to serve. A hypothetical model of
      what Corps should be in 1970 or 1980 is then presented. The often
      neglected subjects of the draft, an exchange Peace Corps and full
      partnership with higher education through credit for Corps service
      are also examined. In view of the actual changes which the
      agency experienced during the years after 1966, this opinion piece
      provides an interesting window into the thinking of some of the
      administration.

526   WOFFORD, HARRIS. "The Peace Corps, Hijos de Kennedy". Of
      Kennedys and Kings: Making Sense of the Sixties, New York:
      Farrar, Straus & Giroux, 1980: 243-84.
           Composed as part of a larger text examining the overall
      impact of the Kennedy Administration upon the 1960's, this chapter
      attempts to fit "Kennedy's children" into a broader framework.
      Historical treatment is adequate but tending towards anecdotal in
      presentation. Of particular interest are the accounts of Sargent
      Shriver's journey to leading Third World nations such as Ghana and
      India to sell the idea of Corps assistance.

527   "Workshop Discusses Peace Corps and Women's Role in
      Development". AA1.13:4/12. InterACTION, 4, n.2 (September
      1976): 1-2.
           On July 21, 1976, a workshop was held at ACTION headquarters
      in Washington, D.C. examining three major questions: the assign-
      ment of female volunteers to non-traditional roles for women in
      host nations, what role Corps should play in the improvement of
      women's social position in host nations and the reasons for the
      low numbers of women in senior staff positions overseas. The
      article summarizes the discussions and presents the group's
      conclusions.

528   "Yesterday, Today and Tomorrow". <u>Peace Corps Times</u> (December
       1985): 4-5.
          A brief historical sketch of Peace Corps. Of interest are
       the reports of possible entry to the Maldive Islands, re-entry to
       Brazil and Panama, and negotiations with Equatorial Guinea.
       Coverage of the Africa Food Systems Initiative is also included.

529   ZIMMERMAN, ROBERT FREDERICK. <u>Peace Corps/Philippines: Image
       or Performance?</u> Ph.D. dissertation, American University,
       1968.
          Written by a specialist in the field of international
       relations, this dissertation examines and evaluates the first two
       to three years of Peace Corps work in the Philippine system of
       education (1961-1963) assessing seven basic premises of the
       original program statement. From the beginning, Peace Corps "co-
       teachers" and "educational aides" emphasized the fields of English
       instruction, science and mathematics. Questions prompting this
       research stemmed from criticism of the Peace Corps work in the
       archipelago by both host country officials and the volunteers
       themselves and a case study carried out by the author in his
       former site, the province of Samar. Assuming that the Peace Corps
       "is essentially a substantive program of assistance in economic
       and social development rather than a mere propaganda effort" (p.
       10), Zimmerman measures the problems in Philippine education,
       stated objectives of Corps in that field, and the actual actions
       taken by the agency. A "wide gap . . . between the image . . .
       and . . . actual performance" (p. 14) is delineated and
       conclusions for improvement presented. The case study of the
       response of Filipino teachers to the first two years of Peace
       Corps educational presence in the province of Samar provides an
       excellent example of both the difficulties of effectively
       implementing assistance and professional obstacles which may
       contribute to such problems. Limitations on the conclusions
       reached here are the special relationship existing between the
       United States and the Philippines, lack of comparison with other
       aspects of Peace Corps/Philippines programming, the rapid rates of
       change in Peace Corps/Philippines, lack of comparison with other
       aspects of Peace Corps/Philippines programming, and the rapid
       rates of change in Peace Corps development which have made the
       conclusions of this work almost obsolete before they were printed.
       A sample questionnaire from the Samar study is included in an
       appendix.

530   ZUNIGA, RICARDO BURMESTER. The Peace Corps As A Value-Oriented
       Movement. Ph.D. dissertation, Harvard, 1968.
         Done as a dissertation in the field of social psychology,
       with special emphasis on the transmission of and formulation of
       specific social values, this document utilizes data from the Peace
       Corps training program in Puerto Rico. Noting "the Peace Corps
       incoherence" as to objectives and motivations, Zuniga explores
       "the major task facing the Peace Corps . . . the discovery and
       transmission of its own meaning, and the attempt to project its
       discoveries into other agencies of both the United States and the
       host country" (p.228). The agency is viewed as being valuable
       "more in terms of its meaning than of its concrete accomplishment"
       (p. 228). The literature issued by the Peace Corps between 1961
       and 1968 is surveyed and the total training process is drawn into
       the discussion.

Country Programs

531   U.S. Department of State. <u>Afghanistan. Peace Corps Program.</u>
<u>Agreement Effected by Exchange of Notes Signed at Kabul</u>
<u>September 6 and 11, 1962</u>. U.S. Treaties and Other
International Agreements, vol. 13, p.2, 1962, Washington, D.C.:
Government Printing Office, 1963, pp. 2100-04. S9.12: 12 Part
2.

        The full text of notes exchanged between Mr. J. M. Steeves,
American ambassador to the Kingdom of Afghanistan and His
Excellency Sardar-a-'Ala Ali Mohammed, acting minister of foreign
affairs, which laid the foundation for the entrance of Peace Corps
into that country. Privileges granted to the volunteers include
waiving of import duties, legal protection under Afghani law, and
acceptance of a country representative to speak for them.

532   "Afghanistan: Volunteers Gain Acceptance in Kabul". <u>Peace</u>
     <u>Corps Volunteer</u>, 2, n.3 (January 1964): 10-21. S19.11/2:2/3.
        A collection of short articles written by members of Peace
Corps/Afghanistan's first contingent of thirty-five volunteers,
covering problems of adaptation to culture and the harsh climate
of the land. Assignments include nursing, teaching and
mechanics.

533   "Around the World". <u>Washington Post</u> (7 February 1972): A9.
        Thirty-three members of the Peace Corps are en route to
Afghanistan to assist in the rebuilding of the nation from a
severe drought. They will work on water management projects and
irrigation systems, with the additional responsibility of aiding
in the distribution of 100,000 tons of wheat sent by the United
State as food assistance. Widespread starvation has followed upon
two successive years of abnormally low rainfall, and many Afghans
are fleeing to the cities in search of food.

534   CANNON, GLENN. "English and Other Languages in Afghanistan".
      Modern Language Journal, 47, n.7 (November 1963): 314-318.
          A concise overview of the present state of language usage
      and linguistic instruction in Afghanistan. Noting that "Exclusive
      of diverging dialects, some thirty languages are spoken in the
      country" (p. 314), the author outlines the forms of instruction in
      Pashto, Persian, German, French, Russian and English, as well as
      the Arabic required for the reading of the Koran. The number of
      qualified teachers is seen as negligible, and national unity is
      predicated upon the choice of a national language. The example of
      the adoption of Hindi as the national language of India is noted.
      The public school course in English is given in detail. The
      author formerly taught linguistics in Afghanistan, and provides an
      excellent background to the issues facing those volunteers who
      have taken over the described activities of teaching English.

535   DUPREE, LOUIS. "Moving Mountains in Afghanistan". The
      Cultural Frontiers of the Peace Corps, Robert B. Textor, ed.,
      Cambridge: M.I.T. Press, 1966: 107-24.
          A profile of the first three groups of volunteers to serve
      in Afghanistan between September, 1962 and January, 1964, together
      with a detailed presentation of the general history and social
      structure of Afghan society as it was in those years. Attitudes
      towards the volunteers were ones of extreme suspicion, which
      gradually altered as the periods of contact became more
      widespread. Postings of these Corpsmen included auto mechanics in
      Kabul, nurses working in provincial hospitals and clinics, and
      teachers in various schools and ministry facilities. Researchers
      will find this article an essential window into both the
      anthropology and politics of the earliest days of Peace
      Corps/Afghanistan.

536   "Energetic Nurse Improves Child Care in Afghanistan".
      AA1.13:1/10. InterACTION, 1, n.10 (July 1973): 1.
          A profile of the efforts of Mary Simpson, a nurse of 65 who
      has served several tours of duty in Afghanistan. Her six-day work
      schedule covers family health clinics in several cities in Baghlan
      Province--many of which she was instrumental in founding--and
      includes checking patient status, community health education and
      encouraging Afghan women to venture out from their traditional
      isolation in family compounds. In her reflections upon her work,
      she notes that veneration for age assists her in gaining a
      hearing. A brief summary of health problems facing most Afghan
      communities is also given.

537   ENTESER, M. EHSEN. Intermediate Dari for Peace Corps
      Volunteers. Washington, D.C.: Peace Corps, May, 1966.
          An eight-unit advanced text designed for use in-country by
      members of Peace Corps/Afghanistan but also applicable to the
      final phases of training. Contents stress conversation drills.
      In 1963, when the author took charge of language training for the
      Afghanistan III group, no basic level Dari materials were
      available. Enteser created a Farsi Reference Manual Basic Course
      as a first step, which has been used by the Peace Corps since

1964. The present text was first used for the Afghanistan VII and
IX training groups at the University of Texas and represents a
second phase based on the 1963 text. The complete text of this
manual has been entered into the ERIC database as document
ED131692.

538   "Holiday from Peace Corps". Christian Science Monitor (12
        October 1965): B11: October 13, 1965: 15.
        A graphic and colorful account by a member of Peace
Corps/Afghanistan of her first holiday. The route included the
areas of Rawalpindi, the then-incomplete capital of Islamabad,
Lahore, Peshawar and finally Swat. This two-part letter is both a
portrait of these cities as they were in 1965 and a first-person
account of the shocks and humor of cultural adaptation.

539   LUKETICH, DOROTHY. "The Amoebas are Lovely". S19.11/2:2/3.
        Peace Corps Volunteer, 2, n.3 (January 1964): 14.
        A personal account by a nurse working at the Masturat
Hospital in Kabul as part of Afghanistan I. The title comes from
a statement made by a medical technician there that Kabul has the
most beautiful amoebas in the world.

540   "PCV's Aid Plane Crash Victims". AA1.13:1/11. InterACTION, 1,
        n.11 (August 1973): 6.
        On April 18, 1973, a tour plane carrying several Americans
crashed just after lift-off for the flight to Kabul. This article
covers the text of a letter written by one of the survivors
covering the assistance rendered to her party by the members of
Peace Corps/Afghanistan. This ranged from clothing and medicine
to simply someone to speak English with. The letter was sent to
Senator Charles Percy of Illinois and was inserted by him in the
Congressional Record of June 20, 1973.

541   "Protest in Afghanistan". Volunteer, 8, n.3-4 (March-April
        1970): 13, 22.
        A news report on the quiet protest staged by members of
Peace Corps/Afghanistan in Kabul hours before the arrival of Vice
President Spiro Agnew and its management by in-country staff.

542   SILVERBERG, MARGARETE V. "In the Land of Ghenghis Khan--Below
        the Khyber Pass: Experiences of a Peace Corps Volunteer in
        Afghanistan". Journal of Obstetric, Gynecologic and Neonatal
        Nursing, 1 (June 1972): 49-51.
        Working as an obstetric nurse in several hospitals in the
Kabul region of Afghanistan, Margaret Silverberg provides graphic
illustrations of the rigors of nursing volunteer life through the
sharing of her personal qualms and growing. A brief background on
the problems of women's health care in Afghanistan is also
included. Despite all the recorded difficulties, the writer
declares that she would do it again.

543   SIMPSON, MARY H.   "With the Peace Corps, Half a World Away".
      American Journal of Nursing, 74 (August 1974):   1464-66.
         A Peace Corps nurse in the Hindu Kush range near Kabul,
      Afghanistan describes her work in Baghlan City and some of the
      obstacles set in her way by the host culture.   Much of the article
      explores general health problems of Afghanistan and efforts being
      made to cope with them.   The author had been in country for some
      six years at the time this article was written.   Especially
      interesting are the folk beliefs of the conservative Muslim
      culture of the countryside and various coping strategies employed
      by the volunteer to promote better health care for women.

544   VIORST, MILTON.   "Tim Thompson's Private Cold War".
      Progressive, 40 (September 1976):   38-9.
         The situation of a volunteer stationed in Sheberghan,
      Afghanistan as a teacher is examined.   The "cold war" of the title
      refers to the presence in his community of 400 Russians working at
      developing the region's supplies of natural gas and their
      ostracism of the volunteer.   Living conditions, sexual mores and
      history of Peace Corps involvement in Afghani culture are also
      noted.

545   ZAKI, MAHFOUZ H.   "Health Programming for the Peace Corps in
      Afghanistan: Family Planning".   American Journal of Public
      Health, 64, n.11 (November 1974):   1098-99.
         During a year of service as Peace Corps physician and
      advisor for health programming, the author was requested to
      respond to a host country request for assistance in operating
      provincial family planning and health clinics.   Travelling some
      2,000 miles across Afghanistan to visit local hospitals and
      consult professional colleagues the writer raised serious doubts
      as to the advisability of Corps involvement, due to high infant
      mortality and emotional resistance to the idea of birth control.
      Four volunteer nurses were eventually involved in a more general
      program of maternal and child health care.   A useful look behind
      the scenes at a Corps program in the planning stages.

546   U.S. Department of State.   Peace Corps: Agreement Between the
      United States of America and Anguilla Effected by Exchange of
      Letters Dated at Washington February 19 and June 24, 1981.
      Treaties and other International Acts Series 10169.
      Washington, D.C.:   Government Printing Office, 1982.
      S9.10:10169.
         A full text of the notes exchanged between Sir Nicholas
      Henderson, ambassador of Great Britain and William G. Sykes,
      acting Peace Corps Director, which made possible service by
      volunteers on Anguilla.   Legal protections to be extended to both
      staff and volunteers are specified.

547   U.S. Department of State. <u>Antigua. Peace Corps. Agreement</u>
       <u>Effected by Exchange of Notes Signed at Bridgetown and Antigua</u>
       <u>December 19 and 28, 1966</u>. United States Treaties and Other
       International Agreements Series, n.6195, vol. 18, p. 1,
       Washington, D.C.: pp. 25-7. S9.12:18 Part 1.
            This document contains the complete texts of notes given
       between the American charge d'Affaires, George Dolgin, and H.
       Burrowes, acting administrator of Antigua, which set the foun-
       dations for the entrance and service of Peace Corps personnel to
       that island nation.

548   "She Shuns Retirement, Joins the Peace Corps Instead". <u>Aging</u>,
       274 (August 1977): 22.
            An interview with Martha L. Daniell, a senior volunteer
       serving as a curriculum development specialist for the Ministry of
       Education on the island of Antigua in the Caribbean. Topics
       discussed involve the advantages of age in carrying out her work
       as a volunteer and reflections on local life and customs.

549   U.S. Department of State. <u>Bahrain. Peace Corps. Agreement</u>
       <u>Effected by Exchange of Notes Signed at Manama April 24 and</u>
       <u>June 12, 1973</u>. United States Treaties and Other International
       Agreements Series, n. 7684, vol. 24, p. 2, Washington, D.C.:
       pp. 1762-66. S9.12:24 Part 2.
            The complete texts of notes exchanged between Robert A.
       Stein, American charge d'Affaires, and His Excellency Shaikh
       Mohamed bin Mubarak Al-Khalifa, minister of foreign affairs,
       concluding the legal terms under which Peace Corps personnel would
       serve in Bahrain. This treaty lasted until the departure of Corps
       from Bahrain in 1979.

550   U.S. Department of State. <u>Bangladesh. Peace Corps. Agreement</u>
       <u>Signed at Washington, July 13, 1978</u>. United States Treaties
       and Other International Agreements Series, n.9283, vol. 30, p.
       2, Washington, D.C.: Government Printing Office, 1980, pp.
       1734-36. S9.12:30 Part 2.
            The English text of an agreement between the governments of
       the United States and Bangladesh establishing a Peace Corps
       presence in that nation. Signatories were Sam Brown, Director of
       ACTION, and M. R. Siddigi of Bangladesh. Researchers seeking
       further information upon Corps activities in this region should
       consult the treaties with Pakistan and India.

551   U.S. Department of State. <u>Barbados. Peace Corps. Agreement</u>
       <u>Effected by Exchange of Notes Signed at Bridgetown July 15 and</u>
       <u>August 9, 1965</u>. United States Treaties and Other International
       Agreements Series, n. 5887, vol. 16, p. 2, Washington, D.C.:
       pp. 1647-49. S9.12:16 Part 2.
            The complete text of notes given between Frank J. Walters,
       acting principal officer of the United States consulate, and His
       Excellency Sir John Stow, governor of Barbados, creating the legal
       base upon which all subsequent Peace Corps service in that island
       nation would rest.

552   U.S. Department of State. <u>Peace Corps: Agreement Between the</u>
       <u>United States of America and Barbados Effected by Exchange of</u>
       <u>Notes Signed at Bridgetown and Hastings May 10 and June 8,</u>
       <u>1982</u>. Treaties and International Acts Series 10413,
       Washington, D.C.: Government Printing Office, 1985.
       S9.10:10413.
           The full text of notes exchanged between Louis R. Tull,
       minister of foreign affairs of Barbados, and Milan D. Bish, U. S.
       ambassador, which laid the legal foundation for the entry of Peace
       Corps into that country. A noteworthy item in the agreement is
       the limitation of privileges and exemptions to the volunteers,
       with staff and country representatives being required to conform
       to Barbadian law.

553   "Marine Biology Graduate of the University of Pittsburgh Helps
       Develop Underwater Park off the Island of Barbados".
       <u>Congressional Record</u>, 122, Part II (11 May 1976): 13479-480.
           As one of thirty Peace Corps volunteers serving on the
       island of Barbados, David Magiske has been working at underwater
       surveying and sea life assessment pursuant to the creation of an
       environmental education park. Among his accomplishments has been
       the creation of a set of slides illustrating the rich fish and
       plant life off the Barbadian coast.

554   U. S. Department of State. <u>British Honduras. Peace Corps</u>
       <u>Program. Agreement Effected by Exchange of Notes Signed at</u>
       <u>Belize July 26 and August 15, 1962</u>. United States Treaties and
       Other International Agreements Series, no. 5137, vol. 13, p. 2,
       Washington, D.C.: Government Printing Office, 1962, pp. 1868-
       70. S9.12:13 Part 2.
           The full text of notes exchanged between the Governor of
       British Honduras. His Excellency Sir Peter H. G. Stallard, and
       Harrison Burgess, United States ambassador, creating a legal
       framework for the entry of Peace Corps into the country. Legal
       benefits accruing to both volunteers and staff are clearly
       defined. This agreement has remained in force since that date.

555   "Belize PCV Gets Assist From VDC". AA1.13:49-10. InterACTION,
       4, n.9-10 (June-July 1976): 13.
           An account of the contribution made to the work of a
       volunteer in the field of beekeeping in Belize by a member of the
       Volunteer Development Corps, an organization focusing on the
       provision of expert aid to cooperative business enterprises.

556   "Belize Track Athletes Trained by Volunteer". AA1.13:1/11.
       InterACTION, 1, n.11 (August, 1973): 7.
           A news story covering the work of Ted Cox, a volunteer
       serving as national track and field director for the country of
       Belize. His activities have included training athletes for
       possible international competition, writing a track and field
       course for the Belize school system and holding coaching clinics
       throughout the country.

557   CLARK, RAYMOND C. AND JON P. DAYLEY. Belizean Creole:
       Teacher's Handbook. Washington, D.C.: Peace Corps, 1979.
       Developed by the Experiment in International Living, this
volume is intended for native speakers of Belizean Creole working
as language instructors for the Peace Corps. Thirty teaching
methods are set out, each corresponding to a unit in the
workbooks. Special communication guidelines are also given, as
well as an outline of each volume in the series on Belizean
Creole. Full text of this document is entered as ED 221 015 in
ERIC system.

558   DAYLEY, JON P. Belizean Creole: Communication and Culture
       Handbook. Washington, D.C.: Peace Corps, 1979.
       Developed by the Experiment in International Living at
Brattleboro, Vermont under Peace Corps contract, this sequence of
forty-one lessons on the Creole language of Belize provides basic
grammar and vocabulary through structured thematic situations.
Complete text is available as ERIC document ED 221 016.

559   DAYLEY, JON P. Belizean Creole: Glossary. Washington, D.C.:
       Peace Corps, 1979.
       Part of a four-volume set of teaching materials for Peace
Corps/Belize, this glossary includes both common Creole words and
terms present in both Creole and English but with different
meanings. Intended as a reference volume, the full text can be
found on the ERIC system as document ED 221 017.

560   DODD, DIXIE. "Success Story in Belize". Peace Corps Times
       (March/April 1985): 9.
       The development and financial success of the Cayo
Businessmen's Organization in Belize is described. The CBO was
set up originally with assistance from a volunteer, and the story
of its development is written by his successor in posting. This
is an example which can answer the question of "what does the
Peace Corps do?" in familiar and quantifiable terms.

561   "PCV Studies, Advises Belize Conch Industry". AA1.13:3/5.
       InterACTION, 3, n.5 (February 1975): 3.
       An account of the assignment of John Frederick of Peace
Corps/Belize to that nation's efforts at planning the utilization
of its conch population. The shellfish is of significant value to
both the export trade and as a domestic food source. Educating
the fishermen and having them assist in the surveys has also had
beneficial effects on marine management.

562   "Volunteer, 70, Is Acclaimed". AA1.13:1/12. InterACTION, 1,
       n.12 (September 1973): 4.
       Bea Alford, PC/Belize, received a citation from that
nation's Ministry of Local Government, Community and Social
Development for her work in 1965 initiating the 4-H club movement
in Belize. At the time of the award, Alford was serving as an
ACTION staffer.

563   U. S. Department of State. Bolivia. Peace Corps Program.
      Agreement Effected by Exchange of Notes Signed at La Paz June
      19, 1962. United States Treaties and other International
      Agreements Series, no. 5086, vol. 13, p. 2, Washington, D.C.:
      Government Printing Office, 1962, pp. 1312-17. S9.12:13
      Part 2.
          This document contains the complete English and Spanish
      texts of notes exchanged between the United States ambassador to
      Bolivia, Ben S. Stephansky, and the Bolivian minister of foreign
      affairs and worship, His Excellency Jose Fellman Velarde. The
      acceptance of these notes by both governments created the legal
      base upon which all subsequent Peace Corps activity in Bolivia
      would be founded. This agreement remained in force until the
      departure of Peace Corps from Bolivia in 1971.

564   ANDERSON, ANN. "A Clinic for Penas". Journal of Practical
      Nursing, 16 (March 1966): 33-4.
          The work of two volunteer nurses, Nancy Crawford and Mary
      Cross, in the Bolivian Altiplano village of Penas, is presented,
      with photographs used to illustrate both living conditions of the
      region and community health work being done. The article also
      provided background on the health problems of Bolivia. Their
      placement in Penas provided primary health care to a group of
      several villages as part of a national effort in this direction.

565   "Bolivia: Impetus is to East in Land Beset by Geography".
      S19.11/2:3/3. Peace Corps Volunteer, 3, n.4 (February 1965):
      8-16.
          Introduced by an article by Richard Griscom, Deputy Director
      of Peace Corps/Bolivia, this group of eight short articles covers
      the involvement of volunteers in Bolivia's resettlement plans east
      of the Andes, in teaching science and nursing, and promoting
      agricultural development.

566   "Bolivia Volunteers Make a Go of Urban Job". Congressional
      Record, 109, p.8 (13 June 1963): 10811-12.
          An article which originally appeared in the Peace Corps
      Volunteer magazine, this report covers the work being done by five
      public health workers in the city of Sucre, Bolivia. Their tasks
      involved contracting families through a milk distribution program,
      the renovation of an orphanage, operating local clinics and
      broadcasting nutrition and public health information over the city
      radio stations in both Spanish and English. Their initial
      difficulties of being accepted and finding ways of adapting their
      skills to Bolivian needs are frankly discussed.

567   "Bolivian Miners Hold 4 Americans Hostage for Reds: 3
      Officials and Peace Corps Volunteer Kidnapped in Reprisal for
      Arrests". New York Times (8 December 1963): 1.
          Robert Fergerstrom, a member of Peace Corps/Bolivia, was
      among twenty-one persons taken hostage at Siglo Veinte, some 150
      miles south of La Paz. The action was take as a protest against
      the seizure by the Bolivian government of four labor leaders.

568   "Bolivian Tribute to Peace Corps Volunteer Sandra Smith".
       Congressional Record, 115, p.21 (3 October 1969): 28546.
       A reprint of an article originally appearing in the Miami
News of September 16, 1969, describing the tributes paid to Sandra
Smith of Peace Corps/Bolivia upon her death from a brain
hemorrhage at the age of twenty-three. Her posting was as a
teacher in a barrio school on the outskirts of La Paz. Extensive
quotations from the Bolivian press are included.

569   COHEN, ANDREW. "In The Andes, a Discovery of a Compromise Verb
       Tense". The Peace Corps Reader: 126-29. Washington, D.C.,
       Peace Corps, 1969.
       "Without a doubt the Incas adopted Quechua as their tongue
because they could not learn Aymara." With these words, the
author, a veteran of Peace Corps/Bolivia, begins his colorful
exploration of the perils of applying language training to actual
daily life in one's host country. Invoking such linguistic
problems as the dubitative potential tense, and suffixes which
change the geographical locale of action, this essay conveys the
frustrations of second language experiences in Corps life
extremely well.

570   "Corpsmen, Out!". Christian Science Monitor (1 June 1971):
       3.
       The first of over 100 Peace Corps Volunteers expelled from
Bolivia have begun to arrive in Lima, Peru. They tell of an
organized campaign by the Bolivian leftist extremists to discredit
the agency. Among charges made were that Corps was spying on
Bolivia for the CIA, conducting sterilization and birth-control
programs, and spreading drug addiction among teenagers.

571   "Costa Rica Offers to Take Ousted Peace Corps Unit".
       Congressional Record, 117, p.15 (10 June 1971): 19326.
       A news report from the Washington Daily News of May 26,
1971, on the offer by President Jose Figueres of Costa Rica to
accept any of the members of the recently ousted Peace Corps
Bolivia group who wish to serve in Costa Rica. When Bolivia's
military government requested the departure of Corps due to
pressure by Marxist elements at the national university, Figueres
stated that a plane of the Costa Rican national airline would be
sent to La Paz to bring its personnel to a new host country. Of
the 107 persons expelled, only half would be in a position to
accept this invitation due to completion of service. Senator
Church of Idaho asked that this item be inserted in the Record as
an example of the value of Corps work and to "confound the fervid
anti-Yankees." 93 volunteers were already at work in Costa Rica
when this offer as made.

572   DENNISON, EDWARD S. "Bolivia". National Geographic (September 1964): 314-19.
       A member of Peace Corps/Bolivia recounts an episode of his service involving a visit to a village near Cochabamba, reluctant sheep, and agricultural customs. The article is illustrated with photographs of the author and his partner carrying sheep, bargaining in the Cochabamba market, and an overview of the village accepting the sheep as an effort to improve local livestock.

573   ELLIOTT, LAWRENCE. "All We Had to Give was Ourselves". Redbook, 127 (May 1966): 58-9, 127-31.
       An account of the work done by Don and Linda Bullock at the Los Negros leper colony near Cochabamba, Bolivia. Conditions at the colony are graphically described, along with attitudinal problems regarding leprosy presented by Bolivian culture. The assignment was from 1962 to 1964. The article also conveys a vivid feeling of what it meant to be a part of one of the earliest groups of volunteers sent to Latin America.

574   ELLIS, SUSAN. "Peace Corps Forestry". American Forests and Forest Life, 77 (May 1971): 36-8.
       Forestry is among the most-requested skills for the host nations in which Peace Corps serves, as many of them move to address issues such as reforestation, watershed management, and wildlife conservation through national parks. Specific skills asked for are forest pathology, forest management, wood utilization, fire control, forest recreation, and instructors for schools of forestry. In some cases, volunteers will be their host nation's only trained foresters. A joint plan with the Food and Agriculture Organization of the United Nations has been at the base of many countries' requested for volunteers. An example from Peace Corps/Bolivia for the reforestation of the Altiplano illustrates the scope of projects in which volunteers may find themselves involved.

575   HAVERTY, KEVIN. "A Cliff-Hanging Tale of a Sunday Ascent to La Paz". S19.11/2:4/10. Peace Corps Volunteer, 4, n.10 (August 1966): 12-3.
       A vivid description of truck travel through the Bolivian Andes by a member of Peace Corps returning to station.

576   HEATH, DWIGHT B. "The Emerging Volunteer Subculture in Bolivia". The Cultural Frontiers of the Peace Corps, Robert B. Textor, ed. Cambridge, M.I.T. Press, 1966: 271-97.
       As training officer, project consultant and visiting lecturer, the author of this chapter was intimately involved with Peace Corps/Bolivia from its inception in 1962. This analysis of the subculture evolved by the volunteers of Bolivia One, Two and Three between 1962 and 1965 exhibits certain patterns which are present in the volunteer culture: energetic activity, egoistic altruism, proud humility, local identification, realistic idealism, planned expediency, situational austerity and organizational loyalty. Initial programming difficulties such as

misassignment and background information on Bolivian geography and
anthropology are also included. As one of the few attempts to
define the life of Peace Corps in categories suitable for
comparative analysis, this article provides a window into exactly
what it meant--and means--to be a volunteer.

577   HERBERGER, JAMES P. "Bees for Bolivia Peace Corps Project".
       Gleanings in Bee Culture, 91 (September 1963): 540.
           A volunteer stationed in Santa Cruz in the eastern lowlands
of Bolivia describes the arrival of four hives of bees as part of
the Heifer Project, Inc. contribution to improving Bolivian
agriculture. Having studies apiculture, the author used the bees
for demonstrations at 4-S clubs (equivalent to the American 4-H)
near the town of Cochabamba, as well as taking some to his posting
at the Agricultural Experiment Station at Santa Cruz. Hives were
used as club projects and proved popular and effective.

578   "Iowa Peace Corps Nurse Tells of Work in Bolivia".
       Congressional Record, 110, p.4 (7 August 1964): 18533.
           This article, reprinted from the Des Moines, Iowa Sunday
Register relates the experiences of Priscilla Buaguess, a Peace
Corps nurse serving as a rural public health worker in the
community of Coroico, Bolivia. Living with another volunteer, her
efforts at coping with endemic tuberculosis, being paid in
chickens, and doing inoculations to curb yellow fever form a
graphic account of ingenuity and growth. Buaguess is one of 138
volunteers currently working in the fields of nursing,
agricultural extension programs, and education in Bolivia.

579   "10 Million Youngsters Are Benefiting from a Child-feeding
       Program Called Operation Ninos". Today's Health, 42 (September
       1964): 58-61.
           A profile of the Alliance for Progress program aimed at
reducing the poverty and malnutrition facing many of Latin
America's children. Administered by the Agency for International
Development, in some countries Peace Corps volunteers assist in
the management and distribution of the school breakfasts and food
supplies. A volunteer in Bolivia relates her experiences with the
program, and an example of a girl from the slums of Chile is used
to illustrate potential improvements.

580   "RPCV Reflects on Return to Bolivian Village". AA1.13:4/1.
       InterACTION, 4, n.1 (October 1975): 8, 13.
           After an absence of seven years, two members of Peace
Corps/Bolivia who had worked in agriculture and public health in
the village of Tiquina on Lake Titicaca returned to their site.
The changes in the community and the survivals--and failures--of
projects they had begun are frankly discussed.

581   SELBY, JOHN. "The Role of the Peace Corps in U. S. Foreign
      Policy". IDOC Bulletin, 40 (February 1976): 7-12.
      This is the complete text of a paper read at the Third
Session of the B. Russell Tribunal II in Rome on January 11, 1976.
Stating that "one of the primary purposes of the Peace Corps is to
paint onto the United States' image abroad a more human facade",
Selby reviews the creation of the Peace Corps and links it to
other organizations such as AID. Volunteers working with host
institutions often find themselves working for groups founded at
the urging of or supported by American interests. The gap between
the actuality of Corps life overseas and the mythologies spread
about it in the American media is also noted. Accepting the three
aspects of the role of a volunteer-high-level cultural and
linguistic proficiency, a low economic level of life and middle-
level job experiences--as valid, "the question that then arises of
who is determining the direction of . . . changes and in whose
interests they are taking place" is then examined, with most of
the agencies with which Corps works being heavily pilloried.
Examples are offered from the author's own experiences as a member
of Peace Corps/Bolivia, ranging from a fiasco with Bolivian tin
miners to the final expulsion of Corps from that nation in 1971.
Selby was one of the last group to serve in Bolivia, and his views
offer a useful historical counterweight to the information
provided by Peace Corps Washington during the Vietnam era.

582   WEXLER, PAUL, ed. Beginning Aymara (A Course for English
      Speakers). Seattle: Washington University, 1967.
      A manual compiled in 1966-1967 by a team of Bolivian
nationals for use in training Peace Corps personnel bound for
Bolivia in the rudiments of the Aymara language. Following an
historical introduction to the language and its importance in
regional cultural development (in both contemporary and colonial
times) lessons present gradually more complex subjects with
vocabulary, grammatical analysis, substitution and completion
drills and dialogues. With a mass of related literature reaching
back to 1603, Aymara poses challenges to speakers themselves
bilingual in Spanish and thus may not have addressed many
technical points. Researchers should note that this manual has
been entered in the ERIC database as document ED 019630.

583   U. S. Department of State. Botswana. Peace Corps. Agreement
      Effected by Exchange of Notes Sighed at Gaborone May 14, 1971.
      United State Treaties and other International Agreements
      Series, n.7145, vol. 22, p. 1, Washington, D.C.: 1025-29.
      S9.12:22 Part 1.
      This document contains the full texts of notes given between
W. Kennedy Cromwell, ambassador to Botswana, and His Excellency
Seretse Khama, president of the Republic of Botswana, setting
forth the legal basis upon which the Peace Corps would come to
that country.

584   ALVERSON, HOYT. "Peace Corps Volunteers in Rural Botswana".
       Human Organization 36, n.3 (Fall 1977):   274-81.
            From June 3 to June 29, 1974, Hoyt Alverson conducted a
       study of Peace Corps volunteers in Botswana relating to their
       problems of cultural adaptation. The present article analyses the
       results of this work, focusing on two aspects of the information
       obtained: reasons for ineffectiveness of volunteers and the
       anthropological methodology by which this data was gathered.
       Chief among the difficulties experienced by the volunteers was
       misinterpretation of behavior patterns among the Tswana into
       American categories. Examples of this include approaches to time,
       presentation of face, the use of language inflections to mark
       social status (and thereby influence behavior), opinions regarding
       space and privacy, the conception of an "oral contract", intimacy,
       the considerations of hospitality and sociability. The author
       makes no recommendations as to possible remedies for such
       problems, as they are considered part of inevitable stresses in
       adapting to a different social milieu.

585   "American Teacher in Botswana Learns Too". Encore, 61
       (12 September 1977):   23.
            The recounting of experiences by Janet Rudolph, a black
       volunteer posted to the Maun Secondary School in northern Botswana
       as an English teacher. Cross-cultural adventures included several
       proposals of marriage (which she countered by making her bride
       price 1,000 cattle, too rich for her suitors to pay), setting an
       example for the local girls that life might hold new
       possibilities, and enduring an examination by elders who could not
       believe that she was, in fact, twenty-six, unmarried, with no
       children, and unable to speak Setswana.

586   "At Age 63, Peace Corps Volunteer from Vermont Manages Vast AG
       Complex in Botswana". Congressional Record, 119, p.28 (7
       November 1973):   36121-122.
            A reprinted article from ACTION News covering the work being
       done by Ellwyn Miller at the government agricultural complex at
       Sebele, Botswana. After working as a manager of the research
       division, Miller was promoted to administer the entire operation.
       Functions of the program are experimentation in dry-land farming,
       running a rural training center for farmers and conducting classes
       at the Botswana Agricultural College. Crop and livestock
       supervisors work closely with Miller. At the time of writing,
       there were eighty-five volunteers serving in Botswana.

587   "Close-Up: Botswana: A Diversity of Talent to Meet a Critical
       Need". AA1.10:1/11. Transition, 1, n.11 (December 1972):   28-
       32.
            An overview of the highly diverse Peace Corps program in the
       southern African nation of Botswana. Expanding from a modest
       beginning in 1967 to 65 categories in 1972, Peace Corps volunteers
       are working in fields as diverse as teaching, water resources
       management, community development, nursing and pest control.

588 GIBSON, HELEN. "Peace Corps Volunteer's Life in Botswana: Hard, but Happy". <u>Christian Science Monitor</u> (15 December 1983): 76.
An interview with Sam Miller, a member of Peace Corps Botswana serving in the town of Shashi as part of a government plan to expand and support the crafts industry. He recounts his first months of adjusting to both Setswana, living conditions, and the artistic issues of advising on traditional craft styles.

589 "Mr. and Mrs. Peace Corps Volunteers in Africa". <u>American Journal of Nursing</u>, 74 (March 1974): 394.
The activities of three registered nurses serving in the Peace Corps in the Republic of Botswana, in southern Africa are described. Two of them are working as nursing instructors at the National Health Institute in Gaberone while the third is a travelling public health nurse, termed "the needle nurse" by the Batswana, based on the eastern village of Serowe. Their husbands are also serving in the country. Included in their duties are practicums in surgical nursing, inoculations of school children, operation of "bush clinics", teaching family planning, nutrition, hygiene and first aid, and organizing the library of the National Health Institute.

590 "The Peace Corps in Botswana". <u>Congressional Record</u>, 114, p.18 (26 July 1968): 23497-498.
A letter from the Honorable Q. K, Masire, Acting President and Minister for Development of the Republic of Botswana to Senator Bartlett of Alaska, detailing the views of that government on the work done by the first group of volunteers to serve there. Accomplishments mentioned include establishment of a handicrafts centre and the invention of a hand-operated washing machine which could be made from local materials. Many of the members of Botswana I requested an extension of service. A larger and more expanded group of volunteers has been requested by the government.

591 U. S. Department of State. <u>Peace Corps. Setswana: Communication and Culture Handbook</u>. Washington, D.C.: 1979.
Based upon the experiences of members of Peace Corps/Botswana, twenty-five lessons present numerous aspects of Tswana culture through dialogues and social situations. A glossary of English and Setswana and picture dictionary are provided. The full text is available on the ERIC database as document ED 205 046.

592 U. S. Department of State. <u>Peace Corps. Setswana: Grammar Handbook</u>. Washington, D.C.: 1979.
A text of fifteen units with descriptions of the basic structure and patterns of Setswana, intended for use with volunteers serving in that country. Each unit introduces a point of grammar followed by oral and written exercises. Verb reference charts and a Setswana and English dictionary are also provided. Full text is available on the ERIC database as document ED 205 044.

593   U. S. Department of State. <u>Peace Corps. Setswana: Special</u>
        <u>Skills Handbook</u>. Washington, D.C.: 1979.
            This volume is a collection of readings in both English and
        Setswana providing data on the culture and problems of Botswana,
        development and natural resources, agriculture, livestock and
        health. The full text is available on the ERIC database as
        document ED 205 045.

594   U. S. Department of State. <u>Peace Corps. Setswana: Teacher's</u>
        <u>Handbook</u>. Washington, D.C.: 1979.
            A guide to native speakers of the language of Botswana who
        will be serving as instructors for Peace Corps volunteers. Course
        organization and philosophy, structure of the handbooks on
        grammar, special skills and communication and culture and teaching
        techniques are presented. The full text is entered on the ERIC
        database as document ED 305 047.

595   U. S. Department of State. <u>Brazil. Peace Corps Program.</u>
        <u>Agreement Effected by Exchange of Notes Signed at Rio de</u>
        <u>Janeiro November 11, 1961</u>. United States Treaties and Other
        International Agreements, n. 4909, vol. 12, p. 3, Washington,
        D. C.: 3102-06. S9.12:12 Part 3.
            This document contains the full texts of notes given between
        the Brazilian minister of foreign affairs, Francisco Clementino
        San Thiago Dantas, and Lincoln Gordon, ambassador for the United
        States, creating the legal basis for the service of Peace Corps
        volunteers in Brazil. A later emendation of this agreement was
        written in 1973.

596   U. S. Department of State. <u>Brazil. Peace Corps Program.</u>
        <u>Agreement Effected by Exchange of Notes Signed at Brasilia</u> June
        <u>18, 1973</u>. United States Treaties and Other International
        Agreements Series, no. 7669, vol. 24, p. 2, Washington, D.C.:
        Government Printing Office, 1973, 1650-54. S9.12:24 Part 2.
            This document contains the exchange of notes resulting in a
        new Peace Corps agreement between the Federative Republic of
        Brazil and the United States. The chief differences between this
        agreement and its predecessor, Treaty 4909, lie in the provision
        that "The withdrawal of a Peace Corps volunteer can be requested
        at any time by the host country" and in the inclusion of an
        annual review meeting by both Corps officials and Brazilian
        representatives, as well as the provision to volunteers by the
        Brazilian government of special identification documents. This
        agreement was in force until the departure of Peace Corps from
        Brazil in 1981.

597   "Brazil: Peace Corps Expands In A Giant Land". Peace Corps
      Volunteer, 3, n.11 (September 1965): 5-19. S19.11/2:3/11.
         A collection of ten articles introduced by the Corps Repre-
      sentative for Brazil which covers everything from road building in
      the Amazon Basin to population control and community development.
      Together, they provide a fascinating look at Peace Corps personnel
      engaged in coping with the gargantuan process of Brazilian
      modernization.

598   "Librarians for Brazil". Wilson Library Bulletin, 38 (February
      1964): 459.
         This news note reports that the government of Brazil has
      requested the services of six Peace Corps librarians for positions
      at the new University of Brasilia. Duties will include
      establishing a central reference library, an education library,
      and a collection for the University's Science Institute.
      Instruction in library science will also be a part of their
      assignment. An outline of training topics is included.

599   FALLERT, ROBERT. "900 Miles From Any Buddy". Peace Corps
      Volunteer, 2, n.11 (September 1964): 6-7. S19.11/2:2/11.
         The only Peace Corps volunteer in the Amazon region of
      Brazil, some 900 miles from his nearest compatriot, discusses his
      work as a forester and instructor at a research station and trade
      school. The goals are all connected with the establishment of a
      successful regional forestry industry. Bathing in rivers full of
      piranhas and coping with "a serenade from the jungle creatures
      that would shame a Tarzan movie" provide background details.

600   GOODSELL, JAMES NELSON. "Girl Team Project". Christian
      Science Monitor (18 May 1964): 9.
         In the San Cristovao section of Rio de Janeiro, a group of
      20 Peace Corps women is engaged in community development work.
      This area contains several of the favelas of Rio, and their
      populations are the target of health, sanitation and community
      action projects. Known as the Guanabara project--after the
      Brazilian state which encompasses Rio--this effort is one of five
      areas of Brazil in which volunteers are concentrated, with
      scattered postings to interior locations as well as urban sites.
      The women of Guanabara have been warmly received by the favela
      residents and, while admitting to doubts about their
      contributions, relish each day's challenges. George Coleman,
      country representative for Brazil, acknowledges that briefings on
      the culture and customs of that nation must reflect current
      conditions as well as historical background.

601   HOLTZMANN, WAYNE H.   The Peace Corps in Brazil: An Evaluation
       of the Sao Francisco Valley Project.   Final Report, Contract
       PC-(W) 116 Between The Peace Corps and the University of Texas.
       Austin: International Office, University of Texas, 1966.
          "In the spring of 1962, plans were made to train over a
       hundred Americans to serve as Volunteers in nearly two dozen
       isolated communities scattered throughout the range of the Sao
       Francisco River" (p. 219).   These were the members of Brazil II,
       and this project provided an opportunity for one of the first
       large research projects involving the Peace Corps.   Project design
       called for selected control and experimental communities to be
       assessed prior to the arrival of the volunteers, halfway through
       their residence, and following their completion of service two
       years later.   The initial assignments of the 91 arrivals to this
       region of northeastern Brazil were highly varied, ranging from
       home economics and medical nursing to farming and electrical
       repair.   Initial data surveys later proved to have been taken
       without careful checking as to local resources actually available.

          The final report begins with a description of the training
       given to the members of Brazil II in preparation for their work in
       the Sao Francisco Valley, followed by a detailed plan of the
       original research design and a history of the region.   A survey of
       each individual community involved in highland, coastal and
       northeast zones of the valley drainage system, reviewing actual
       contributions made by the volunteers posted there, comprises the
       bulk of the work.   Chapters on interview data from 57 volunteers,
       taken six months after arrival on site, parallel interviews from
       local people assessing the Peace Corps impact and scales used to
       predict field performance provide further details of the project.
       A summary chapter illustrates that screening of applicants to
       Corps can be made efficient through inclusion of psychological
       variables not presently being employed in the selection process.
       After the first period of adjustment, a high degree of mobility
       from sites became necessary, and by the end of the two years, only
       20 of the original 91 volunteers were still at their first
       assigned communities.   Factors contributing to Corps frustration
       included an inaccurate preliminary survey of the region, while the
       presence of a common language and culture throughout Brazil made
       cultural adjustment easier.   This study stands as an excellent
       window into a time when the Peace Corps was new and finding its
       own techniques.   Researchers interested in the issue of Peace
       Corps and community development may wish to consult a similar
       study done on Peace Corps Peru by the Department of Anthropology
       at Cornell.

602   MUKAVITZ, SUSAN. "I was a Med Tech in Brazil's Back Country".
       Medical Laboratory Observer, 10 (June 1978): 33-42.
          An engaging account by a member of Peace Corps/Brazil of her
       life and professional challenges serving in the city of Montes
       Claros, 600 miles northwest of Rio de Janeiro. Details on the
       public health problems and supply difficulties of the area are
       included, together with accounts of training local counterparts
       and improving diagnostic procedures. Photographs by the author
       illustrate the types of communities served and the clinic staff,
       as well as the countryside of interior Brazil. The author served
       from 1971 to 1973.

603   "Peace Corps Librarians Get Intensive Training". Library
       Journal, 89 (November 15, 1964): 4490-91.
          The training program being conducted at the University of
       Wisconsin-Madison for the six librarians who will be serving at
       the University of Brasilia is reviewed. Topics included in the
       curriculum are organization of university libraries, librarianship
       in Brazil, bibliographic resources and applications of the Dewey
       classification system. A practicum at both the Milwaukee and
       Madison campuses and the John Crerar Library at the University of
       Chicago is also part of the training schedule. Participating as
       training staff are faculty members from the University of
       Wisconsin, New York University and the University of Illinois, as
       well as Dr. Abner Vicentini of the University of Brasilia. The
       names of the volunteers and their library schools complete the
       article.

604   WATKINS, CAROLE. "Peace Corps Parteira". American Journal of
       Nursing, 70 (October 1970): 2160-63.
          Carol Watkins recounts a situation during her service as a
       health services volunteer in the sertao country of northeast
       Brazil when she was forced to act as midwife. Attention is paid to
       local beliefs and practices of medical care and the strategies
       used to instruct the people in alternative methods.

605   "Working in the Hills of Rio". Peace Corps Volunteer, 3, n.2
       (December 1964): 12-13. S19.11/2:3/2.
          A photo essay describing the involvement of twenty women of
       Peace Corps/Brazil as visitadoras (community health nurses) in the
       urban slums of Rio de Janeiro.

606   U. S. Department of State. Peace Corps: Agreement Between the
       United States of America and Burundi Effected by Exchange of
       Notes Dated at Bujumbura August 31, 1982. Treaties and Other
       International Acts Series 10465. Washington, D.C.: Government
       Printing Office, 1985. S9.10:10465.
          The full texts of the aides-memoires exchanged between the
       ministry of foreign affairs and cooperation of the Republic of
       Burundi and the United States Embassy at Bujumbura formalizing the
       proposed creation of Peace Corps/Burundi. Legal guarantees and
       rights extended to both staff and volunteers are clearly spelled
       out.

607   U. S. Department of State. Cameroon, Peace Corps Program.
       Agreement Effected by Exchange of Notes Signed at Yaounde July
       23 and September 10, 1962. United States Treaties and Other
       International Agreements Series, n.5171, vol. 13, p.2,
       Washington, D.C.: Government Printing Office, 1962, 2114-19.
       S9.12:13 Part 2.
            The full text in both French and English of notes exchanged
       between Charles K. Moffly, acting charge d'Affaires of the U. S.
       Embassy to Cameroon, and His Excellency Nzo Ekhah-Nghaky, deputy
       minister of foreign affairs of the Federal Republic of Cameroon.
       These documents comprise the basic legal agreement between the
       host nation and the United States which permitted Peace Corps
       members to serve in Cameroon. This treaty has remained in force
       since its original adoption.

608   HENRY, C. F. "Peace Corps in West Cameroon". Christianity
       Today, 9 (1 January 1965): 29.
            This article is both a criticism of the assignment of Peace
       Corps teachers to mission-related schools in Cameroon and
       retraction of objections printed in an earlier editorial comment
       on August 28, 1964. These latter included the charges that six
       new schools were to open with total Peace Corps staffing
       (including headmasters) and that Peace Corps was bringing pressure
       on the schools to accept volunteers they neither needed nor
       wanted. Further investigation showed these charges to be false.
       The chief matter of dispute here is the relationship of church and
       state, with the writer objecting to the usage of public funds to
       pay Peace Corps teachers serving at sectarian institutions.
       Charles Woodward, associate director of the Corps, responds that
       although volunteers may at times be posted to religiously
       affiliated institutions, "this is invariably because in the
       specific situation this is the best, if not the only, way to carry
       out our primary function-- helping the people in that community to
       improve their own lives."

609   MORETON, REBECCA L., et.al. Cameroon Basaa. Washington, D.C.:
       Center for Applied Linguistics, 1968.
            This teaching manual for the language of the Basaa people of
       Cameroon was prepared by the Center for Applied Linguistics under
       Peace Corps contract in September, 1968. Its format is the
       "microwave" approach comprising many small units. The 265 which
       form this manual have been oriented to basic social and survival
       needs, with a special section for those volunteers who will be
       working in the health field. Researchers should note that this
       manual is also available as ERIC document 048593.

610   "'No Two Days Alike' Says PCV". AA1.13:1/4. InterACTION, 1,
       n.4 (January 1973): 4.
       Rich Munson, a member of Peace Corps/Cameroon, describes his
work in education for the Cooperative Department of West Cameroon.
His chief responsibility is to supply over 300 local organizations
with information as to their rights under the government system of
economic development. The cooperative system was designed and set
in place by the government in Yaounde, but many of the regional
people are unfamiliar with the concept. The groups focus on the
production of Arabic coffee, one of the nation's main export
crops. Munson also included information on his adaptation to his
host nation.

611   "Sacred Statue Returns Home". AA1.13:2/4. InterACTION, 2, n.4
       (January 1974): 1, 13.
       After seven years, the sacred Afo-A-Kom statue of the Kom
nations of the grasslands in Cameroon is being returned to its
place in the palace of the Fon in Bamenda. The article details
the story of the involvement of Craig and Merry Kinzelman, members
of Peace Corps/Cameroon, with the search for the stolen art work
and its subsequent location in the hands of a private dealer in
New York City.

612   U. S. Department of State. Central African Republic. Peace
       Corps. Agreement Effected by Exchange of Notes Signed at
       Bangui September 9 and November 24, 1966. United States
       Treaties and Other International Agreements Series, n. 6157,
       vol. 17, Washington, D.C.: Government Printing Office, 1968,
       2205-09. S9.12:17, Part 2.
       The complete French and English texts of documents given
between the American Ambassador, Claude G. Ross, and His
Excellency Colonel Jean Bedel Bokassa, president of the Central
African Republic, creating the legal basis for Peace Corps service
in that country.

613   "Central African Republic Decorates Peace Corps Coach".
       AA1.13:2/12. InterACTION, 2, n.12 (September, 1974): 3.
       President Jean-Bedal Bokassa of the Central African Republic
awarded the medal of: "Officer de la Reconnaisance de la
Republique Centrafricaine" to volunteer Lu Verne Grussing in a
ceremony at the presidential palace. Grussing had been serving as
coach of the national men's basketball team, which won over
Senegal in the African championship tournament held in Bangui in
April, 1974. The contingent of volunteers in the Central African
Republic was inaugurated with the arrival of Grussing's group in
August, 1972.

614   "Foreign Aid Appropriations, 1979". <u>Congressional Record</u>, 124,
       p.19 (14 August 1978): 25916-19.
           This text of debates on foreign aid appropriation covers the
       opposition to further funding of Peace Corps efforts in the
       Central African Empire due to the outrageous human rights record
       amassed by Jean Bedel Bokassa, self-styled "Emperor" of that
       nation. Representative Ashbrook of Ohio introduced this
       amendment, with Representatives Conte, Fenwick, McHugh and Bonker
       rising in opposition. Their points were based upon the basic
       statement that the Peace Corps was never intended to be an arm of
       United States foreign policy. Two articles demonstrating
       Bokassa's megalomania and extravagant style of living are
       included. The amendment was not passed.

615   <u>Voices of Experience in Central America: Former Peace Corps
       Volunteers Insights into a Troubled Region</u>. Washington, D.C.:
       National Council of Returned Peace Corps Volunteers, 1985.
           Compiled by the Returned Peace Corps Volunteer Committee on
       Central America, this document reports on a survey taken of some
       2,600 former Corps personnel from that area. Five questions were
       addressed: the main community problems of one's former host area
       and the role, if any, played by the government in alleviating
       them: awareness of instances of individuals being forced to
       emigrate, becoming victims of violence or disappearing without
       trace: United States misconceptions of the host nations and media
       coverage: assessment of U. S. foreign policy actions during the
       period of service and their reception by host nationals, and what
       recent policy initiatives taken by the United States were most and
       least positive. Countries covered in this document are Belize,
       Costa Rica, El Salvador, Guatemala, Honduras, Nicaragua and
       Panama. Chapters are composed of the questions and representative
       answers drawn from the respondents and United States statistical
       information used in the text and its sources. The Committee
       intended the report to serve to educate the public regarding the
       realities of Central America as well as to tap the experience of
       the volunteers, feeling that "if it is worth sending Peace Corps
       Volunteers to Central America during a 22-year period to aid the
       people there, it is worth learning . . . whether the work has
       brought lasting results" (p. i).

616   U. S. Department of State. <u>Ceylon. Peace Corps Program.
       Agreement Effected by Exchange of Notes Signed at Colombo
       November 21, 1962</u>. United States Treaties and Other
       International Agreements Series, no. 5245, vol. 13, Washington,
       D.C.: 2722-28. S9.12:13 Part 3.
           The complete texts, in both the language of Ceylon and
       English, of notes exchanged between Francis Willis, United States
       ambassador, and the Honorable Sirimavo R. D. Bandaranaike, prime
       minister of Ceylon, laying the fundamental understandings upon
       which Peace Corps service in that nation could be constructed.
       This agreement remained in force until the departure of volunteers
       from Ceylon in 1964, and served as the basis for subsequent
       returns in 1967 and 1983.

617 "Ceylon Group is Welcome Despite Row in Parliament". Peace
Corps Volunteer, 1, n.1 (November 1962): 24. S19.11/2:1/1.
On September 6, 1962, thirty-five volunteers arrived in
Colombo, Sri Lanka to take up teaching and teacher education
positions through-out the island. Attacks in Parliament on the
government (lead by a Communist member) for inviting Corps made
their entry front page news. As part of their service, each
volunteer will spend one month of each year at Ceylon's work
camps, organized to carry out the concept of sramadana (the
voluntary giving of one's labor).

618 The Peace Corps Again: A New Invasion of Ceylon. Colombo:
Tribune Publications, 1967.
This pamphlet was printed upon the occasion of the return to
Sri Lanka of the U. S. Peace Corps in 1967, and "focusses
attention on the dangers of allowing a contingent of the Peace
Corps to operate in any country." Among the charges leveled at
the agency is one that would be heard again and again--that some
members of each group were in fact agents of the Central
Intelligence Agency, bent upon subversive acts against the host
nation government. From the very first page, the qualifications
of the volunteers are attacked, and examples are offered of
purported Peace Corps actions in other host nations, notably India
and Ethiopia. The authors of the pamphlet are adamant that Sri
Lanka does not need the Peace Corps, and that its entry was a
proposition that the government dared not refuse for fear of
offending the United States. Volunteers are seen to have been
imposed upon the island for furthering the foreign policies of the
United States. This text serves as an unusual example of the
types of resistance and stereotyping with which volunteers in may
countries were forced to contend in the years when the image of
"the ugly American" foreign expert was rampant in the Third
World.

619 U. S. Department of State. Chad. Peace Corps. Agreement
Effected by Exchange of Notes Signed at Fort Lamy August 31,
1966. United States Treaties and Other International
Agreements Series, no. 6094, vol. 17, p. 1, Washington, D.C.:
1384-89. S9.12:17 Part 1.
The complete texts of documents exchanged between Brewster
H. Morris, ambassador of the United States, and His Excellency
Antoine Bangui, Chad minster of coordination, which created the
legal framework upon which all subsequent Peace Corps work would
in Chad would be based. This agreement remained in force until
the departure of Corps from Chad in 1979. Both French and English
tests are provided.

620 ABSI, SAMIR ABU and ANDRE SINAUD. Spoken Chad Arabic.
Washington, D.C.: Peace Corps, 1966.
The texts of one hundred lessons aimed at promoting both
listening comprehension of the sounds of Arabic as spoken in Chad
and active practice in using the dialect in structured situations.
All transcriptions follow a phonetic alphabet. The full text can
be located under the ERIC document number ED144356.

621   "Chad To Get PCVs". Peace Corps Volunteer, 4, n.6 (April
       1966):   4. S19.11/2:4/6.
            Thirty-seven volunteers are scheduled to arrive in the
       Republic of Chad in the fall of 1966 for assignments including
       land reclamation, public health, nursing and education.

622   "Peace Corps Volunteer Brings Pit Silos to Chad Farmers".
       AA1.13:2/7. InterACTION, 2, n.7 (April 1974):   1-2.
            A report covering the success of introducing pit storage for
       animal fodder to the farmers of Chad. Prior to the experiment,
       cattle feed had not been sufficient to last through the dry
       season, resulting in substantial loss of stock. Following the
       success of the pit silos project in the Canton of Bessad, the
       Chadian government has endorsed the idea for application
       throughout the nation. Volunteer Jim Diamond was responsible for
       the first nineteen silos which began the project.

623   "Pit Silos: Silage For Livestock". AA1.13:2/11. InterACTION,
       2, n.11 (August 1974):   3-4.
            This is a reprint of an article written by James Diamond, a
       volunteer in Chad from 1971 to 1973 who served as an agricultural
       extension agent. Among his projects was the construction of pit
       silos to preserve feed for livestock into the dry season. This
       technical discussion provides background on the production of
       silage and the practical details of construction and maintenance.
       An expanded version of this article in booklet form was made
       available to other volunteers through the ICE office of Peace
       Corps.

624   THAYER, JAMES E. and JULIEN MARABY. Sara Intermediate Course.
       Washington, D.C.: Peace Corps, 1966.
            Created at the Intensive Language Training Center at Indiana
       University in September, 1966 under Peace Corps contract, this
       manual on the Sara language of the Republic of Chad is intended to
       be used following the completion of a basic three hundred hours of
       instruction. Forty lessons include both cultural materials and
       vocabulary. Full text is available from the ERIC database as
       document ED 152 113.

625   RAULIN, GEORGE. Kanouri. Washington, D.C.: 1966.
            During the training given to volunteers bound for Niger and
       Chad at San Francisco State College in the summer of 1966, it
       became necessary to familiarize them with the Kanouri language of
       that region. As no linguistic materials were available, the
       present text was created for the twelve-week course. Format is
       intended to be used in a classroom setting with a fluent native
       speaker of Kanouri as instructor. Transcriptions are in French,
       with translations in both French and English. The full text has
       been entered on the ERIC database as document ED131695.

626   U. S. Department of State. Chile. Peace Corps Program.
       Agreement Effected by Exchange of Notes Signed at Santiago
       October 3 and 4, 1962. United State Treaties and Other

International Agreements Series, no. 5199, vol. 13, p. 2,
Washington, D.C.:   2307-11.   S9.12:13 Part 2.
　　The complete texts in both Spanish and English of notes
exchanged between the Chiliean acting minister of foreign
relations, Sotero del Rio Gundian, and Charles W. Cole, United
States ambassador, forging the basis for entrance of Peace Corps
personnel for service in the Republic of Chile.

627　　BOEGLI, JANET CLAIRE. "My Life As A Peace Corps Girl".
　　　　Catholic Digest, 27 (August, 1983): 19-24.
　　Janet Boegli was part of the first group of volunteers to go
to Chile and served in the southern settlement of Rio Negro as a
community development worker. Her account includes group training
at Notre Dame, in-country briefings by local officials, and
adapting to rural Chilean life and customs. Of particular
interest is her attempt at improving nutrition through sharing a
recipe for apple pie. Her account provides a brief if thoughtful
look at one of the earliest Peace Corps projects in South
America.

628　　"Chile". S19.11/2:1/12. Peace Corps Volunteer, 1, n.12
　　　　(October 1963): 10-18.
　　A collection of brief articles and sketches by members of
Peace Corps/Chile covering their projects, problems and learning
experiences. Typical assignments in Chile include teaching,
health care, housing development and business cooperatives. A
varied look at the first two years of Peace Corps work in Chile.

629　　"Chile Team Ends Grueling Tour". AA1.13:1/4. InterACTION, 1,
　　　　n.4 (January 1973): 5.
　　A brief survey of a recent scheduled tour of the United
States by the Chilean National Basketball Team, coached by PCV Dan
Peterson, formerly coach at the University of Delaware. The
objectives were to promote the development of the sport in Chile,
as well as to prepare for the Pan American Games in 1975 and to
gain experience for the players. Sports-related assignments from
other nations are also mentioned.

630　　"A Conservationist In Chile". American Forests and Forest
　　　　Life, 75 (April 1969): 24-5.
　　In 1968, a request was received at the Peace Corps head
quarters from the government of Chile, asking for volunteers with
experience in forest management and national parks and recreation
to assist in preparing plans for that country's park system.
Although large areas had been designated as refuges and set aside,
no general concept for their utilization had been drawn up. This
news item notes the work of one of these volunteers, Gary
Wetterberg, in the Vicente Perez Rosales Park in the Chilean Lake
District. Several striking photos are included.

631   CRAIG, MARY E.   "Person to Person".   Social Action, 30 (January
       1964):   24-8.
       A reflection by a volunteer home economist and nutritionist
from Chile IV on her experiences in that country and the personal
sense of growth and community she experienced there.   A re-
examination of commitment to service is a main theme of her
essay.

632   DIUGUID, LEWIS H.   "Chile Still Wants U. S. Peace Corps".   Los
       Angeles Times (20 January 1972):   28.
       The government of President Salvador Allende has increased
its request for Peace Corps volunteers.   Although the majority of
the members of Peace Corps/Chile are serving in the area of
forestry, specialists are also being requested in such fields as
electronics.   Involvement in community development has been
specifically prohibited.   Representative Donald Boucher, himself a
veteran of Peace Corps/Chile, reviews the history of the program.
Under President Eduardo Frei, in-country complement of volunteers
reached 400, before declining to an all-time low after the early
months of the Allende regime.   Fifty new volunteers are requested,
which will bring the total complement to seventy-six.

633   FARRAR, FRED.   "Peace Corps to Get Tough Test in Chile--Young
       Volunteers Undergo Stiff Training".   Chicago Tribune (7 August
       1961):
       The fourth Peace Corps project to go abroad was a group of
community development workers for the central valley of Chile.
This article reviews their training at Notre Dame University in
South Bend, Indiana and outlines their assignments in country.
The training curriculum is presented in detail, making this
unusual and a valuable picture of the earliest days of Peace Corps
training methods.

634   "International Understanding and the Peace Corps in Chile".
       Hispania, 45 (May 1962):   301-2.
       This is a letter from one of the two directors of training
for the Chile I group of Peace Corps volunteers, detailing the
process of language learning to which they were exposed.   This
ranged from intensive classes in grammar and vocabulary at Notre
Dame University and work in the language laboratory there to in-
country conversational sessions.   All forty-five of the volunteers
achieved functional proficiency for their particular work
assignments by the end of the classes, and some have even acquired
a smattering of the Mapuche Indian tongue as well.   Most of them
are firm in their opinion that their children should grow up
knowing a language other than English.   Dr. Smith notes that these
are the same concerns that foreign language teachers have been
voicing for years without notable success.

635 MEYER, JAMES H. "Two-Way Sharing". <u>Christian Science Monitor</u>
   (21 May 1986): 31.
   "How does a volunteer communicate . . . that he and his host
   have lessons to learn from each other?" Drawing upon his
   experiences as a member of Peace Corps/Chile, James Meyer
   illustrates this process using daily incidents and adapting to a
   new culture slowly, providing time for each side to give and
   receive.

636 "PCV Makes Physics Lab Equipment from Inexpensive Materials".
   AA1.13:5/4. <u>InterACTION</u>, 5, n.4 (January 1977): 11.
   Working as a science instructor in a Chilean university with
   future high school teachers, Leroy Nawrot attempted to overcome
   the absence of adequate demonstration equipment by teaching his
   students how to construct their own. Examples of his class
   materials are given.

637 RAMSEY, PETER. "The Peace Corps: Sneakers and Levis For Me".
   <u>Harvest Years</u>, 9 (July 1969): 10, 25.
   "By their dress you shall know them . . . sneakers and levis
   have become synonymous with Peace Corps volunteers." A senior
   volunteer in the field of performing arts relates his experiences
   in Peace Corps/Chile as part of teaching drama at a university in
   Santiago and setting up drama groups and putting on a Spanish
   version of the Three Bears. Drama was seen as a way of stirring
   up new possibilities and stimulating the imagination. Older
   volunteers are seen as having much to contribute, including
   offering an example to younger volunteers of how to deal with
   frustration.

638 U. S. Department of State. <u>Colombia. Peace Corps. Agreement
   Signed At Bogota April 2, 1963</u>. United States Treaties and
   Other International Agreements Series, no. 8134, vol. 26, p. 2,
   Washington, D.C.: Government Printing Office, 1976, 1764-72.
   S9.12:26 Part 2.
   The complete texts in both English and Spanish of one of the
   first host country agreements ever written, establishing a legal
   basis for the presence of Peace Corps workers in Colombia.
   Representatives signatory to this basic agreement were Dr. Aurelio
   Camacho Rueda, minister of the interior of the Republic of
   Colombia, and Christopher B. Sheldon, director of Peace Corps/
   Colombia.

639 ASHABRANNER, BRENT. "Business Volunteers for Developing
   Countries". <u>Personnel</u>, 46 (January 1969): 68-70.
   Peace Corps' increasing use of volunteers with special
   skills and qualifications is examined, using the business
   administration workers of Peace Corps/Colombia as example. Known
   as the "Grupo Cali", their charge was to work with the University
   del Valle in the city and its small business sector. Among the
   aims of this project were the creation of courses for small
   business executives, expanding the flow to credit to this portion
   of the Colombian economy, and establishing technical and
   consulting services. Their success prompted the Colombians to

request a second group to expand the program to the cities of
Medellin, Pereire, Cartagena, Bucaramanga, and Pasto. Other
similar programs in Swaziland, Turkey, Peru and the Ivory Coast
are also noted.

640   BRAESTRUP, PETER. "Peace Corps Gets Colombia Project". New
       York Times (17 May 1961): 11.
          On May 16, 1961, President Kennedy announced the second
Peace Corps project--a program of rural development in Colombia.
Working with CARE under a plan recently completed by that agency
for the Colombian government, 64 volunteers will work in a variety
of areas, such as developing farm-to-market roads, stocking fish
ponds, livestock raising and digging wells. The President
remarked that he was impressed with the quality of the individuals
who had volunteered for the Corps thus far. Following two months
of training at Rutgers University, participants would receive one
further month of briefings at a school of community development
near Bogota.

641   "Casey in Colombia With Peace Corps". Congressional Record,
       123, p.3 (7 February 1977): 3875-76.
          A reprinted article from the Scranton Tribune describing the
volunteer work being done by Andy Casey in the city of Cartagena,
Colombia. Casey's work has included working with two cooperatives, one an agricultural organization and the other a
factory group, doing accountancy and teaching statistical methods.
Results include the purchase of a bus by one co-op and limited
loan capacities to members in the other. At the time, 143
volunteers were serving Colombia in various capacities ranging
from health and education to conservation and business programs
such as Casey's.

642   "Colombian Rebels Offer Talks on U. S. Hostage". Washington
       Post (25 September 1977): A24.
          An offer of negotiations has been received by a Colombian
radio network from a rebel group which has been holding a Peace
Corps botanist as hostage for the past seven months. Richard
Starr, 31, was abducted from his post in the town of La Macarena
in February, 1977. The group also claimed that Starr had
confessed to being an agent of the CIA, a charge heatedly denied
by ACTION officials in Washington, D.C.

643   COMSTOCK, GEORGE A. A Boomerang In A Peace Corps Attempt At
       Persuasion. RAND Report P-4032 (February 1969), Washington,
       D.C.: RAND Corporation, 1969.
          This investigative research report takes as its subject the
techniques used to advance the cause of educational television in
Colombia as part of the ETV project initiated with government
funding and Peace Corps staff assistance. The "boomerang" of the
title is of the indirect sort, producing a change in perception
incompatible with the desired result. In the Colombian case, it
can best be described as defense arousal of the host country
teachers. The basic criteria and expectations of the study are
outlined, and field methodologies stated. Concepts of "efficacy"

and "professionalism" were involved in a plan of motivation, with the television seen as either a small or large departure from traditional instruction. The results indicated that, when the ideas were presented as a great departure from established patterns of classroom activity, host country teachers claimed that their methods of teaching were very similar to the proposed addition. This attitude was a serious bar to compliance, indicating that no changes were necessary. The underlying mechanism was seen as a threat to professional identity and self-esteem. This indicates that arguments acceptable at one level of a society may completely backfire at their intended population. Hence, when the Peace Corps personnel introduced the ETV materials, their Colombian hosts indicated that, as it was already in use, they were willing to support it, but not to make extensive actual use of the technique. With the value of traditional methods in question, the reaction was one of defense and refusal.

644   COMSTOCK, GEORGE A. The Peace Corps Volunteer and Achieving Educational Change with New Media. RAND Report P-4174 (August 1969) Washington, D.C.: RAND Corporation, 1969.
        This research report covers the period from 1964 to 1966 in the educational television project set up in Colombia by Peace Corps volunteers. Specific recurrent issues encountered are discussed in the context of the overall impact of Corps person-nel on the Colombian systems of education. Colombia received eighty full-time volunteers to augment this programming on the national television system through following the required syllabus via expanded coverage to new schools. The majority of volunteers were in "utilization"--advising their Colombian counterparts as to the most effective applications of ETV in the classroom. The remainder were in production, installation and maintenance. It is the utilization group which provided the subject group for the paper. Background information on the Colombian teacher and teaching system is also provided. Increased use of field information occasioned a change in the second year of study. Through comparing schools with volunteers and those without, "the conclusion is that the 'help' helped" (p. 17). Precisely how ranged from repairs and better application of existing facilities to obtaining official aid. A final survey to determine the degree of self-sufficiency gained by Colombians in this program showed a shift in the second year from reliance on the volunteer to Colombian host groups, reflecting a new level of training and expertise not previously present.

645   FERRELL, DAVE. "New Outlook At La Picota". Peace Corps Volunteer, 3, n.2 (December 1964): 16-18. S19.11/2:3/2.
        At the La Picota prison in Bogota, Colombia, volunteers have been involved with a literacy program involving the use of educational television as well as classroom instruction. This article provides an overview of the project's history.

646   FREEMAN, FULTON. "Community Development in Colombia". Peace
        Corps, Pauline Madow, ed. New York: Wilson, 1964: 69-80.
           Written by the U. S. Ambassador to Colombia at the time of
      the arrival of the first volunteers of Colombia I, this article
      provides background information on the CARE--Peace Corps
      collaboration, the structure of the community development effort
      planned by the host government in 1959, and the nature of the
      partnerships involved. As the information included gives figures
      on the first year's results of schools built, reforestation
      programs and literacy classes and the like, it supplies a rare
      glimpse into the diversity behind the name "community
      development."

647   HATCH, JOHN. "Mr. John Was 'El Patron'". Peace Corps
        Volunteer, 3, n.8-9 (June-July 1965): 25-27.
           A volunteer who served in Colombia reflects on his term of
      service and notes approaches which would have been more effective.
      His posting was a community development worker in a barrio on the
      outskirts of the city of Medellin.

648   HELGESON, BEE. "Months and Miles Between". Parks and
        Recreation, 7 (December 1972): 20-22, 51-52.
           An interview with Fran Brewer, serving in the Peace Corps in
      Colombia, detailing the camp for street orphans she runs as part
      of the YMCA program in the city of Bogota. Her efforts at
      establishing outreach classes to the neighborhood in south Bogota
      where she was assigned as director of a community center are also
      detailed. The title refers to the fact that, in order to attend
      the 1972 Congress for Recreation and Parks in Anaheim, California,
      she hitchhiked and rode in various conveyances across Panama,
      Costa Rica, Nicaragua, El Salvador, Guatemala and Mexico.

649   KENNEDY, JOHN FITZGERALD. "Statement By the President
        Announcing A Peace Corps Project in Colombia". Public Papers
        of The Presidents: John F. Kennedy, 1961, Document 187, May
        16, 1961, pp. 187-8. GS4.113:961. Washington, D.C.,
        Government Printing Office, 1962.
           The formal announcement by President Kennedy of the second
      project of the Peace Corps, as requested by the Colombian
      government. Sixty-four volunteers were to be trained in the areas
      of small farming, handicrafts, sanitation and rural construction.
      Trainees will be drawn from those who successfully pass the Peace
      Corps qualifying examination, which Kennedy urged all interested
      persons to take on May 27, 1961. This announcement and its
      accompanying treaty of agreement marked the birth of Peace Corps
      activities in Latin America.

650 KUBIC, MILAN J. "Senor Ron". Peace Corps, Pauline Madow, ed.
New York: Wilson, 1964: 86-8.
Reprinted from the June 3, 1963 issue of Newsweek, this
article profiles the work done by volunteer Ronald Atwater of
Peace Corps/Colombia in the village of Lenguazaque sixty miles
from Bogota. Among his activities was the formation of a
marketing co-operative for locally made ruanas for the tourist
shops in the capital.

651 LA BELLE, TOM. "The Peace Corps in Colombia". Journal of
Health, Physical Education, and Recreation, 37 (November 1966):
57-9.
The role facing the Peace Corps in providing assistance to
the universities of Colombia in developing a programme of physical
education integrated with the established curriculum is discussed.
Case histories are included from the Universidad del Valle in Cali
and the Universidad Industrial de Santander in Bucaramanga,
providing detailed information on the structure of Colombian
higher education. Progress made between 1963 and 1966 in the area
of physical education is reviewed, with the plans gaining
increased acceptance at other schools.

652 "The News, Briefly". Christian Science Monitor (1 March 1969):
2.
A news report on a riot by approximately 500 students
against the U. S. Peace Corps in the Colombian city of Pereira.
Windows were broken, cars set afire and several policemen
injured.

653 "PC Nurses In Colombia Praised". AA1.13:4/12. InterACTION, 4,
n.12 (September 1976): 14.
A description of the range of work being done by nurses who
are serving as members of Peace Corps/Colombia by a Texas
journalist working with that state's nurses association. In 1976
she was invited to be a Peace Corps traveler, visiting trainees,
hospital-based nurses and volunteers working in village health
care. Duties performed by personnel include inoculations,
operating public health clinics and training nursing auxiliaries.

654 "PCV Instrumental in Preserving Colombia's Archaeological
Heritage". AA1.13:5/3. InterACTION, 5, n.3 (December 1976):
3, 6.
Serving in Colombia for four years, Carson Murdy has worked
with the government to investigate and preserve archaeological
sites in Tayrona National Park and on the island of Salamance on
the Caribbean coast. His surveys and publications have made the
public more aware of their heritage, as have the lectures Murdy
delivers at the Museum of Natural History in the city of Cali,
where he is director.

655   "PCV Works in Dental Hygiene". AA1.13:3/5. InterACTION, 3,
       n.5 (February 1976): 1.
          An account of the work done by a dental hygienist teaching
       at the Pontifica Universidad Javeriana in Bogota, Colombia. She
       stresses the uniqueness of her assignment and the types of
       patients and disorders treated, as well as commenting on being a
       volunteer in a semi-urban environment.

656   "Peace Corps Sets Up Program of Visits to Volunteers".
       American Journal of Nursing, 74 (May 1974): 817.
          In 1974, the Peace Corps inaugurated a program aimed famil-
       iarizing members of the professions with the actual conditions and
       challenges of volunteer life and experiences. Nurses, engineers,
       architects and city planners are sent to host countries for
       periods ranging from two to four weeks to meet and talk with
       volunteers in their respective fields. The goal of the program is
       to "prepare the representative to answer questions from potential
       volunteers". A visit by a nurse to Colombia is used as
       illustration of this effort, with volunteers visited working in
       Bogota, Pereira and outlying communities.

657   "Peace Corps Volunteer from North Falmouth Assists Pre-School
       Education in Colombia". Congressional Record, 122, p.12 (24
       August 1976): 27369-70.
          An ACTION press release reporting on the work done in
       Manizales, Colombia, at a facility for pre-school children by
       Debbie Eldridge. Her posting was as an education and child
       development consultant to the Corporacion of the Sacred Family,
       which provides day care for some 550 children and classes in
       cooking, sewing and home improvement for their mothers. Among her
       projects has been the writing of an instruction book for pre-
       school classroom supplies made out of materials locally available.
       At this time there were 194 volunteers serving in Colombia.

658   RITTER, LARRY. "Yanqui, Si". International Wildlife, 8 (July
       1978): 36-41.
          This is a survey article on the Peace Corps environmental
       workers in Colombia, and their contributions to preserving that
       nation's flora and fauna. Projects discussed include public
       education on environmental subjects, designing new national parks,
       writing a field guide to the fish of the Colombian Caribbean
       coastal regions, breeding capybara as possible food animals,
       monitoring tourist development with ants, tracking and
       inventorying the more than one hundred lizard species native to
       Colombia, and writing an environmental plan for the reparation of
       Providencia Island.

659   ROBBINS, CARLA JANE. "After the Yankees Left For Home". U.S. News and World Report, 101 (29 September 1986): 76-8.
      An examination of the town of Zipacon, Colombia, site of one of the first Peace Corps projects in that country, and the people's memory of the volunteers who served there two decades later. Changes in the intervening years are described, along with the reasons for the departure of Peace Corps from Colombia in 1981. The latter included the kidnapping and detention for three years of a volunteer by left-wing terrorists. Photographs of the town and its volunteers then and now are included. Among the townspeople, many of the younger generation had never heard of Peace Corps or were uncertain as to its nature and objectives.

660   SAMUELS, GERTRUDE. "Peace Corps Trains in New York". New York Times Magazine (21 October 1962): 36-7.
      A photo essay covering the participation of community development volunteers in training for service in Colombia in New York City's social work agencies active in Hispanic neighborhoods. The Henry Street Settlement on the lower East Side is the focus of the article. Volunteers and their Colombian counterparts in accion comunal form an intense network of exchange.

661   SANDERS, GENEVA. The Gringo Brought His Mother. San Antonio: Corona Publishing Company, 1986.
      In 1967, Geneva Sanders traveled from her home in southern Texas to visit her son on site in the small town of Mistrato in the mountains of Colombia. This book is an account of Peace Corps life viewed from the outside looking in for fifteen days which proved to be, in the author's words, "a blast, a real mind-blower" (p. 191). Her forthright admissions and descriptions of her own varieties of culture shock offer an interesting and useful comparison with similar experiences of Peace Corps volunteers themselves.

662   "Sister Carries On Brother's Work in Peace Corps". Congressional Record, 110, p.21 (7 January 1964): A17.
      An article from the Chicago Sun-Times consisting of an interview with Elena Radley. Her brother, Lawrence, was one of the first Peace Corps volunteers to die while on site, perishing in a plane crash in Colombia. Elena stated that she wanted to work doubly hard in her efforts so as to make up for her brother's untimely death. She will be posted to aid in the construction of an educational television network in Colombia. A Peace Corps training camp in Puerto Rico has been named after her brother.

663   "Two Peace Corps Dead to Be Left in Colombia". New York Times (1 May 1962): 14.
      Two Peace Corps volunteers, Lawrence Radley and David Crozier, were killed in late April when their AVISPA airliner crashed in the mountains of Colombia. Searchers stated that the bodies would remain with the wreckage due to the peril of landslides. Crozier and Radley were the first two members of the Peace Corps to die while serving a host nation.

664   "Volunteers Give A Push to Fashion". Peace Corps Volunteer, 2,
       n.3 (January 1964):   9.   S19.11/2:2/3.
          An account of the promotion of a weaving co-op in the
       Colombian town of Lenguazaque by the two volunteers stationed
       there and the subsequent success of the marketing effort in both
       Bogota and the United States.

665   WHITE, PATRICIA M.   "Uphill All the Way For Peace Corps
       Veteran". Christian Science Monitor (12 February 1973):   10.
          An interview with Reka Matthews, who became the oldest Peace
       Corps volunteer on the rolls when she joined in 1966 at age 69.
       She discusses her posting in the city of Mariquita, Colombia and
       her work in the adult literacy program there.

666   WINNIE, JOHN R.   "The Peace Corps ETV Project in Colombia".
       Audiovisual Instruction, 10 (January 1965):   27-9.
          In December of 1962, the government of Colombia requested
       Peace Corps assistance in determining the viability of
       establishing a country-wide system of educational television
       programming. Details of the unique conditions in Colombia making
       it possible for such an effort to be considered are noted, among
       them the difficulty of land travel and a shortage of trained
       teachers. Problems of designing a training program for ETV
       volunteers and the enthusiastic reception of the resultant classes
       by the Colombian schools and the public in general are detailed.
       Volunteers also worked with Colombian counterparts via the
       television screen to aid them in improving their own teaching
       skills. Personal notes included the volunteer whose village
       donated a horse for her to use in reaching her outstations--with
       Peace Corps providing the saddle--and the volunteer assigned to La
       Picota, one of Colombia's largest jails, who found the ETV a great
       stimulus to her work in literacy promotion.

667   U. S. Department of State. Peace Corps. Spanish for Peace
       Corps Volunteers In Specialized Technical Jobs. Washington,
       D.C.: 1966.
          Developed at George Washington University as part of the
       training program for Peace Corps/Colombia, this manual focuses on
       basic Spanish vocabulary and grammar before proceeding to the
       technical terms. Sections on cultural notes and regional Spanish
       dialects are also included. This document has been entered on the
       ERIC database as item ED 230 017.

668   U. S. Department of State. Peace Corps. Agreement Between the
       United States of America and the Cook Islands Effected by
       Exchange of Notes Signed at Wellington and Rarotonga April 28,
       1981. Treaties and Other International Acts Series 10093,
       Washington, D.C.: Government Printing Office, 1982.
          This document contains the full texts of the letters
       exchanged between Her Excellency Mrs. Anne C. Martindell,
       ambassador of the United States, and Dr. P. Robati, deputy premier
       of the Cook Islands, which opened the way for volunteers to serve
       in that nation. Legal benefits to be extended to the Peace Corps
       are clearly specified.

669 U. S. Department of State. Costa Rica. Peace Corps.
Agreement Effected by Exchange of Notes Signed at San Jose
November 21 - 23, 1962. United State Treaties and Other
International Agreements Series, no. 5719, vol. 15, p. 2,
Washington, D.C.: 2317-21. S9.12:15 Part 2.

The complete Spanish and English Texts of notes exchanged
between the Costa Rican minister of foreign relations, Daniel
Oduber Quiroa, and Raymond L. Telles, United States ambassador,
creating a legal basis for service by Peace Corps volunteers in
the Republic of Costa Rica.

670 "PCV Forester Develops Products". AA1.13:2/1. InterACTION, 2,
n.1 (October 1973): 7.

A chief problem of many developing nations is an
agricultural economy which emphasizes one or more export crops
over basic needs. This article reports on a project initiated by
volunteer Jerry Kemperman in the Turrialba region of Costa Rica
involving introduction of fast-growing tropical trees to
supplement the local wood supply, fish farms to augment local
dietary deficiencies, and nuts as a new cash crop.

671 "Volunteers Create Beautiful Music In Costa Rican Program".
InterACTION, 4, n.1 (October 1975): 3, 13.

An unusual account of the participation of six Peace Corps
personnel to a music education project in Costa Rica. Among other
duties are the provision of free music lessons (as part of a
government-sponsored effort at public education) and playing with
the Costa-Rica Symphony Orchestra. The program of auditions and
training set up by the conductor (himself a Peace Corps veteran)
is also outlined and background on the music education plans of
the government provided.

672 ZENTELLA, ANNA. "Who's Lonesome? I Never Left Home".
S19.11/2:1/9. Peace Corps Volunteer, 1, n.9 (July 1963): 4.

An account by a teacher at the Liceo San Carlos in Ciudad
Quesada, Costa Rica, of her numerous projects and the realization
that Costa Rica "is more a family than a country." In addition to
teaching English and physical education, holding swimming classes
and working with the Alliance For Progress medical teams, Zentella
has also experienced a somewhat unique reaction to her audiovisual teaching aids in the classroom. Projects underway by other
members of her group are also profiled.

673   U. S. Department of State.   Cyprus. Peace Corps Program.
       Agreement Effected by Exchange of Notes Signed at Nicosia
       August 23, 1962.   United States Treaties and Other
       International Agreements Series, no. 5166, vol. 13, p. 1,
       Washington, D.C.: Government Printing Office, 1962, 2089-93.
       S9.12:13 Part 2.
          The full text of the notes given between the Cypriote
       minister of foreign affairs, His Excellency Spyros Kyprianou, and
       Fraser Wilkins, ambassador of the United States, laying the legal
       foundation on which Peace Corps would come to Cyprus. Legal
       rights and limitations of Corps in that country are set forth.

674   "Cyprus . . . Its Problems Are Different".   S19.11/2:1/4.
       Peace Corps Volunteer, 1, n.4 (February 1963): 20-2.
          A collection of four articles by members of Peace
       Corps/Cyprus serving as geologists, English teachers and
       vocational education instructors and agricultural extension
       workers (animal husbandry). Together they offer insight into the
       Peace Corps' experience in one of the most divided of its host
       nations.

675   SNOW, JAMES A.   Levantine Arabic: Introduction to
       Pronunciation, Washington, D.C.: Peace Corps, 1981.
          Issued by the Foreign Service Institute of the State Depart-
       ment, this text focuses on points of difference between Arabic and
       American English. Nineteen drill sections use familiarization,
       reading, dictation, discrimination, recognition, mimicry and
       transference as teaching techniques. This manual was used by
       members of the Peace Corps stationed in Arabic-speaking regions
       where a specific dialect was not handled by a specific tool, such
       as the volume Chadian Arabic. Full text is available from the
       ERIC database as document ED 054 667.

676   U. S. Department of State.   Dahomey. Peace Corps. Agreement
       Effected by Exchange of Notes Sighed at Cotonou June 30 and
       July 3, 1967.   United States Treaties and Other International
       Agreements Series, no. 6302, vol. 18, n.2, Washington, D.C.:
       Government Printing Office, 1968, 1606-11. Sp.12:18 Part 2.
          The complete French and English texts of documents exchanged
       between John R. Clingerman, ambassador of the United States, and
       His Excellency Dr. Emile-Derlin Zinsou, minister of foreign
       affairs, which set forth the legal framework within which Peace
       Corps would function in Dahomey.

677   "'Everything I Know, I Teach' Says PCV".   AA1.13:1/3.
       InterACTION, 1, n.3 (December 1972): 7.
          A profile of Ljube and Stefanie Ivanovich, a couple serving
       as part of the Lower Oueme river development project in southern
       Dahomey. In addition to teaching proper care and use of heavy
       equipment, they have begun a class in English, started a soccer
       team, and planted fruit trees which will be of long-term benefit
       to their host village of Houeda.

678   "Farmers In Dahomey Get Concrete Help Via Peace Corps Volunteer
       from Lewiston". Congressional Record, 120, p.24 (25 September
       1974): 32573-74.
           A reprint of an ACTION press release profiling the work of
       Laurier Nadeau in the Pobe district of southern Dahomey. Assigned
       to the area as an agricultural construction worker, he teaches
       silo building and design to host country counterparts, and has
       introduced a new concrete silo which has permitted a massive
       increase in the storage capacity of the province. Commenting upon
       his enjoyment of Dahomean culture and customs, Nadeau admits a
       preference for egba, described as "a mixture of manioc, flour and
       water served with bush rat." At that time, sixty-one volunteers
       were serving in Dahomey.

679   U. S. Department of State. Dominica. Peace Corps. Agreement
       Effected by Exchange of Notes Signed at Bridgetown December 16,
       1966, and at Dominica January 11, 1967. United States Treaties
       and Other International Agreements Series, no. 6206, vol. 18,
       p. 1, Washington, D.C.: Government Printing Office, 1968,
       109-11. S9.12:18 Part 1.
           The complete texts of documents given between George Dolgin,
       American charge d'Affaires, and His Honor Geoffrey Guy, adminis-
       trator of Dominica, setting forth the legal basis upon which Peace
       Corps would serve in that island country.

680   U. S. Department of State. Peace Corps. Agreement Between the
       United States of America and Dominica Effected by Exchange of
       Letters Signed at Bridgetown and Roseau May 15 and 22, 1980.
       Treaties and International Acts Series 10016, Washington, D.C.:
       Government Printing Office, 1981. S9.10:10016. S.9.12:32 Part
       5, 1986.
           The full texts of notes exchanged between Sally Shelton,
       United States ambassador to Dominica, and Oliver J. Seraphin,
       prime minister, replacing the earlier agreements of December 16,
       1966 and January 11, 1967, and providing the legal framework
       within which Peace Corps would operate in that nation.

681   U. S. Department of State. Dominican Republic. Peace Corps
       Program. Agreement Signed at Washington, May 2, 1962. United
       States Treaties and Other International Agreement Series, no.
       5007, vol. 13, p. 1, Washington, D.C.: Government Printing
       Office, 1962, 447-51. S9.12:13 Part 1.
           This document contains the complete text of both the Spanish
       and English agreements signed by Sargent Shriver, George Bell,
       ambassador to the Dominican Republic, and Bonilla Atiles of that
       nation, which created the legal framework within which the Peace
       Corps would function in the Dominican Republic.

682   "Blind Texas Girl Assumes Peace Corps Teaching Post."
       Congressional Record, 109, p.23 (25 February 1963): A938.
          A reprint article from the Washington Evening Star of
       February 20, 1963, profiling Marilyn Brandt, the first blind Peace
       Corps volunteer. Currently serving as a teacher for the blind in
       the Dominican Republic, Ms. Brandt's history and training are
       briefly summarized.

683   BRANDT, MARILYN DEE. "They Love Bingo-in Braille". Peace
       Corps Volunteer, 1, n.11 (September 1963):   20.
       S10.11/2:1/11.
          One of the first blind volunteers to serve describes her
       life and teaching in the Escuela Nacional de Ciegos in Santo
       Domingo, the Dominican Republic. Details of her curriculum, such
       as ways of coping with daily life, are included.

684   BRUNO, PAULINE and MARILYN SHANAHAN. "Teaching Peace Corps
       Volunteers". American Journal of Nursing, 65 (April 1965):
       96-9.
          A University of Washington training session for nurses
       intending to serve as volunteers in the Dominican Republic is
       reviewed by the two instructors. Orientation was towards
       practical problem-solving through simulating actual field
       conditions. Resources utilized included materials provided by the
       Peace Corps itself, data supplied from other nurses who had lived
       and worked in Latin America and basic health science and hygiene
       source publications. Training was intended to show the reactions
       of the volunteers to stress, hence the long days. Issues
       discussed included training the volunteers in teaching skills,
       reviewing nursing skills where necessary, and intensive language
       training. Due to the situation in the Dominican Republic,
       administrative skills were also seen to be useful. Throughout the
       ten week period, the course was constantly being revised, and
       further input was planned after the participants had been in the
       field for nine and eighteen months respectively.

685   "'Cuerpo de Paz' In A Troubled Land". S19.11/2:3/8-9. Peace
       Corps Volunteer, 3, n.8-9 (June-July 1965):   5-8.
          An overview of the manner of Peace Corps life in the
       Dominican Republic following the political violence of mid-1965.
       The acceptance of staff and volunteers by both sides is noted.
       Photographs of the contemporary Santo Domingo situation are
       included.

686   "Dominican Republic". S19.11/2:1/11. Peace Corps Volunteer,
       1, n.11 (September 1963):   16-23.
          A collection of brief articles and sketches by members of
       the Dominican Republic contingent of Peace Corps illustrating
       their problems with work and accidents with adaptation to a new
       host culture. The background provided to later Peace Corps
       programming prior to the 1965 political troubles is particularly
       valuable.

687   "Dominican Republic: The Work Goes On".   S19.11/2:4/7.   Peace
        Corps Volunteer, 4, n.7 (May 1966):   4-9.
        A summary article reviewing the state of the Peace Corps in
the Dominican Republic one year after the civil disturbances of
1965.   Volunteers in both Santo Domingo and the countryside are
interviewed.

688   FIXX, JAMES F.   "Behind the Scenes".   Saturday Review, 48
        (12 June 1965):   32.
        A brief sketch of the role played in the Dominican Republic
crisis by Lowell Robert Satin, Director of Peace Corps operations
there.   During the fighting, Satin was able to move freely about
Santo Domingo due to the familiarity with which he was regarded by
both sides.   He was also able to act as negotiator for eight
hostages who were released to the custody of the OAS.

689   JONES, KIRBY.   "The Peace Corps Volunteer in the Field-
        Community Development".   Annals of the American Academy of
        Political and Social Science, 365 (May 1966):   63-71.
        The process of "community development", a major theme of the
early years of the Peace Corps, is explored in this article, using
two case studies from the Dominican Republic as examples.
Problems of determining the felt needs of people in a host
community include understanding local political systems and what
barriers these may pose to community improvement.   Jones states
that "community development as practiced by the Peace Corps
volunteers in a process aimed not at material ends but rather at
the poverty in men's minds" (p. 70).   While this article has an
undeniable elitist tone to it, it serves to illustrate some of the
issues facing volunteers in the 1960's who were precipitated into
such projects.   Few details of actual projects in the Dominican
Republic are outlined beyond the discussion of process.   The
author served in that country as a volunteer in an urban community
development area from 1963 to 1965.

690   "Land Project Develops Frontier".   AA1.13:3/4.   InterACTION, 3,
        n.4 (January 1975):   2.
        As part of the land development plans of the Dominican
Republic, members of the Peace Corps are being posted to frontier
districts.   This article illustrates such assignments with the
experiences of a married couple in Rio Pimpio, a rural district
some 400 kilometers from Santo Domingo near the Haitian border.

691   "Report from Santo Domingo".   Saturday Review, 48 (July 3,
        1965):   18.
        In reply to the news item about his actions during the
Dominican crisis which appeared in the June 12, 1965 issue of
Saturday Review, Robert Satin, in-country director of Peace Corps
work in the Dominican Republic, writes to correct several
incomplete statements.   Noting that he had gone from a rebel news
conference to the American Embassy, he proceeds to set the action
in context as a rebuttal to any suggestion that Peace Corps was
involved as an intelligence-gathering agency during that time.
"My reason for being in rebel headquarters . . . was to discuss

relief needs and insure the freedom of movement for Peace Corps
volunteers and staff who were going about their work in all parts
of the city." The contribution of other members of the
multinational aid effort is also acknowledged.

692   THURBER, ALAN. "UA Graduate Plays Games to Nurture
       Illiterates' Health". Congressional Record, 132, n.137 (7
       October 1986): S15530-31.
          A reprint of an article originally appearing in the Arizona
Republic covering the work of Judy Carr, a volunteer serving as a
rural health promoter in the Dominican Republic. Her task is to
train local people in basic health techniques so that the clinic
can be maintained after her departure. As many of her audiences
are illiterate, she uses home-made audiovisuals to help her in the
classroom. She reflects upon her adventures in getting government
employees and the rural people to work together.

693   "Volunteers Play Neutral Role In Dominican Republic Strife".
       S19.11/2:3/7. Peace Corps Volunteer, 3, n.7 (May 1965): 3-4.
          At the height of the domestic political fighting in the
Dominican Republic, the 102 volunteers stationed there maintained
a low profile, functioning as nurses, physicians and supply
officers. Director Robert Satin also served as mediator at
several points in the turbulence.

694   U. S. Department of State. Peace Corps. An Active
       Introduction to Swahili: Geography. Washington, D.C.: 1966.
          A text of thirty-eight lessons based upon an experimental
course in Kiswahili developed in 1965 by the Foreign Service
Institute. Coverage is limited to geographical names and
situations encountered in daily life in East Africa. Specific
sections deal with place names, map reading and travel. The text
is available from the ERIC system as document ED 012 898.

695   U. S. Department of State. Peace Corps. Swahili: An Active
       Introduction: General Conversation. Washington, D.C.: 1966.
          Produced by the Foreign Service Institute of the State
Department under Peace Corps contract, this text of eighty-seven
lessons uses the microwave approach to teaching new elements of
language. it was successful enough to become the model for a
microwave course in Spanish (ED 157 372). Full text is available
as ERIC document ED 144 351.

696   U. S. Department of State. Ecuador. Peace Corps Program.
       Agreement Effected by Exchange of Notes Signed at Quito August
       3, 1962. United States Treaties and Other International
       Agreements Series, no. 5145, vol. 13, p. 2, Washington, D.C.:
       Government Printing Office, 1962, 1903-08. S9.12:13 Part 2.
          This document contains the full text of notes given by the
Ecuadorean minster of foreign affairs, Dr. Benjamin Peralta Paez,
and the United States ambassador, Maurice M. Bernbaum, which laid
the foundation for Peace Corps service to Ecuador. Both Spanish
and English texts are included.

697   BLANK, JOSEPH P.   "John F. Kennedy School No. 1".   Reader's
       Digest, 86 (March 1965):   54-8.
            In 1963, Edward Whalen arrived at the pioneer settlement of
       El Esfuerzo in the province of Pichincha in coastal Ecuador to
       become the first teacher in the local school. After the
       assassination of President Kennedy, the people of the town decided
       to rename their school after him. This article chronicles the
       changes occurring during Whalen's first year there and the growing
       both he and his neighbors experienced.

698   BROOKS, EARLE and RHODA.   The Barrios of Manta: A Personal
       Account of the Peace Corps in Ecuador. New York: New American
       Library, 1965.
            In this intensely personal account, two members of Ecuador I
       tell the story of their investigation of Peace Corps, their
       training at the camps in Puerto Rico, and the frustrating,
       infuriating and always vivid years they spent as community
       development workers in the town of Manta. The text is illustrated
       with drawings by Rhoda Brooks. In their time, they coped with
       such issues as malnutrition, bubonic plague, literacy and sewing
       classes, and how to sail one of the massive bongos used as fishing
       vessels. The volume is a window into a time when the phrase
       "Cuerpo de Paz" was new in the world and unfamiliar in Latin
       America.

699   BROOKS, RHODA and EARLE.   "Ecuador".   National Geographic
       (September 1964):   338-45.
            A volunteer couple recount their lives as community
       development workers in Manta, a small port on the Ecuadorian
       coast. Their contributions include adjusting to a new standard of
       time, setting up a local school lunch program, and organizing a
       weekly regatta of bongos, sailing canoes used for fishing and
       transportation.

700   COWAN, PAUL.   The Making of an Un-American: A Dialogue With
       Experience. New York: Viking Press, 1967.
            Prior to becoming a volunteer in Ecuador in 1966, Paul Cowan
       had participated in civil rights work in Mississippi and begun to
       question seriously accepted definitions of reality. This book is
       the chronicle of his continuing intellectual dialogue and disputes
       with both other volunteers and the Peace Corps itself as part of a
       massive program of community development work set out for the
       barrios of the city of Guayaquil. While the tone is somewhat
       acrid at times, this is possibly the only account of the political
       conflicts which faced aware volunteers who served during the
       beginning of America's involvement in Viet Nam. The descriptions
       of rigid training styles and apathetic trainees is instructive in
       light of subsequent changes in Corps policies.

701   COWAN, RACHEL. <u>Growing Up Yanqui</u>. New York: Viking Press,
       1975.
           A politically aware former member of Peace Corps/Ecuador
       describes her involvement with public life and issues. The
       second, third and fourth chapters of the book cover her partic-
       ipation in (and criticism of) the community development programme
       in Guayaquil to which she and her husband were posted.
       Researchers should read Paul Cowan's <u>The Making of an Unamerican</u>
       to provide a background for the information in <u>Growing Up Yanqui</u>.

702   "Doin' What Comes Naturally". AA1.13:4/12. InterACTION, 4,
       n.12 (September 1976): 11.
           An article originally printed in <u>La Bocina</u>, a publication of
       Peace Corps/Ecuador, recounting the experiences of setting up ways
       of discouraging the use of prepared formula and bottle feeding at
       the expense of breast-feeding as a solution to that nation's
       problems of infant malnutrition.

703   "Ecuador PCV Transcribes Dialects". AA1.13:1/8. InterACTION,
       1, n.8 (May 1973): 2.
           As part of his assignment as a teacher in the mountain
       village of El Cercado, Ecuador, Lawrence Carpenter and two other
       volunteers have developed a transitional program of introducing
       Spanish to students whose first language is Quechua. The problem
       is further complicated in that many of the Quechuan dialects are
       mutually unintelligible. This has forced the team to devise an
       alphabet for Quechua, write and publish textbooks and consider
       familiar situations to bring across the points of the various
       subject lessons.

704   "Ecuador: Volunteers Serve in 'Country of Contrasts'".
       S19.11/2:2/10. Peace Corps Volunteer, 2, n.10 (August 1964):
       6-21.
           A series of thirteen articles covering the first years and
       then-contemporary programs of Peace Corps/Ecuador. Introduced by
       the deputy director of the Ecuadorian office, topics covered
       include roadbuilding, community development, rabbit raising and
       oven manufacture.

705   ENDE, EDWARD. "A Volunteer Finds Work". S10.11/2:1/12. Peace
       Corps Volunteer, 1, n.12 (October 1963): 24.
           A personal account of the necessity of creating projects in
       unstructured situations by a member of Peace Corps/Ecuador who
       started a boy's club in the city of Ambato after discovering that
       his community-development post at the Andean Mission had no
       precise duties.

706   ERNST, JULIA. "A Day in the Peace Corps". Dairy Goat Journal,
       41, (November 1963): 9.
           A letter from a volunteer serving as a participant in
       Ecuador's livestock improvement effort, detailing one recent day
       in her field life. Involvement with local agricultural clubs and
       co-operatives is highlighted.

707 "4-F Program and Small Business-Ecuador". Peace Corps Times, (September/October/November 1985): 13-15, 24.
    This article is an expansion of notes from a presentation given by Mike Goldberg, Peace Corps/Ecuador, at a recent job conference in Ecuador. Details of the process of marketing, resource analysis, organizational structuring and identifying local networks are given in detail. The 4-F clubs correspond substantially to American 4-H organizations.

708 "In Memory of Mickey Fedor, A Very Special Peace Corps Volunteer". Congressional Record, 129, n.138 (20 October 1983): E5043.
    A tribute to Mickey Fedor, a blind volunteer who served in Ecuador. While working at an orphanage in Quito, he designed and implemented a "Special Olympics" plan for five schools in the city. His idea was then expanded to the national level, a project in which he became deeply involved. Within one year of the beginning of the Quito program, Ecuador held its first Special Olympics. In addition to this, his work involved organizing sports, recreational and physical education classes for the blind, retarded and handicapped. Following his service and the completion of a Peace Corps Fellowship, Fedor returned to Ecuador in 1983 as assistant director of that nation's program. He was forced to leave before his work with the blind could be effectively resumed, and died of cancer on October 17, 1983. Rep. Bruce Morrison of Connecticut delivered his speech honoring Fedor in the House of Representatives on October 20, 1983, and expressed condolences "to his parents, his eight brothers and sisters, and to the Peace Corps."

709 LUCEY, ROSE. "Our Daughter Works for World Peace". Marriage, 45 (December 1963): 36-41.
    An article written by the mother of a member of Peace Corps Ecuador, containing excerpts form her daughter's letters home. These latter touch on everything from the problems of training at the Corps camps in Puerto Rico to the posting to a school of social work in Guayaquil, Ecuador.

710 "Methane Gas Digesters Proven As Viable Energy Source in Ecuador". AA1.13:5/2. InterACTION, 5, n.2 (November 1976): 6.
    A detailed account of the design and construction of a methane gas production unit using solid waste in the community of Araque in rural Ecuador. Pat Doherty began planning and experimenting with such a facility in 1974, the first time any such research had been done applying this method of energy generation to local needs.

711   MONROE, MARGARET. "My Sun-Drenched Dream". S19.11/2:2/7,2/8.
      Peace Corps Volunteer, 2, n.7 (May 1964): 19-22: 2, n.8 (June
      1964): 17-20.
          The wife of a Peace Corps staff physician in Ecuador
      recounts her problems of adjustment and adventures in following
      her 'sun-drenched dream' to Guayaquil. Her narrative provides a
      view of the volunteers from a perspective not usually represented
      in the literature on the Peace Corps. The time period covered is
      from 1962 to mid-1964.

712   "Ohio Farmer in Peace Corps For Third Year". AA1.13:1/12.
      InterACTION, 1, n.12 (September 1973): 4.
          Leon Winget, 76, a member of Peace Corps/Ecuador, will serve
      a third year of duty in the Galapagos Islands, participating in
      the construction of an elementary school and teaching
      blacksmithing at a vocational center he helped to erect. He also
      plans to visit a village reputed to have people living to 150
      years of age "to find out what their diet is."

713   PARSONS, CYNTHIA. "Bees, and the Courage to Do What's Never
      Been Done". Christian Science Monitor (29 June 1981): 17.
          A review of the beekeeping project being guided by Ned and
      Julie Strong of Peace Corps/Ecuador among teenagers in the
      country. With eucalyptus, lemon, lime and avocado serving as
      sources of nectar, local demand has quickly risen far beyond
      supply. This project has been running more than one year and is
      part of the Partners of the Americas Network.

714   "PCV Writes Island Guidebook". AA1.13:1/9. InterACTION, 1,
      n.9 (June 1973): 3.
          An illustrated guide book detailing the history, flora and
      unique natural history of the Galapagos Islands was created by two
      members of Peace Corps/Ecuador. Following a period of six months
      residence in the archipelago, each island was covered in depth.
      With the success of the initial English edition, a Spanish
      printing is planned.

715   SHUTE, NANCY. "After a Turbulent Youth, The Peace Corps Comes
      of Age". Smithsonian, 16, n.11 (February 1986): 80-9.
          In an attempt to survey the changes which the Peace Corps
      has experienced since its foundation in 1961, this article
      provides a brief historical background, interspersed with detailed
      reportage on the history of volunteers and their work in Ecuador.
      Shute notes that "to fathom how well the Peace Corps works today,
      it must be seen incountry, where success or failure is judged by
      the people who live with it" (p. 86). Ecuadorean volunteers are
      working at everything from special education for the deaf and
      blind, to serving as public health nurses inoculating
      schoolchildren, and include handicapped among their own members.
      The article is lavishly illustrated with photographs giving an
      excellent picture of Peace Corps Ecuador as it was in 1986.

716   THOMSEN, MORITZ. Living Poor: A Peace Corps Chronicle.
      Seattle: University of Washington Press, 1969.
           "It may seem to some that this story is scarcely typical of
      the Peace Corps experience. Actually, there is no typical story
      to tell." With these words Moritz Thomsen begins his account of
      life as an agricultural volunteer in the community of Rio Verde on
      the coast of Ecuador from 1965 to 1968. The frustrations and
      problems of adjusting are frankly shared and thus make this one of
      the most absorbing of all accounts of Peace Corps life.

717   "A Tour At Tarqui". S19.11/2:2/1. Peace Corps Volunteer, 2,
      n.1 (November 1963): 8-9.
           A photo essay covering the work done by three volunteers at
      Manta, Ecuador. Two of them, Rhoda and Earle Brooks, wrote an
      expanded account of their time there in The Barrios of Manta.

718   TRAIL, JO ANN. "Peace Corps Volunteers Learn New Techniques".
      Journal of Home Economics, 58 (June 1966): 462.
           This is a report on a workshop conducted for volunteers in
      Ecuador stressing certain practical projects in the field of home
      economics. They include building ovens out of lard tins and
      turning old oil cans into stovepipes, planning home gardens and
      promoting the eating of raw vegetables. The author served as a
      special consultant to Peace Corps/Ecuador in the field of home
      economics. Workshops are seen as building morale as well as
      sharing ideas for application in various host country settings.

719   "Wildlife on Galapagos Still in Danger". New Scientist, 106
      (5 June 1965): 7.
           A fire started by unknown factors was brought under a degree
      of control in the Galapagos National Park off the Ecuadorean
      coast. This news note details the altered conditions in the park
      due to increased vegetation and lower-than-normal rainfall. Fire
      management workers from the Peace Corps participated in the
      emergency work force.

720   WINGET, LEON. Life Begins At 73: Two Years Three Months In
      the Peace Corps In Ecuador. Kingston, Ohio: Zane Commercial
      Printing, 1974.
           Leon Winget entered the Peace Corps on October 1, 1970, and
      immediately became that agency's oldest volunteer. Life Begins At
      73 is an account of his service and training based upon his daily
      journal.

721   "Wisconsin Peace Corps Volunteer Serves in Ecuador".
       Congressional Record, 121, p.5 (12 March 1975):   6424.
           A reprint of a press release from ACTION describing the
       agricultural extension work being done by Daniel Matthias at the
       experimental station of Rancho Ronald in northern Ecuador.   The
       project centers on livestock and dairy breeding and crop and grass
       experimentation to enable Ecuador to increase its food supply.
       Matthias describes his problems with learning Spanish and
       adjusting to the rain forest environment.   At this time, 230
       volunteers were in Ecuador serving in health and education
       programs as well as agricultural projects.

722   U. S. Department of State.   El Salvador. Peace Corps Program.
       Agreement Effected by Exchange of Notes Signed at San Salvador
       August 11 and November 13 and 20, 1961.   United States Treaties
       and Other International Agreements Series, no. 4899, vol. 12,
       p. 3, Washington, D.C.:   Government Printing Office, 1961,
       2983-88.   S9.12:12   Part 3.
           This document contains the full texts of letters exchanged
       between Dr. Rafael Eguizabal Tobias, Salvadoran minister of
       foreign affairs and Murat Williams, United States ambassador,
       which laid the framework for Peace Corps service to that nation.
       Both Spanish and English texts are included.

723   HANCOCK, RICHARD H.   "Volunteers A 'New Presence' In El
       Salvador".   S19.11/2:1/2.   Peace Corps Volunteer, 1, n.2
       (December 1962):   6-9.
           A review article covering the arrival of the first twenty-
       four volunteers in El Salvador on May 3, 1962 and detailed
       information on their postings with the Salvadoran Ministry of
       Agriculture.

724   "Marine Fisheries Program Flourishes in El Salvador".
       AA1.13:3/3.   InterACTION, 3, n.3 (December 1974):   3, 8.
           Since 1968, the Peace Corps has been working in El Salvador,
       assisting local fishing cooperatives to increase their catches and
       improve management techniques.   The town of El Tamarindo in
       southeast El Salvador is used as illustration and the volunteers
       serving there are interviewed.

725   "PCV 'Reinvents' Watermelon".   AA1.13:5/7.   InterACTION, 5,
       n.7 (April 1977):   12.
           Upon arrival at the national agricultural college of El
       Salvador in 1974, Richard Figoni was obliged to develop both a
       course in genetics and a text suited to local environmental
       conditions.   He decided to use watermelons as an example of
       applied genetics, an idea which resulted in the appearance of
       seedless watermelons on the market and created attention for his
       subject in a rather dramatic fashion.

726 "Second Time Around Proves Better". AA1.13:1/7. InterACTION,
1, n.7 (April 1973): 2.
With a one-year hiatus caused by the withdrawal of the Peace
Corps from his first country of assignment, Panama, volunteer Ed
Schiffer is presently working in El Salvador as one of four
corpsmen on the staff of the National Association of Scouts. All
have backgrounds in the Boy Scout movement in the United States.
The bulk of this article is an interview with Schiffer and his
host country supervisor, Gilbreth Gonzalez.

727 U. S. Department of State. Ethiopia. Peace Corps Program.
Agreement Effected by Exchange of Notes Signed At Addis Ababa
May 23, 1962. United States Treaties and Other International
Agreements Series, no. 5067, vol. 13, p. 2, Washington, D.C.:
Government Printing Office, 1962, 1227-30. S9.12:13 Part 2.
This document contains the full texts of notes exchanged
between Arthur L. Richards, ambassador of the United State and His
Excellency Ato Ketema Yifru . . . acting foreign minister of the
imperial Ethiopian government, setting forth the legal framework
under which Peace Corps would enter the host nation. This
agreement remained in force until the departure of Peace Corps
from Ethiopia in 1977.

728 BARTLETT, BEULAH D. and BLYTHE F. MONROE. "Reading A Foreign
Culture: The Peace Corps in Ethiopia". Claremont Reading
Conference Yearbook, 29 (1965): 66-72.
Blythe Monroe and Beulah Bartlett, two English teachers
posted to the Harar Teacher Training Institute in Addis Ababa as
part of Ethiopia I, relate their problems of learning to "read"
Ethiopian culture accurately. In addition, they present the
mirror image of the Peace Corps experience through cultural
discrimination difficulties encountered by their students in
attempting to understand English and to prepare themselves for
careers as elementary school teachers. Ranging from goats locked
in taxi trunks and belief that the earth was flat to coping with
local foods and their effect on child development, this article
states the "ever-present problem of the Peace Corps teacher . . .:
how to teach yet not offend" (p. 70). Background data on the
languages, religions and system of education in Ethiopia in 1962
is included.

729 BERGTHOLD, GARY D. The Impact of Peace Corps Teachers on
Students in Ethiopia. Ed.D. dissertation, Harvard, 1969.
Between 1962 and 1969, some 1400 members of the U. S. Peace
Corps served as teachers in the school system of Ethiopia. To
ascertain what impact these volunteers had made upon their
students, 3,500 tenth graders were selected as a representative
sample of a total school population of six thousand at that level.
Performance skills (English fluency, English antonyms and problems
solving) and psychological dimensions (achievement motivation,
empathy and modernity) were measured on a scale of those who had
experienced intensive interaction with a volunteer teacher versus
those who had not. In all but one area (empathy) students who had
a large number of volunteer teachers scored higher than those who

had lacked such instruction. To further explore the impact of the
Peace Corps personnel, comparison was made between having
volunteers teaching and the full expense of hiring a contract
teacher. A survey of teaching styles employed by members of Peace
Corps/Ethiopia was also included, with volunteers utilizing a
combination of learner-centered and teacher centered styles. Four
case studies of individual volunteers who had developed teaching
techniques designed to foster the elements of the study suggested
that "if volunteers were trained in specific techniques for
promoting skills, motives and attitudes" (p. 7), their impact
would be heightened.

    Researchers examining the Peace Corps in Ethiopian education
should also consult Through Ferrengi Eyes for a viewpoint from
within the dying imperial system.

730   BOYER, NEIL A.   "In Ethiopia, Teaching and Much More".
      American Teacher Magazine, 48 (February 1964):   7-8, 18.
    The arrival of 416 teachers as part of the Yesalem Gwad,
otherwise known as Peace Corps/Ethiopia, doubled the number of
college graduates teaching in the secondary and elementary schools
of that nation. In many cases, these volunteers permitted schools
to open where there had been none before, and substantially
enriched the curriculum of others with classes and extra-
curricular activities which staff shortages had previously
precluded. Details of the problems encountered in the Ethiopian
school system are discussed, such as the reluctance of school
graduates to take their skills back to the provinces. The idea of
beginning an Ethiopian version of Peace Corps is also covered.

731   BOYER, NEIL A.   "Volunteers in the Field: Great Expectations".
      Annals of the American Academy of Political and Social Science,
      365 (May 1966):   55-63.
    Written by a member of Ethiopia I, this article discusses
the problems which face volunteers when they arrive in their host
countries. Despite all the information which has been provided
them in training, difficulties of adjustment abound, ranging from
coping with a negative image and suspicions of the host peoples
that Corps members may be CIA agents, ill-defined assignments, and
other factors involved in living "life in the goldfish bowl". By
contrast, it is this very difference and constant example that
permits the volunteer to act as a catalyst for change in
attitudes. Issues such as over-identification with the local
expatriate community and questions of discretion in using one's
personal freedoms are also considered. These issues are liberally
illustrated with incidents from the author's time in Ethiopia.

732   COVINGTON, ANN.   "Negro Volunteer In Ethiopia Finds Color An
      Advantage". S19.11/2:2/6. Peace Corps Volunteer, 2, n.7 (May
      1964):   4-5.
    Reflections on being a black volunteer in an African nation
are shared by a member of Peace Corps/Ethiopia stationed in
Asmara. Of particular interest are the views traditionally held
of other Africans by the Ethiopians.

733 "Ethiopia-Teaching and Much More". S19.11/2:1/5. Peace Corps
Volunteer, 1, n.5 (March 1963): 12-22.
A collection of eight articles by members of Peace
Corps/Ethiopia discussing the cultural contexts of their teaching
assignments. Communities represented include Jimma, Tesserai and
Yirgalem as well as Addis Ababa.

734 "Ethiopian Students Repair 10 Schools". AA1.13:1/6.
InterACTION, 1, n.6 (March 1973): 4.
A report on a summer vacation project in the city of Dessie
in eastern Ethiopia designed by four industrial arts teachers to
provide both assistance to a local high school in repairs to
buildings and facilities, and actual work experience for their
students.

735 "Kansas Woman Extends Peace Corps Service as Home Economics
Teacher in Ethiopia". Congressional Record, 119, p.26
(12 October 1973): 33959-60.
The extension of service granted to Beverly Smith, an home
economics teacher serving in Dessie, Ethiopia, is noted. Details
of her methods of teaching--such as using a bottle of cooking oil
as illustration of gradual change--and her views of the Ethiopian
system are included. At this time, 300 volunteers were serving in
Ethiopia.

736 KLEIN, HENRY. Through Ferrengi Eyes: The Diary of A Peace
Corps Volunteer in Ethiopia, 1974-1976. Hicksville, New York:
Exposition Press, 1979.
This volume consists of excerpts from the diary kept by one
of the final group of volunteers to serve in Ethiopia. The period
in question covers the revolution which toppled the aging Haile
Selassie from his throne and the subsequent civil ware with
Eritrean separatists. Information on Ethiopia's attempt at
correcting abuses of the imperial period is detailed and
colorfully expressed.

737 LESLAU, WOLF. An English-Amharic Dictionary of Everyday Usage.
Washington, D.C.: Peace Corps,
Created as "the first modern English-Amharic dictionary",
this work is intended for students who are already familiar with
the essential features of the language's script and grammar. Its
compilation was occasioned by the inception of Peace Corps
training for the teaching program in Ethiopia. The author
emphasizes that the present text is an experimental version. Only
essential items of spoken and written Amharic are included, with
ambiguous items illustrated in contextual sentences. The
dictionary has been entered in the ERIC database as documents ED
12044 and 12045.

738   LETA, DEJENIE. <u>Oromo For Beginners: Language Materials</u>.
       Washington, D.C.:   Peace Corps, 1975.
            This text was prepared by the author for a series of two-
       week in-service language workshops for volunteers held at Awassa,
       Ethiopia in the summer of 1975. Standard Oromo has been taken to
       be the dialect spoken in the Ethiopian provinces of Illubabor,
       Kaffa and Woolega. Twenty units covering everything from basic
       pronunciation to conversation comprise the work. It can be found
       in the ERIC system as document ED 226 615.

739   "One Career Leads to Another". AA1.13:1/12. <u>InterACTION</u>, 1,
       n.12 (September 1973):   3.
            A report on the work of Ernest Franz, late of Boeing,
       serving as an electrical theory and shop teacher in Mekelle,
       Ethiopia. Having set Corps aside until retirement, his entry was
       hastened by the crisis in the aerospace industry.

740   SLAGER, WILLIAM R., et. al. <u>Amharic and English. An
       Introduction to the Principles of Language Teaching and
       Language Learning</u>. Washington, D.C.:   Peace Corps, 1966.
            This document was prepared as part of an experimental
       program bringing together the TESL and language components of the
       Peace Corps training program for Ethiopia. Used by the English
       and Amharic teaching staffs, awareness of structured control and
       vocabulary is stressed. The document is entered in the ERIC
       system as ED 132 839.

741   "Smallpox Battle Nears End". AA1.13:2/5. <u>InterACTION</u>, 2, n.5
       (February 1974):   1, 4.
            In 1971, Peace Corps members began a co-operative effort
       with the Ethiopian public health service to inoculate the
       population against smallpox and to eradicate the disease from the
       country. This article profiles the effort of the World Health
       Organization at smallpox control and the reception of the teams
       fanning out across the regions of Ethiopia, as well as the
       etiology and occurrence of smallpox within Ethiopian culture.

742   "Volunteer Doctor Serves in Ethiopia". AA1.13: 1/12.
       <u>InterACTION</u>, 1, n.12 (September 1973):   5.
            A profile of the medical work being done in a teaching
       hospital by volunteer Dana Larson. By serving in this capacity,
       she enables many interns to have valuable experiences of bedside
       instruction. Many of her students are in their second to fourth
       years of study. Among her observations are the frustration of
       coping with a belief in fatalism and faulty equipment.

743   "We Peace Corpsmen Work Cheaper". <u>Senior Scholastic</u>, 100
       (10 April 1972):   10.
            An interview with volunteer Marc Weishaus which explores his
       work as an advisor for an irrigation project in Ethiopia and
       provides some observations on both the difficulties facing
       volunteers in that country and changes occurring in Ethiopian
       culture due to Western influence.

744   U. S. Department of State. <u>Fiji. Peace Corps. Agreement</u>
      <u>Effected by Exchange of Notes Signed at Suva June 25, 1968.</u>
      United States Treaties and Other International Agreements
      Series, no. 6515, vol. 19, p. 4, Washington, D.C.: Government
      Printing Office, 1969. 5208-10. S9.12:19 Part 4.
         The full text of notes given between Louis J. Link, American
      consul, and His Excellency Sir Derek Jakeway, governor of Fiji,
      laying the legal foundation upon which Peace Corps service to that
      island nation would rest.

745   BERNON, GARY. "Environmental Education in Fiji". <u>Journal of</u>
      <u>Environmental Education</u>, 9, n.3 (Spring 1978): 12-7.
         Beginning with a general consideration of the increasing
      importance of environmental education programs in the Third World,
      this article moves to examine one such effort in Fiji. The Colo-
      i-Suva Recreation Area, the first such park and wildlife refuge
      established in Fiji, is located on a peninsula on the southern
      coast of the island of Viti Levu. Drawing upon the large
      population of the Suva region--including the University of the
      South Pacific--Bernon describes the trial program he developed
      with the Ministry of Education, Youth and Sport. The unit
      consisted of fifteen experiences, culminating in the consideration
      of what was being done to protect and preserve Fijian species
      which were or could become endangered. Cross-cultural plans for
      environmental education are seen as necessary for the management
      of planetary resources and possible to be fitted into Third World
      programs of tourism. The Fijian program is then set in context
      with similar programs in countries such as Kenya. Peace Corps
      involvement is this effort is explained in detail.

746   "Fijian Handicrafts Sales Boom". <u>Christian Science Monitor</u>
      (5 September 1970): 14.
         A crafts cooperative organized by a member of Peace Corps
      Fiji has succeeded in capturing a share of the Pacific market.
      Items most in demand are Fijian war clubs, kava bowls, outrigger
      canoes and <u>tapa</u> (bark cloth). Wages of co-op members have risen
      to four times previous earnings.

747   "Peace Corps Calls for Volunteers". <u>Physics Today</u>, 27
      (February 1974): 77-8.
         A call for the participation in Peace Corps of trained
      members of the physics profession as part of the Corps' new shift
      towards skilled volunteers. Most postings involve teacher
      training. A case study of a lecturer at the University of South
      Pacific in Suva, Fiji is offered as an example.

748   U. S. Department of State. <u>Peace Corps. Lessons In Colloquial</u>
      <u>Hindustani for Fiji.</u> Washington, D.C.: 1968. Sheela Smith.
         Developed by the Pacific and Asian Linguistics Institute at
      the University of Hawaii, this volume contains eighty-nine lessons
      useful in preparing Peace Corps personnel for service in Fiji.
      The full text of this manual has been entered on the ERIC database
      as document ED 144 353.

749   U. S. Department of State. Peace Corps. Lessons in Fijian by
       Albert J. Schutz and Ratu Komaitai. Washington, D.C.: 1978.
          Developed at the Peace Corps training center in Hawaii, this
       is a basic grammar of the Fijian language. A section on spelling
       and pronunciation is followed by eighteen chapters with dialogue,
       substitution drills and vocabulary. The full text has been
       entered on the ERIC database as document ED 131 693.

750   U. S. Department of State. Gabon. Peace Corps Program.
       Agreement Effected by Exchange of Notes Signed at Libreville
       October 4, 1962. United States Treaties and Other
       International Agreements Series, no. 5189, vol. 13, p. 2,
       Washington, D.C.: Government Printing Office, 1962, 2233-37.
       S9.12: Part 2.
          The full French and English texts of the notes exchanged
       between M. Jean-Hilaire Aubame, minister of foreign affairs, and
       Charles F. Darlington, United States ambassador, creating a legal
       base for the entry of Peace Corps workers to service in Gabon.

751   JACKSON, NORMAN. "Another Technical Manual: How to Build a
       Peace Corps School in Gabon". Peace Corps Reader, Washington,
       D.C.: Peace Corps, 1969, 84-9.
          An account by a volunteer in Gabon of the actual experiences
       encountered in the course of assisting in the construction of
       several village schools. These include his recollections of his
       first day in his village of being greeted by an old man who had
       walked a long distance to bring him a calabash of palm wine as a
       welcome, as well as falling through the outhouse floor.

752   MURPHY, JOHN F. "Gabon". National Geographic (September
       1964): 324-29.
          In the west African nation of Gabon, Peace Corps volunteers
       participated in a construction program to build thirty rural
       schools and ninety houses for teachers. Because of this, they
       became know as les blancs qui travaillent, "the whites who work."
       One of them describes the adventures encountered by the group,
       including wife-purchase, and coping with a large number of
       national languages. Photographs illustrate the type of schools
       being built, their predecessors, and an historic visit by Corpsmen
       to Dr. Albert Schweitzer at his home at Lambarene.

753   "The News, Briefly". Christian Science Monitor (8 December
       1967): 2.
          The fifty-seven members of Peace Corps/Gabon are being
       withdrawn from that country at government request. Although a
       formal note of thanks has been received, no reason was given for
       the removal by the Gabon authorities.

754   "Peace Corps Wins Gabon Praise". Christian Science Monitor,
      (21 May 1064): 3.
          An interview with William Wilkes, an ex-Marine and country
      director of Peace Corps/Gabon. With the exception of sixteen
      teachers, all seventy-one volunteers in country were engaged in
      the construction and planning of schools. Thirty schools had been
      planned and, in one case, the Fang people celebrated the
      completion of the work by presenting Wilkes with baskets of
      mangoes and oranges. Initial frictions with both the French
      business community and racial stereotyping appear to have been
      overcome.

755   U. S. Department of State. Peace Corps. Technical Dictionary,
      English-French, French-English. Washington, D.C.: 1967.
          Developed as part of the training materials for Peace
      Corps/Gabon in September, 1967, this text presents more than two
      thousand terms, chiefly relating to mechanics. Available as ERIC
      document ED 014 924.

756   U. S. Department of State. Gambia, Peace Corps, Agreement
      Effected by Exchange of Notes Signed at Bathurst November 26
      and December 5, 1966. United States Treaties and Other
      International Agreements Series, no. 6181, vol. 17, p. 2,
      Washington, D.C.: Government Printing Office, 1968, 2346-50.
      S9.12:17 Part 2.
          The complete texts of documents given between John G.
      Gossett, American charge d'Affaires of the United States Embassy
      and His Excellency Sir Dawda Jawara, prime minister of The Gambia,
      laying the foundation for Peace Corps service in that nation.

757   "Drought-Stricken Gambia Gets New Wells". AA1.13:2/2.
      InterACTION, 2, n.2 (November 1973): 1, 4.
          With the spread of the Sahelian drought to the Gambia,
      methods of efficient water use and conservation were required.
      Traditional water sources and wells were failing and proving
      insufficient for both livestock and people. Two volunteers in the
      arid Basse region of eastern Gambia drew up a plan for wells based
      upon a successful model in use in Peace Corps/Niger. In one year,
      they rebuilt or strengthened fifty-one wells for both humans and
      cattle. The projects were so successful that a similar plan was
      adopted on a country-wide basis with requests for more volunteers
      as part of the plan.

758   SESSEH, HAYIB. A Basic Wolof Course with Cultural Notes.
      Washington, D.C.: Peace Corps, 1965.
          The manual was prepared from the actual experiences of
      volunteers serving in the Gambia, West Africa, and is based on
      proficiency in oral communication, emphasizing repetition. A
      preface to the lessons emphasizes the objectives of cross-cultural
      training. Full text is available as ERIC document ED 131 733.

759   JAMES SOSSEH. U. S. Department of State. Peace Corps. A
        Basic Mandinka Course with Cultural Notes. Washington, D.C.:
        1965.
             Prepared under a contract to Peace Corps/Gambia, this series
        of lessons in basic Mandinka is grounded in actual experiences of
        volunteers in that country. Emphasis is on oral facility and
        gaining an understanding of Mandinka culture. The full text has
        been entered on the ERIC database as document ED 131 734.

760   MUHAMMAD I ASHRIF. U. S. Department of State. Peace Corps.
        English-Mandinka Dictionary. Washington, D.C.: 1965.
             A basic dictionary of the Mandinka dictionary of the Gambia,
        compiled at Yundum in 1965 and used in in-country training. The
        complete text is available from the ERIC system as document ED 131
        732.

761   JOSEPH NICOL. U. S. Department of State Peace Corps. Lexicon
        Mandinque-Francais. Washington, D.C.: 1968.
             A dictionary of French and Mandinka, used to enable Peace
        Corps volunteers to adapt to Francophone Africa more easily.
        Sample entries include sentences illustrating usage. The full
        text is entered on the ERIC database as document ED 144 352.

762   U. S. Department of State. Ghana. Peace Corps Program.
        Agreement Effected by Exchange of Notes Signed at Accra July
        19, 1961. United States Treaties and Other International
        Agreements Series, no. 4811, vol. 12, p. 1, Washington, D.C.:
        Government Printing Office, 1961, 1066-70. S9.12:12 Part 1.
             This document contains the full texts of letters exchanged
        between Imoru Egala, and Francis Russell, ambassador of the United
        States, which formalized the request of Ghana for Peace Corps
        volunteers. It was this agreement which opened the way for the
        beginnings of Corps service in West Africa.

763   "An African Odyssey On Tap". Los Angeles Times (9 January
        1972): E3.
             A news item on the departure of Penny and Mike Ruchs for
        Ghana as part of the joint Smithsonian Institution--Peace Corps
        environment program. Their assignment will be to study elephant
        behavior patterns with a view toward managing the wildlife
        resources in harmony with agriculture. Upon completion of their
        studies, recommendations will be made to the government of Ghana.
        The qualifications lie in the areas of biology and zoology.

764   "Asantehene Visits Peace Corps". Peace Corps Times
        (January/February 1986): 7.
             In October, 1984, the Asantehene Opoku Ware II, cultural and
        spiritual leader of the Ashanti people of Ghana, paid a state
        visit to the United States to open an exhibition entitled "Asante:
        Kingdom of Gold." Following upon the successful celebrations of
        the history of Ghanaian goldcraft at the Museum of Natural History
        in New York, he traveled to Washington, D.C. to visit the head-
        quarters of the Peace Corps. A special reception was held for the
        Asantehene on Capitol Hill, with many returned members of Ghana's
        Peace Corps in attendance. At the ceremony, a replica of the
        Golden Stool, symbol of the hereditary power of the Asantehene and
        of the Asante people, was presented to the Peace Corps.

765   "Corpsmen in Ghana". Time, 78 (17 November 1961): 20-21.
             A review of the reception and accomplishments of the first
        group of Peace Corps men and women to arrive anywhere after some
        two months of residence in Ghana. Most of the volunteers are
        serving the Ghanaian school system as science and English
        instructors. A brief outline of their training in Twi, Ghanaian
        history and customs and health care at the University of
        California is also given. Overall reaction from both staff and
        students to the volunteers is extremely favorable.

766   DENTEH, A. CRAKYE. Spoken Twi for Non-Twi Beginners.
        Washington, D.C.: Peace Corps, 1974.
             Sixty-five lessons oriented to instruction in the Twi
        language of Ghana under the guidance of a fluent native speaker
        comprise the manual. Each lesson is structured about a particular
        topic or situation. Review questions are interspersed at
        intervals. The full document is available as ERIC document ED 140
        609.

767   DENTEH, A. CRAKYE and K. K. KEELSON. Spoken Fante for Non-
        Fante Beginners. Washington, D.C.: Peace Corps, 1974.
             Sixty-six lessons for the beginning student of the Fante
        language of Ghana comprise this manual. Emphasis is on inter-
        action with a native speaker and each lesson is structured about a
        specific topic, such as the marketplace and greetings. Review
        lessons are interspersed. The full text can be found as ERIC
        document ED 140 608.

768   "Fresh From Africa to Speak on Children's Literature".
        AA1.13:2/4. InterACTION, 2, n.4 (January 1974): 8-9.
             Mary O'Neill, author of several children's books and veteran
        of Peace Corps/Ghana, shares her thoughts on the universality of
        the needs of children, illustrating her points with examples from
        her service. Her description of storytelling as an art form which
        even the youngest children may participate in is of particular
        interest.

769   "Ghana, the First Peace Corps Country". Peace Corps Times
       (January/February 1986): 4-8.
            An historical article and photo essay covering the
       beginnings and contemporary work being done by members of the
       Peace Corps in Ghana. Among the traditions which have arisen in
       the twenty-five years of service is that all volunteers take the
       oath of service wearing garments of kente cloth. The number of
       volunteers in Ghana has dropped to seventy, while programming has
       diversified widely into areas such as beekeeping, fisheries, and
       village development. The photographs illustrate several
       volunteers from the 1960's and the 1980's and the present staff of
       Peace Corps Ghana.

770   "Ghana Food Complex Set to Open". AA1.13:1/11. InterACTION,
       1, n.11 (August 1973): 3.
            In the early 1960's, the government of Ghana began
       construction of a food processing complex at Tema, only to have
       construction halted by a change of government in 1966. Subsequent
       governments decided to continue the project, and requested
       assistance from the Peace Corps. The present article details the
       work done by Harold Seaman, a refrigeration mechanic teaching in
       Accra, to revive the factories while providing on-the-job training
       for the students in his care. Among the difficulties were the
       absence of original instructions (except in German) and equipment
       which had been neglected since 1966. Three other volunteers also
       participated in the project under Seaman's direction. Upon
       completion, the plant would enable Ghana to reduce substantially
       its imports of fish and fish meal, but also to preserve large
       amounts of its own catch, thus stabilizing the price structure of
       that part of its market.

771   "Ghana Newspaper Terms the Peace Corps 'A Godsend'".
       Congressional Record, 109, p.31 (4 November 1963): A6866.
            An article from the Ghana News of August 6, 1963 is
       reprinted here, covering the warm reception and value which the
       people of Ghana have extended to the first group of volunteers to
       serve anywhere. At the end of their tour of service, the forty-
       one members of the group were honored at a reception hosted by Dr.
       Kwame Nkrumah, President of Ghana. Also recorded is a reception
       at Philadelphia hosted by Milton Shapp, at which His Excellency M.
       A. Ribeiro, Ambassador of Ghana, addressed a group of returned
       volunteers. Excerpts from the ambassador's remarks are included.

772   "Ghana Receives 12 Peace Corps Geologists to Assist in Survey
       Work on Back Country". S19.11/2:1/10. Peace Corps Volunteer,
       1, n.10 (August 1963): 4.
            At the request of the Ghanaian government, ten Peace Corps
       geologists arrived in Accra in May, 1963 for assignment to the
       Geological Survey. The principal goal of their project is the
       mapping and evaluation of nickel, bauxite, colombite and diamond-
       bearing deposits.

773   JONES, VIRA. "The Toughest Job You'll Ever Love". Seventeen
       (March 1982): 72-3.
           In the summer of 1978, Vira Jones found herself in an
       airliner descending to the Accra airport. She had come to serve
       as a volunteer in the mountain village of Agogo. Her
       reminiscences cover learning Twi, picking out the tadpoles from
       her drinking water before boiling, and adjusting her thinking to
       being considered both white and extremely rich. "Most of all, I
       miss my African friends, who let me into their lives--and who made
       it so hard for me to come home."

774   KENNEDY, JOHN FITZGERALD. President. "Remarks To A Group Of
       Peace Corps Volunteers Before Their Departure For Tanganyika
       and Ghana." Public Papers of the Presidents: John F. Kennedy
       1961, Document 331 (28 August 1961) Washington, D.C.: Govern-
       ment Printing Office, 1962, 569-70. GS4.113:961.
           On August 28, 1961, President Kennedy held a reception in
       the Rose Garden of the White House for the first group of Peace
       Corpsmen to complete training and depart for service anywhere in
       the world. At that time, he made the statement that "There are a
       great many hundreds of millions of people scattered throughout the
       world. You will come in contact with only a few, but the . . .
       impression of what kind of country we have and what kind of people
       we are will depend on their judgment, in these countries, of you."
       The members of these first groups were assigned to work on the
       surveying of a network of secondary roads to Tanganyika and to
       teach in the school system of Ghana. Due recognition of the
       invitations by Presidents Nkrumah and Nyerere of these respective
       nations is given.

775   "PC Volunteers Pledge Commitment to Ghana at Traditional
       Ceremony". AA1.13:5/2. InterACTION, 5, n.2 (November 1976):
       1.
           In a ceremony at the town of Akropong, fifty-two volunteers
       were sworn into service in Ghana in accordance with that country's
       cultural traditions. All volunteers wore traditional Ghanaian
       attire, and the complete proceedings were translated into Twi.
       The Ghanaian people were represented by the local chief and the
       director of the Ghana Education Service. This was the first time
       in the history of Peace Corps Ghana that such a ceremony had been
       held at a swearing-in.

776   "The Peace Corps". Congressional Record, 107, p.13 (31 August
       1961): 17873-74.
           A comment by Representative Hiestand of California noting
       the departure of the first two groups of Peace Corps Volunteers to
       Ghana and Tanganyika. Contrasting the "lofty ideals" of Corps
       with its practicability, the question of the consequences of this
       new program are raised, with the view that "every American abroad
       is a representative of our nation" (p. 17874) emphasized. While
       supportive, Rep. Hiestand calls for a close watch on Corps
       progress and activity, so that it will not become "another
       children's crusade."

777   "Peace Corps Allays Prejudice, Suspicion in Ghana". Congres-
       sional Record, 111, p.13 (20 July 1965): 17410-11.
          A reflective article by an RPCV from Ghana looking at not
       only the contributions made by the two generations of Corps who
       had served in Sunyani at his secondary school, but also giving a
       larger view of Peace Corps activities in Ghana and elsewhere in
       Africa. An interesting note is the camaraderie existing between
       Corps personnel and Russian aid workers also invited to Ghana by
       Kwame Nkrumah. The wide travels of volunteers and problems with
       some of the vacation projects required of them are also recounted.
       This article originally appeared in the Honolulu Star-Bulletin and
       was inserted in the Record by Senator Daniel Inouye of Hawaii.

778   "Peace Corps Group in Ghana". Christian Science Monitor
       (13 July 1972): 2.
          A group of forty-eight volunteers has arrived in Accra.
       Following their briefing in-country, they will be posted to
       secondary and higher education institutions. Among their number
       are laboratory technicians, computer technicians and science
       teachers.

779   "The Peace Corps in Ghana". Congressional Record, Appendix,
       108, p.30 (31 January 1962): A725.
          This entry is a reprint as part of the Congressional Record
       of an article originally issued in the Chicago Defender examining
       the Peace Corps in Ghana. Chief attention is paid to George
       Carter, country director, and the growing rapport which the
       volunteers are creating with their host country colleagues,
       friends and students.

780   "Peace Corps Volunteers on Race Relations". School and
       Society, 94 (5 February 1966): 56-8.
          A brief report on research conducted among members of Peace
       Corps/Ghana on the effect of service upon their concepts and ideas
       regarding race relations. Reactions include the category of race
       becoming irrelevant, refusal to raise children in a segregated
       American system, and increased awareness through being labeled
       with stereotypes by their African students and colleagues. The
       image of America abroad, such as the rioting in Birmingham,
       Alabama, also played a part in determining that racism should not
       be tolerated in the United States.

781   GROBEL, LAWRENCE. "Second Dawn in Ghana". S19.22/2:8/1-2.
       Volunteer, 8, n.1-2 (January-February 1970): 18-20.
          A description of the ceremonies attendant upon the
       restoration of civilian rule in Ghana following the collapse of
       Kwame Nkrumah's government and three years of military rule by a
       member of Peace Corps/Ghana.

782   SAM, ISAAC. "Binationalism in Ghana".   S19.11/2:8/7-8.
       Volunteer, 8, n.7-8 (July-August 1970):   13-14.
           Upon assuming the position of Director of the Peace Corps in
       May, 1969, Joseph Blatchford made the concept of binationalism--
       involving host country nationals on Peace Corps staffs in-country
       at the policy-making level--a key part of his "New Directions"
       package. This article examines the way in which this policy was
       carried out in Peace Corps administration in Ghana. The author is
       associate Peace Corps Director for that country and a Ghanaian
       national.

783   "Science Dictionary Compiled". AA1.13:2/5. InterACTION, 2,
       n.5 (February 1974):   3, 11.
           A report of the compilation of the first science dictionary
       in both Twi and English for use in the schools of Ghana by
       volunteer Rudolph Sovinee. It was created as part of a response
       to an appeal by the Ghanaian Commission of Education, Sports and
       Culture for more books in the local languages. Many of the
       spellings are, of necessity, phonetic.

784   SMITH, ED. Where To, Black Man? Chicago: Quadrangle Books,
       1967.
           Written by a black volunteer serving in the Ghana of Kwame
       Nkrumah over a period of some eighteen months as diary entries,
       this politically aware account illustrates clearly the ambiguous
       position of Afro-Americans in the 1960's as viewed by newly
       independent African states. Of particular interest are the
       descriptions of the activities of the Young Pioneer organizers and
       the differences--sometimes sharp--between public statement and
       private opinion concerning the success of Nkrumah's remaking of
       Ghanaian society.

785   THURBER, ALAN. "Peace Corps Couple in Ghana Bring Abundant
       Instant Results". Congressional Record, 132, n.137 (7 October
       1986): S15529-30.
           Placed in the Congressional Record by Senator Dennis
       DeConcini of Arizona, this article is one of a series looking at
       the contributions of citizens of that state to the Peace Corps.
       This case is from Ghana, where a couple with experience in
       drilling wells are working to bring safe sources of water to a
       large region of west-central villages near the town of Wenchi.

786   ZEITLIN, ARNOLD. To the Peace Corps, with Love. New York:
       Doubleday, 1965.
           In October, 1961, Arnold Zeitlin arrived in Ghana to become
       part of the first group of Peace Corps volunteers to serve
       anywhere in the world. Invited by Kwame Nkrumah, Ghana I was to
       demonstrate just how well the promises made by President Kennedy
       could be carried out. This account chronicles his experiences and
       those of this wife--also a volunteer--as they adapted to
       everything from mammy lorries, British education standards and
       ebullient nationalism to the niceties of international politics.
       As a window into the earliest days of the Peace Corps experience,
       this work is uniquely valuable.

787   U. S. Department of State. Gilbert and Ellice Islands. Peace
       Corps. Agreement Effected by Exchange of Notes Signed at Suva
       and Tarawa November 12 and 20, 1974. United States Treaties
       and Other International Agreements Series, no. 7991, vol. 25,
       p. 3, Washington, D.C.: Government Printing Office, 1975,
       3383-85. S9.12:25 Part 3.
          This document contains the full texts of notes given between
       Walter V. Hall, American charge d'affaires, and His Excellency
       John H. Smith, governor of the Gilbert and Ellice Islands, setting
       forth the framework within which the Peace Corps workers would
       serve that archipelago.

788   U. S. Department of State. Peace Corps. Kiribati
       (Gilbertese): Communication and Culture Handbook. Washington,
       D.C.: 1979.
          Forty situations drawn from the life of the Gilbert Islands
       are used to present basic cultural structures and to provide
       conversational practice. The full text is entered on the ERIC
       database as document ED 205 003.

789   U. S. Department of State. Peace Corps. Kiribati
       (Gilbertese): Grammar Handbook. Washington, D.C.: 1979.
          Forty lessons on the grammar of the Kiribati language of the
       Gilbert Islands archipelago, including examples, practice
       exercises (both written and oral) and an English/Kiribati
       glossary. Developed as part of a series for the Micronesian
       languages at the Experiment in International Living, the full text
       of this document is available on the ERIC database as item ED 205
       004.

790   U. S. Department of State. Peace Corps. Kiribati
       (Gilbertese): Special Skills Handbook. Washington, D.C.:
       1979.
          A collection of readings intended to acquaint the volunteer
       in the Gilbert Islands with the region's history, geography and
       culture. Texts in both Kiribati and English include mythology,
       plant names, maps and a gazetteer. Developed by the Experiment in
       International Living, the full text is available on the ERIC
       database as document ED 205 006.

791   U. S. Department of State. Peace Corps. Kiribati
       (Gilbertese): Teacher's Handbook. Washington, D.C.: 1979.
          Intended as an accompaniment to the Peace Corps texts for
       the acquisition of Kiribati, this volume assists the native
       speaker in understanding the perspective of the volunteers and
       discusses useful teaching techniques. Three sections present
       course outlines and organization, commentaries and lesson notes
       for the handbooks on grammar and communication and culture. The
       full text is available on the ERIC database as document ED 205
       005.

792   U. S. Department of State. <u>Grenada. Peace Corps. Agreement</u>
        <u>Effected by Exchange of Notes Signed at Bridgetown, Barbados,</u>
        <u>December 19, 1966 and at Grenada December 16, 1967</u>. United
        States Treaties and Other International Agreements Series, no.
        6398, vol. 18, p. 3, Washington, D.C.: Government Printing
        Office, 1969, 3073-77. S9.12:18 Part 3.
        The complete texts of notes given between George Dolgin,
American charge d'affaires, and His Honor E. M. Gairy, premier of
Grenada, setting forth the basis upon which volunteers would serve
in that island nation. Researchers will note that diplomatic
personnel changed between the first and second documents.

793   "Grenada: Now the Peace Corps". <u>Christian Science Monitor</u>
        (3 January 1984): 23
        An editorial on the United States invasion of Grenada and
the role and obligations assumed. While many Grenadians
appreciated the removal of the Marxist government, the island
nation requires more aid in the form of economic and social
assistance. The U. S. is called upon to honor the request of
Grenada for Peace Corps volunteers "as soon as possible". Their
projected assignments will be in restoring the island road
network, agriculture and education. Such a move would disprove
assertions by critics that the only priority of the government in
the Caribbean is the displacement of Communism.

794   "Peace Corps/Grenada". <u>Peace Corps Times</u>. (March/April 1986):
        12.
        An invitation to return was received by the Peace Corps from
the government of the island nation of Grenada in January, 1984.
This article reviews the progress made in the period 1984-1986 on
re-establishing volunteers in the fields of secondary school
teaching and nursing, the latter involved in teaching as well as
patient care. Agriculture and small business development are also
part of the requested assistance from the Grenadian government. A
photograph showing President Reagan visiting the assembled
volunteers on the twenty-fifth anniversary year of Corps
accompanies the article.

795   U. S. Department of State. <u>Guatemala. Peace Corps Program.</u>
        <u>Agreement Effected by Exchange of Notes Signed at Guatemala</u>
        <u>December 28 and 29, 1962</u>. United States Treaties and Other
        International Agreements Series, no. 5307, vol. 14, p. 1,
        Washington, D.C.: Government Printing Office, 1962, 280-84.
        S9.12:14 Part 1.
        This document contains the full texts, in both English and
Spanish, of notes exchanged between John O. Bell, United State
Ambassador to Guatemala, and His Excellency Jesus Unda Murillo,
minister of foreign relations. The exchange and acceptance of
these documents created a legal basis for the presence and work of
Peace Corps personnel in Guatemala.

796   BLAIR, ROBERT W. <u>Cakchiquel Basic Course</u>. Washington, D.C.:
       Peace Corps, 1969.
       Developed at Brigham Young University as preparation for
volunteers posted to the Mayan regions of Guatemala, this course
manual uses the principle of "overchallenge" (constant demands on
the students at their maximum rate of learning). Twelve units are
presented, prefaced by a brief historical background on Cakchiquel
and language learning myths. Appendixes contain dialogues, verb
conjugations, games contests and vocabulary list. The complete
text of the document may be found as ERIC document ED 028 325.

797   "The Earth Roared: Walls Turned to Rubble". AA1.13:4/8.
       <u>InterACTION</u>, 4, n.8 (May 1976): 3, 5.
       An eyewitness account of the earthquake which devastated
large sections of Guatemala in 1976 and the response of Peace
Corps members to the havoc in their towns and regions.
Participation ranged from serving as translators for other aid
groups to reburying bodies in a ravaged cemetery.

798   "Earthquake". AA1.13:4/7. <u>InterACTION</u>, 4, n.7 (April 1976):
       1-2.
       A summary account of the effect of the Guatemalan earthquake
of February 4, 1976 on both the Peace Corps volunteers serving in
that nation and their response to aid its victims. With
acceptance by local people as an assist, they filled diverse role
as translators for the Guatemalan governmental survey. Peace
Corps nurses from neighboring Honduras were also flown in to
assist.

799   HOYT, ANTHONY and CARLYLE STOUT. "Organic Methods Bring Hope
       to Guatemala". <u>Organic Gardening and Farming</u>, 23, n.1 (January
       1976): 168-72.
       Two volunteers detail the program of school gardens and
nutritional education currently underway in highland Guatemala.
The objective of this plan is to provide an increased level of
nutrition for the population through utilizing demonstration
gardens at local schools as catalysts for introducing new plants
and practices. Guatemala is noted as having a massive problem
with child nutrition, as well as some twenty-nine languages,
making national efforts difficult to carry out. Organic methods
were adopted due to the increase in the prices of chemical
fertilizers and their more appropriate roles for the regional
ecology. Full details of the logistics of the program are
included.

800   "Life and Times of A Forester in Guatemala". <u>American Forests
       and Forest Life</u>, 84, n.5 (May 1978): 27.
       An interview with Michael Finity, serving as a volunteer in
the highlands of northwestern Guatemala in the area of soil and
forest conservation. Forty volunteers are working for the
National Forest Institute of Guatemala in a widespread program of
natural-resources conservation. Details of both the plan and
Finity's training and adaptation are also included.

801 "PCV's Join Guatemala Earthquake Relief". AA1.13:4/5.
  InterACTION, 4, n.5 (March 1976): 1.
    The 132 members of the Peace Corps assigned to Guatemala at
the time of the February 15, 1976 earthquake have been fully
integrated into disaster relief efforts of such agencies as the
Red Cross and CARITAS. Working as health care providers,
communications translators and delivering food supplies to
stricken areas, Corps members are rotated between assistance work
and recovery centers set up in Quetzaltenango and Guatemala City.
Members of Peace Corps/Honduras and Nicaragua with medical
backgrounds, including thirty nurses, have been brought in to ease
the strain on in-country personnel.

802 "Senior Peace Corps Volunteers Aid Workers and Students in
  Central America". Aging, 255 (January 1976): 17.
    Interviews with Klaus Schocken and Janet Klepper, senior
volunteers serving in Honduras and Guatemala. Their views on the
contributions which seniors can and are making to their host
nations provide a different perspective on the benefits of Peace
Corps service. Schocken teaches physics and Janet Klepper works
with women craftspeople in the area of quality control.

803 U. S. Department of State. Guinea. Peace Corps Program.
  Agreement Effected by Exchange of Notes Signed at Conakry
  December 11 and 14, 1962. United State Treaties and Other
  International Agreements Series, no. 5246, vol. 13, p. 3,
  Washington, D.C.: Government Printing Office, 1962, 2729-34.
  S9.12:13 Part 3.
    The complete texts of notes exchanged between the United
States ambassador, William Attwood, and the Guinean minister of
posts, telephones and telecommunications, A. Diop, which created a
legal basis for the presence of Peace Corps in Guinea. Volunteers
entered that country in 1963, 1969 and 1985.

804 U. S. Department of State. Peace Corps. French for West
  Africa. Washington, D.C.: 1966.
    Prepared at George Washington University in 1966 as part of
a training program for Peace Corps/Guinea, this text presents
French as it is used in Senegal, Mali, Dahomey, Upper Volta,
Niger, Ivory Coast and the Cameroons as well. Emphasis is on
pattern drills of repetition and progressive substitution of new
elements. The full text has been entered on the ERIC database as
document ED 153 464.

805   U.S. Department of State. <u>Guyana. Peace Corps. Agreement</u>
        <u>Effected by Exchange of notes Signed at Georgetown May 31 and</u>
        <u>June 7, 1967</u>. United States Treaties and Other International
        Agreements Series, no. 6277, vol. 18, p. 2, Washington, D.C.:
        Government Printing Office, 1968, 1259-61. S9.12:18 Part 2.
           This document contains the full text of notes given between
        Delmar R. Carlson, ambassador of the United States, and His
        Excellency S. S. Ramphal, minister of state, setting out the basic
        format of legal relations covering the Peace Corps presence in
        that country. This treaty remained in force until the departure
        of Peace Corps from Guyana in 1971.

806   "PCV's to Guyana". S19.11/2:4/7. <u>Peace Corps Volunteer</u>, 4,
        n.7 (May 1966):   3.
           In September, 1966, fifty volunteers will arrive in newly-
        independent Guyana to serve as math, science, commercial and
        physical education teachers in government schools on the coast and
        in the capital. Several architects are also planned for later
        deployment.

807   U. S. Department of State. <u>Peace Corps: Agreement Between the</u>
        <u>United States of America and Haiti Effected by Exchange of</u>
        <u>Notes Signed at Port-au-Prince August 12 and 13, 1982</u>.
        Treaties and Other International Acts Series 10445, Washington,
        D.C.: Government Printing Office, 1985. S9.10:10445.
           This document contains the full text of the two notes whose
        exchange between Earnest Preeg, the U. S. ambassador to Haiti and
        Jean-Robert Estime, secretary of state for foreign affairs of the
        Republic of Haiti, formalized the acceptance of an invitation for
        volunteers to serve in that country. Specific areas of assistance
        are not given.

808   U. S. Department of State. <u>Honduras. Peace Corps Program.</u>
        <u>Agreement Effected by Exchange of Notes Signed at Tegucigalpa</u>
        <u>July 16 and 20, 1962</u>. United States Treaties and Other Inter-
        national Agreements Series, no. 5142, vol. 13, p. 2,
        Washington, D.C.: Government Printing Office, 1962, 1892-97.
        S9.12:Part 2.
           The full text, in both Spanish and Enlgish, of the notes
        exchanged between the Honduran minister of foreign affairs, His
        Excellency Andres Alvarado Puerto, and Charles R. Burrows,
        ambassador of the United States, which created a legal basis for
        the entry of Peace Corps to Honduras. This agreement has remained
        in force since its original signing.

809   "Close-Up: Honduras--Education as Experience". AA1.10:2/6.
       Transition (June 1973): 18-21.
              This survey article of the variety and types of educational
       volunteer placement in Houduras was written by the volunteers
       themselves, and presents a summary of involvement in primary,
       secondary, university and vocational education. Detailed accounts
       of problems encountered in each area are also included. Nursing
       and fine arts and physical education programs are also included as
       well. Researchers will find this a concise picture of the state
       of Peace Corps participation in the Honduran system of education
       as of 1973.

810   DWYER, MARYANN. "Peace Corps Assists Houduras in Wildlife
       Conservation". Conservation News, 40, n.24 (5 December 1975):
       4-5.
              A case study of the work of Earl Klein, Peace Corps/
       Honduras, in aiding the nation of Honduras to set up its first zoo
       for the breeding and preservation of endangered species of
       wildlife. Among his contributions were participating in the
       drafting of the first proposed conservation laws. Other
       volunteers are at work in this field in Thailand and Kenya: their
       projects are profiled.

811   GREGG, CAROL and STEW. "Keeping Busy in Honduras".
       S19.11/2:2/3. Peace Corps Volunteer, 2, n.3 (January 1964): 6-
       7.
              A social work couple assigned to the community center in San
       Pedro Sula, Honduras describe their projects--and some failures--
       as well as a sampling of the other projects being carried out by
       members of one of the first groups to serve in that nation.
       Pictures of several of the activities are included.

812   "PCV Sparks Special Olmypics". AA1.13:5/4. InterACTION, 5,
       n.4 (January 1977): 1.
              In August, 1976, the first Special Olympics held in
       Honduras took place in Tegucigalpa. This article covers the
       efforts put forth by volunteer Jim Cristie in interesting
       Hondurans in holding such an event for the students at CIRE, the
       only public school for the deaf and retarded in the country.

813   "PCV Unearths Archaeological Treasures In Honduras".
       AA1.13:4/4. InterACTION, 4, n.4 (January 1976): 1.
              A member of PC Honduras assisting in relief efforts
       following Hurricane Fifi located a large archaeological site in
       the Choloma Valley near the north coast. A description of the
       ruins and their mapping by James Sheehy as an assist to the
       Archaeological Institute of Honduras, which had no field staff at
       this time, is provided.

814   "PCV's Weather Storm: Help With Relief Work". AA1.13:3/2.
       InterACTION, 3, n.2 (November 1974): 1-2.
          On September 20, 1974, Hurricane Fifi struck northern
       Honduras, bringing widespread destruction and wiping out ninety
       percent of the banana crop. This article recounts the efforts of
       the members of Peace Corps/Honduras to aid their host country to
       rebuild and inoculate the population against typhoid and
       smallpox.

815   "Peace Corps Nurses Help Hondurans Help Themselves".
       Hospitals, 37 (16 March 1963): 51-7.
          This article examines the daily duties and life of four
       Peace Corps nurses serving in Honduras as part of a group of
       twenty-five nurses and social workers. Clinical conditions,
       problems of Honduran public health and solutions evolved by the
       volunteers are discussed. The article is lavishly illustrated
       with photographs and maps.

816   "Peace Corps Seeks RN Volunteers". Hospital Progress, 45 (June
       1964): 40.
          Saint Louis University agreed to serve as the training site
       for a new Peace Corps project for the Republic of Honduras.
       Twenty-one nurses are needed to work in community medical centers
       and design an in-service training system for hospital auxiliary
       nurses. Details of training in the United States and in
       Tegucigalpa are provided.

817   "Varied Skills Help Honduras Develop Resources". AA1.13:2/6.
       InterACTION, 2, n.6 (March 1974): 12.
          A group of three photographs and accompanying text which
       illustrate the work of three members of Peace Corps/Honduras who
       serve as foresters, nutrition experts and beekeepers.

818   "What It's Like to be a Peace Corps Volunteer". American
       Forests and Forest Life, 91 (July 1985): 25.
          This short article focuses on the work being done by Phillip
       Rodbell, a forestry volunteer in the town of Sabanagrande,
       Honduras. Overall goals of the reforestation scheme and personal
       changes in the individual perspective of the volunteer are set
       out.

819   U. S. Department of State. India. Peace Corps Program.
       Agreement Effected by Exchange of Notes Signed at New Delhi
       November 13 and 21, 1962. United States Treaties and Other
       International Agreements Series, no. 5247, vol. 13, p. 3,
       Washington, D.C.: Government Printing Office, 1962, 2735-38.
       S9.12:Part 3.
          The complete texts of notes given between the United States
       ambassador to India, John Kenneth Galbraith, and His Excellency
       Jawaharlal Nehru, prime minster of India, which laid the legal
       basis upon which Peace Corps volunteers and staff would work in
       that nation. This agreement remained in force until the departure
       of Peace Corps from India in 1976.

820 BERNSTEIN, JUDITH, et.al. Conversational Tamil. Washington,
     D.C.: Peace Corps, 1961.
     Designed for Peace Corps programs in agriculture in the
     Tamil-speaking regions of India, this manual of language drills
     and dialogues is intended to develop conversational skills. The
     complete text is available as ERIC document 148 158.

821 BERNSTEIN, JUDITH, et.al. Conversational Telugu. Washington,
     D.C.: Peace Crops, 1962.
     A general manual aimed at the development of conversational
     skills in Telugu, a Dravidian language of southern India.
     Beginning with mimicry of patterns and listening comprehension,
     the text moves to drill exercises and task-oriented dialogues.
     The full text is available as ERIC document ED 152 110.

822 BOYER, PETER. "Sunsets, Smiles, 101 Strings". Congressional
     Record, 110, p.24 (11 May 1964): 2400.
     A report from a volunteer stationed at Osmania University in
     the city of Hyderabad, in central India, as an English instructor.
     The article reports on his efforts at organizing a summer course
     in English for high school seniors who would soon enter
     university. Although eventually successful in a limited fashion,
     the experience of attempting to set up such a program taught Boyer
     several lessons. In his view, "often a country is judged by the
     scope of its problems and not by its attempt to overcome them."

823 CARTER, LILLIAN. Away From Home: Letters to My Family. New
     York: Simon and Schuster, 1977.
     This volume is a reprinted collection of the letters Lillian
     Carter sent home to her family in Georgia during her tour of duty
     as a Peace Corps nurse in a clinic near Bombay from 1966 to 1968.
     Due to her son's subsequent election to the Presidency, "Miss
     Lillian" became one of the best known and familiar figures of the
     Carter administration. Her letters speak for themselves of
     culture shock, emotional involvement with her host country and new
     friends, and adapting to an environment containing everything from
     fire gods to streets full of sacred cows.

824 CARTER, WOODY. "The Volunteer in the Gray Flannel Suit".
     S19.11/2:9/3-4. Volunteer, 9, n.3-4 (March-April 1971): 6-
     11.
     An account by a married couple, members of India 63, as to
     the success and redefinitions experienced by their group involved
     in family planning efforts in the Indian state of Punjab. Issues
     raised include effectiveness of training, redefinition of possible
     roles for the volunteers in their bureaucratic situations, and
     suggestions as to the goals and objectives of Peace Corps
     involvement in such an extended and frustrating program. The
     India 63 group arrived in country in November, 1968.

825   CLAES, THOMAS. "'Something Stuck'". S19.11/2:8/5. <u>Volunteer</u>
       8, n.5 (May-June 1970): 14-5.
            A former member of India VII involved in poultry raising in
       the Indian state of West Bengal in 1964 returns to his site. A
       local industry in poultry is examined and impact of Corps work in
       the region assessed.

826   "The Clarence Pickards Are Still Going Strong--As Peace Corps
       Volunteers in Their 70's". <u>Aging</u>, 165 (July 1968): 15.
            An interview with Clarence and Mildred Pickard, serving at
       an agricultural training center near the city of Bulanshahr in the
       state of Uttar pradesh. At seventy-eight, Clarence Pickard was
       the oldest member of the Peace Corps at that time. Of the 12,300
       volunteers then serving, eighty-five percent were in their
       twenties. Note is made of a second couple, the Frank Herriots,
       also senior volunteers, serving in the Kingdom of Lesotho.

827   "Co-Op Tool Factory Makes Implements For India's Farms".
       S19.11/2:1/9. <u>Peace Corps Volunteer</u>, 1, n.9 (July 1963): 5.
            In the Indian state of Uttar Pradesh, four members of Peace
       Corps/India have set up a co-operative manufacturing farm
       implements for their local region around the town of Bisauli. All
       shareholders are local residents, and the project will be turned
       over to Indian management following their departure. Orders for
       two dozen of the farm implement they designed have already been
       received.

828   "From Judgement Ridge to India". S19.11/2:4/10. <u>Peace Corps</u>
       <u>Volunteer</u>, 4, n.10 (August 1966): 7-11.
            An account of the training being given at Judgment Ridge,
       Vermont, to volunteers assigned to food production projects in
       India. Most of the postings are to be in the southern state of
       Andhra Pradesh. Goals are to alter food habits on the village
       level. Photographs of the training are included.

829   GAUDINO, ROBERT L. <u>The Uncomfortable Learning: Some Americans</u>
       <u>in India</u>. Bombay: Popular Prakashan Ltd, 1974.
            This volume reports on a group of sixty-eight volunteers who
       served in India from September, 1966 to June, 1968 assigned to an
       applied nutrition project. In July and August of 1967, Gaudino,
       director of the training program which prepared them, visited
       fifty-four surviving members of the original group and discussed
       their experiences with them. In addition to lengthy taped
       interviews, all fifty-six received and responded to a fifty-item
       questionnaire. <u>Uncomfortable Learning</u> opens with letters written
       by the PCVs commenting upon their situation in India from October,
       1966 to June, 1968. The situation in India with regard to
       nutrition and the participation of Peace Corps workers in it is
       next reviewed. A chapter on training notes language facility,
       cultural studies and technical skills as the three emphases of the
       program. Questionnaire responses, volunteer expectations and
       reasons for feelings of failure comprise the remaining sections of
       the book. A useful case study of an early project with all its
       attendant problems.

830 "India: The Winds of Change Are Blowing". S19.11/2:2/6.
Peace Corps Volunteer, 2, n.6 (April 1964): 8-21.
     A collection of brief articles written by members of Peace
Corps/India serving in capacities ranging from village health
nurses and English teachers to printing shop instructors.
Observations on the importance of learning the host languages well
and questions based on racial backgrounds are also raised.

831 "Jimmy Carter's Mother". Newsweek, 88 (4 July 1976): 17-8.
     A brief interview with Lillian Carter, discussing how she
decided to go to the Peace Corps, her family's reaction, and her
own thoughts on the meaning of her time in India.

832 "Miss Lillian Returns to India". AA1.13:5/7. InterACTION, 5,
n.7 (April 1977): 1, 11.
     Upon the death of Indian President Pakhruddin Ali Ahmed,
President Jimmy Carter asked his mother to serve as head of the
United States delegation to the funeral observances. Following
completion of her diplomatic duties, Lillian Carter met with Prime
Minister Indira Gandhi and then traveled to the village of
Vikhroli, fifteen miles north of Bombay, her site as a Peace Corps
nurse from 1967 to 1969. This expression of interest in her old
friends and community was favorably viewed by the Indian press.

833 MOAG, RACHEL and RODNEY. A Course In Colloquial Malayalam.
Milwaukee, Wisconsin: University of Wisconsin/Milwaukee/U. S.
Peace Corps, June, 1967.
     The present work was begun by the authors in July, 1965 in
preparation for the arrival of the members of India 20 in
Milwaukee for three months of training in language and culture.
Following the completion of this period they visited the state of
Kerala and received assistance in linguistics from the university
faculty in Trivandrum, which stimulated massive revision of the
original text. It is this revised version which is represented by
the present work. The text can be found in the ERI system as
document ED 030 093.

834 "The News, Briefly". Christian Science Monitor (29 March
1969): 2.
     The government of the Indian state of West Bengal, dominated
by members of the Indian Communist Party, ordered the immediate
expulsion of all Peace Corps volunteers. Most had been assigned
to constructing rural wells.

835 "Peace Corps Couple Typify New Trend". Peace Corps, Pauline
Madow, ed., New York: Wilson, 1964: 88-91.
     An interview with Carl and Jane Gibson, chemists serving at
the Uttar Pradesh Agricultural University at Pantanagara as
part of Peace Corps/India. In addition to their faculty
duties, they also work in the area of community development.
Part of the article is a discussion of the contributions of
technically trained volunteers with Jules Pagano, director of
the professional and technical division of the Peace Corps.

836   "Peace Corps To Double Farm Workers in India". Washington
       Post, (2 April 1966): A15.
            President Lyndon Johnson has directed that the number of
       agricultural workers in service in India be doubled by the end of
       1966. This recommendation came following a conference with the
       prime minister of India, Mrs. Indira Gandhi. Presently, a
       complement of four hundred volunteers are already at work in
       increasing food production, and another five hundred will be in
       place by September.

837   "Peace Corps Worker Called CIA Agent". Christian Science
       Monitor (3 April 1967): 6.
            Joyce Russell, regional director of Peace Corps/India in the
       state of Andhra Pradesh, was attacked as a "U. S. Mata Hari" by
       The Blitz, a leading leftist periodical. Prior to her assignment
       Russell had taught home economics at two colleges in southern
       India. Corps officials denied the charges and viewed them as a
       personal grudge against Russell by a disgruntled official.

838   "Peace Corps Works Quietly in India". AA1.13:1/11.
       InterACTION, 1, n.11 (August 1973): 4.
            An interview with John Pupols, serving as an agricultural
       and farming advisor in Rajasthan, one of the ninety-four PCVs
       remaining in India at this time. The Indian government has set a
       ceiling of no more than fifty volunteers in-country from any
       foreign assistance program similar to the Peace Corps:
       accordingly, the number assigned to India is expected to decline
       to lower level by December, 1974. At present, Corps personnel are
       assigned to six states of India and are involved in teaching
       English and science as well as animal husbandry.

839   POPE, CARL. Sahib: An American Misadventure in India. New
       York: Liveright, 1972.
            This volume chronicles the experiences of Carl and Judy
       Pope, volunteers assigned to a family planning project in Barhi, a
       village in the southern hill country of the Indian State of Bihar.
       Their reactions to--and affection for--the world of arranged
       marriages and caste regulations is clear in the text. Sahib
       recounts their efforts to remain and the reasons underlying their
       early termination.

840   RAU, SANTHA RAMA. "It's A Long Long Way from Old Camp
       Shawnee". New York Times Magazine (13 November 1966) Section
       6: 52-3, 122-40.
            A former boy's camp in the Pocono Mountains of Pennsylvania
       was transformed into a pseudo-Indian village by the University of
       Pennsylvania in the summer of 1966. Its aim was to serve as a
       base for the preparation of sixty volunteers for servie in the
       state of Gujarat as food production and applied nutrition workers.
       The author, a noted writer on her native India, records her
       impressions of Camp Shawnee--the training regimen--involving
       everything from morning yoga classes to construction of a Hindu
       temple, acclimatization to Indian food and growing rice--and feels

that, despite all the efforts, the camp cannot convey the real feeling of life in Gujarat. She then sketches such a village world and recounts an experience of her own with village culture to illustrate problems the volunteers will face.

841 "Resigning from Peace Corps". AA1.13:2/4. InterACTION, 2, n.4 (January 1974): 13.
Excerpts from an article written by David Rogers, Director of Peace Corps/India for an expatriate publication in Delhi. Reasons advanced for resignation of service include inability to handle individual responsibility and inexperience with working as part of a bureaucracy.

842 SABAVALA, SHAROKN. "Peace Corps Clicks in India". Christian Science Monitor (9 November 1966): 6.
By early 1967, some fourteen hundred members of Peace Corps/India were serving that nation in the fields of agriculture, health and nutrition in fifteen of its states. Their presence came at a time of increased student unrest and general political agitation, including fabricated "incidents" involving volunteers. Despite such pressures, defense of Corps personnel and their contributions has been firm, even in India's parliament. Proposals such as that of Ambassador Chester Bowles for a "reverse Peace Corps" of young Indians in the United States seem to be one option for engaging the interests of many of India's youth who feel isolated and useless. A program known as the "shanti sena", proposed by a follower of Mahatm Gandhi, is also under study.

843 SHARMA, D. N. and JAMES W. STONE. Hindi: An Active Introduction. Washington, D.C.: Peace Corps, 1970.
A text of basic Hindi used in training for Peace Corps/India using the microwave approach to language instruction. Developed at the Foreign Service Institute of the State Department, the Hindi is introduced in the Devanagari script, with emphasis on geography and personal information. Cultural notes and grammar are given in English. Full text is included in the ERIC database as document ED 044 665.

844 SHUBIN, S. "A Conversation with Lillian Carter, RN". Nursing 78 (September 1978): 62-6.
An interview conversation with Lillian Carter covering her professional history as a nurse, highlighting her philosophy of service and caring. Her time as a Peace Corps nurse in India is of particular importance to her.

845 VISEL, ADELE. Of Brahmins and Lesser Folk. New York: Vantage Press, 1979.
Adele Visel describes herself as "a retired English teacher looking for a new challenge", a search which lead her to training in the South Indian city of Bangalore, lessons in Tamil, and walking through a new culture. Her account is at once poignant and humorous.

846   WEATHERALL, ERNEST. "'Graduate' Recalls Peace Corps Days".
       Christian Science Monitor (11 November 1967):   3.
           An interview with Tomas and Mary Ann Senett, veterans of
       Peace Corps/India, discussing their two years working on rural
       development and nutrition projects in a Rajasthan village. Issues
       noted range from social adjustment in village life to charges of
       working for the CIA.

847   U. S. Department of State. Indonesia, Peace Corps Program.
       Agreement Effected by Exchange of Notes Dated at Djakarta March
       8 and 14, 1963. United States Treaties and Other International
       Agreements Series, no. 5489, vol. 14, p. 2, Washington, D.C.:
       Government Printing Office, 1964, 1789-93. S9.12:14 Part 2.
           This document consists of the response of the Department of
       Foreign Affairs of the Republic of Indonesia to a note given by
       the American Embassy in Djakarta, dated November 13, 1962, which
       offered the services of the Peace Corps to Indonesia. The
       provisions of that note are stated to be acceptable to the
       Indonesian government.

848   "Ambassador Bunker Concludes Meetings With Indonesian Leaders".
       Department of State Bulletin, 52 (April-June 1965):   654-55.
           A joint communique released on April 15, 1965 at Jakarta,
       Indonesia, by Ambassador Ellsworth Bunker and His Excellency
       President Sukarno of Indonesia, touching upon various matters
       lying between their respective nations. Owing to the dispute over
       the questions of whether the states of British Borneo favored
       union with Malaysia or Indonesia, the two agreed "that in light of
       the current situation the Peace Corps should cease operations in
       Indonesia". Volunteers were to terminate their activities and be
       out of the country within several weeks.

849   DOUGHTY, DICK. "Indonesia Volunteer Finds Smiles and Djeruk
       Juice". Peace Corps Volunteer, 2, n.1 (November 1963):   22.
       S19.11/2:2/1.
           In May, 1963 a group of seventeen athletic coaches arrived
       in Indonesia for posting to KOGOR, that nation's sports
       association. This article details the life of one of them in the
       city of Bandung.

850   "Indonesians Ask More Corpsmen". Congressional Record, 109,
       p.28 (30 July 1963):   A4853.
           A reprint of an article from the New York Times of July 28,
       1963, reporting that thirty-three more volunteers are being
       requested by the government of Indonesia. Types of postings of
       the initial seventeen volunteers include athletic instructors and
       lecturers at the University of Jogjakarta. Opposition to their
       presence by the Communist Party of Indonesia is noted.

851   U. S. Department of State. <u>Iran. Peace Corps. Agreement</u>
      <u>Effected by Exchange of Notes Signed at Tehran September 5 and</u>
      <u>16, 1962</u>. United States Treaties and Other International
      Agreements Series, no. 7078, vol. 22, p. 1, Washington, D.C.:
      Government Printing Office, 1971, 434-40. S9.12:13 Part 1.
          This document contains the full texts, in both Farsi and
      English, of the notes exchanged between His Excellency Abbas Aram,
      minister of foreign affairs, and J. C. Holmes, ambassador to Iran,
      which laid the foundation for Peace Corps service in that country.
      This agreement remained in force until the departure of Peace
      Corps from Iran in 1976.

852   "Age, Business Experience Aid in Improving Communications in
      Iran". AA1.33:3/2. <u>InterACTION</u>, 3, n.2 (November 1974): 12.
          An account of the work being done by Prabhu Sondhi, seventy-
      four, as an English instructor in Teheran. In addition to newly-
      learned Farsi, Sondhi, a recent immigrant from India, also speaks
      Hindi and Punjabi.

853   "The Beautiful American: A Peace Corps Volunteer Who Couldn't
      Come Home". S19.11/2:9/3-4. <u>Volunteer</u>, 9, n.3-4 (March-April
      1971): 12-5.
          A profile of the work done by Barkley Moore in the Iranian
      city of Gonbad-e-Kavus, during his six years and four months in
      the Peace Corps. Among his accomplishments were founding a
      kindergarten and library, teaching English and assisting in school
      construction. Upon his departure, the citizens of Gonbad
      presented him with some thirty-two pieces of weaving, including
      saddlebags, prayer rugs and carpets.

854   DURFEY, JAMES. "Masjeds: The Architecture of Meditation".
      S19.11/2:8/9-10. <u>Volunteer</u>, 8, n. 9-10 (September-October
      1970): 19-21.
          In the earthquake of August 31, 1968, a massive mosque in
      the village of Kakh in the province of Khorasan, Iran was badly
      damaged. An architect serving in Peace Corps/Iran was asked to
      design a new structure. In this article he comments on the
      traditional system of theology as exemplified by buildings which
      makes up a <u>masjed</u> complex and which influenced his own work.

855   <u>Glossary of English-Farsi Agricultural Terms</u>. Washington,
      D.C.: Peace Corps, 1964.
          Five hundred useful terms in English and Farsi for volun-
      teers working as agricultural extension agents in Iran are
      listed. The full text is available as ERIC document ED 228
      833.

856   "Grandfather, 74, Starting New 2-Year Duty Tour in Iran".
       Aging, 243 (January 1975):   11.
           An interview with Prabhu Sondhi, a volunteer serving in Iran
       at the College of Mass Communications in Tehran.   In the beginning
       of his seventh year as a Peace Corps member, he discusses the
       advantages of age in carrying out both cultural adaptations and
       the practical work of his assignment.   His position was as an
       English instructor, as part of Iran's effort to modernize.

857   HART, NEIL. "The Kutchee, the Highway and the City in Iran".
       S19.11/2:8/9-10. Volunteer, 8, n.9-10 (September-October
       1970): 14-5.
           The design of the Persian city of the immediate future is
       among the questions addressed in this article by a Peace Corps
       architect posted to the Iranian city of Hamadan.   His observations
       on the possible integration of traditional neighborhood structures
       into a more generalized city plan pose interesting questions.
       Background on the city planning efforts of Iran are also
       included.

858   HUF, TOM and ROGER CAVANNA. "A College of Dentistry For
       Mashad". S19.11/2:8/9-10. Volunteer, 8, n.9-10 (September-
       October 1970): 16-8.
           An account by two architects in Peace Corps/Iran of the
       factors to be considered when designing structures for a culture
       which possesses its own needs and concepts of spatial
       organization.   Their project for Mashad University is offered as
       both learning experience and example.

859   "Iran". S19.11/2:3/1. Peace Corps Volunteer, 3, n.1 (November
       1964):   6-13.
           An overview collection of articles on the roles and contri-
       butions made by members of Peace Corps/Iran.   Factors affecting
       their work include an ethnically diverse population, widely varied
       assignments (from English teaching to soil desalinization) and
       problems of transportation.   This collection presents a valuable
       picture of the ways in which Corps could adapt to a host nation
       where cultural change was well under way in many areas backed by
       mineral wealth.

860   LAMPEL, ARDEN. "Volunteers Around the World: the Peace Corps
       Is Into Vocational Education". American Vocational Journal, 47
       (December 1972): 56-7.
           In 1972, twenty-eight host countries had volunteers who were
       serving in the capacity of occupational instructors.   Ministry
       requests for such personnel involve operating school shops,
       curriculum development, supervision and administration, elec-
       tronics and welding, engineering and a wide variety of other
       vocational areas.   Examples are given from Iran and Swaziland.
       The process of setting up a school partnership program is also
       outlined.

861 "Living In the City: the Iran Municipal Development Project".
S19.11/2:8/9-10. <u>Volunteer</u>, 8, n.9-10 (September-October
1970): 11-21.
This extended article examines the varied projects being
conducted by five members of Peace Corps/Iran, including city
planning, designing a college of dentistry for the city of Mashad
and restoration work on a damaged mosque in Khorasan state. Each
contribution has been entered separately under its own title.

862 "The News, Briefly". <u>Christian Science Monitor</u> (6 October
1966): 2.
Thomas Dawson, the twenty-four-year old volunteer arrested
for violating the Soviet border with Iran, was released after more
than three weeks detention. Dawson departed immediately for
Washington, D.C.

863 "Peace Corps". <u>New Statesman</u>, 71 (4 March 1966): 296.
A letter from a correspondent at Pahlavi University in
Tehran complaining about the volunteers sent to that country. The
author is very much of the opinion that "Kennedy's election
gimmick has turned into a nationalistic scheme designed to . . .
propagate the American gospel." Corps members are described as
having little scope for individual initiative and as being
cautiousness itself. This is seen as ironic since the volunteers
are suppose to be introducing needed changes.

864 "Peace Corps 'Trial' Hinted". <u>Christian Science Monitor</u>
(26 September 1966): 2.
On September 11, 1966, Thomas Dawson, a member of Peace
Corps/Iran, waded across the Astara-Chai River intending to gather
shells on the north bank. The river forms the boundary between
the Soviet Union and Iran, and Dawson was promptly arrested by a
border patrol. He is being held in Baku, in Soviet Azerbaijan,
pending decision on a possible show trial. Representation has
been made to Soviet officials by Peace Corps and the Secretary of
State Dean Rusk to obtain his release.

865 "Peace Corps Volunteer Ends Six Year Stay in Iran". <u>New York
Times</u> (3 January 1971): 49.
An interview with Barkley Moore, a member of Peace
Corps/Iran recently returned from six years and four months of
service in the Iranian city of Gunbad-i-Qawus. The roster of his
accomplishments is extremely impressive, with the city having
bestowed citizenship upon him prior to his departure. His was the
longest period of service of any of the 37,00 volunteers presently
in service or returned as veterans.

866   SITOMER, CURTIS J.   "The Peace Corps Fails Only When
       Selfishness Comes In".   Christian Science Monitor (25 March
       1971):   21.
           An interview with returned volunteer Barkley Moore, who
       spent 6 1/2 years in the Iranian city of Gonbad-e-Kavus, fifty
       miles from the Soviet border.   In his tour of duty he focused on
       education, teaching English classes,, participating in the
       foundation of a library, and constantly prodded villagers and
       local mullahs on the value of educational improvements for their
       children.

867   STILO, DONALD L.   Introductory Persian, Washington, D.C.:
       Peace Corps, 1966.
           A basic course in the Persian language, with emphasis on
       skills useful in teaching of English as a foreign language.
       Materials included here were developed during the Peace Corps/Iran
       Summer Training Course at the University of Texas in 1966.   The
       lesson format includes dialogue, text can be found as ERIC
       document ED 131 694.

868   SVARE, HOMA, et. al.   Conversational Persian, Washington, D.C.:
       Peace Corps, 1966.
           Originally prepared at the State University of Utah in
       connection with the Peace Corps language instruction in Persian,
       the present edition was modified for use in the Peace Corps/Iran
       Pahlavi University Training Project at the University of
       Texas/Austin from November 15, 1965 to January 29, 1966.   Seven
       chapters cover Persian language and expressions for law and
       government (including practical bureaucracy), professions and
       trades, economics, biology, physics, chemistry, arts and
       humanities and basic information such as greetings.   The format
       reflects the placement of the group of volunteers using the
       document.   The full text has been entered into the ERIC database
       as document ED 132 838.

869   TONGE, PETER.   "The Letters Begin: 'My Dear Teacher'".
       Christian Science Monitor (8 July 1971):   15.
           An account of the letters being received by Barkley Moore,
       Peace Corps/Iran, from his former students in the city of Gonbad-
       e-Kavus in northeastern Elburz mountains.   His reminiscences of
       sharing ideas on the value of literacy are illustrative of Corps
       programming in that country.

870   U. S. Department of State.   Ivory Coast.   Peace Corps Program.
       Agreement Effected by Exchange of Notes Dated at Abidjan April
       5 and 21, 1962.   United States Treaties and Other International
       Agreements Series, no. 5561, vol. 15, p. 1, Washington, D.C.:
       Government Printing Office, 1962, 345-8.   S9.12:15   Part 1.
           This document contains the full text of notes exchanged
       between the United States Ambassador and Felix Houphouet-Boigny,
       president of the Republic of Ivory Coast, which laid the
       groundwork for the entry of Peace Corps volunteers and staff to
       that nation.   Both French and English texts are included.   This
       agreement remained in force until the departure of Corps in 1981.

871   "Ivory Coast". S19.11/2:1/10. <u>Peace Corps Volunteer</u>, 1, n.10
       (August 1963): 10-19.
           Ten articles on the work of the Peace Corps in the Ivory
       Coast, written by teachers of everything from English to physical
       education. An outline of the Ivorien educational system is
       included for reference.

872   "Voici Le Peace Corps". <u>Congressional Record</u>, 110, p.21 (13
       February 1964): A658-659.
           An article by a volunteer teaching at Port Bouet in the
       Ivory Coast, relating her adventures in adapting to both the
       French system of education and students who sing "Sur le pont
       d'Abidjan". A typical series of classroom activities is listed.

873   "Volunteer in Ivory Coast Relocates Remote Village".
       AA1.13:1/4. <u>InterACTION</u>, 1, n.4 (January 1973): 1, 8.
           Bob Burke, posted to work with the Ministry of Construction
       and Urbanism for the Agboville region of the Ivory Coast, some
       eighty kilometers north of Abidjan, has been involved in a
       modernization and relocation project for sixty-five villages. In
       this article, he describes the shift in rail lines and the
       resultant typical day of preparing a site for the creation of a
       new settlement.

874   "Volunteers Cover 9 Towns in 10 Days With Ivory Coast Athletic
       Caravan". S19.11/2:2/1. <u>Peace Corps Volunteer</u>, 2, n.1
       (November 1963): 4.
           Five members of Peace Corps/Ivory Coast participated in a
       traveling caravan consisting of a group of coaches intent upon
       competing with and training local athletes in several communities
       of the central Ivory Coast.

875   U. S. Department of State. <u>Jamaica. Peace Corps Program.</u>
       <u>Agreement Effected by Exchange of Notes Signed at Kingston</u>
       <u>February 15 and 22, 1962</u>. United State Treaties and Other
       International Agreements Series, no. 4954, vol. 13, p. 1,
       Washington, D.C.: Government Printing Office, 1962, 166-70.
           This document contains the full text of notes given between
       Robert G. McGregor, United States consul general in Jamaica, and
       N. W. Manley, premier of Jamaica, which laid the foundations for
       Peace Corps service in that country. Legal rights and exemptions
       extended to volunteers are specified.

876   BAILEY, BERYL LOFTMAN. <u>Jamaican Creole Language Course</u>.
       Washington, D.C.: Peace Corps, 1968.
           One hundred and twenty six cycles of lessons in the dominant
       version of English spoken on the island of Jamaica. Topics of the
       lessons include basic grammar and vocabulary, as well as cultural
       items such as folk songs. Full text is available as ERIC document
       ED 130-535.

877   "Beyond the Beaches of Jamaica--Another Way of Life".
       S19.11/2:3/12. Peace Corps Volunteer, 4, n.1 (November 1965):
       7-12.
            Work in the world of the two Jamaicas--that of Kingston and
       the rural land of "soon come" is portrayed in this set of five
       articles, including a vivid description of storytelling in the
       season known as "browndust."

878   COMITAS, LAMBROS. "Lessons from Jamaica". The Cultural
       Frontiers of The Peace Corps, Robert B. Textor, ed., Cambridge:
       M.I.T. Press, 1966, 201-19.
            The problems of administration, programming, organizations
       and cultural preparation which beset the members and staff of
       Jamaica One are outlined. The background data on Jamaican
       cultural similarities and sharp differences is included. The
       difficulties which these first Jamaican volunteers encountered are
       seen as similar to many other programs rather than as unique to
       that country. Factors contributing to the high degree of
       dissatisfaction evinced by these volunteers were a great turnover
       in senior staff positions, in-country staff who were not
       conversant with Jamaican mores and culture, poor timing of
       volunteer arrival, administrative communications breakdown and
       logistical frustrations. The Program Development and Operations
       office of Peace Corps is called upon to play a more important role
       in planning of actual country logistics when possible. The
       author, an anthropologist with specialization in the Caribbean,
       served as advisor for several programs in that region in 1961 and
       1962, as well as directing the training program for Jamaica One
       and visiting them in the field.

879   LAWTON, DAVID. "Some Problems of Teaching A Creolized Language
       to Peace Corps Members". Language Learning, 14, n.1-2 (1964):
       11-9.
            Using the case of Jamaican Creole as example, the issues
       surrounding the definition of a "creolized" Language and the
       problems this can pose for both language instructor and pupil are
       raised. The absence of adequate instructional materials for such
       languages, debate over definitions of exactly what constitutes a
       "base" language versus a "creolized" variant, and tonal variations
       of meaning are discussed. The author had worked as part of a team
       training volunteers for service in Jamaica, and notes that, in
       some cases "Peace Corps Volunteers are being sent to areas for
       which there are no adequate pedagogical materials" (p. 12). Use
       of bilingual informants and native speakers who are aware of the
       cultural issues involved for an outsider attempting to speak
       Creole are seen as necessary parts of such a training plan.
       Preliminary linguistic instruction should begin in the United
       States, with the bulk of learning taking place in-country.

880   "Making Music In Jamaica . . . From Scratch". <u>Peace Corps</u>
       <u>Times</u> (July/August 1985): 11.
       The story of the foundation of a small business specializing
in the manufacture of drums by Frank Treadwell, member of Peace
Corps/Jamaica, as a secondary project. Treadwell's principal
posting was as an agricultural and woodworking volunteer.

881   "Peace Corps Librarians in Jamaica". <u>Wilson Library Bulletin</u>,
       37 (December 1962): 319.
       Reporting on the arrival and posting of seven librarians to
Peace Corps/Jamaica, this new note mentions one factor with which
they will have to deal--the local language. Known as "Jamaican
Creole", it is virtually a distinctive language rather than merely
a dialect of English. Several examples of typical library
situations are given as illustrations. The volunteers received
help in their language training from a guide to the patois
compiled by the Research Institute for the Study of Man, the group
responsible for the stateside phase of their training.

882   "Peace Corps Volunteer for Bessemer Teaches New Farm Methods in
       Jamaica". <u>Congressional Record</u>, 121, p.16 (25 June 1975):
       20902.
       An account of the agricultural extension activities of
Robert Sabol, a volunteer stationed in Mt. Horeb, Jamaica. The
focus of his assignment is the improvement of local vegetable
crops and the introduction of new varieties. His living
conditions are described, and his acceptance by the community,
both via willingness to discuss many topics and his command of
Jamaican patois, pointed up as an example of integration with a
host culture. At the time this was written, 195 volunteers were
at work on Jamaica.

883   RAINE, PATTI. "PCV Presents Paper At IHC". <u>Peace Corps Times</u>
       (July/August 1985): 10.
       At the 12th International Health Conference in Washington,
D.C., June 3-5, 1985, the theme of discussion was "Management
Issues in Health Programs in The Third World". Among the papers
given at that time was one by Jeremy Clark of Peace Corps/Jamaica,
reporting on a system of access and data presentation in graphic
form used by the Public Health Department. Clark is currently
serving his second term of assignment as a volunteer.

884   "Recruiting, Jamaican Posts Filled By Peace Corps". <u>Christian</u>
       <u>Science Monitor</u> (4 October 1967): 3.
       Two staff appointments were announced by Peace Corps, Elaine
Cassell as director of specialized staff recruiting and Henry L.
Smith as deputy director for Peace Corps/Jamaica.

885   SCHNEBEL, CAROL. "Jamaica: No Place Like Home".
       S19.11/2:2/1. Peace Corps Volunteer, 2, n.1 (November 1963):
       10-11.
            A review article of the activities of the volunteers who
       arrived in Jamaica in June, 1962 by one of their number. Postings
       include agricultural work in extension, cataloging the library of
       the Jamaica Library Service, crafts work and teaching machine
       shop. Learning the attitude of "soon come" makes the experience
       easier.

886   "Soldier Becomes PCV". AA1.13:1/12. InterACTION, 1, n.12
       (September 1973):   4.
            An Army surveyor-turned Peace Corpsman, Bernard Loeffler
       served as an instructor in blueprint reading, English and
       mathematics at a vocational training center in Jamaica's north
       coast city of Falmouth. He recounts his views on joining and his
       contributions to Jamaica.

887   SMITH, MARVIN. "Jamaica Volunteer Afloat in Caribbean Maps".
       S19.11/2:1/5. Peace Corps Volunteer, 1, n.5 (March 1963):   5.
            A Peace Corps librarian assigned to the West India Reference
       Library at the Institute of Jamaica in Kingston discusses his
       cataloging and identification of several thousand maps and rare
       prints. He feels he is "creating an image for myself . . . my
       profession, the Peace Corps and the country I represent."

888   U. S. Department of State. Kenya. Peace Corps. Agreement
       Effected by Exchange of Notes Signed at Nairobi August 26,
       1964. United States Treaties and Other International Agree-
       ments, no. 5666, vol. 15, p. 2, Washington, D.C.:   Government
       Printing Office, 1964, 1906-12. S9.12:15 Part 2.
            The complete text of notes exchanged between William
       Attwood, ambassador to Kenya and His Excellency Jomo Kenyatta,
       prime minister of Kenya, creating the legal foundation for Peace
       Corps service in that nation.

889   BEATTY, RICHARD. "Travel As Transition, or the Shortest
       Distance Between Two Points Isn't Always the Most Interesting".
       AA1.10:2/5, 2/6. Transition (May 1973):   9-16:   (June 1973):
       3/10.
            This two-part article recounts the homeward journey of a
       member of Peace Corps/Kenya and his companions overland from
       Pakistan to England. Their trip included crossing the Khyber
       Pass, visiting the Blue Mosque in Isfahan, examining the
       underground cities of Anatolia and watching the famed Lippizaner
       stallions at the Spanish Riding School in Vienna. The author
       reflects on the overseas life of the Peace Corps and offers an
       example of one method of transition chosen by volunteers en route
       home.

890   "Kenya Volunteers Will Take Part In RCA, Education".
        S19.11/2:2/12. Peace Corps Volunteer, 2, n.12 (October 1964):
        3.
            A brief description of the projects and skills for which the
        members of Kenya I, to arrive in-country at the end of 1964, were
        recruited. Stress has been placed upon education (in the areas of
        history, geography, English, mathematics and science) and on
        assisting rural co-operatives.

891   "PCV Introduces 'Total Care' Idea". AA1.13:4/4. InterACTION,
        4, n.4 (January 1976): 2.
            The concept of regarding hospital patients as persons
        requiring a regimen of total care to be implemented by one nurse
        is being introduced to students at Kisii General Hospital in
        Kenya. The students' usual approach is to divide up tasks and
        minister to a group of patients as a team.

892   "School Complex Built in Kenya". AA1.13:1/3. InterACTION, 1,
        n.3 (December 1972): 6.
            Working with the Tharakan tribesmen of central Kenya over a
        period of three years, Wilbur James, a history graduate of
        Colorado College, developed plans for and supervised the con-
        struction of a multi-building agricultural school. Included in
        the plans was an irrigation system and the region's first
        electrical generator. This article provides background on the
        project, which was partly funded by Peace Corps Partnership
        monies. Photographs of the complex located at the foot of Mt.
        Kenya are also included.

893   "Severna Park Resident Peace Corps Volunteer in Kenya".
        Congressional Record, 123, p.30 (15 December 1977): 39667-8.
            An ACTION news release covering the work of Patricia Reidy,
        a volunteer working as manager of a jewelry cooperative for the
        blind and handicapped in Mazeras, Kenya. The history of the
        business, known as Bombolulu, and the problems of supplies,
        visibility and marketing are discussed, as well as the contri-
        bution to human dignity it gives to people who would otherwise be
        forced to beg.

894   U. S. Department of State. Republic of Korea. Peace Corps.
        Agreement Effected by Exchange of Notes Signed at Seoul
        September 14, 1966. United States Treaties and Other Inter-
        national Agreements Series, no. 6097, vol. 17, p. 1,
        Washington, D.C.: Government Printing Office, 1967, 1396-1400.
        S9.12:17 Part 1.
            This document contains the complete text of documents given
        between George S. Newman, American charge d'Affaires at the United
        States embassy to Korea, and His Excellency Tong Won Lee, minster
        of foreign affairs. Together, these notes form the legal base
        upon which all Peace Corps activity in Korea would be conducted.

895   CHANG WHAN KIM. <u>Lessons In the Korean Language and Culture For
       Teachers of English as a Second Language</u>. Washington, D.C.:
       Peace Corps, 1970.
            This text is aimed at introducing Korean to volunteers who
       will be serving as TEFL instructors in school settings. Kim's
       manual contains one hundred lessons covering language, cultural
       points and grammar. Full text is available from the ERIC system
       as document ED 131 696.

896   "Country Close-Up: Korea--Teaching English As An International
       Language". AA1.10:2/4. <u>Transition</u>, 2, n.4 (April 1973): 20-4.
            The majority of the three hundred volunteers serving in
       Korea in 1973 were working as English language instructors in
       middle schools and colleges. This article reviews their programs
       and problems and the approaches taken to their host nation and
       culture. Three volunteers share their own experiences as both
       travelling teachers and advisors to government planning bodies.

897   "Country Director Seeks 'Extra Spark'". AA1.13:4/11.
       <u>InterACTION</u>, 4, n.11 (August 1976): 10.
            An interview with Jon Keeton, current Director, Peace
       Corps/Korea, exploring both his philosophy of service and plans
       for the future utilization of personnel in that nation. In
       celebration of the tenth anniversary of Peace Corps service in
       Korea, Keeton plans to offer all veterans from Korea a special
       travel package to Seoul in August of 1976.

898   "Focus On Education". <u>Christian Science Monitor</u> (23 September
       1969): 1.
            A news report on a group of volunteers completing ten weeks
       of training for Korean service at Fairleigh Dickinson University.
       The chief element of their training as science teachers has been
       the construction of laboratory equipment from materials which will
       be locally available in Korea in their secondary schools.

899   KAILIAN, GREGORY SHAHAN. <u>English Test and Attitude Measures
       Among Korean Students of United States Peace Corps Volunteers.</u>
       Ed.D. dissertation, University of Southern California, 1980.
            This dissertation reports on evaluative research conducted
       on two groups, volunteers currently serving as English instructors
       in Korean schools and co-teachers of English using the
       instructional method handbook developed for the teaching of
       English by Peace Corps Korea. The objective of the research was
       to ascertain comparable levels of ability in reading
       comprehension, grammar and translation and pronunciation. While
       similar scores on these areas were noted in the study, certain co-
       factors such as host teacher perception of the abilities of the
       volunteers and location of schools (urban and private versus rural
       and public) were uncovered bearing upon the overall success of the
       volunteers. Recommendations are made for the improvement of
       volunteers in Korean education with regard to placement, and
       further testing of the results of this study is advised.

900   "Korea Hosts Ten Year PC Reunion". AA1.13:5/1. InterACTION,
      5, n.1 (October 1976): 1-2.
      A tenth year anniversary celebration of Peace Corps work in
Korea was held in Seoul from August 1-3, 1976. Attending were
some eighty-one former members of Peace Corps/Korea, both
volunteers and staff. A description of the receptions and
ceremonies sponsored by the Korean government is provided.

901   Korean Phrase Book. Washington, D.C.: Peace Corps, 1973.
      A guide to proper pronunciation of the Korean language,
originally intended for use by U. S. Navy personnel. Nine
headings cover emergencies, personal needs, location and terrain,
roads and transportation, communications, signage, military terms,
letters and numbers and general information. Full text is
available from the ERIC system as document ED 131 691.

902   "Next Stop For PCV's: Korea". S19.11/2:4/5. Peace Corps
      Volunteer, 4, n.5 (March 1966): 3.
      Ninety volunteers are scheduled to arrive in South Korea in
September, 1966 as English, science and physical education
teachers. Korea thus becomes the fiftieth host nation of the
Corps.

903   "Not Lusty But Sound--Peace Corps Here One Year".
      Congressional Record, 113, p.20 (27 September 1967): 27047.
      This article is reprinted from the Korea Herald newspaper,
one of Korea's English-language presses, and describes the entry
and activities of Korea I. The Director, Kevin O'Donnell, and
Deputy Director Loren Cox discuss the progress and distribution of
the volunteers. At this writing, 113 volunteers were in Korea
serving as teachers in colleges, high schools and middle schools.
Regional offices of the Corps had been opened in Taegu, Kwangju,
Taejon and Chunchon to better serve the scattered personnel. As
O'Donnell noted, Peace Corps had come "to serve the Korean people,
not to lead them".

904   "One-Year-Old Peace Corps--'Sincerity To Learn'".
      Congressional Record, 113, p.20: 27027-48.
      A reprinted article from the Korea Times of September 16,
1967, written upon the first anniversary of Peace Corps/Korea,
detailing the types of training and service which the volunteers
are providing to that nation. Most are serving as teachers in the
fields of science, English and physical education. Reception of
the volunteers by their Korean hosts has been positive, with the
language facility particularly appreciated.

905   "PCV Teaches 'Living Language'". AA1.13:1/7. InterACTION, 1,
      n.7 (April 1973): 8.
      A report on the work being done by Randall Kawamoto of
Honolulu, serving as an English instructor with the Pusan City
Board of Education. A general overview of the Korean system of
education and the planned importance of the acquisition of an
international language such as English is also included.

906   "PCV Therapist Treats Leprosy". AA1.13:1/9. <u>InterACTION</u>, 1,
       n.9 (June 1973): 1.
           In Sunchon, Korea, volunteer Susan Kram works with patients
       suffering from leprosy as a physical therapist. Part of the
       philosophy of the leprosy center where she works is to treat and
       demythologize the disease from its popular terrors and
       stereotypes. A brief outline of a typical day is included.

907   "Wyoming Peace Corps Volunteer Helps Korea Fight Tuberculosis".
       <u>Congressional Record</u>, 120, p.24 (24 September 1974): 32302-3.
           A news release from ACTION describing the work being done by
       volunteer Martha King in Cholla Namdo province of Korea as part of
       that nation's campaign to control and eradicate tuberculosis. Her
       views on Korean culture and problems of patient care are vividly
       portrayed. At the time, there were 321 volunteers serving in
       Korea.

908   U. S. Department of State. <u>Peace Corps. A Glossary of
       Agricultural Terms, Spanish-English, English-Spanish</u>.
       Washington, D.C.: 1960.
           Created by the American Language Center of American
       University in Washington, D.C., this text was originally put out
       for the International Cooperation Administration and adopted for
       use by the Peace Corps in 1965. Issued as part of the Program and
       Training Journal Reprint Series, it was designed "to provide
       technical support . . . and to share material on 'intermediate
       technology'" (p. 3). Used as a training guide for volunteers who
       were to serve as agricultural extension workers and posted to
       rural areas, the full text is included on the ERIC database as
       document ED 138 121.

909   U. S. Department of State. <u>Peace Corps. A Microwave Course in
       Spanish for English Speakers</u>. Washington, D.C.: 1968.
           Modeled on a "microwave" course in Swahili developed by the
       Foreign Service Institute in 1965, this text is composed of one
       hundred and six "cycles" of lessons. This approach stresses
       communicating and using a new element of grammar as soon as it is
       presented. Developed by a private firm in La Jolla, California,
       the full text is available form the ERIC database as document ED
       157 372.

910   U. S. Department of State. <u>Peace Corps. Spanish Programmatic
       Text: Instructor's Manual</u>. Washington, D.C.: 1970.
           A manual covering those portions of the basic Spanish course
       which have not been recorded in the main text but are available on
       the teaching dialogue tapes. The main course (entered as ERIC ED
       055 499) was developed jointly by the Foreign Service Institute
       and the Peace Corps Development and Training Center in Escondido,
       California. This adjunct text has been entered on the ERIC system
       as document ED 055 524.

911 U. S. Department of State. Peace Corps. Spanish Programmatic
     Text, v.2. Washington, D.C.: 1970.
        A text of twenty-five lessons prepared by the Foreign
     Service Institute as an intensive course in Spanish. Format
     includes dialogues, grammar and practice drills. An index of
     grammatical features and vocabulary are appended. This document
     has been entered in the ERIC system twice, as ED 022 397 and
     ED 055 524.

912 U. S. Department of State. Lesotho. Peace Corps. Agreement
     Effected by Exchange of Notes Signed at Washington September
     22, 1967. U. S. Treaties and Other International Agreements,
     no. 6339, vol. 18, p. 3, Washington, D.C.: Government Printing
     Office, 1968, 2357-61. S9.12:18 Part 3.
        This document contains the full text of notes exchanged
     between Jack Vaughn, director of the Peace Corps, and His
     Excellency Chief Leabua Jonathan, prime minister of the Kingdom of
     Lesotho, which form the legal basis for Peace Corps presence in
     that country. Legal benefits extended to the volunteers are
     spelled out in detail.

913 "Construction PCV Runs Unique Firm". AA1.13:2/2. InterACTION,
     2, n.2 (November 1973): 9.
        Robert Poynter, Peace Corps/Lesotho, is currently running a
     training school for construction workers at Matsieng in the
     western lowlands. The unique aspect of the school is that it is
     being run as a business, to give students training in both
     technical and business skills. By rotation of the artisans and
     masons to different work teams, Poynter attempts to provide the
     classes with a general package of useful skills.

914 "Lesotho". S19.11/2:7/8. Peace Corps Volunteer, 7, n.8 (July
     1969): 9-14.
        A collection of photographs of the land and people of the
     Kingdom of Lesotho taken by Peace Corps volunteers assigned to
     that southern African nation. Commentaries are included written
     by their students.

915 "Lesotho Gets New Roads". AA1.13:2/12. InterACTION, 1, n.12
     (September 1973): 1, 6.
        For two years, Mark Nelson, a civil engineer in Peace Corps
     service in the Kingdom of Lesotho, surveyed road sites and helped
     to supervise construction of a new road system for the Thaba Tseka
     district of mountainous eastern Lesotho. Construction crews were
     formed of local women through a food-for-work program. A
     photograph of a typical work crew is included, as well as an
     outline of the planned development of the region.

916 MELVIN, WILLIAM. "Going Home". Christian Science Monitor
     (25 November 1980): 21.
        A vivid and moving account of a volunteer's return to his
     post at St. Louis' Mission near Thaba Telle in the lowlands of
     Lesotho. After three years' service, and six months home leave,
     he decided to return to what had become his home.

917   NUSSBAUM, LOREN V. and GERSHON T. LIJANE. An Introduction to
        Spoken Sesotho. Washington, D.C.: Center For Applied
        Linguistics, 1968.
            This manual of 176 lessons was prepared for the Peace Corps
        by the Center for Applied Linguistics for Peace Corps volunteers
        serving in the Kingdom of Lesotho. Sesotho materials are
        presented in a phonemic fashion, along with English glosses.
        Researchers should be aware that the document is also available on
        the ERIC system as entry ED 048 592.

918   "PCV Trains Lesotho Mechanics". AA1.13:2/3. InterACTION, 2,
        n.3 (December 1973): 9.
            A summary of the instruction in practical shop mechanics
        given by Jim Kelly at the Lerotholi Technical Institute in Maseru,
        capital of Lesotho. Initially assigned as a mechanics supervisor,
        Kelly switched to LTI so as to improve the experiential component
        of mechanical training. Most of his students maintain the
        government fleet of Landrovers and trucks. Prior to this time,
        instruction centered on mechanical theory.

919   "Peace Corps to Send Volunteers to Lesotho". Christian Science
        Monitor (7 April 1967): 17.
            Jack Vaughn, Director of the Peace Corps, announced that the
        newly-independent Kingdom of Lesotho in southern Africa had
        requested eighty-eight Peace Corps volunteers in the areas of
        education, health, agriculture and rural development. Their work
        would begin in late December, 1967 under the guidance of David R.
        Sherwood. Sherwood's experience with the Peace Corps included
        directing the training camps in the Virgin Islands and serving as
        deputy director of projects for Africa. Emphasis in the Lesotho
        program will be on education, with fifty of the volunteers
        assigned to teacher-training colleges and secondary schools.

920   "Robert N. Poynter, Jr., Peace Corps Volunteer in Lesotho,
        Africa". Congressional Record, 119, v.24 (25 September 1973):
        31267.
            This entry is a reprinted news release from the Peace Corps
        detailing the vocational training work in the field of con-
        struction being done by Robert Poynter at the Matsieng Vocational
        School in the Kingdom of Lesotho in Southern Africa. Believing
        that the best way to train artisans in management techniques was
        to actually run a firm, Poynter set up the school following a
        request from the Ministry of Education. Employing some fifteen
        Basotho, the focus of the new business has been modular
        construction in concrete, with the first project several faculty
        houses for the Lerotholi Training Institute in Maseru, the capital
        city. At the time of writing, there were forty-five volunteers
        serving in Lesotho.

921   SCIESZKAM, GREG and MARGIE. "PCV's in Lesotho Write
      Impressions". AA1.13:2/1. InterACTION, 2, n.1 (October 1973):
      4.
          Memoirs of two years service spent teaching history and
      biology at the mission school of St. Monica's in the northern
      lowlands of Lesotho. The diligence of their students and the
      warmth of the Basotho are especially noted. Government plans for
      a national teacher training college in Maseru, Lesotho's capital,
      are also mentioned.

922   U. S. Department of State. Liberia. Peace Corps Program.
      Agreement Effected by Exchange of Notes Signed at Monrovia
      March 5 and 8, 1962. United States Treaties and Other Inter-
      national Agreements Series, no. 4980, vol. 13, p. 1,
      Washington, D.C.: Government Printing Office, 1962, 308-11.
      S9.12:13 Part 1.
          This document contains the complete text of notes exchanged
      between His Excellency Elbert G. Matthews, United States
      ambassador, and J. Rudolph Grimes, secretary of state of the
      Republic of Liberia. This set of notes and their mutual accep-
      tance by both governments laid the legal foundation for the
      genesis of Peace Corps/Liberia.

923   CUTLER, SUE A. and ABU VARFLAI TALAWOLEY. A Learner Directed
      Approach to Maniyaka. Washington, D.C.: Peace Corps, 1981.
          Created at the African Studies Center of Michigan State
      University, this teacher's manual and textbook of twenty lessons
      presents texts, exercises and cultural information. Full text has
      been entered on the ERIC database as document ED 217 692.

924   CUTLER, SUE A. and DAVID J. DWYER. Maniyaka: A Reference
      Handbook of Phonetics, Grammar, Lexicon and Learning
      Procedures. Washington, D.C.: Peace Corps, 1981.
          This volume is intended for students who are already in an
      environment where Maniyaka (also known as Mandingo), a Mande
      language of Liberia, is spoken, but where no experienced teachers
      are available. A basic overview of the languages of Liberia is
      followed by advice for the independent student, a reference
      grammar and dialogues and a detailed presentation of the Mande
      language sound system. Done at the African Studies Center of
      Michigan State University, the full text of this document is
      available on the ERIC system as ED 247 767.

925   DE ZEEUW, PETER and REXANNA KRUAH. A Learner Directed Approach
      to Mano. Washington, D.C.: Peace Corps, 1981.
          Done at the African Studies Center of Michigan State
      University, this text contains twenty-one lessons in Mano, a
      language of Nimba County, Liberia and adjoining regions of Guinea.
      Each lesson contains text and dialogues, grammar, vocabulary
      drills and practice exercises. An appendix contains background on
      self-instruction and general data on the languages of Liberia.
      The full text of the document is available as ERIC ED 217 691.

926   DWYER, DAVID J., et. al. <u>A Learner Directed Approach to Lorma</u>.
       Washington, D.C.: Peace Corps, 1981.
           A product of the African Studies Center at Michigan State
       University, this text gives a basic vocabulary of one thousand
       terms, along with grammar exercises, texts for reading and
       exploration of cultural features of the Lorma-speaking regions of
       Liberia. Full text is available from the ERIC database as
       document ED 247 766.

927   DWYER, DAVID JAMES. <u>Lorma: A Reference Handbook of Phonetics,
       Grammar, Lexicon and Learning Procedures</u>. Washington, D.C.:
       Peace Corps, 1981.
           Written at the African Studies Center at Michigan State
       University, this volume covers basic Lorma, a Mande language of
       Liberia for Peace Corps volunteers learning without structured
       assistance. An introduction sets out the language families of
       Liberia, followed by a reference grammar covering phonology,
       phrase structure and verb tenses. Transcription exercises are
       also included. Full text is available from the ERIC database as
       document ED 227 691.

928   ENOANYI, BILL FRANK. "Peace Corps Helps Staff New Liberian
       Hospital". <u>American Journal of Nursing</u>, 72 (April 1972):
       754-6.
           The staffing of the John F. Kennedy Medical Center in
       Monrovia by a team of Peace Corps nurses, pediatricians,
       obstetricians and an electro-medical repairman is reviewed in this
       article. Host country reactions to the volunteers is very
       favorable. Volunteers were requested to serve at the staff level
       to reinforce instruction in the use of technology brought back by
       the senior personnel from their overseas training. As the
       director of the nursing service expressed it, "they fill a gap in
       a critically short staff and bring a zest which the Liberain staff
       is motivated to match" (p. 756).

929   KELLER, MIKE. "The Peace Corps in Liberia: Frustration,
       Little Support". <u>Congressional Record</u>, 123, p.30 (15 December
       1977): 39474-7.
           An article drawn from the <u>Washington Post</u> of 12 December,
       1977 on the absence of significant material support present in the
       structure of Peace Corps/Liberia. Problems include ill-defined
       jobs, lack of response by in-country staff to volunteer requests
       for assistance, and a monthly wage which was unrealistically low.
       The basic problem is the cutting of the Peace Corps budget overall
       and the gradual removal of support services and critical materials
       needed by the volunteers. A history of the volunteers and their
       contribution to the development of Liberia is also included. This
       article was placed in the <u>Record</u> by Senator Hubert Humphrey as
       evidence that further fiscal support of renewed efforts at
       rebuilding Peace Corps should be allocated.

930   KRAL, BARBARA. "Diary of a Hitchhike Across the Sahara".
       Life, 56, n.16 (17 April 1987): 92-107.
       On January 12, 1964, four Peace Corps women left, Monrovia,
Liberia bound across the Sahara. This photo essay and accompanying text describe a journey which include train derailments in
Niger, dancing the "High Life" in Ouagadougou, riding atop a load
of peanut oil drums to Agades, and leaving a distinctive memory in
the minds of their many hosts along the way.

931   "Liberia Holds Farm Worker In Death of Peace Corpsman". New
       York Times (1 September 1971): 10.
       Robert Toe, a farm worker, has confessed to the murder of
Marsha Ann Ragno, Peace Corps/Liberia, at the agricultural station
at Gbedin.

932   "Liberia Lauds the Peace Corps". AA1.13:3/6. InterACTION, 3,
       n.6 (March 1975): 1.
       In January, 1975, the announcement was made on Radio Liberia
that the government had selected the members of that nation's
Peace Corps contingent to receive an award as the most outstanding
of the international organizations serving it. At this time,
Peace Corps/Liberia was the largest program in Africa, with some
three hundred volunteers working in the fields of education,
agriculture, health, public administration and rural development.

933   "Liberia: Volunteers Are Working in Africa's Oldest Republic".
       S19.11/2:2/9. Peace Corps Volunteer, 2, n.9 (9 July 1964): 8-
       21.
       Introduced by an article by the Peace Corps Representative
for Liberia, Thomas Quimby, this is a collection of short pieces
by volunteers working in capacities as road construction
engineers, architects, carpenters and teachers, all of whom report
doing "a ka-hell-of a thank-you job." An interesting portrait of
the early years of Peace Corps/Liberia.

934   "Liberian Rural Newspapers Spread Information by Mimeo".
       S19.11/2:2/12. Peace Corps Volunteer, 2, n.12 (October, 1964):
       5.
       In an effort to cope with the absence of newspapers in the
rural areas of Liberia, several members of that country's Peace
Corps contingent initiated the use of mimeographic equipment as a
means of beginning such efforts. Several of the papers have since
become self-supporting, and a UNESCO study of the project has also
been written for use in other nations. Some thirty communities
are represented in the project.

935   MCANDREWS, ROBERT L. "Liberian Village Trial and 'American
       Justice'". Practical Anthropology, 14 (May-June 1967): 103-
       9.
       A description of a village trail in the Kpelle region of
western Liberia which obliged a Peace Corps couple to question
their own ideas about justice and practices structuring a
society.

936   MCANDREWS, SUELLEN. "Some 'Marriage Business'". S19.11/2:2/6.
       Peace Corps Volunteer, 2, n.7 (May 1964): 6-7.
            An account by a Peace Corps bride of being wed in the tradi-
       tional fashion by the Kpelle people of Liberia to her husband, and
       the participation of her relatives.

937   "PCV's Offer Help to Child". AA1.13:1/4. InterACTION, 1, n.4
       (January 1973): 8.
            An appeal for donors of A- positive blood for a five-year-
       old girl with severe anemia by a hospital in Monrovia, Liberia
       having failed, a request was made to the Peace Corps physical for
       lists of volunteers with the needed blood type. Three volunteers
       supplied blood to enable the child to be evacuated to Boston for
       further treatment.

938   "Scholarship Fund Established by Sahara Hitchhikers".
       S19.11/2:2/9. Peace Corps Volunteer, 2, n.9 (July 1964): 3.
            The five members of Peace Corps/Liberia who garnered fame by
       hitching across the Sahara have placed the money paid them by Life
       magazine into a scholarship fund for Liberian teachers. The funds
       will permit two-year sponsorship of candidates to obtain their
       certification at the colleges and the University of Liberia.
       While the Liberians are completing these programs, their places
       will be filled by volunteers.

939   SINGLER, JOHN VICTOR. An Introduction to Liberian English.
       Washington, D.C.: Peace Corps, 1981.
            A manual designed to introduce Peace Corps personnel to the
       variety of English used in the West African nation of Liberia,
       with texts based upon the dialect of the capital, Monrovia. Two
       sections comprise the text: the first dealing with the history of
       Liberian English, while the second presents examples. Emphasis
       here is on comprehension rather than achieving fluency. The full
       text may be found in the ERIC system as document ED 226 617.

940   "3 In Peace Corps Killed in Auto Crash in Liberia". New York
       Times (12 December 1971): 35.
            Three members of Peace Corps/Liberia died when an unlighted
       truck rammed into their car some twenty miles east of Monrovia. A
       fourth volunteer survived the crash with relatively minor
       injuries.

941   THACH, SHARON V. and J. DWYER. Kpelle: A Reference Handbook
       of Phonetics, Grammar, Lexicon and Learning Procedures.
       Washington, D.C.: Peace Corps, 1981.
            Created for the Peace Corps under contract by the African
       Studies Center at Michigan State University, this text on the
       Kpelle language of northern Liberia is intended for use by
       students who have already completed several hundred hours of
       classroom instruction. Following a brief overview of the
       languages of Liberia and their distribution, the work contains a
       dictionary, a summary reference grammar, advice on self-teaching
       of languages and the sound systems of the Mande language group to
       which Kpelle belongs. The full text is available as ERIC document

ED 217 690.

942   THACH, SHARON V., et. al. <u>A Learner Directed Approach to</u>
       <u>Kpelle</u>. Washington, D.C.: Peace Corps 1981.
            This volume on the Kpelle language of Liberia presents the
       equivalent of a first year college course in the subject. One
       thousand common vocabulary items were introduced along with
       syntactic constructions. Each unit has text and vocabulary,
       grammar and cultural information. A list of readings in Kpelle is
       appended. The complete text is available as ERIC document ED 247
       765.

943   UNGER, MARVIN H. <u>Pawpaw, Foofoo and Juju: Recollections of a</u>
       <u>Peace Corps Volunteer</u>. New York: Citadel Press, 1968.
            This account of Peace Corps service was written by a
       volunteer in Liberia IV group who was posted to the Zorzor
       Technical Institute as a chemistry teacher from 1964 to 1966.
       Included in the work are vivid descriptions of the culture and
       educational system of Liberia, relations between the United States
       and Africa in the early 1960's, and pungent tales of the first
       years of being a Peace Corps volunteer at "palaver" with West
       Africa.

944   "Woman in the Peace Corps Found Murdered in Liberia". <u>New York</u>
       <u>Times</u> (27 August 1971): 68.
            The body of Marsha Ann Ragno, a twenty-three-year old home
       economist from Winthrop Park, Illinois, was found in her living
       quarters at the government agricultural station at the village of
       Gbedin, some 210 miles east of the capital of Monrovia. She had
       been stabbed in the head, chest, neck, and arms. Two suspects are
       in custody. Ragno had been in country since December, 1970.

945   "Yank Brings Hope to Leper Colony in Liberia". <u>Congressional</u>
       <u>Record</u>, 114, p.8 (11 April 1968): 9740.
            An article from the <u>Washington Daily News</u> of April 1, 1968,
       reporting on the work of Thomas Bartlett, a volunteer teacher who
       became involved with a leprosarium in Suakoko, Liberia. Through
       his attentions, and fundraising activities, housing just for the
       infectious patients was constructed, additional staff hired, and
       increased medical care instituted. By Liberian custom, the
       families of those driven from their villages out of fear of
       leprosy accompany them, thus running the risks of further
       infection. Upon his return to the United States, Bartlett plans
       to attend medical school.

946   U. S. Department of State. <u>Malawi, Peace Corps. Agreement</u>
        <u>Effected by Exchange of Notes Signed at Blantyre and Zomba</u>
        <u>March 4 and April 20, 1965</u>. United States Treaties and Other
        International Agreements Series, no. 5811, vol. 16, p. 1,
        Washington, D. C.: Government Printing Office, 1966, 784-8.
        S9.12:16 Part 1.
             The complete texts of notes given between Sam P. Gilstrap,
        ambassador to Malawi, and His Excellency Ngwazi Dr. H. Kamuzu
        Banda, prime minister of Malawi, setting forth the legal basis for
        the presence and service of Peace Corps personnel to that nation.
        This agreement was renegotiated in 1971.

947   U. S. Department of State. <u>Malawi, Peace Corps. Agreement</u>
        <u>Effected by Exchange of Notes Signed at Blantyre and Zomba</u>
        <u>September 14, 1971</u>. United States Treaties and Other Inter-
        national Agreements Series, no. 7191, vol. 22, p. 2,
        Washington, D.C.: Government Printing Office, 1972, 1633-40.
        S9.12:22 Part 2.
             This document contains the full texts of notes exchanged
        between William C. Burdett, United States ambassador and the
        Honorable Aleke K. Banda, minister of finance, creating the legal
        basis for Peace Corps presence in that nation.

948   "Banda Scolds Peace Corps on Attire". <u>Washington Post</u> (5
        January 1966): 8B.
             Dr. Hastings Kamuzu Banda, President of Malawi, objected to
        the moral, political and aesthetic behavior of the two hundred
        volunteers serving in his country in a private conversation with
        the American charge d'affaires. Problems beyond issues of dress
        and manners were also raised involving Corps criticism of regional
        politics of the ruling Malawi Congress Party. This castigation
        had an immediate effect and the volunteers in Malawi have
        smartened up their appearance.

949   BEHRS, JAN, et. al. <u>Learning Chichewa: Teacher's Manual</u>.
        Washington, D.C.: Peace Crops, 1980.
             Intended to accompany the Peace Corps basic texts in
        Chichewa, this manual on the dominant language of Malawi consists
        of three sections. The first covers basic concepts of language
        instruction and methods, while the second and third treat outlines
        of Chichewa materials and effective classroom strategies and notes
        on individual lessons in the series. The full text is available
        on the ERIC database as document ED 206 159. A related two-
        volume set of classroom instruction text is also on ERIC as ED 206
        157 and 206 158.

950   "Focus--Malawi". <u>Peace Corps Times</u> (March/April 1985): 4-7.
             An outline of the involvement of Peace Corps with the devel-
        opment of Malawi since its arrival in 1963 and its return in 1979.
        Co-ordinated with the host policy of localization while retaining
        expatriates in posts, Corps personnel are working in areas of
        technical support, education, rural development, and services to
        the handicapped. The economic and political status of Malawi in
        the world economy is briefly reviewed.

951   GIRARDET, EDWARD. "American Volunteers in Malawi--They're The
      Cream of the Crop". Christian Science Monitor (16 May 1986):
      1, 10.
         A brief look at the contemporary personnel of Peace
      Corps/Malawi. Presently the third time Corps has served in that
      nation, the previous groups were obliged to leave due to political
      reasons and differences over programs. With a heavy emphasis on
      specialists, the program--referred to by other officials of the
      agency as the "Cadillac Corps" is the most sophisticated and
      varied of any outside of the program of Peace Corps/Belize.
      Volunteers in horticulture, physical education and audio-visual
      equipment maintenance are interviewed in Lilongwe and Zomba.

952   "Help for Malawi Pupils". Christian Science Monitor (9 August
      1965): 17.
         As a result of letters to the Monitor by several members of
      Peace Corps/Malawi, funds were raised in the United States to
      assist the Secho Hill Secondary School. While a portion of these
      funds was spent for equipment, most went for school fees for able
      students who would otherwise have been forced to withdraw. One of
      these volunteers, Paul Theroux, would later be expelled for a
      claimed involvement in an assassination plot against President
      Banda. A photograph of the students, their headmaster, Theroux
      and Dr. J. E. Blackwell, Director of Peace Corps/Malawi, is also
      included.

953   "In Malawi, Bad News from Banda". Peace Corps Volunteer, 7,
      n.13 (December 1969): 4. S19.11/2:7/13.
         In September, the ruling party of President Hastings Banda
      of Malawi adopted eleven resolutions, one of which cited
      "complaints against the influence which the Peace Corps Volunteers
      have over our children because of their bad conduct . . .
      behavior and slovenliness." All volunteers were to leave Malawi
      within the next eighteen months.

954   "Making TB Taboo In Malawi". S19.11/2:4/4. Peace Corps
      Volunteer, 4, n.4 (February 1966): 5-6.
         An account of the adaptation by two members of Peace
      Corps/Malawi to the local system of health care in their work
      against tuberculosis.

955   MORRIS, DAVID. "PCV's Work in Park Master Plan Will Help
      Preserve Land, Water and Animals in Malawi". AA1.13:5/7.
      InterACTION, 5, n.7 (April 1977): 7.
         A volunteer recounts his two-year tour in the East African
      nation of Malawi as part of a development planning effort for
      national parks and game reserves. Among his accomplishments was
      the creation of nine master plans for the country. A history of
      prior efforts in this field and public attitudes in Malawi towards
      conservation are also included.

956   "Nyasaland". S10.11/2:2/1. Peace Corps Volunteer, 2, n.1
       (November 1963): 12-21.
          A group of short articles written by members of Peace
       Corps/Malawi who arrived in the first contingent in January, 1963
       at the request of President Hastings Banda. Their stories recount
       activities as diverse as teaching and training future teachers,
       art instruction, dressmaking, English classes and operating local
       clinics.

957   "Nyasaland Leaders Visit United State--Nyasaland Newspaper
       Praises American Peace Corps Volunteers". Congressional
       Record, 109, p.24 (28 March 1963): A1833-34.
          A visit to the United States by the minister of local
       government and the minister of education of Malawi is reported to
       the House of Representatives. At that time, Rep. Brademas of
       Indiana was shown a copy of an article from the Malawi News
       describing the address given to the newly-arrived contingent of
       volunteers by Ngwazi Dr. Hastings Kamuzu Banda, President of
       Malawi. While emphasizing the recent political history of that
       country under the Central African Federation, his speech was
       welcoming. These volunteers were invited to serve as secondary
       school teachers and received orientation in-country at Soche Hill
       College in Blantyre.

958   SCOTTON, CAROL MYERS and GREGORY JOHN ORR. Learning Chichewa,
       Books One and Two. Washington, D.C.: Peace Corps, 1980.
          A two-volume set of manuals for instruction in the official
       language of Malawi, with pen and ink drawings, stressing practice.
       Emphasis is on basic grammar in the first volume, with vocabulary
       acquisition dominating lessons in the second. Lesson format
       includes dialogues, monologues, riddles, proverbs and readings.
       The full text is entered on the ERIC database as documents ED 206
       157 and 206 158. A companion teacher's manual is available as ED
       206 159.

959   THEROUX, PAUL. "The Killing of Hastings Banda: Spying for the
       Free World in the Peace Corps". Esquire, 76 (December 1971):
       22-40.
          An interesting and complicated story of a Peace Corpsman in
       Malawi who through a series of favors for friends inadvertently
       becomes involved with the political underground opposing President
       Hastings Banda. The volunteer was deported after Dr. Banda
       charged him with being implicated in an assassination plot. The
       events recounted took place in 1965.

960   U. S. Department of State. Peace Corps. Chinyanja Basic
       Course. Washington, D.C.: 1965.
          Created by the Foreign Service Institute of the State
       Department under Peace Corps contract, this text of sixty-three
       units covers pitch and tone, acquisition of basic grammar and
       vocabulary and useful social skills for volunteers serving in
       Malawi. All dialogues are based upon a series of tapes made by
       the Malawian co-authors. The full text is available on the ERIC
       database as document ED 012 445.

961 U. S. Department of State. Peace Corps. Health Vocabulary,
     1966: Guide of the Host Country, Malawi. Washington, D.C.:
     1966.
     A list of English health terms and their counterparts in
Chinyanja intended for Peace Corps volunteers serving as medical
personnel in Malawi. The full text is entered on the ERIC
database as document ED 161 241.

962 U. S. Department of State. Malaya. Peace Corps Program.
     Agreement Effected by Exchange of Notes Signed at Kuala Lumpur
     September 4, 1961. United States Treaties and Other Inter-
     national Agreements Series, no. 4843, vol. 12, p. 2,
     Washington, D.C.: Government Printing Office, 1961, 1236-9.
     S9.12:12 Part 2.
     This document contains the full texts of letters between
Charles F. Baldwin, ambassador to the Federation of Malaya, and
His Excellency Muhammad Ghazali Bin Shafie, minister of external
affairs, defining the conditions of service for Peace Corps volunteers in the Federation.

963 CONKLIN, PAUL. "2 Volunteers In Sabah". S19.11/2:4/2. Peace
     Corps Volunteer, 4, n.2 (December 1965): 12-5.
     A photo essay and text describing the activity and lives of
two members of Peace Corps/Malaysia stationed in Tambunan and
Sunsuran as an elementary teacher and nurse respectively.

964 FAUZI HALIM, MOHAMMED. "'I Found An American Eating with His
     Hands'". S19.11/2:62/11. Peace Corps Volunteer, 2, n.11
     (September 1964): 23-4.
     This article is a condensation and translation of a piece
originally printed in Utusan Saman, the largest Malaysian newspaper. Its author is a former student at the Language Institute
at Kuala Lumpur and is presently serving as a Malay instructor in
the Peace Corps training program at Northern Illinois University.
It provides a host national's view of some of the members of Peace
Corps/Malaysia and the manner of their adaptation to their new
nation.

965 GAWENUS, JANET. "Selamat Pagi". Seventeen, 33 (January 1974):
     38.
     Writing from the perspective of a PCK (Peace Corps Kid),
Janet Gawenus relates her experiences as part of a family serving
in Malaysia. Her essay includes living as a teenager in Malaysia,
her language lessons, and reflections of the value of her time in
the land of "Selamat pagi." The title is the common greeting in
Bahasa Malaysia, meaning "good morning".

966   GORMAN, JOHN. "Peace Corps In Malaysia Works Itself Out of a
       Job". Congressional Record, 130, n.59 (4 May 1984): S5495-6.
            An insertion of an article originally appearing in the
       Chicago Tribune of April 24, 1984, covering the departure of Peace
       Corps from the Federation of Malaysia, completing an association
       which began in 1962. Interviews with Sargent Shriver, Loret
       Miller Ruppe and returned volunteers such as Senator Paul Tsongas
       chart the changes which Corps has experienced in those twenty-one
       years. In the years of its existence, Peace Corps Malaysia
       personnel worked in the areas of public health, road construction,
       education, nursing, architecture and surveying.

967   KOVACS, MARY. "With the Peace Corps Nurses in Malaya".
       Nursing Outlook 11, n.12 (December 1963): 890-4.
            Mary Kovacs, stationed at the General Hospital School of
       Nursing in Kuala Lumpur, Malaysia, describes the overall programs
       in which nursing volunteers in Malaysia are involved. These range
       from public health nursing care and classroom instruction to
       working in such specialized facilities as a leprosarium, local
       clinics and a tribal hospital. Detailed information on the
       diseases endemic to Malaya and problems which face the nursing
       profession is also given. At the time this article was written,
       there were some forty nursing personnel serving in this particular
       country.

968   LOVATT, DON and CLAYTON GILL, eds. The Best of Pokok-Pokok
       From Peace Corps Volunteers In Malaysia. Kuala Lumpur,
       Malaysia: United States Peace Corps, 1981.
            A collection of pieces originally appearing in Pokok-Pokok,
       the newspaper of Peace Corps Malaysia. Coverage extends from the
       arrival of Malaya I to the departure of the volunteers in the
       1980s.

969   LUBASCH, ARNOLD H. "Peace Corps Aide Cleared in Court:
       Dismissal Over Marijuana Charge Ruled Illegal". New York Times
       (13 August 1972): 23.
            In a nineteen-page decision, Judge Murray Gurfein found that
       the Peace Corps had in fact violated its own regulations and due
       process of law and suffered from "bureaucratic myopia" in the
       dismissal in 1970 of William Michael O'Shea from his teaching post
       in North Borneo. Having received permission from in-country staff
       to survey volunteers in North Borneo on their attitudes toward
       marijuana, a letter prepared by O'Shea to accompany the question-
       naire mentioned that he had recently smoked "my first and only"
       marijuana cigarette. In view of Corps regulations on drug usage
       this was held to be in violation, and O'Shea was expelled. Judge
       Gurfein ordered O'Shea's record cleared and the possibility of
       reinstatement opened to him if he so desired. This was believed
       to be the first time a federal court told a government agency that
       marijuana use off duty could not be grounds for dismissal.

970   "Malaya". S19.11/2:1/6. Peace Corps Volunteer, 1, n.6 (April 1963): 10-22.
      A group of nine articles, introduced by Lewis Butler, Representative in Malaya, written by nurses, biology teachers, doctors, laboratory technicians and foresters serving in that nation.

971   MAPES, SUSAN. "School for Aborigine Children". S19.11/2:2/8. Peace Corps Volunteer, 2, n.8 (June 1964): 4.
      Working at Rumah Sakit Orang Asli, the Aborigine Hospital outside Kuala Lumpur, a volunteer has begun a school for the children of the patients, many of whom cannot speak Malay and are fluent in their own tongues, such as Temiar or Semai.

972   "'Marco Polo Expedition' Sets Sail". S19.11/2:3/12. Peace Corps Volunteer, 3, n.12 (October 1965): 4.
      A dozen members of the Malaysia contingent of Peace Corps plan to return to the United States by sailing a self-built craft through the Indian Ocean, the Mediterranean and over the Atlantic. Details of the project's history and costs are given.

973   "Marijuana-Use Dismissal By Peace Corps Challenged". New York Times (1 January 1971): 32.
      A suit has been filed in federal court in New York City by the American Civil Liberties Union challenging the dismissal of William Michael O'Shea, a member of Peace Corps/Malaysia, who admitted to having smoked a cigarette "that might have contained marijuana." The ACLU claims that the dismissal violated O'Shea's constitutional rights, as this act was in no way related to his responsibilities as a volunteer. In fact, O'Shea had been highly critical of drug use by other volunteers in the past.

974   MARYANOV, GERALD S. "The Representative Staff as Intercultural Mediators in Malaya". The Cultural Frontiers of the Peace Corps, Robert B. Textor, ed. Cambridge: M.I.T. Press 1966, 63-86.
      The focus in this article is on the founding of Peace Corps structure and systems in what was then the Federation of Malaya and on the roles played by the three-person staff sent from Washington. Following a brief section of historical and political factors influencing decisions in placement of Malaya One, the duties of the staff are outlined and their problems presented. Advantages in this particular setting were the genuine goodwill on both sides to make Peace Corps a success in the country, an intensive briefing of school officials, hospital matrons and other officials of the states of Malaya as to the purposes and goals of Peace Corps, and the fact that two of the staff members had extensive training in and familiarity with the Malay languages and cultures. This latter is credited with keeping the rate of position shifts for volunteers far below other new country programs. Problems of interpreting Washington to not only Kuala Lumpur--but also to the volunteers--are discussed. Among these were the fact that the colonial heritage of British expectations caused difficulties in assessing professional qualifications and keeping in

close touch with the training program to provide improved information and feedback. The author was the Associate Representative
for these years: thus, this is a rare look inside the nascent
bureaucracy of a Corps country program by a participant.

975   "North Borneo/Sarawak".   S19.11/2:1/9. Peace Corps Volunteer,
       1, n.9 (July 1963):   8-9.
          A frank account of a thought-provoking day by a nurse
       stationed at Tambunan in the foothills of Mt. Kinabalu. Her
       encounter with the culture and health ethics of the local people
       is graphic.

976   "PCV Discovers Tin Off Malaysia". AA1.13:1/4. InterACTION, 1,
       n.4 (January 1973):   5.
          For the past two years, David Muerdter, a volunteer assigned
       to the Geological Survey Department of Malaysia, has participated
       in and led diving expeditions to map the off-shore mineral
       resources near the western coasts. Peace Corps has been able to
       assist Malaysia in this area due to a shortage of trained geolo-
       gists in-country. The deposit discovered by Muerdter appears to
       be rich enough to warrant serious investigation by the Ministry.
       As of 1973, only 65% of Malaysia had been studied geologically and
       mapped, with many of the known tin deposits being exhausted.

977   "PCV Teaches Welding in Malaysia". AA1.13:1/8. InterACTION,
       1, n.8 (May 1973):   4.
          At Malaysia's Industrial Training Institute, Robert Olson
       serves as one of six skilled tradesmen instructors provided by the
       Peace Corps. His students are apprentices in their crafts, sent
       to Kuala Lumpur by employers to acquire advanced proficiency in
       welding and other practical workshop techniques. The participato-
       ry style of Olson's teaching is a sharp departure from familiar
       practices.

978   "PCV's Train Malaysian Pre-School Teachers". AA1.13:5/2.
       InterACTION, 5, n.2 (November 1976):   5-8.
          Two members of Peace Corps/Malaysia recount the varied
       teaching techniques and games they have used to equip their
       students at a family training center at Kuala Lumpur as pre-school
       teachers. Basic curriculum points and attitudes are discussed.
       The chief problem lies in imagining that their seventeen - thirty-
       five-year old students are preschoolers.

979   "Peace Corps '64". Look (16 June 1964):   70-3.
          This article and photo essay focuses on Fred and Anne
       Schmidt, volunteers serving in Malaya, and traces their progres-
       sion from their stateside training at Northern Illinois University
       to assignment on site. Emphasis is placed upon their experiences
       at the model Malay village established in the Waipio Valley of
       Hawaii, where they learned to manage water buffalo, cope with
       daily situations in Malay, and bargain in a transplanted market,
       as well as continuing physical training and digging wells.

980   "Peace Corps Veterinarian Helps Build Swine Unit in Southeast
      Asian Jungle". Journal of the American Veterinary Medicine
      Association, 146 (15 February 1965): 383-5.
         The work of Dr. D. L. Jeffries as a Peace Corps veterinarian
      in Sabah is profiled. Most of the article is a discussion of the
      various tropical livestock diseases which the region forces local
      people to cope with. His work in establishing a swine screening
      station near the city of Kudat is given special attention.

981   "Peace Corps Volunteer from Melrose Park Serves with Forestry
      Program in Malaysia". Congressional Record, 123, p.15 (10 June
      1977): 18541-2.
         A report on the activities of Tom Thake, a volunteer posted
      to Malaysia working on the development of silviculture in that
      nation. Stationed in Kuala Lumpur, his work deals with the estab-
      lishment, management, care and reproduction of forest lands, one
      of Malaysia's most vital sources of revenue. Inventorying avail-
      able resources and upgrading methods of assessment, setting up
      experimental plots on the eradication of bamboo--regarded as a
      weed by Malaysians--and training colleagues occupy most of Thake's
      time. Following his tour of duty he plans to work for the U. S.
      Forestry Service.

982   PIERCE, ESTHER. "A Top Story From Kelantan". S19.11/2:3/3.
      Peace Corps Volunteer, 3, n.3 (January 1965):   6-7.
         A report on the sport of main gasing, top spinning, as
      practiced among the people of Kelantan state on Borneo. A Peace
      Corps nurse who works as part of a mobile leprosy unit wrote the
      story and took the photographs.

983   QUAID, MICHAEL J. The United States Peace Corps in Malaysia
      1962-1983. Washington, D.C.: Peace Corps, 1983.
         Written by a training officer and project co-ordinator of
      Peace Corps/Malaysia, this is a history of the programs, problems
      and achievements of the twenty-one year involvement of Peace Corps
      with the nation of Malaysia. Following a review of programs by
      area of interest (agriculture, education, health care and indus-
      trial arts) sample letters by members of various groups portray
      the human face of this experience.

984   "Sandra Kusumoto Teaches Malay Children--In Malayan".
      Congressional Record, 123, p.23 (13 September 1977):   29130.
         A reprint of an article from the bilingual paper The Hawaii
      Hochi covering the work of an Hawaiian volunteer teaching biology
      in the town of Lemal on the west coast of the Malayan peninsula.
      Her adjustments to the slower pace of Malaysian life and adven-
      tures in learning Bahasa Malaysia are recounted.

985   SHAFTEL, FANNIE R.   "A Report on the Peace Corps Teachers in
       Malaya".   Educational Leadership, 21 (March 1964):   347-51,
       397-8.
           At the request of the Corps, Fannie Shaftel arranged to
       interview many of the volunteer teachers then serving in Malaya
       during her own travels.   Most of these teachers were serving as
       mathematics, English and science instructors.   As a professor of
       education Shaftel was interested to ascertain how these
       generalists, in some cases with little or no formal training in
       education, would compare with professional teachers.   Most of the
       schools she visited were located in urban areas, chiefly in Johore
       Baru, Kuala Lumpur, Ipoh, Kuala Kangsar and Penang.   Although
       impressed by her observations, several immediate problems surfaced
       through her interviews.   The principal advantage of teacher train-
       ing seemed to be an ability to get beyond traditional and
       minimalist curriculum plans.   An outline of needed information for
       improving volunteer preparation is also included.

986   "Volunteer Wins First Prize in Malay Contest".   S19.11/2:2/10.
       Peace Corps Volunteer, 2, n.10 (August 1964):   25.
           Barbara Guss, a mathematics teacher assigned to Ipoh, won
       first place in an elocution contest held in Batu Gajah for non-
       Malay women.   She received a silver cup and a scroll of award.

987   U. S. Department of State.   Mali. Peace Corps. Agreement
       Effected by Exchange of Notes Dated at Bamako December 23, 1969
       and April 17, 1971.   United States Treaties and Other
       International Agreements Series, no. 8178, vol. 26, p. 3,
       Washington, D.C.:   Government Printing Office, 1977, 2611-15.
       S9.12:26 Part 3.
           The complete French text of the agreement established by G.
       Edward Clark, ambassador of the United States, and His Excellency
       Sory Coulibaly, minister of state for foreign affairs of Mali,
       which provided a legal basis for Peace Corps service in that
       country.

988   URBAN, RUTH.   "Cookstoves/Mali".   Peace Corps Times
       (March/April 1985):   13-5.
           A member of Peace Corps/Mali recounts her work at Segou in
       developing a type of local stove to improve cooking conditions via
       the local women's cooperative organization chapter.   Utilizing the
       traditional three stones as a basis, a mud stove could be con-
       structed which significantly reduced the amount of wood needed to
       supply flames.   Urban notes that her training classes always
       include members of previous classes as instructors, so as to
       continue the program after her departure.   A series of traditional
       and appropriate technology stoves from both Mali and elsewhere are
       illustrated.

989   U. S. Department of State. Peace Corps, Soninke Communication
       and Culture Handbook. Washington, D.C.: 1980.
            Thirty lessons presenting Soninke phrases and vocabulary via
       a structured situations based upon daily life in Mali. Developed
       by a team from the Experiment in International Living, the text
       also provides a glossary and bibliography. The full text has been
       entered on the ERIC database as document ED 203 706.

990   U. S. Department of State. Peace Corps, Soninke Grammar
       Handbook. Washington, D.C.: 1980.
            Twenty-eight lessons on the grammar and phonology of the
       Soninke language based on items gathered from volunteers and staff
       of Peace Corps/Mali. Topics covered include the sound system,
       tonal variations and basic dialogues to introduce vocabulary. A
       glossary and a short bibliography are also provided. The full
       text has been entered on the ERIC database as document ED 203
       705.

991   U. S. Department of State. Peace Corps, Soninke Special
       Skills Handbook. Washington, D.C.: 1980.
            Prepared by a team from the Experiment in International
       Living, this text covers samples of the Soninke language of Mali
       in the form of legends and stories. Much of the material in this
       text was created by members of Peace Corps/Mali and sent to the
       United States for assembly. Subjects covered include a specific
       profile of Peace Corps involvement in Mali, as well as assessments
       of potential situations likely to be encountered by volunteers.
       The full text is entered on the ERIC database as document ED 203
       707.

992   U. S. Department of State. Malta. Peace Corps Agreement
       Effected by Exchange of Notes Signed at Valletta April 29 and
       June 24, 1970. United States Treaties and Other International
       Agreements Series, no. 6907, vol. 21, p. 2, Washington, D.C.:
       1486-90. S9.12:21 Part 2.
            The full texts of notes given between John C. Pritzlaff,
       ambassador of the United States, and His Excellency Dr. Giorgio
       Borg Olivier, minister for commonwealth and foreign affairs of
       Malta. These documents comprised the legal basis for the presence
       and service of volunteers to that island republic.

993   U. S. Department of State. Mauritania. Peace Corps.
       Agreement Effected by Exchange of Notes Signed at Nauakchott
       September 19 and October 17, 1966. Untied States Treaties and
       Other International Agreements Series, no. 6143, vol. 17, p. 2,
       Washington, D.C.: 2046-9. S912:17 Part 2.
            The complete French and English texts of documents given
       between Richard W. Faville, American charge d'affaires, and His
       Excellency Maloum Ould Braham, minister for foreign affairs and
       rural economy, creating the legal foundation for Peace Corps
       service to Mauritania. After a sudden departure, Peace Corps
       returned to that country in 1971.

994   DOWNING, MICHAEL B. "Mission to Mauritania". America, 142 (17
       May 1980): 424.
           Written by a student at Harvard, this article is a thought
       piece based on an interview with Jerry Sternin, newly-appointed
       country director for Peace Corps/Mauritania. Describing the Peace
       Corps as "one of the Federal Government's precious anomalies", it
       gives the flavor of the environment of the early 1980's and the
       public sense of bemusement that there still was a Peace Corps.
       Details about the sedentarization of nomadic peoples in Mauritania
       and a years-long drought there provide some background. Sternin
       states his perspective on the Peace Corps thus: "You can live
       your life being very true to your ethical standards and keep your
       hands very clean, or you can decide that you are willing to get
       your hands dirty."

995   "Peace Corps, UNICEF Aid Refugees in Mauritania". AA1.13:3/3.
       InterACTION, 3, n.3 (December 1974): 1, 4.
           An account by James Collbran, who is serving in the
       Mauritanian capital of Nouakchott as administrator of UNICEF aid
       funds to refugees from the drought in the Sahel. Beginning as a
       rural development worker, a nutrition survey of Mauritania for the
       Centers for Disease Control confronted him with the brutal reali-
       ties of a land where seventy per cent of the population was for-
       merly nomadic and has seen their environment collapse.

996   U. S. Department of State. Mauritius. Peace Corps. Agreement
       Effected by Exchange of Notes Signed at Port Louis March 18,
       1971. United States Treaties and Other International Agree-
       ments Series, no. 7080, vol. 22, p. 1, Washington, D.C.:
       Government Printing Office, 1972, 453-7. S9.12:22 Part 1.
           The full texts of notes exchanged between William D. Brewer,
       American ambassador to Mauritius, and Dr. the Honorable Sir
       Seewoosagur Ramgoolam, prime minister of Mauritius, setting forth
       the legal basis upon which Peace Corps personnel would serve in
       that island nation.

997   GOODMAN, MORRIS F., et. al. Mauritian Creole: An
       Introduction. Washington, D.C.: Peace Corps, 1971.
           Twenty-three units of lessons on the Creole language of the
       island nation of Mauritius, based on an earlier volume Spoken
       Mauritian Creole which was used in the first training program for
       the Peace Corps personnel assigned there. Following a brief
       introduction covering the history of Creole and the languages of
       Mauritius in general, basic grammar and vocabulary is presented.
       A glossary completes the text, which can be found in the ERIC
       system as document ED 048 598.

998   "Mauritius". Christian Science Monitor (2 October 1970):   20.
       A letter to the Monitor correcting an assertion by Congress-
man Gross of Iowa that Peace Corps brought ten citizens of
Mauritius to the United States to serve as language instructors,
only to find that the "native tongue" of the island nation was
English. Although English and French are used, the actual daily
language is a Creole derived from French and the Bhojpuri dialect
of Hindi.

999   "PCVs Aid Cyclone Relief". AA1.13:3/7. InterACTION, 3, n.7
       (April 1975): 1.
       On February 6, 1975, Cyclone Gervaise struck the island
nation of Mauritius, causing extensive damage to crops and livestock and killing nine people. This article recoints the role
played by the ten volunteers stationed on Mauritius in the
recovery effort.

1000   ". . . While Mauritius Asks For Aid". S19.11/2:7/13. Peace
       Corps Volunteer, 7, n.13 (December 1969): 4.
       A group of agricultural extension volunteers has been
requested by the island nation of Mauritius. Goals include diversification of the economy away from a dependence on sugar production.

1001   "Crocodiles in the Bath Water". AA1.13:2/8. InterACTION, 2,
       n.8 (May 1974): 12.
       A vignette from the service experiences of Dona Riley, a
member of Peace Corps/Micronesia. Her bathtub is a neighboring
river which boasts not only crocodiles but three-foot lizards as
well.

1002   DETWEILER, RICHARD A. "Intercultural Interaction and the
       Categorization Process: A Conceptual Analysis and Behavioral
       Outcome". International Journal of Intercultural Relations, 4
       (1980): 275-93.
       The dynamics of analysis as applied to the phenomenon of
"culture shock" are carried out in the framework of categorization
theory. With the hypothesis that persons with a broader set of
categories would find adjustment to a new and different culture
easier than those whose sets of limits were somewhat more strict,
the writer's research is recounted. The present research was
conducted on the twenty-nine volunteers in training at Truk,
Micronesia in 1972. Results indicated that the categorization
approach was a valid way of gaining better control over the
factual basis of the issues involved when passing from one culture
to another.

1003   "Hula Dancers in Florida Keys: Youths Train in Tropic Setting
        for Peace Corps in Micronesia".   Congressional Record, 112,
        p.14 (10 August 1966):   18858.
            An article from the Washington Post describing the training
        site of three hundred ten volunteers in the Florida Keys where
        they are preparing for service in the archipelagos of Micronesia.
        Intended as English teachers and community development workers,
        they are receiving cross-cultural briefing from sixty-four
        Micronesians flown in to serve as instructors in everything from
        languages to sailing outriggers and climbing coconut palms.   The
        site was chosen due to its similarity with Micronesia in climate.
        Another two hundred forty trainees are preparing for service in
        Hawaii, specializing in public health and sanitation.   Originally
        scheduled for 1961, the Micronesian project was revived due to
        criticisms leveled at the United States by Micronesians them-
        selves, charging that the Trust Territory had been neglected.

1004   Lessons in Ponapean.   Washington, D.C.:   Peace Corps, 1962.
            Thirty-five lessons in beginning Ponapean, a language of
        Micronesia, for native speakers of English comprise this text.
        Format is a presentation of structured dialogues based upon
        aspects of Ponapean culture and grammar.   Full text is available
        as ERIC document ED 152 112.

1005   "PC, SCORE Aid Small Businesses".   AA1.13:2/3.   InterACTION, 2,
        n.3 (December 1973):   9, 11.
            An account of the joint project conducted by the Peace Corps
        and the Service Corps of Retired Executives in Micronesia.   The
        two SCORE volunteers trained PCVs in accounting and business
        management techniques to aid the islands' industries in trochus
        shells, copra, poultry and tourism.   The program began in July,
        1973.

1006   "PCV In Micronesia Moves Forward By Going Backward".
        AA1.13:5/7.   InterACTION, 5, n.7 (April 1977):   3.
            Utilizing the concept of appropriate technology with a
        different twist, this article recounts the involvement of a Peace
        Corps teacher in Micronesia with an outreach program emphasizing
        traditional methods of coping with the environment.   The program
        was modelled on the Outward Bound school structure and is intended
        as a counterweight to the over-education being given the popula-
        tion by the present school systems.

1007   "Peace Corps Takes On Micronesia".   S19.11/2:4/8.   Peace Corps
        Volunteer, 4, n.8 (June 1966):   4-5.
            A summary announcement of Peace Corps entry to the Trust
        Territory of the Pacific Islands.   Four hundred volunteers will
        initially serve as teachers, with more specialized workers follow-
        ing in the second group.

1008   "Saipan Museum Launched". AA1.13:3/2. InterACTION, 3, n.2
        (November 1974): 4.
        James Moses, posted to the island of Tinian as a science
teacher, has amassed a large collection of artifacts from the
Chamorro culture, the dominant civilization of pre-contact Saipan.
As well as creating a museum collection and serving as its
curator, he has been recording some ninety stories and legends.
While the materials are presently housed at the Oleai School where
Moses teaches, a permanent facility is being renovated and a law
mandating a museum board is on the books.

1009   "The Trust Territory of the Pacific Islands". Department of
        State Bulletin, 55 (July-September 1966): 387-401.
        This entry is the full texts of three statements made to the
United Nations Trusteeship Council on June 27, 1966, by Eugenie
Anderson, U. S. Representative to the Council, William R.
Norwood, Acting High Commissioner of the Trust Territory of the
Pacific Islands, and Francis Nuuan, adviser to the American
delegation. In their statements, both Mrs. Anderson and
Commissioner Norwood note the contribution of American assistance
to the region and detail the next steps in such aid. Among these
is the entry of between four and five hundred Peace Corps
volunteers to the Trust Territory in October, 1966, to serve as
teachers on the elementary level and as community development
workers, nurses, pharmacists, engineers, surveyors, lawyers and
urban planners. Later phases are envisioned with volunteers
working in agricultural extension assignments and in such varied
fields as radio broadcasting and credit union development.

1010   "The Trust Territory of the Pacific Islands". Department of
        State Bulletin, 57 (July-September 1967): 365-78.
        A summary of statements made at the June 8, 1967 session of
the United Nations Trusteeship Council by Eugenie Anderson, United
States representative to the Council, Mr. William Norwood, High
Commissioner of the Territory, and Lazarus Salii, advisor to the
U. S., delegation. In his remarks, Mr. Norwood summarizes the
accomplishments of the first year of Peace Corps work in
Micronesia and estimates that, by the end of 1967, some seven
hundred volunteers will be at work in the archipelagoes. Most are
working as English instructors, with others assigned to hospitals
as nurses and X-ray technicians, and still others to the government as community development workers and architects.

1011   U. S. Department of State. Montserrat. Peace Corps.
        Agreement Effected by Exchange of Notes Signed at Bridgetown
        and Montserrat April 3 and May 16, 1968. United States
        Treaties and Other International Agreements Series, no. 6493,
        vol. 19, p. 4, Washington, D.C.: Government Printing Office,
        1969, 4889-91. S9.12:19 Part 4.
        The complete text of documents given between Charles P.
Torrey, United States Consul General, and the Honorable Dennis R.
Gibbs, administrator of Montserrat, creating the foundation for
the presence of Peace Corps volunteers and staff in that island
nation.

1012   U. S. Department of State. Peace Corps. Agreement Between the
       United States of America and Montserrat Effected by Exchange of
       Letters Signed at Bridgetown and Plymouth January 13 and
       February 9, 1981. Treaties and Other International Acts Series
       10092. Washington, D.C.: Government Printing Office, 1982.
       S9.10:10092.
          The full text of letters exchanged between His Excellency
       Mr. David Kenneth Hay Dale, governor of Montserrat, and Sally
       Shelton, United States ambassador, creating the legal basis for
       Peace Corps presence in Monserrat. This agreement supersedes an
       earlier understanding between the two nations published as
       Treaties and Other International Acts Series 6493.

1013   BISHOP, ANN and BILL BURNS. "Special Education in Marrakech".
       Peace Corps Times (March/April 1985): 11-2.
          The authors are volunteers working in a school for children
       with cerebral palsy they began in a hospital outside the city of
       Marrakech, Morocco. Cultural attitudes towards the specially
       handicapped child or adult in the host culture are described,
       together with the frustrations and triumphs of the job.

1014   COOLEY, JOHN C. "A Bold Vision Realized". Christian Science
       Monitor, (8 January 1964): 9.
          A news report profiling Peace Corps/Morocco as it was after
       barely one year of operations. Following stateside training at
       the University of Utah, volunteers undergo further training at a
       government farm and rural training center. Morocco's initial
       request was for surveyors, irrigation specialists, teachers of
       art, English and music and athletic coaches. Frederic C. Thomas,
       country representative, acknowledged language as the primary
       problem, with fluency in both French and Arabic highly desirable.
       Inherited French technology has also posed challenges for the 107
       volunteers presently serving in Morocco, as have border skirmishes
       with Algeria.

1015   MCDOUGAL, JOHN M. "In Morocco, A Welding School Teaches More
       Than Welding". Christian Science Monitor (8 September 1983):
       B8-9, 14.
          An interview with Dallas Bowen and Steve Scarfati, volun-
       teers living in the town of Chichaoua west of Marrakech as part of
       a Moroccan government plan for improving vocational education in
       the country. Bowen teaches arc and acetylene welding, while
       Scarfati trains students in woodworking. Language confusions
       arise from having to cope with Berber, Moroccan Arabic and French,
       as well as English. Forty workshops in thirteen cities are
       involved in the vocational education plan, many of them staffed by
       members of Peace Corps. While the involvement of Corps personnel
       will phase out by late 1983, Bowen has extended service and will
       depart for Tonga.

1016   "Morocco: Volunteers Face Problems In A Proud Country".
      S19.11/2:3/3. <u>Peace Corps Volunteer</u>, 3, n.3 (January 1965):
      8-19.
      A collection of six articles on the varied and colorful
experiences of members of the Peace Corps assigned to Morocco,
including shopping for eggs (and forgetting the crucial word),
becoming known as "the slave of the mosquito" on entomological
work and running summer camps by the Mediterranean. Photo
illustrations are also provided.

1017   O'DONNELL, MIKE. "Climate Contrasts Create Varied Lots for
      Volunteers Assigned to Morocco". <u>Peace Corps Volunteers</u>, 1,
      n.12 (October 1963):
      The varied climatic zones and environments of Morocco are
used as introduction to this account of a volunteer surveyor's
work in the city of Ain-El-Hjar as an instructor for the Moroccan
forestry service. A survey of the placement of the other volunteers and assignments is also included. Much of the information
in this article originally appeared in the news letter of Peace
Corps/Morocco, <u>Harka</u>.

1018   THOMAS, FREDERIC C. "The Peace Corps in Morocco". <u>Middle East
      Journal</u>, 19, n.3 (1965): 273-83.
      This article provides a brief overview of the history of
Peace Corps Morocco and some of the problems faced by volunteers,
both in training and in actual on-site experiences. Among these
are the necessity to become adequate in both French and Arabic
simultaneously, French systems of education and professional
influence, poor matching of personnel to host country require-
ments--particularly in the technical service sector--and the
reaction of other expatriates. Changes in planning over the first
three years are also noted. This is an excellent example of the
ways in which an in-country program can and should adapt to maxi-
mize both the benefits for the host country and the effectiveness
of the volunteers.

1019   U. S. Department of State. <u>Nepal. Peace Corps Program.
      Agreement Effected by Exchange of Notes Signed at Kathmandu
      August 24, 1962</u>. United States Treaties and Other
      International Agreements Series, no. 5146, vol. 13, p. 3,
      Washington, D.C.: 1909-13. S9.12:13, Part 3.
      The complete texts of documents exchanged between Henry E.
Stebbins, American ambassador to Nepal, and His Excellency
Rishikesh Shaha, minister for foreign affairs of the Court of
Nepal, laying the foundation for entry of Peace Corps volunteers
to serve in that nation.

1020   "Bio-gas Digestor Serves as Prayer Wheel".   AA1.16:2/2.
        Reconnection, 2, n.2 (September 1979):   5.
            While stationed in Nepal, volunteer Alex Fazio designed and
        built a bio-gas digestor based on four public latrines in a
        Tibetan refugee camp. Using the idea of the prayer wheel which
        when turned sends up a petition, Fazio mad the agitator of the
        bio-gas system into a community prayer wheel. This represents an
        effective blend of traditional cultural elements with appropriate
        technology. The bio-gas plant provides energy for the resettle-
        ment camp and fertilizer for local crops. Fazio is currently
        working with a Pittsburgh firm on implementing ideas of methane
        usage based in part on his experiences in Nepal. An illustration
        of the plant accompanies the article.

1021   "Bridging Nepal's Kali Khola". AA1.12:2/12. InterACTION, 2,
        n.12 (September 1974): 1, 6.
            An account by Paul Benjamin, Peace Corps/Nepal, of the
        construction and design of a suspension bridge across the Kali
        Khola River. In the course of overcoming numerous obstacles, the
        necessity for inventive use of materials is made apparent. Such
        bridges as this are a priority of Nepal's economic development.

1022   U. S. Congress. House of Representatives. Committee on
        Foreign Affairs. U. S. Foreign Assistance and Peace Corps
        Activities: Report of a Staff Study Mission to Indonesia,
        Bangladesh and Nepal, November 16 to December 6, 1978.
        Washington, D.C.: Government Printing Office, 1979.
        Y4.F76/1:F76/56
            The title of this document is somewhat misleading: the
        focus of the study mission was chiefly to ascertain the effective-
        ness of work being done by the Agency for International Develop-
        ment; only incidentally was the work of the Peace Corps
        considered, and then only in one host nation, Nepal. The problems
        of that country--ecological degradation due to increased demand
        for fuel wood, transportation networks under construction or non-
        existent, basic human needs programming such as water, education
        and health measures and conservation are presented as a framework
        for the mission results. The discussion of Peace Corps/Nepal is
        limited to the degree to which Corps members are engaged in joint
        projects with UNICEF, FAO and AID. Of the one-hundred thirty
        volunteers in Nepal at the time of the study, seventy were so
        involved. Details of the precise placement of these people or the
        rest of Peace Corps/Nepal are not given.

1023   DEUTSCHLE, PHIL. The Two-Year Mountain. New York: Universe
        Books, 1986.
            This unusual volume is the story of both a volunteer's life
        as a science instructor in the high school in the Nepali town of
        Aiselukharka and his solo expedition to climb several of the
        Himalayan peaks near Everest following his completion of service.
        As such, it offers a glimpse of the cultural dynamics of adapting
        to life in a land as varied in landscape and social norms as
        Nepal.

1024   DOERR, ROBERT.   Ice and Curry: A Peace Corps Volunteer's
       Images of Nepal. San Francisco: The Company and Sons, 1970.
       A collection of poems written by a member of Peace
Corps/Nepal during his tour of service.

1025   "Elephants Walk, PCVS Follow". AA1.13:4/2-3. InterACTION, 4,
       n.2-3 (November-December 1975):   7.
       Two photographs of members of Peace Corps/Nepal forty-eight,
a conservation education and ecology project, at work in the
Chitwan National Park. Transportation within the park is safely
accomplished only upon elephant back due to the large populations
of rhinoceros, tiger and deer in the towering grasslands. One
photo shows the height of the grass by having a volunteer stand up
atop his elephant and still be overshadowed by the foliage.

1026   "Focus-Nepal". Peace Corps Times. (September/October/November
       1985):   4-7.
       A profile article discussing the history of Peace
Corps/Nepal and where the programs sponsored by that agency fit
into the development objectives of the nation. Focusing on education, rural community development projects such as water supply,
suspension bridges and fish farms and a newly introduced effort in
special education and reforestation, Corps has become an accepted
part of the work of changing Nepal. The first volunteers arrived
in Kathmandu in 1962. Photographs of several volunteers at their
sites illustrate the life and culture of the land.

1027   GORMAN, JOHN. "A Commitment Bearing Fruit: Couple Planting
       Good Will In Nepal Countryside". Congressional Record, 130,
       n.59 (9 May 1984):   S5494-5.
       An article reprinted from the Chicago Tribune of April 23,
1984, interviewing Lee and Karen Altier, volunteers serving in the
village of Panchkhal, Nepal. Their assignment was to work with
the local farmers to introduce new methods of fruit crop production and protection. Among their other projects has been the
construction of a bio-gas plant at the local orphanage.

1028   "Learning from Pashupati". Congressional Record, 109, p.8 (13
       June 1968):   10811-12.
       Originally printed in the magazine Peace Corps Volunteer of
May, 1963, this article recounts the experiences of two members of
Peace Corps/Nepal in their attempts to organize and carry out a
school construction project. Pashupati, a colleague, pointed out
following the construction's completion--by the volunteers--that
their approach was not the Nepali way. The latter involves calling community meetings and garnering community support. The
volunteers involved offer their experience as an object lesson in
community development.

1029   "Nepal". Peace Corps Volunteer, 1, n.7 (May 1963): 8-20.
       S19.11/2:1/7.
            Eleven articles on Peace Corps life and experiences in the
       Kingdom of Nepal, introduced by a survey piece from Robert Bates,
       the Representative. Areas covered include teaching, architecture
       and rural development.

1030   "Nepal Peace Corps Official One of Pair Traversing Everest".
       Peace Corps Volunteer, 1, n.7 (May 1963): 3. S19.11/2:1/7.
            William Unsoeld, Deputy Peace Corps Representative in Nepal,
       and his climbing partner ascended Mt. Everest via the previously
       unscaled West Ridge. Frostbitten feet forced their evacuation to
       Katmandu.

1031   "Nepal Sees Gobar Gas Plants as Answer to Energy Shortages".
       AA1.13:5/2. InterACTION, 5, n.2 (November 1976): 7.
            Since the early part of 1975, gobar (cow dung) plants have
       been developed as part of an ongoing effort by the government of
       Nepal to provide viable energy sources for its people. This
       article covers the work of a member of Peace Corps/Nepal in the
       project and obstacles to the widespread adoption of this technolo-
       gy by the population in general.

1032   Nepali Supplement. Washington, D.C.: Peace Corps, 1962.
            A volume of songs, dialogues in Devanagari script, an
       English-Nepali and Nepali-English glossary, numerals and a techni-
       cal English-Nepali glossary for surveyors, intended for use as
       part of formal instruction in Nepali. The complete text is avail-
       able as ERIC document ED 152 115.

1033   "Peace Corps Teacher Weds Sherpa in Nepal". New York Times.
       (23 May 1966): 14.
            Barbara Wylie, a Peace Corps teacher stationed at Phaphu,
       made history by marrying Gyale Lama, a Sherpa, on May 23, 1966.
       This was the first such marriage on record in the Kingdom of
       Nepal.

1034   ROBERTS, TOM and GARY ARROWSMITH. Lessons in Nepali.
       Washington, D.C.: Peace Corps, 1966.
            A revision of 1965 text originally developed at the Univer-
       sity of Washington, this manual was created at the University of
       Hawaii Peace Corps Training Center and used with Nepal VIII, IX,
       X, and XI. Seven units of lessons use an audiolingual approach
       with pattern drills. Glossaries of technical terms and language
       for surveyors are included as well as basic vocabulary. Both
       script and Romanized spellings of Nepali are given. Full text is
       available on the ERIC database as document ED 143 237.

1035   STEVENS, LLOYD A. "Volunteer Launches Education System for
        Nepalese Blind". S19.11/2:54/8. Peace Corps Volunteer, 4, n.8
        (June 1966): 11-3.
            An account by a blind volunteer requested by the Kingdom of
        Nepal to develop a pilot project of special education for blind
        children. The article explores the history of the school and
        problems such as teacher training and locating likely students.

1036   "Stripes You See On the Roads in Nepal May Be On A Tiger".
        S19.11/2:1/2. Peace Corps Volunteer, 1, n.2 (December 1962):
        3.
            A brief article outlining the projects training and postings
        of Peace Corps/Nepal as it was in 1962.

1037   "Volunteer Forester in Nepal Killed in Fall from Train".
        S19.11/2:2/12. Peace Corps Volunteer, 2, n.12 (October 1964):
        3.
            A description of the death of Bruce McKeen, a volunteer
        forester assigned to Biratnagar in a fall from a mountain train at
        night. He was the ninth volunteer to die in service since the
        inception of the Peace Corps.

1038   U. S. Department of State. Nicaragua. Peace Corps. Agreement
        Effected by Exchange of Notes Signed at Managua May 23 and 25,
        1968. United States Treaties and Other International
        Agreements Series, no. 6507, vol. 19, p. 4 Washington, D.C.:
        Government Printing Office, 1969, 5073-8. S9.12:19 Part 4.
            The full Spanish and English texts of notes exchanged be-
        tween Kennedy M. Crockett, ambassador of the United States, and
        His Excellency Don Lorenzo Guerrero, minister of foreign rela-
        tions, which laid the legal foundation for the presence and ser-
        vice of Peace Corps personnel in Nicaragua.

1039   "PCVs Praised". AA1.13:2/1. InterACTION, 2, n.1 (October
        1973): 5.
            A Department of State Award of Valor was presented to the
        Staff of the American Embassy in Managua, Nicaragua, in recogni-
        tion of assistance rendered during the December, 1972, earthquake.
        Tony Thielen, acting director of Peace Corps/Nicaragua, received a
        letter of commendation as well. This article relates the partici-
        pation of volunteers in Managua at that time in relief efforts,
        some working up to fifty-six hours without sleep as interpreters,
        cooks, electricians and assistants in food distribution centers.

1040   U.S. Department of State. Niger. Peace Corps. Agreement
        Effected by Exchange of Notes Signed at Niamey July 23, 1962.
        United States Treaties and Other International Agreements
        Series, no. 5368, vol. 14, p. 1, Washington, D.C.: Government
        Printing Office, 1962, 868-73. S9.12:14 Part 1.
            The complete texts, in both French and English, of notes
        exchanged between the American ambassador to the Republic of
        Niger, Mercer Cook, and His Excellency Hamani Diori, President of
        the Republic, which laid the foundations for the service of Peace
        Corps workers in that nation.

1041   COOPER, PAUL V. and OLIVER RICE. Djerma Basic Course,
        Washington, D.C.: Peace Corps, 1966.
            This manual presents the basic structural features of Djerma
        as it is spoken in the western region of Niger. Thirty units
        cover basic dialogues, structural drills and phonology. Construc-
        tion of the manual makes it applicable to both classroom use and
        self-instruction. The full text is available as ERIC document ED
        143 238.

1042   "Life in Niger: Science and Mud House". New York Times (30
        November 1970): 12.
            An interview with laboratory technician Luella Foster, a
        member of Peace Corps/Niger stationed at Dosso, some 200 miles
        south of the Sahara. Prior to arriving on site, she spent six
        weeks training at the Center for Disease Control in Atlanta
        studying hematology and serology. She exemplifies the shift in
        Peace Corps recruiting from generalists to specialist volunteers
        with clearly defined skills. Speaking of her life in Niger and
        her work at the Dosso public dispensary, Foster feels that "the
        whole world is like a play . . . You can change the costumes and
        some of the lines but the characters are the same all over."

1043   "PCVs Develop, Preserve Lush Parkland in Niger". AA1.13:1/6.
        InterACTION, 1, n.6 (March 1973): 7.
            Parc W., a wildlife refuge straddling the Niger River, is
        being developed as a future resource and tourist attraction for
        Niger. This article details the works being done by the park's
        Nigerien administrator and his Peace Corps assistant in the con-
        struction, repair and maintenance of roads, classification of the
        wildlife and flora, and patrolling the refuge against poachers by
        foot and boat. Both volunteers must import their food supplies
        and drinking water.

1044   RASPBERRY, WILLIAM. "Peace Corps and Niger". Washington Post
        (17 July 1972): A21.
            This column examines the programs of Peace Corps/Niger and
        the impact the appropriations debate in Congress in 1972 had upon
        them, interrupting planning and recruiting and forcing emergency
        measures with the host government. The Nigerien volunteers are
        working in four areas, public health education foremost, followed
        by forestry and land preservation, well digging and instruction in
        English. Most of the complement is generalists, as "Niger simply
        hasn't the infrastructure to support highly skilled technicians."

1045   "Volunteer Fights Infant Deaths". AA1.13:1/2. InterACTION, 1,
        n.2 (November 1972): 3.
            An article focusing upon the work being done in the Nigerien
        town of Tera by volunteer Nancy Riordan in the fields of community
        health and infant malnutrition. Background is provided upon the
        health problems and customs of Niger as well as the training in
        Djerma which Riordan and her fellow volunteers received.

Nigeria
    The inception of the Peace Corps' assignment and assistance
to the Federation of Nigeria took place under a program agreement,
rather than the treaty format that would subsequently become
standard procedure. The first Annual Peace Corps Report notes
that "the leaders of Nigeria--His Excellency the Rt. Honorable Dr.
Nnamdi Azikiwe, Governor-General and Commander-in-Chief: Alhaji
the Rt. Honorable Sir Abubakar Tafawa Balewa, Prime Minister and
Alhaji the Honorable Sir Ahmadu Bello, Sardauna of Sokoto, Premier
of the Northern Region . . . requested programs" (p. 32).
Researchers desiring information on the exact provisions of this
agreement should contact the Peace Corps Office of General
Counsel.

1046   AKAMBA, BAWAH and A. CRAKYE DENTEH. Spoken Hausa for Non-Hausa
       Beginners. Washington, D.C.: Peace Corps, 1974.
       A manual of sixty-two lessons in the Hausa language of
Nigeria, emphasizing developing skills in the spoken language
through drills with a fluent native speaker as instructor. All
lessons are built in the thematic framework around particular
subjects or situations. The complete text is found in the ERIC
database as document ED 142 070.

1047   AWBREY, STUART and PAT BROWN. "The Issues of Nigeria, and
       Beyond". Peace Corps Volunteer, 5, n.2 (December 1966): 2-6.
       S19.11/2:5/2.
       In October, 1966 Peace Corps Director Jack Vaughn spent
three weeks visiting volunteers in Nigeria. While issues of
hostels, living allowance and vehicle policies were discussed, it
was clear that deeper problems affecting definition of mission and
country structure were involved. This article explores the
problems and details suggested solutions.

1048   AWOBULUYI, A. OLABELE. Peace Corps Yoruba Course, Washington,
       D.C.: Peace Corps, 1965.
       This course in the Yoruba language of Nigeria was designed
at the Columbia University Teachers College in New York City for
use in Peace Corps training. It is structured to be used in a
setting where the classroom instructors have Yoruba as their first
language and consists of "cycles" of lessons. Each cycle emphasizes pronunciation, conversation and comprehension. Topical
arrangement presents grammatical points with personal introduc-
tions, food, professions, buying and selling, time, weather,
directions, travel, kinship terms and illness. The complete text
is available from the ERIC database as document ED 210 923.

1049   CARROLL, ERROL. "Education By Air Wave". <u>Peace Corps</u>
        <u>Volunteer</u>, 2, n.11 (September 1964): 16-7. S19.11/2:2/11.
            A volunteer working with the educational television network
        of Nigeria in Kaduna details the problems of his assignment.
        Carroll broadcast four program per week to forty schools between
        Kano and Kaduna. Plans for the future development of the technol-
        ogy are discussed. Researchers will want to compare this article
        with the materials on the educational television program conducted
        by volunteers in Colombia.

1050   COWAN, L. GRAY. "The Nigerian Experience and Career
        Reorientation". <u>The Cultural Frontiers of the Peace Corps</u>,
        Robert B. Textor, ed. Cambridge: M.I.T. Press, 1966, 157-69.
            Written by an academic advisor to many of the Peace Corps'
        West African programs, this article explores the experiences of
        the secondary school teachers who represented the bulk of assign-
        ments in Peace Corps/Nigeria and the problems they encountered.
        Among these latter were an unfamiliar structure of education,
        expectations of status which clashed with the egalitarian ideals
        of their Corps oath of service, expatriate heritages and their
        influence, and intense frustration with rote learning. The author
        served as an interviewer for Study Fellowships in International
        Development, in which capacity he interviewed perhaps half of the
        country complement for eligibility for scholarships. For many
        members of this group, the discovery of teaching as a vocation and
        a shift from the hard sciences to the social was noticed.

1051   DALBEY, E. GORDON. "The Technicolored Christian". <u>Practical</u>
        <u>Anthropology</u>, 15 (May-June 1968): 86-90.
            This article explores the question of what, if anything,
        Americans believe in, and how they act on their beliefs.
        Recounting incidents out of his own two years as a teacher in
        Nigeria, the Ibo and American systems of Christianity and juju are
        compared. Nigerian perceptions of foreigners are also explored
        and the Peace Corps placed in context.

1052   DALBEY, E. GORDON. "To Bear Witness As A Man". <u>Volunteer</u>, 8,
        n.7-8 (July-August 1970): 9-11. S19.11/2:8/7-8.
            An account by a member of Peace Corps/Nigeria of a collision
        of Western health methods with traditional Igbo belief systems and
        the learning experienced by both sides in the situation.

1053   FRANK, GINNA. "'Vacation' Is Teacher's Plight". <u>Peace Corps</u>
        <u>Volunteer</u>, 2, n.1 (November 1963): 6-7, 24. S19.11/2:2/1.
            During the vacation periods in the school terms of their
        host nations, PCVs were encouraged to design or participate in a
        project of a constructive nature different from their usual
        duties. This article follows the eighty volunteers assigned to
        the Western Region of Nigeria as they scattered to a wide variety
        of tasks during August and September of 1963. These ranged from

assisting public health nurses and university courses in Ibadan to collecting historical documents and filling in as teachers in the system of the Northern Region. Such projects are seen to have proved their value as a needed break in routine and as ways for the volunteer to learn more about levels of the host culture not encountered on site.

1054   GODSELL, GEOFFREY. "Peace Corps Man Tells of Nigeria".
       Christian Science Monitor (19 March 1964): 15.
            An interview with Dr. William Saltonstall, director of Peace Corps/Nigeria. His recruitment to Corps by Sargent Shriver and his views on Nigerian reactions to Peace Corps are particularly interesting. At this time, four hundred forty-five volunteers were serving in Nigeria, as teachers at virtually every level from university to elementary, making it the second largest program after the Philippines. Ninety volunteers presently in training will add the areas of agriculture and community development. The Ibadan incident involving Margery Michelmore in the early days of Peace Corps/Nigeria is now referred to humorously by Nigerians themselves.

1055   MCCLURE, H. DAVID and JOHN O. OYEWALE. Yoruba: Intermediate
       Texts. Washington, D.C.: Peace Corps, 1967.
            Based upon a series of monologues recorded by a native Yoruba speaker from the Oyo region of Nigeria, this course was developed for the Peace Corps under contract by the Foreign Service Institute in Washington, D.C. in 1966. Stress is laid on the mastery of tonal control. The presentation was intended for volunteers who would be using Yoruba in the less Westernized regions of Nigeria. Lessons are structured about daily situations, travel and cultural events. The complete document has been placed on the ERIC database as item ED 012 899.

1056   MISCHEL, WALTER. "Predicting the Success of Peace Corps
       Volunteers in Nigeria". Journal of Personality and Social
       Psychology, 1, n.5 (1965): 510-17.
            This article reports the results of several types of psychological tests done to evaluate possible successful volunteers in the first group to go to Nigeria. Types of measurements used included self-evaluations during training, peer opinion, faculty ratings, interviews, final assessment board ratings, and grades during training. The self-reporting data were gathered in late August of 1961, at the training site of Harvard University. In April, 1962, ratings of the relative success of each group member were made by in-country staff in Nigeria, using such dimensions as appreciation of Nigerian culture, representation of American culture, teaching effectiveness and adjustment to the individual postings. The staff admitted that much of what these volunteers had been doing since arrival had not been observed by any staff members and that their data were at best fragmentary. Results of the correlation of final opinions of the various stateside groups show significant correlations only between the self reports and the listed criteria, and no correlation with data obtained by the training staff through other types of measurements. "Global"

techniques of assessment are seen to be inappropriate for such
evaluation: this fits with the results of other similar studies
done using different populations.

1057   MURRAY, LOIS. "Peace Corps Girl 'Discovers' Nigeria".
       Congressional Record, 108, p.3 (26 February 1962): 2866.
       Reprinted from the Great Falls, Montana Tribune, this
article relates the experiences of Roberta Jones, a volunteer
assigned as an English instructor at the University of Nigeria.
Emphasis is laid on the international character of the faculty,
the development of Nigeria, and the positive attitude taken by
both volunteers and their hosts as to the contribution being made
by the Peace Corps.

1058   A New Peace Corps for a New Nigeria: Proceedings of the U. S.
       Peace Corps Senior Staff Seminar, Ibadan, May 13-16, 1968.
       Edited by Sam A. Carradine and Peter A. Flynn. Ibadan:
       Abiodun Printing Workd, 1968.
       This volume contains the full texts of twenty-two papers and
addresses given at a staff meeting of Peace Corps/Nigeria staff
and volunteers, ministry officials and representatives of external
research organizations held in the city of Ibadan during the
period of governmental reorganization which followed the inception
of civil war in 1967. The documents collected here cover four
topics: programming, policy and administration; agriculture and
rural development, urban community development and education for
development (including the roles of volunteers in Nigeria's
universities). The basic goal of this conference was to develop
"a set of programs and policies that will enable us to look
outward, not inward . . . to become, not a Peace Corps in Nigeria,
but a Nigerian Peace Corps" (p. 11).

1059   "Nigeria Counts Heavily on Eduction". S19.11/2:2/11. Peace
       Corps Volunteer, 2, n.11 (September 1964): 8-21.
       Introduced by a short piece written by William Saltonstall,
Director of Peace Corps/Nigeria, this is a collection of short
pieces written by volunteers in a variety of assignments within
the educational system of that nation. Projects represented range
from summer camps through familiar jobs of mathematics instruction
to court inspector of the Northern Region. Communities included
in this collection are Ilesha, Lagelu, Buguma, Kaduna and Owerri.

1060   "Nigeria: The Peace Corps Revisited". Congressional Record,
       109, p.27 (6 June 1963): A3673.
       The full text of a cable from Robert P. Smith, American
Consul to Nigeria relating the experiences of the twenty-three
volunteers who served at the University of Nigeria at Nsukka. An
article from the Nsukka Record, the campus newspaper, dated May
18, 1963 expressing the appreciation for the shift in attitudes
toward Peace Corps, is also included in the reprinted cable.

1061   "Peace Corps Girl Likes Shagamu, Nigeria". Congressional
       Record, 108, p.2 (5 February 1962): 1634-5.
          A reprinted account of the life and adjustment of Cynthia
       Bery of Philadelphia, presently serving as a teacher at the Ramo
       Secondary School in Shagamu, Nigeria, some forty miles west of
       Lagos. The article originally appeared in the Washington Evening
       Star of February 2, 1962. As a first-person view of coping with
       everything from learning Yoruba to cadging transportation, it is
       an invaluable part of the history of Peace Corps/Nigeria.

1062   "The Peace Corps in Nigeria". Sepia, 14 (March 1965): 60-5.
          During their first period of vacation, two volunteers in
       Nigeria participated in a survey of Abakaliki and Ogoja provinces
       in the eastern portion of the country. The objective was to
       determine which schools could serve as centers for a school food
       services program aimed at easing the food shortages which occur
       during the dry season. Working from dawn to dusk in some cases,
       over one thousand miles of travel yielded basic information from
       headmasters and directors for the survey workers. The bulk of
       this article is a photographic essay describing the volunteers and
       the various locations in Nigeria visited during the survey.
       Noting that an inter-racial team "is regarded as quite normal" in
       Nigeria, background information on both volunteers completes the
       article.

1063   "Peace Corps Skid". Christian Science Monitor (12 December
       1967): 5.
          Peace Corps/Nigeria, once one of the largest programs of the
       agency, is gradually fading out, due to what country director John
       McConnell terms "general feeling against the Peace Corps."
       General Yakubu Gowon, military leader of the federal government of
       Nigeria, cancelled the arrival of thirty-four volunteers for
       teaching posts in secondary schools the day prior to their depar-
       ture from New York. The present complement of Corps personnel in
       Nigeria is three hundred twenty-seven, down from a high of seven
       hundred ninety in May, 1967. No replacements are planned.

1064   "Postcard 'Gone Astray'". America, 106 (28 October 1961):
       109.
          An opinion piece issued in the "Current Comments" section of
       this periodical, the subject being the uproar occasioned by
       Margery Michelmore in Peace Corps/Nigeria. Miss Michelmore wrote
       a postcard with a description of the city of Ibadan to which the
       Nigerians took violent exception. Her situation is sympathized
       with but criticized, with the author viewing her action as conse-
       quent to an insufficient preparation for "the realities behind the
       words' developing nation". Volunteers are seen to require dedica-
       tion similar to that of missionary personnel. Blame for the
       incident is placed equally with the young lady and with the Peace
       Corps itself.

1065   SALTONSTALL, KATHARYN W. Small Bridges to One World: A Peace
        Corps Perspective, Nigeria, 1963-1965. Portsmouth, New
        Hampshire: Peter Randall, 1986.
            This story of the years of the Peace Corps in Nigeria imme-
        diately before the civil war of 1966 is told by the wife of the
        country Representative and is based upon her journal and her
        husband's daily record. Ranging from the difficulties of
        adjusting to a new climate and culture to frank and vivid accounts
        of travels across the rivers, mountains and plains of Nigeria and
        visits with volunteers at their sites, this work presents a view
        of the inner workings of a country office from a staff perspec-
        tive. Of particular interest are interviews with President Nnamdi
        Azikiwe and the account of the installation of the Emir of Kano.

1066   SCHUMM, RUTH. "Blackboard in the Jungle". Science Teacher,
        32 (October 1965): 40-1.
            The work of several Peace Corps science teachers serving
        under various working conditions in the schools of Nigeria is
        profiled. Personal interviews with the volunteers include
        accounts of coping with the British system of education and exami-
        nations, improvising facilities and writing syllabi for the
        science curricula. Communities discussed in the article are
        Katsina Ala, Yabba (a suburb of Lagos) and several bush schools in
        the Lagos-Ibadan area.

1067   SHURTLEFF, BILL. A Peace Corps Year with Nigerians. Frankfurt
        an Main: Moritz Diesterweg, 1966.
            A collection of monthly letters written by the author, a
        volunteer teaching calculus and physics at a boy's school in
        Okigwi, Eastern Region, from 1963 to 1966.

1068   SIMS, ALBERT G. "A Certain Quality of Free Enterprise".
        Overseas, 1 (July 1961): 11-3.
            An account by the first liaison officer to universities of
        the Peace Corps of the visit by Sargent Shriver to Nigeria for the
        purposes of negotiating service to that country. His meeting with
        the Sardauna of Sokoto in Kaduna and background on life in Nigeria
        from expatriate teachers already there serve as a useful window
        into the attitudes and environment of one of the first host
        nations during preliminary consideration of the benefits of having
        Corps personnel.

1069   "The Story of a Postcard". Newsweek (30 October 1961): 28-
        30.
            Margery Michelmore, a volunteer in Ibadan, Nigeria, became
        the center of controversy when a postcard she had written to a
        friend in the United States was inadvertently lost before it could
        be mailed. In the message, Michelmore made several statements
        about her host country to which the students at the University
        College in Ibadan took violent exception. Copies of the message
        were circulated across the campus, resulting in anti-Peace Corps

and anti-American demonstrations. In the interest of international amity, it was felt that Michelmore should leave Nigeria. After
apologizing to Dr. Nnamdi Azikiwe, Governor-General of Nigeria,
she was reassigned to the Peace Corps training in Arecibo, Puerto
Rico. Peace Corps personnel remained in Nigeria after this
incident.

1070   U. S. Department of State. Peace Corps. Introductory Kanuri
        by Oladele Awobuluyi et. al., Washington, D.C.:   1969.
            This course in Kanuri, a widely spoken language of Nigeria
        and Niger, was developed by the Center for Applied Linguistics in
        Washington, D.C. under Peace Corps contract. Designed for use
        with fluent speakers of Kanuri, the text of twenty lessons covers
        situations based on actual Peace Corps field experience, supplying
        vocabulary, grammar notes and usage drills. Standard Kanuri has
        been taken to be the Yerwa (Maiduguri) dialect. The full text has
        been entered on the ERIC database as document ED 051 717.

1071   "Volunteers Leave Eastern Region of Nigeria". S19.11/2:5/11.
        Peace Corps Volunteer, 5, n.11 (September 1967):   21.
            All one hundred thirty-nine volunteers assigned to the
        former Eastern Region of Nigeria were withdrawn in July, 1967,
        three weeks after fighting broke out between federal troops and
        the seceding Republic of Biafra. Most chose reassignment to
        thirteen other African host nations.

1072   "Volunteers Leave Midwest Nigeria". S19.11/2:5/12. Peace
        Corps Volunteer, 5, n.12 (October 1967):   19.
            In mid-August, 1967, all operations of the Peace Corps were
        suspended in the Midwestern state of Nigeria, which bordered on
        the rebelling Republic of Biafra. Schools had been closed in the
        region and project maintenance was becoming difficult. Peace
        Corps/Lagos ordered the withdrawal "because the uncertainty of the
        situation put the safety of the volunteers in jeopardy." The
        evacuees were reassigned while the remaining three hundred twenty-
        nine volunteers in the Northern and Western states were not dis-
        turbed. Two groups trained for service in Nigeria were posted
        elsewhere and two suggested training programs were also
        cancelled.

1073   WEISS, ALAN. High Risk/High Gain: A Freewheeling Account of
        Peace Corps Training. New York: St. Martin's Press, 1968.
            In the nomenclature of the Peace Corps, a "high risk/high
        gain" volunteer was one who had the potential, in the view of the
        training staff, for either a major contribution or becoming a
        major problem upon assignment. This volume presents the story of
        one training group of volunteers for Nigeria as seen through the
        eyes of one of the members who fell into this category. Research-
        ers will find the views expressed here range from the politically
        extreme to the patriotic and comprehensible. The flavor of the
        intensity with which training staff and volunteers alike regarded
        the situation is clearly presented.

1074   WELMERS, BEATRICE F. and WILLIAM E. Igbo. Washington, D.C.:
        Peace Corps, 1964.
            This is a teaching manual for the acquisition of Igbo, the
        largest single language in the Eastern Region of Nigeria.
        Contents have been based upon the instruction and analysis of
        Peace Corps trainees between 1961 and 1964. Twelve lessons
        covering pronunciation, major patterns of grammar and conversa-
        tional practice are provided. Researchers will find the complete
        text in the ERIC system as document ED 233 567.

1075   WELMERS, BEATRICE F. and WILLIAM E. Igbo: A Learner's
        Dictionary. Washington, D.C.: Peace Corps, 1968.
            A two-part dictionary for the student of Igbo who is already
        somewhat familiar with basic patterns and grammatical structures.
        The standard of Igbo used here is commonly known as "Central
        Igbo," although regional usages from the provines of Owerri and
        Umuahia are included. Orthography used is the official transcrip-
        tions of the government of Nigeria. The text has been entered
        into the ERIC database as document ED 024 938.

1076   "What Peace Corps Is Doing in Nigeria". Congressional Record,
        109, p.24 (25 March 1963): A1689-90.
            This is a reprinted article from Nigeria's government news-
        paper, the Morning Post, discussing the reaction of officials of
        the Ministry of Education to Peace Corps volunteers and assessing
        their contributions to a developing Nigeria. The willingness of
        volunteers to take on assigned tasks with enthusiasm, no matter
        their educational level, is remarked upon. Satisfaction with the
        performance of the personnel sent is expressed, with the comment
        that "the sincerity with which the young men and women . . .
        devote their energies to the assignment they have been given is
        one which makes it difficult to call them foreigners in Nigeria"
        (p. A1689).

1077   FITZGERALD, OWEN RAY. Psychodynamics of Volunteers Serving
        Overseas: Religious Vocation Workers and Peace Corps
        Volunteers in a North African Country. Ph.D. dissertation,
        Boston University, 1969.
            This dissertation examines Peace Corps activity in a broader
        context, that of voluntary programs of overseas service, and
        compares the Peace Corps volunteer with workers acting as part of
        religious groups. The chief problem explored here was "to develop
        a comparative study of Religious Vocation Workers . . . and Peace
        Corps Volunteers . . . which will look for statistically signifi-
        cant differences and . . . similarities in the two groups" (p.
        3). Eight factors were considered in the psychological analysis:
        1.) needs, interests and personality typologies; 2.) demographic
        factors (birth order, income level, etc.); 3.) higher education
        level attained and major field of study; 4.) motivation for
        service; 5.) problems reported in the host country; 6.) personal
        associations in the host country (both group and individual); 7.)
        life goals and 8.) self-image. Data were collected on two groups
        of volunteers in the spring of 1967 in the North African countries
        of Morocco, Tunisia and Libya, testing six hypotheses. Results

indicated more similarities than differences, with differences appearing in such areas as motivation, educational background, age of decision to serve and patterns of association. Appendixes to the text illustrate research guides and values listings employed in the survey, and a lengthy bibliography is also provided.

1078   U. S. Department of State. United Kingdom of Great Britain and Northern Ireland. Peace Corps Program in North Borneo. Agreement Effected by Exchange of Notes Signed at London October 23, 1962. United States Treaties and Other International Agreements Series, no. 5201, vol. 13, p. 3, Washington, D.C.: Government Printing Office, 1962, 2389-93. S9.12: Part 3.
      The complete text of the notes given between the British secretary of state for foreign affairs, the Earl of Home, and David Bruce, ambassador of the United States, which laid the foundation of Peace Corps service in North Borneo, at that time under British administration.

1079   U. S. Department of State. United Kingdom of Great Britain and Northern Ireland. Peace Corps Program in Sarawak. Agreement Effected by Exchange of Notes Signed at London October 25, 1962. United States Treaties and Other International Agreements Series, no. 5202, vol. 13, p. 3, Washington, D.C.: Government Printing Office, 1962, 2394-8. S9.12: Part 3.
      The complete texts of notes exchanged between David Bruce, ambassador to the United Kingdom, and the Right Honorable the Earle of Home, secretary of state for foreign affairs, which formed a legal framework for the entry and activities of Peace Corps volunteers and support personnel in Sarawak.

1080   PRICE, EDWIN C. "Sarawak". National Geographic (September 1964): 334-7.
      A volunteer working in the Kanowit district of Borneo shares this thoughts on adapting to the life and customs of the Iban, former headhunters. His posting was as rural development and extension worker, involving transporting by boat "seed, fertilizer, cement, fruit trees, rabbits, chickens, pigs, or anything else needed for the various projects along the river" (p. 334). Various photographs show the environment of the area and the Ngemah river, as well as the author experimenting with Iban tattooing.

1081   LANDGRAF, JOHN L. "Aspects of Anthropology and Language Study in the Peace Corps". Modern Language Journal, 47 (November 1963): 305-10.
      Examining the use of local languages in a fluent manner by both field anthropologists and members of the Peace Corps, the author-former Representative in charge of the establishment of the North Borneo-Sarawak program--compares the ways in which both groups have approached the matter. Noting that most anthropologists have a much longer period of linguistic training prior to service in the field, and are trained to assimilate unfamiliar dialects quickly, problems encountered by volunteers are

discussed, using examples from the Sarawak program. In one case, training was given to volunteers in Malay, while their host groups were speaking Hakka, a dialect of Chinese. But away from the school environment, most people in the area of the example spoke a dialect of Murut. For the bulk of the languages which Peace Corps personnel must master, inadequate information was available in the United States for instruction, whether from scholars of the regions or from native speakers. The course of language training given to volunteers is then outlined, with increasing stress being laid on oral facility, with written comprehension and abilities to perform technical translations coming only later. A list of the thirty-four languages in which Corps members were being taught in 1963 is provided. Noting that "in many of our schools, it is still the language courses which are the core of our overseas outlook" (p. 310), a great deal of stimulation and change is anticipated upon the return of the first groups of volunteers.

1082   U. S. Department of State. Oman. Peace Corps. Agreement
        Effected by Exchange of Notes Dated At Muscat November 15 and
        28, 1972. United States Treaties and Other International
        Agreements Series, no. 7614, vol. 24, p. 1, Washington, D.C.:
        Government Printing Office, 1974, 1013-5. S9.12:24 Part 1.
            The complete text of an agreement given between C. J.
        Quinlan, charge d'affaires of the United States embassy, and His
        Excellency Sayyid Fahad bin Mahmoud al Said, minister of state for
        foreign affairs of the Sultanate of Oman, creating a legal basis
        for Peace Corps service to that nation. This agreement was
        amended in 1977.

1083   U. S. Department of State. Oman. Peace Corps. Agreement
        Amending the Agreement of November 15 and 28, 1972. Effected
        by Exchange of Notes Signed at Muscat May 4 and August 25,
        1977. United States Treaties and Other International
        Agreements Series, no. 9116, vol. 29, p. 5, Washington, D.C.:
        Government Printing Office, 1980, 5358-62. S9.12:29 Part 5.
            The complete text of an agreement between William D. Wolle,
        ambassador of the United States and His Excellency Qais Abd al
        Munilm al-Zawawi, minister of foreign affairs of the Sultanate of
        Oman, updating and amending the original understandings reached
        between their respective governments in 1972 on matters touching
        the Peace Corps.

1084   U. S. Department of State. Pakistan. Peace Corps Program.
        Agreement Effected by Exchange of Notes Signed at Karachi May
        31, 1962. United States Treaties and Other International
        Agreements Series, no. 5113, vol. 13, p. 3, Washington, D.C.:
        Government Printing Office, 1962, 1563-7. S9.12:13 Part 3.
            The complete texts of documents exchanged between William O.
        Hall, charge d'affaires at the American embassy to Pakistan, and
        Mr. M. A. Mozaffar, acting secretary of the economic affairs
        division of the government of Pakistan, which laid the legal basis
        for the entry and service of Peace Corps volunteers to that
        nation. This agreement remained in force until the departure of
        Corps from Pakistan in 1967.

1085   ELLICKSON, JEAN. "Librarian in the Peace Corps". <u>Wilson</u>
        <u>Library Bulletin</u>, 36 (June 1962): 833-4.
            On October 28, 1961, Jean Ellickson arrived in Dacca, East
        Pakistan as part of the first Peace Corps group to be assigned
        anywhere in Asia. Her site was at the Academy for Village Devel-
        opment in the city of Comilla, concentrating on extending adult
        literacy into the villages and producing one hundred pamphlets for
        villagers on all aspects of technological improvement. To do
        this, the original texts in simplified English were first composed
        and then translated into Bengali. A brief outline of the group's
        training through the Experiment In International Living and
        Ellickson's reception by her host community is also included. As
        the author says, "in this country of Islam and purdah and the
        barely emerging female, just being a woman takes as much time as
        being a librarian."

1086   "A Glimpse of Forestry in the Peace Corps". <u>Journal of</u>
        <u>Forestry</u>, 65 (August 1967): 572-3.
            A letter from Gerald Jensen, a volunteer with two years of
        completed service in West Pakistan as a forester. The assignment
        was to work with host country foresters in two capacities: as a
        trainer of technical personnel and as a participant in a compre-
        hensive survey of the forest resources of that nation. The Aerial
        Forest Inventory Scheme involved the mapping of large areas which
        had not been assessed in this fashion from a forestry perspective.
        One facet of Jensen's experience involved the creation of new
        volume assessment tables for the measurement of standing timber.
        Upon completion of his tour of duty, he was commended by the
        Government of Pakistan for his work in this area. The time period
        covered is from 1965 to 1967.

1087   "Pakistan". S19.11/2:1/3. <u>Peace Corps Volunteer</u>, 1, n.3
        (January 1963): 10-23.
            A collection of twelve articles written by members of Peace
        Corps/Pakistan discussing their challenges and problems of adapta-
        tion. The introductory background article was done by the country
        representative, F. Kingston Berlew.

1088   "Pakistan Volunteers Attend Conference". S19.11/2:1/1. <u>Peace</u>
        <u>Corps Volunteer</u>, 1, n.1 (November 1962): 3.
            An in-service conference was held in Dacca, East Pakistan
        for that nation's Corpsmen, covering Bengali language and culture
        and current political events.

1089   "The Peace Corps Will Receive a Friendly Welcome in Pakistan".
        <u>Congressional Record</u>, 107, p.24 (29 June 1961): 4955-7.
            This entry in the <u>Congressional Record</u> is the full text of a
        letter received by the Director of the Near East and South Asia
        Division of the Peace Corps from a friend in Pakistan. The
        author, Fazl-I-Ahmad, is president of the West Pakistan TB Associ-
        ation and active in his country's efforts at development. The
        letter outlines the ways in which Peace Corps volunteers might be
        of benefit to Pakistan and the problems of agriculture, health

care and community work which will face them. Particular stress
is laid upon the learning of Urdu, because, in the writer's
words, "a link between hearts is only possible through a link
between tongues" (p. 4956).

1090   "Psychiatry Comes to Pakistan". Roche Medical Image, 6 (June
        1964): 18-9.
            A profile of the work being done by volunteer Janet Hanneman
        at the Government Medical Hospital in Lahore, West Pakistan.
        Changes introduced via her suggestions and the actions of the new
        hospital administration affected patient care and diet, living
        quarters, and health. Adopting the shalwar dress of the country
        and living with a host family, Hanneman decided to remain in
        Lahore for a third year following her initial period of service.
        A brief history of psychotherapy in Pakistan is also included as
        background.

1091   ROSIAK, ALBERTA. "An Interview with Akhtar Hameed Khan".
        S19.11/2:2/8. Peace Corps Volunteer, 2, n.8 (June 1964): 6-7,
        24.
            The individual covered in this interview is the vice chair-
        man and former director of the Pakistan Academy for Rural Develop-
        ment at Comilla. His views on the future development of Pakistan
        and some desirable changes in Peace Corps programming there
        provide an assessment from a host country official knowledgeable
        in areas crucial to effective service.

1092   RUECHELLE, RANDALL C. "Communication and the Peace Corps".
        Journal of Communication, 12 (September 1962): 135-41.
            From August 30 to November 1, 1961, a training group of
        volunteers lived at Colorado State University, acquiring skills
        related to their posting to Pakistan. The author was part of the
        team constructing the curriculum for them, and headed the unit on
        communication techniques and problems. The article outlines the
        strategies used to familiarize and sensitize the trainees with
        regard to such issues as thought and behavior related to particu-
        lar languages and the difference between language as a social
        process, amenable to instruction, and its actual use, which is
        something of an art. At the conclusion, results indicated that
        "more was accomplished through discussion, demonstration and
        practice than by lecture presentation." Reports from the field
        indicated that this group of volunteers were adapting well to
        their host country and culture.

1093   U. S. Department of State. Panama. Peace Corps Program.
        Agreement Effected by Exchange of Notes Signed at Panama
        October 30, 1963. United States Treaties and Other
        International Agreements Series, no. 5614, vol. 15, p. 2,
        Washington, D.C.: Government Printing Office, 1964, 1421-7.
        S9.12:15 Part 2.
            This document is composed of the complete texts of the notes
        given between Wallace W. Stuart, charge d'affaires at the United
        States embassy to Panama, and His Excellency, Galileo Solis,
        minister of foreign affairs of the Republic of Panama, which

created the legal basis for Peace Corps service in that country.
Both Spanish and English texts are included. This agreement
remained in force until the departure of Peace Corps from Panama
in 1971.

1094   "Peace Corps Role Ending in Panama". New York Times (25 April
        1971): 17.
        At the request of the Panamanian government, all 120
remaining members of Peace Corps/Panama will leave the country by
May 12. Reasons given were that Panamanian nationals could assume
the duties presently being filled by the volunteers. This program
began in 1962 and reached a peak in 1966 with some 200 volunteers,
the same year that Panama started its own volunteer program with
United States assistance. The bulk of Peace Corps service to
Panama was in the field of agriculture.

1095   "Peace Corps Withdrawal Asked". Christian Science Monitor (13
        February 1971): 2.
        The government of Panama has requested the removal of all
Peace Corps Personnel from its territory. The announcement, made
on February 11, follows eight years of service in that nation.
No official reason was given.

1096   U. S. Department of State. Peace Corps: Agreement Between the
        United States of America and Papua New Guinea Effected by
        Exchange of Notes Signed at Washington October 6, 1980, with
        Related Note. Treaties and International Acts Series, no.
        9882, vol.   , p. 3, Washington D.C.: Government Printing
        Office, 1981, 2889-92. S9.10:9882.
        The full texts of the notes exchanged between Richard
Celeste, director of the Peace Corps, and Sir Noel Levi, minister
of foreign affairs of Papua New Guinea, which formed the legal
foundation for the entry of Corps into that nation. The related
note covers currency and tax matters.

1097   U. S. Department of State. Paraguay. Peace Corps. Agreement
        Effected by Exchange of Notes Signed at Asuncion November 4,
        1966. United States Treaties and Other International
        Agreements, no. 6144, vol. 17, p. 2, Washington, D.C.:
        Government Printing Office, 1968, 2050-4. S9.12:17 Part 2.
        The complete Spanish and English texts of documents given
between William P. Snow, American ambassador to Paraguay, and His
Excellency Dr. Raul Sapena Pastor, minister of foreign affairs of
the Republic of Paraguay. These notes form the base upon which
all subsequent Peace Corps activity in Paraguay would rest.

1098   BLAIR, ROBERT W. Guarani Basic Course, Volumes I and II.
        Washington, D.C.: Peace Corps, 1968.
        A two-volume set of instructional exercises in the indige-
nous language of Paraguay. The first book covers an introduction
to Guarani, general principles of adult language learning and ten
study units: the second, the "core stage" for classroom training
with a native Gurarani speaker, including a short section of
dialogues.

1099   "Cheyenne Peace Corps Volunteer Gives Technical Aid to Farmers
        in Paraguay". <u>Congressional Record</u>, 122, p.21 (24 August
        1976): 27306-7.
            The work being done in crop extension work in Paraguay by
        James Pry of Wyoming is reviewed. A description of Paraguayan
        agricultural practices, crops and geography is included. Aspects
        of Corps life in this nation mentioned are training in both
        Spanish and Guarani and adjustment to a culture where privacy is
        not valued. At this time, some sixty-five volunteers were serving
        in Paraguay in health and education as well as agricultural
        assignments.

1100   MCARDLE, PATRICIA. "Close-Up: Paraguay--A Patchwork of
        Progress in a Tranquil Land". AA1.10:2/7,8. <u>Transition</u>, 2,
        n.7-8 (July-August 1973): 24-8.
            A volunteer serving in the town of Acahay in central
        Paraguay describes not only her own work as an health educator but
        also the overall work done in Paraguay by Peace Corps workers
        since the initial group's arrival in 1966. Emphasis has been
        placed on development of resources in the Guarani-speaking rural
        regions of the nation, with projects ranging from developing a
        silk industry to teaching and health work.

1101   "Paraguay's Biological Inventory Is In Its Sixth Year of
        Collecting Flora and Fauna, Some of the Rarest in the World".
        <u>Peace Corps Times</u> (March/April 1986): 7.
            A photo essay on the work being done by members of Peace
        Corps/Paraguay towards establishing an inventory of the biological
        resources of the country. Begun in 1980, the survey has amassed a
        large collection of specimens ranging from insects through iguanas
        and freshwater stingrays, the latter unique to Paraguay.

1102   "PCV Gould Studies Silvia, A Peccary Thought Extinct". <u>Peace
        Corps Time</u> (March/April 1986): 6.
            This article reports on the original research being done by
        Gina Gould, Peace Corps/Paraguay, on the rare species of peccary
        found in the Chaco region of that nation. She plans to catch
        approximately twenty-five animals to establish a breeding project
        to preserve them as well as other rare species of the Chacoan
        biota.

1103   "Peace Corps Paraguay, in the Heart of South America". <u>Peace
        Corps Times</u> (March/April 1986): 4-6.
            An overview essay on the history and programming of the
        Peace Corps program in Paraguay. Volunteers are posted in the
        areas of agricultural cooperative work, home extension, rural
        health and environmental sanitation, education (teacher training
        and special education), and forestry work with the national parks.
        Corps personnel were first invited to Paraguay in 1967. Photo-
        graphs illustrate the variety of positions occupied by volun-
        teers.

1104   "26 Health PCVs Assist Paraguay". AA1.13:3/6. InterACTION, 3,
       n.6 (March 1975): 7.
       Since 1969, the government of Paraguay has requested Peace
Corps personnel to assist in its efforts to eradicate hookworms,
malnutrition and diarrhea from its population through public
health education. This article assess the types of contributions
being made by volunteers currently on assignment, with three
interviews providing direct experience.

1105   WENTLING, ROGER H. "Organic Farming in Third World Countries".
       Organic Gardening and Farming, 19 (September 1972): 74-7.
       Written by a returned volunteer with experience in Paraguay,
this article focuses on the many applications farmers with experience in using and recycling organic sources of minerals and nutri-
ments for soils can have in the Third World. Examples of waste of
such resources as animal blood which can be used for creating
compost and long-range depletion of soil resources through repeated cash crops such as cotton are drawn from the author's experiences in Paraguay.

1106   U. S. Department of State. Peru. Peace Corps Program.
       Agreement Effected by Exchange of Notes Signed at Lima January
       25, 1962. United States Treaties and Other International
       Agreements Series, no. 5293, vol. 14, p. 1, Washington, D.C.:
       Government Printing Office, 1961, 180-4. S9.12:14 Part 1.
       The complete texts, in both English and Spanish, of the
documents exchanged between James Loeb, ambassador of the United
States, and His Excellency Dr. Richardo Elias Aparicio, acting
minister of foreign affairs, which set the legal basis for the
entry and service of Peace Corps personnel to Peru.

1107   "Airliner With 49 Lost in Andes: 5 Americans Among the
       Missing". New York Times (28 April 1966): 6.
       Three Peace Corps volunteers were among the passengers of a
Peruvian airliner which crashed on a routine flight from Lima to
Cuzco. Searchers were hampered by bad weather over that section
of the Andes. The dead were Gerald Flynn, Paul Bond and Troy
Ross.

1108   "All 49 on Airliner in Peru Crash Dead". New York Times (29
       April 1966): 12.
       The crash site of a LANSA flight from Lima to Cuzco on a
mountain some sixty miles south of Lima yielded no survivors. An
emergency call was received by the Lima airport ten minutes after
takeoff. Three members of Peace Corps/Peru were among the
victims.

1109   ANDERSON, ANN M. "Pioneer in Peru". American Dietetic
        Association Journal, 47 (December 1965): 489-90.
            In 1963, Frances Juanita Constance came to serve in the
        barriadas of the Peruvian city of Puno. She was the first
        volunteer to work in that part of the city. As a trained dieti-
        tian, her work involved managing a school lunch program for the
        school system of Puno, training host country personnel to take
        over the program upon her departure and later, her transfer into
        the barriadas as a community health and child care worker
        assisting an ongoing effort by a local group. Two photographs
        illustrate other dietitians at work in Ecuador and Belize. Of the
        volunteers in Peru, approximately two-thirds are at work in commu-
        nity development projects.

1110   BECKER, TRUMAN. "Helping Hand Boosts Peruvian Businessmen".
        Christian Science Monitor (23 November 1968): 18.
            A profile of the MBA Group, a program launched by members of
        Peace Corps/Peru to offer consulting services to small and middle
        sized businesses. It is geared to training Peruvians in business
        and designing new industrial project, particularly those in the
        fields of agriculture and natural resource development. The
        program is presently active in nine cities, and has assisted
        everything from a freezing plant to a factory making baby shoes.

1111   BONAR, RONALD E. "A Matter of Pride". American Forests, 92,
        n.7 (July 1986): 22-4.
            In 1967, Ronald Bonar participated in a program of community
        improvement in Independencia and Tahuantinsuyo, two of the
        barriadas of Lima, Peru. Among his activities was an effort to
        introduce trees to the then-barren neighborhoods and to promote
        interest in their growth and development as assets and environ-
        mental controls. In 1986, he returned to his host community to
        learn what had become of this plan. In meeting with two old
        friends and community leaders, he learned that, not only had the
        trees become a source of pride, but that when the original plant-
        ings had been bulldozed by the city of Lima, residents had renewed
        them elsewhere, creating a program of their own. In the author's
        words, "they were a testament to the tenacity of Peruvians who
        were determined to have trees in their neighborhood."

1112   CARTER, TOM. "If You Think It Will be Picturesque, Forget
        It!". Peace Corps Reader. Washington, D.C.: Peace Corps,
        1969, 5-8.
            A volunteer serving in the barriada of San Pedro outside the
        Peruvian city of Chimbote comments upon the myth of the exotic and
        romantic which pervades the image of Peace Corps life and which
        causes many volunteers to suffer massive culture shock in their
        first days on site. His work on community development and teach-
        ing in the local school is offered as an example of the real world
        of daily Peace Corps life. "The problem of false motives" for
        joining Corps is seen as underlying some, if not all, of the
        culture shock.

1113   CONGER, LUCY. "Peru: Six-Months After". S19.11/2: 9/1-2.
        Volunteer, 9, n.1-2 (January-February 1971):
        Following the disastrous earthquake of May 31, 1970 in which
two volunteers lost their lives, a varied international effort of
aid and rebuilding began in Peru. This article surveys the damage
in both mountain regions such as the Callejon de Huaylas and
coastal cities such as Chimbote, and notes the roles being played
by both members of Peace Corps/Peru and ex-volunteers in city
planning, construction, health care and population relocation.
Photographs of some of the projects are included.

1114   "Close-up: Peru: Teaching and Learning In Math and Science".
        AA1.10:2/1. Transition 2, n.1 (January 1973): 20-3.
        This article provides a brief summary of the problems faced
by the educational system of Peru and the efforts being made by
Peace Corps workers to alleviate them. These include teaching
formal subject classes, providing training for Peruvian teachers
through formal classes and instruction after school hours, holding
regional workshops, and exchanging methods of approaching topics
through practical as well as theoretical techniques.

1115   DENZLER, EVELYN. "Two Years with Peace Corps in Peru".
        Christian Science Monitor (22 January 1966): 13.
        From 1962 to 1964, Evelyn and Wayne Denzler served in Peace
Corps Peru as part of its community development effort. This
brief reminiscence details their work in school nutrition
programs, sewing classes, construction of new school buildings and
visits to outstations hidden in the Andes. Their assignments
began in the city of Arequipa and shifted later to the Callejon de
Huaylas.

1116   DOUGHTY, PAUL L. "Pitfalls and Progress in the Peruvian
        Sierra". Cultural Frontiers of the Peace Corps. Cambridge:
        M. I. T. Press, 1966, 221-41.
        In December,, 1962, Paul Doughty became field director of a
study sponsored by the Peace Corps assessing the impact and
problems of rural development programs conducted by volunteers in
the Peruvian sierra. This chapter summarizes the results of that
study. Following a brief description of the rural areas of Peru,
the arrival of the first volunteers is placed in the context of
the political developments and social attitudes of the host
nation. Factors of status and prestige, bureaucracy, class
conflict and a language barrier (volunteers were taught Spanish,
only to be posted to areas where the majority of the country
people spoke Quechua) and personal impatience are cited as contributing to a less than optimum program. A case study of the
possible results of this matrix of forces is offered through the
expulsion of the Peace Corps from the community of Vicos, itself
the site of an ongoing project by Cornell University. Suggestions
for improved programming and better language and cultural background training are given.

1117   DOUGHTY, PAUL. "20th Century is Dawning In the Andes".
        S19.11/2:1/9. Peace Corps Volunteer, 1, n.9 (July 1063):   13-
        5.
            Written by a member of the Peace Corps training staff at
        Cornell and an anthropologist with expertise in Peruvian culture,
        this article explores the participation of Peace Corps members in
        the National Plan for the Integration of the Indian Population
        (PNIPA). The work being done in the states of Ancash, Cuzco and
        Puno is reviewed. Researchers wishing a more detailed account of
        Peace Corps work in this nation should also consult the
        monographic report done by Cornell.

1118   DULINE, CHARLOTTE. "Dreams of Powdered Milk". S19.11/2:1/9.
        Peace Corps Volunteer, 1, n.9 (July 1963): 19.
            A volunteer working as part of the School Feeding Program in
        Cuzco, Peru shares her perceptions of the structure of the effort
        and the problems it must deal with. Her involvement with the
        project became so intense and the identification of the Cuerpo de
        Paz with milk so strong that she even dreamed about it on
        occasion.

1119   "A Glimpse of Forestry in the Peace Corps". Journal of
        Forestry, 65 (August 1967): 573.
            A letter from Scott Evans, a volunteer serving in the
        eastern jungles of Peru as the manager of a sawmill. The con-
        struction of the mill by the Peruvian Forest Service, problems of
        adapting to a different life and culture and professional growth
        are detailed. Foresters are also noted as working in capacities
        such as establishing tree nurseries, teaching at the university
        level, organizing a school of forestry and working in planting
        projects and forest re-creation. The time period covered is from
        1965 to 1967.

1120   "In Latin America, The Corps Copes". Christian Science Monitor
        (14 June 1966): 8.
            A visit to three members of Peace Corps/Peru serving in
        community development projects in the barriadas outside Lima.
        Susan Platt, Karen and Ted Howard discuss their projects, which
        range from a successful community newspaper to a sewing coopera-
        tive and community hall.

1121   INSKEEP, RONALD. "Friendship Meets the Test". S19.11/2:1/9.
        Peace Corps Volunteer, 1, n.9 (July 1963): 20.
            A member of a group of volunteers who set up a summer camp
        for children from the barriadas of the city of Arequipa on the
        Peruvian coast recounts the problems and satisfactions of the
        work.

1122   MCCUTCHAN, STEVE. "Peru Gets a New School". Peace Corps
        Volunteer, 4, n.2 (December 1965): 18-9. S19.11/2:4/2.
            The history of a School-To-School project coordinated by a
        member of Peace Corps/Peru serving in the village of La Quebrada
        de Caracharme de Siguas. Ethical questions related to the program
        are explored.

1123   MANGIN, WILLIAM. "City Jobs Yield Profit in Experience".
        S10.11/2:1/9. Peace Corps Volunteer, 1, n.9 (July 1963):   16-
        8.
            A report by the Deputy Peace Corps Representative in Peru on
        the placement of volunteers in the cities of Lima, Chimbote and
        Arequipa. Originally assigned to work with a housing division of
        the government, the one hundred twenty-five personnel assigned to
        these sites have involved themselves in construction projects in
        their barriadas; nearly one-third have since been reassigned to
        other projects.

1124   MORTON, NANCY. "Tu Presidente Esta Muerto!". Peace Corps
        Reader, Washington, D.C.: Peace Corps, 1969, 90-1.
            A letter written by a volunteer teacher in the city of
        Huarocondo, Peru describing the reaction of herself and the towns-
        people to the news of the assassination of John Kennedy. Morton
        and her fellow teacher dressed in black to mourn the President in
        the fashion of their host nation.

1125   PALMER, DAVID SCOTT. "Expulsion from a Peruvian University".
        Cultural Frontiers of the Peace Corps. Cambridge: M. I. T.
        Press, 1966, 243-70.
            David Palmer was one of four volunteers posted to the
        University of Huamanga in Ayacucho, Peru, who were ejected follow-
        ing three weeks of crisis in 1963. The story of that episode is
        related against the very unfamiliar background of powerful student
        political factional battles, an experimental program in English
        instruction implemented by the volunteers, and a series of
        individual incidents which were interpreted by the Peruvians
        vastly differently than they were regarded by the volunteers.
        Although a general call was issued by the Huamanga students to
        expel all Corps personnel from the universities of Peru, this was
        ignored elsewhere. The expelled volunteers returned to Ayacucho
        in other capacities and were well received by the community, which
        came to view the students' actions with some degree of disfavor.

1126   PALMER, DAVID SCOTT. "Peru". S19.11/2:1/9. Peace Corps
        Volunteer, 1, n.9 (July 1063):   10-3.
            A survey article on Peace Corps activity in Peru as it was
        in 1963. Volunteer placements in urban development, housing,
        nutrition and co-operatives are reviewed. Photographs of sample
        projects and the Peruvian landscape are included.

1127   "PC Exits Peru". AA1.13:3/4. InterACTION, 3, n.4 (January
        1975): 1.
            At the request of the Revolutionary Government of the Armed
        Forces, all one hundred thirty-seven volunteers comprising the
        contingent of Peace Corps/Peru and all trainees have been with-
        drawn from that nation. Some three thousand five hundred members
        of Corps have served in the Peruvian agriculture, forestry, public
        health, nutrition, fisheries and disaster relief sectors since the
        beginnings of the program in 1962. Government- controlled news-
        papers charged that some members of the Peace Corps were engaged
        in gathering data for the Central Intelligence Agency.

1128   "Peace Corps Team Finds Friendship". Christian Science Monitor
        (2 September 1964): 12.
            An interview with returned volunteers Chester Wiggins, 67,
        a construction engineer, and his wife Barbara, 65, on their
        service in Peru. Posted to the southern city of Arequipa, they
        worked with barriada leaders to begin an open-air school (which
        eventually acquired a building), install cesspools, water tanks
        and bathrooms. They note that "there are about fifty-seven
        barriadas in Arequipa, and all fifty-five Peace Corps volunteers
        lived in them."

1129   "Peru Tells Peace Corps to Go Home". Washington Post (15
        November 1974): A11.
            The government of Peru has requested that all one hundred
        thirty-seven members of the Peace Corps serving in that nation be
        withdrawn as soon as possible, stating that the agricultural
        development work they are performing can be done as effectively by
        Peruvian nationals. State Department officials denied a statement
        by President Alvarado that some Corps officials had been asked to
        leave in the 1960's for being CIA agents.

1130   "Report Measures Peace Corps Impact". S10.11/2:4/3. Peace
        Corps Volunteer, 4, n.3 (January 1966): 4-24.
            A series of short articles centering on the Cornell
        University study of the impact of Peace Corps programming in
        fifteen sample communities in Peru. The scale of the study is
        presented and accounts of various problems and successes--such as
        language fluency, the Vicos incident and the role gender
        differences played--supplied by both staff and volunteers. The
        full text of the report has been cited elsewhere in this bibliog-
        raphy under its full title.

1131   ROBERTS, BOB. "She Must Walk". S19.11/2:1/9. Peace Corps
        Volunteer, 1, n.9 (July 1963): 16.
            A report on the efforts of a volunteer in Vicos, Peru to
        obtain assistance from the hospital ship Hope for a young girl
        with polio.

1132   WILEY, KARLA H. Assignment Latin America: A Story of the
       Peace Corps. New York: David McKay, 1968.
          Based upon observations by the author of Peace Corps person-
       nel in training at Camps Crozier and Radley in Puerto Rico and on-
       site visits in a Latin America, this novel presents the difficul-
       ties of a volunteer working in community development programs, in
       this case in Peru.

1133   "Young Publisher with Problems: Brooklyn Peace Corps Volunteer
       Puts Out Spanish Newspaper in Slum of Lima, Peru". Ebony, 21
       (November 1965): 101-9.
          St. Clair Bourne, a volunteer in Peru, is profiled in this
       article on his revival and expansion of El Comeno, newspaper for
       Comas, the largest barriada in Lima. Under his direction, the
       paper has promoted a degree of social awareness and community
       projects. Much of the article is a photo essay graphically illus-
       trating living conditions of both volunteers and the people of the
       barriada.

1134   U. S. Department of State. Philippines. Peace Corps Program.
       Agreement Effected by Exchange of Notes Signed at Manila
       October 11 and 31, 1961. United States Treaties and Other
       International Agreements Series, no. 4889, vol. 12, p. 2,
       Washington, D.C.: Government Printing Office, 1961, 1699-1702.
       S9.12:12 Part 2.
          This document contains the full texts of the letters
       exchanged between Felixberto M. Serrano, minister for foreign
       affairs of the Republic of the Philippines, and John D. Hickerson,
       ambassador of the United States, defining the legal basis for the
       presence of Peace Corps in that nation. Legal provisions of
       Philippine law affecting the volunteers are clearly stated.

1135   "Assignment In Oslob". Congressional Record, 109, p.29 (29
       August 1963): A5499.
          The final paragraphs of an article written by Dianne
       Bridges, a volunteer serving at the village of Oslob on the island
       of Cebu in the Philippines, for the Emory University alumni
       magazine. Her affection for and valuing of the Peace Corps
       service and her host nation are very evident.

1136   BAURA, BETTY, et. al. Cebuano Para Sa Mga Peace Corps
       Volunteers. Washington, D.C.: Peace Corps, 1967.
          This text presents the basic structure and vocabulary of the
       Visayan dialect of the Cebuano language of the Philippines in
       twenty-two short dialogues with accompanying cultural materials
       and pattern drills. Situational contexts are based upon experi-
       ences reported by members of Peace Corps/Philippines. No provi-
       sion for practicing the writing or reading of Cebuano is made.
       The full texts and English equivalents of eleven well-known songs
       in Cebuano are also included. The document was produced by Peace
       Corps/Philippines and may be found in the ERIC database as docu-
       ment ED 012 905.

1137   BLANCHARD, JULIET S. Ants Have No Taste. New York: Vantage
        Press, 1980.
            A novel based upon the experiences of the author as a
        volunteer in the Philippines from 1962 to 1964.

1138   BUNYE, MARIA VICTORIA R. and ELSA PAUL YAP. Cebuano For
        Beginners. PALI Language Texts: Philippines. Washington,
        D.C.: Peace Corps, 1971.
            This text for the Cebuano language of the Philippines was
        developed under a contract with the Pacific and Asian Linguistics
        Institutes at the University of Hawaii, with early drafts tested
        in Peace Corps training at Hilo. The dialect of Cebuano spoken in
        Cebu, Negros and Leyte was taken as the standard upon which
        lessons were based. Forty-five lessons using the aural-oral
        method of instruction comprise the text. Appendixes summarize the
        language structure charts, useful common phrases, idioms and
        intonation practice materials. The full text of the document is
        available from the ERIC database as ED 239 485.

1139   CARLIN, GEORGE P. "The Peace Corps Lives". America, 150 (28
        January 1984): 46-7.
            Written by a teacher at Sacred Heart Mission on Cagraray
        Island off the coast of southern Luzon, this article profiles the
        two volunteers who have been assigned to an agricultural develop-
        ment project there. Their efforts include the foundation of a
        tree nursery, veterinary medicine and a water project involving
        wells, pumps and pipelines.

1140   "Center for Students for the Far East". Christian Science
        Monitor (18 April 1964): 15.
            An interview with General Carlos Romulo, president of the
        University of the Philippines, discussing reforms in curriculum,
        student life, academic freedom and other areas which he intro-
        duced. He noted that the Peace Corps was the best refutation of
        the Communist claim that America would not deal equitably with
        people of color. In recognition of the services rendered to the
        Philippines, the 1964 Ramon Magsaysay Award, the Philippines'
        highest honor, was granted to the Peace Corps. Sargent Shriver
        accepted the award in person.

1141   CORT, JOHN C. "Eight Hundred Americans". Commonweal, 81 (25
        September 1964): 7-10.
            A reflective essay by a returning member of Peace
        Corps/Philippines which considers both the frustrations of the
        original assignment as "co-teachers" in the school systems and the
        growth in human qualities experiences by many of the volunteers.
        It places the idea of Peace Corps service in the tradition of such
        humanist thinkers as Teilhard de Chardin. Examples of changes
        seen in both Filipinos and Americans are offered to support this
        viewpoint.

1142   "Daughter of San Sebastian". <u>Congressional Record</u>, 132, n.1
        (21 January 1986):   E3.
        A resolution passed by the Municipality of Matag-ob, Leyte
Province, Republic of the Philippine, formally expressing the
thanks of the people to the American people for having sent them
Lorie Brown, a Peace Corps volunteer from Minneapolis who worked
at an agricultural extension agent. In this document, inserted in
the <u>Record</u> by Rep. William Frenzel of Minnesota, she is formally
adopted "as a true daughter of our Barangay of San Sebastian".

1143   DE LA CRUZ, BEATO A. and R. DAVID PAUL ZORC. <u>A Study of the
        Aklanon Dialect</u>. Volumes I and II. Washington, D.C.: Peace
        Crops, 1968.
        The two-volume set of a grammar and an English-Aklanon
dictionary covering the language of the island of Panay in the
Philippines was jointly prepared by a fluent speaker from the
region and the Peace Corps language coordinator for the Western
Visayan area. The dialect belongs to the Malayo-Polynesian group
of languages and is related to Tagalog and Cebuano, for which
manuals were also prepared as part of the Peace Corps/Philippines
training effort. The complete set can be found in the ERIC system
as documents ED 145 704 and ED 145 705.

1144   "Deaf PCVs Teach Deaf Children to Communicate". AA1.13:4/7.
        <u>InterACTION</u>, 4, n.7 (April 1976):   8-9.
        At the Southeast Asian Institute for the Deaf in Quezon City
in the Philippines, three deaf volunteers are serving as teachers.
All are alumni of Gallaudet College in Washington, D.C. They
relate their experiences with both their students at SAID and
other countries' methods of attempting to teach the deaf. More
participation by deaf Corps personnel in programs is suggested.
Several photographs taken at the school illustrate the article.

1145   "From A Young American, with Love". <u>Look</u> (30 May 1967):   50-
        2.
        This article focuses on Dian Hamilton, a volunteer working
in a school for retarded children south of Manila. Overviews are
given of Peace Corps presence and programming in Malaysia, Thailand, Korea and the Philippines, as well as the effect the milita-
rization of the region is having on the effectiveness of
volunteers. Photographs included illustrate Dian's classes,
colleagues and living conditions.

1146   FUCHS, LAWRENCE H. <u>Those Peculiar Americans: The Peace Corps
        and American National Character</u>. New York: Meredith Press,
        1967.
        Written by the first country director of the Peace Corps
program in the Philippines, this volume attempts to place the
phenomenon of Peace Corps within the larger framework of the
literature of the analysis of the Americans and their national
traits, beginning with the analysis of America offered by Alexis
de Tocqueville in the late eighteenth century. Fuchs intersperses
his view of individual American features with his own account of
the foundation and development of the Peace Corps pilot project in

the Philippines, the teacher-aides program. The absence of clear definition of the assignment was due in part to a radically different view of the role of the volunteers by the Filipinos and the Corps staff in Washington due to the history of the Philippines interaction with the United States and the traditional cultural patterns of Filipino life. Concepts of social structure such as <u>pakikisama</u> and <u>utang na loob</u> which the volunteers were obliged to comprehend and cope with are presented and the varying successes of the volunteers illustrated. The volume closes with an investigation of the cult of individualism as inculcated in the United States. For researchers seeking data on both the history of one of the first major Corps in-country efforts, as well as the problems attendant upon being a volunteer when few understood its challenges, this will prove a useful resource.

1147   "Garcia Backs Corps". New York Times (17 May 1961): 11.
        Following a meeting with Sargent Shriver aboard the presidential yacht in Manila Bay, President Carlos Garcia of the Philippines welcomed the idea of three hundred Peace Corps person- nel as participants in that nation's development. Areas targeted for assistance were education and rural community development.

1148   GORMAN, JOHN T. "Demonstration Farm: Philippines". Peace Corps Times (July/August 1985): 13-4.
        An integrated farm system representing many types of appro- priate technologies suitable for marginal land environments in the Philippines near Davao City on the island of Mindanao is reviewed and critiqued in this article. James Peterson, the PCV involved in the project, describes the layout and functions of the farm and its impact on transmission of effective agricultural technologies in the region.

1149   GORMAN, JOHN. "What We Did There Was Good--A Volunteer Brought Four Decades of Experience". Congressional Record, 130, n.59 (9 May 1984): S5493-4.
        An interview with Emma Brodbeck, at ninety-one the oldest living returned volunteer. Prior to joining the Peace Corps in 1962, she had served for thirty-five years as a missionary in China, finally leaving only in 1952. Her posting was to the Philippines, where she had also done a term in mission life. Her reflections on Peace Corps provide an interesting object lesson for those interested in hearing the voice of one of the founding generation of volunteers.

1150   GUTHRIE, GEORGE M. "Cultural Preparation for the Philippines". The Cultural Frontiers of the Peace Corps, Robert B. Textor, ed. Cambridge: M. I. T. Press, 1966, 15-34.
        George Guthrie was a psychologist at Pennsylvania State University who directed the area studies and assessment programs for Philippines One through Four. With a background in Philippine culture and psychological dynamics, he discusses the historical relationship (and attitudes engendered by it) between the United States and the Philippines, the motivations of the two hundred

seventy-eight trainees who finally reached their posts, the difficulties in creating a training program (covering linguistics and
second-language teaching, science instruction, physical conditioning, briefing on American and Philippine culture, and "Outward
Bound" types of challenges) and the problems encountered in-country. These last included assignment of volunteers to a role of
"educational aide" which was never clearly spelled out by the host
ministry and a "gung ho" approach to their hosts and tasks which
offended many Filipinos, accustomed to a more balanced method of
handling affairs. Pressures from Washington were also in
evidence. Guthries then considers the nature of the helping
relationship in psychology and draws parallels with the activities
of the Peace Corps volunteer. Recommendations for continuous
training and staffing only with personnel informed adequately
about the host culture are then presented.

1151   HARE, A. PAUL. "Factors Associated with Peace Corps Volunteer
       Success in the Philippines". Human Organization, 25, n.2,
       (1966): 150-3.
           From September, 1961 to August, 1962, the author served as
part of the psychological staff of Peace Corps/Philippines
monitoring the performance of the first group of volunteers in
that country. While there, data were gathered to test predicted
correlations between certain personality and background traits and
success as volunteers. To the chagrin of the staff, "none of the
expected relationships between background and personality
variables and rated success appears" (p. 152). This caused the
serious debate of the question as to "who then is the successful
volunteer, and at what point in time do you measure his success?"
(p. 151). Details of the structuring of the first program and
living situations of the Corps is also provided.

1152   HERRING, RONALD BYER. Intercultural Transmission of Work
       Values in a Teacher Retraining Situation: A Case Study of the
       Peace Corps in the Philippines. Ph.D. dissertation, Stanford
       University, 1973.
           The issue examined in this dissertation is the dynamics of
culture trait acquisition and the ways in which this process can
be impeded or stimulated. A group of five provinces in the
Southern Tagalog region of the Philippines--Rizal, Laguna, Quezon,
Cavite and Batangas--was the site of this research involving
schools with and without Peace Corps volunteers, who would work
with Filipino teachers to improve teaching skills. Comparative
study carried out in 1967 and part of 1968 uncovered factors such
as language proficiency, degree of contact, and technical
competency of the volunteer as influential in spurring acquisition
of such values as respect for hard work. A series of
recommendations made to both the Peace Corps and the Philippine
Department of Education is also included, as well as the full text
of survey questionnaires and a full bibliography.

1153   "'Learning By Doing' Taught in Philippines". AA1.13:1/10.
        InterACTION, 1, n.10 (July 1973):8.
             The participatory approach to science education being
        applied by Peace Corps teachers in the Philippines is illustrated
        by the work of Joe Rivera at Silliman University in the central
        portion of the archipelago. His assignment is as a teacher train-
        er to both aid in modernizing the curriculum and to design materi-
        als for the classrooms which are relevant to familiar items in
        Filipino culture.

1154   LYNCH, FRANK, et. al. The Philippines Peace Corps Survey:
        Final Report. Honolulu, Social Science Research Institute,
        University of Hawaii, 1966.
             In 1964, a study was begun at the University of Hawaii to
        assess the impact which the Peace Corps had had on a specific host
        country and to answer certain questions regarding the effective-
        ness of Corps structure and administration. Evaluation of the
        success of Peace Corps activities was to be measured against the
        goals of the organization as set forth in the original Peace Corps
        Act of 1961 and in the country plan. The Philippines was selected
        because the role of the volunteers in that country had been
        regarded as somewhat controversial. A three-part interview of one
        hundred nineteen items was constructed and administered to some
        seventy-five communities, forty-eight of which had had volunteers
        in residence. The remaining twenty-seven were used as a control
        group. Questions centered upon the effect the volunteers had
        exerted upon English competence--the area to which many of them
        had been posted in Philippine schools--attitudes toward Americans,
        teaching, certain introduced facilities and the volunteers and the
        Peace Corps itself. The survey was carried out in both English
        and Spanish, as well as eleven local languages. The present
        document reports on the findings of this effort, as well as
        detailing the various steps and methodological questions faced by
        the investigators.

             Results indicated that the majority of the volunteers
        participating had been successful, both in terms of the Peace
        Corps mandate and the opinion of their local colleagues. Topics
        focused on in the reporting included the "ideal volunteer" image,
        differences in Filipino awareness and knowledge about the Peace
        Corps, characteristics of the respondents, and the degree to which
        volunteers were learning about Philippine culture. Criticism was
        leveled at the degree of preparation given to the volunteer
        teachers, and further professionalism was seen to enhance a volun-
        teer's status in Filipino eyes, rather than detracting from it.
        Levels of acceptability were defined and ways of improving the
        overall in-country program discussed.

1155   MCKAUGHAN, HOWARD and LEATRICE MIRIKITANI. A Report on
        Language Materials Development for Seven Philippine Languages.
        Washington, D.C.: Peace Corps, 1970.
            This report covers the project at the University of Hawaii's
        Pacific and Asian Linguistics Institute to develop teaching
        materials for seven of the Philippine languages: Bikol, Cebuano,
        Hiligaynon, Ilokano, Kampampangan, Pangsinan and Tagalog. For
        each, three hundred hours of classroom work, reference grammars
        and learners' dictionaries were compiled. The text of this report
        also appears in Working Papers In Linguistics, vol. 2, no. 6, July
        1970. Entries for Cebuano, Hiligaynon, Tagalog, Bikol and
        Kampampangan have been entered onto the ERIC database. The full
        text of this report is entered as ERIC document ED 043 873.

1156   MILMOE, MEG. "Happiness is a Warm Pupil". Arizona Teacher, 52
        (January 1964): 22-3.
            A short profile of Peace Corps teachers at work. Two volun-
        teers serving in Malawi and the Philippines are interviewed.

1157   MINTZ, MALCOLM W. Bikol Dictionary. PALI Language Texts.
        Philippines. Washington, D.C.: Peace Corps, 1971.
            A bilingual dictionary of the Bikol language of the
        Philippines, spoken in the southern regions of the island of Luzon
        and the island provinces of Catanduanes and Masbate. An introduc-
        tion covers the Bikol alphabet, emphasizing orthography and
        phonology. The complete text is available on the ERIC database as
        document ED 238 483. The text was produced by Peace
        Corps/Philippines.

1158   MIRIKITANI, LEATRICE T. Speaking Kampampangan. PALI Language
        Texts: Philippines. Washington, D.C.: Peace Corps, 1971.
            Prepared at the Pacific and Asian Linguistics Institute at
        the University of Hawaii, this text is intended to teach conversa-
        tional ability in the language spoken in the Panpanga-Talca region
        of the central plain of the island of Luzon. The fifty lessons
        emphasize vocabulary and basic structures. Researchers will find
        the full text of the document entered into the ERIC database as ED
        144 357.

1159   MARROW, MARGOT. "A Glimpse at Teaching in the Peace Corps:
        Young Volunteer Teaches English in the Philippines". Chicago
        Schools Journal, 45 (October 1963): 1-7.
            Working as an instructor in the rural community of Midsayap
        on the island of Mindanao, Margot Morrow describes her life in
        detail, beginning with roosters crowing at 3 A.M. and reaching to
        considerations of how to cope with being treated as if one is an
        honored guest most of the time. Children's games, local transpor-
        tation systems, curriculum planning and classroom strategies,
        faculty meetings, and languages are all included in this sincere
        portrait. Morrow laments that, after her first six months of
        service, she still does not feel integrated into the barrio
        community as much as she would like, and wonders "if they'll ever
        believe us when we tell them that Peace Corps Volunteers are not
        rich."

1160   MOTUS, CECILE L. Hiligaynon Lessons. PALI Language Texts.
        Philippines. Washington, D.C.: Peace Corps, 1971.
            Prepared at the University of Hawaii's Pacific and Asian
        Linguistics Institute, this text of fifty-four lessons in the
        Hiligaynon language was tested in Peace Corps training sessions at
        Hilo. It is intended to be used with a companion dictionary and
        reference grammar. Hiligaynon is one of the eight major languages
        of the Philippines. The twelve units of the book are each struc-
        tured for four to five hours of classroom work, and are arranged
        by topical and situational themes. The full text is available
        from the ERIC database as document ED 239 484.

1161   NOFFSINGER, JOHN S. "A Teacher for Bayombong".
        S19.11/2:3/12. Peace Corps Volunteer, 3, n.12 (October 1965):
        22-5.
            Reminiscences by a member of the 'first' Peace Corps, the
        group of American teachers who went to the Philippines following
        the Spanish-American War and became known as "Thomasites" after
        the name of the transport ship which brought them to Manila.
        Noffsinger was working with the Peace Corps Office of Public
        Affairs when this article was written. Comparisons of the two
        groups offer an historical perspective on Philippine development.

1162   "Ohio Man Assists Filipino Farmers". AA1.13:1/11.
        InterACTION, 1, n.11 (August 1973): 8.
            A news report on the work done by David Deppner, assigned to
        the province of Bulacan in the Philippines as an assistant to the
        Bureau of Animal Industries to serve as an extension agent to
        improve poultry and livestock. Among other projects, Deppner has
        set up a regional newsletter for informing farmers of market
        prices and other information on animal health usually not avail-
        able to them. Community work through starting one hundred forty
        unemployed youth on home pig-raising projects has also helped
        Deppner and his family fit into their new homes in the Philippines
        and adjust to local customs and traditions.

1163   "PCV Advises Pig Farmers". AA1.13:1/12. InterACTION, 1, n.12
        (September 1973): 4.
            A profile of the work being done by Barbie McDonald, as part
        of the Philippines Bureau of Animal Industry effort to improve and
        increase the quality of swine production. Her duties include the
        demonstration of vaccination techniques, management principles for
        living quarters and breeding plans.

1164   "Peace Corps Intrigue in the Philippines". Christian Century,
        87 (1 January 1970): 4-6.
            A brief summary of a case of suspected "grave coercion"
        involving the country director, Arthur W. Purcell, and a volunteer
        stationed in a province where there had been guerrilla trouble.
        In response to Corps efforts to have him removed from the country
        as a psychiatric case, the volunteer was forced to retain legal
        council and bring suit. The chief cause of the matter is laid at
        the door of the in-country policies of loyalty and co-operation
        with the C.I.A. favored by Purcell. Extensive damage was done to
        the image of Peace Corps by this incident.

1165   "The Philippines: Emphasis Is On Education". S19.11/2:3/12.
        Peace Corps Volunteer, 3, n.12 (October, 1965): 11-21.
            A collection of five articles on Peace Corps service in the
        Philippines as of 1965. Introduced by the country representative,
        topics covered include leper colonies, living conditions, the
        problems of the ill-defined assignments as 'co-teachers' and a
        program overview. Photographs by the volunteers illustrate the
        collection.

1166   RAMOS, TERESITA V. and VIDEA DE GUZMAN. Tagalog for Beginners.
        PALI Language Texts: Philippines. Washington, D.C.: Peace
        Corps, 1971.
            Prepared at the Pacific and Asian Linguistics Institute at
        the University of Hawaii, this text is designed for students
        beginning instruction in Tagalog, the dominant language of the
        island of Luzon. Following an introduction providing brief
        historical information on the influence and origins of Tagalog,
        nine sections of texts address basic constructions, verb forms and
        dialogies. A glossary is also included. The full text of the
        manual has been entered into the ERIC database as ED 144 358.

1167   ROGERS, DAVID. The Peace Corps Girls: A Play in Three Acts.
        Chicago: Dramatic Publishing Company, 1962.
            The only play ever written about the Peace Corps, this
        production depicts several young people as they metamorphose into
        members of Peace Corps/Philippines.

1168   SHAPLEN, ROBERT. "Encounters in Barrios". New Yorker, 39,
        n.32 (28 September 1963): 50-92.
            A frank and thoughtful account of the early years of Peace
        Corps/Philippines, as seen through the eyes of Lawrence Fuchs,
        Director and interviews with volunteers serving on the island of
        Panay, in the Visayan section of the archipelago. Postings ranged
        from "teachers aides" with ill-defined jobs and little to do to
        deeply involved community workers. All belonged to Philippines
        II. Their voices bring out graphically a part of Peace Corps
        history often obscured within the large numbers of the overall
        Philippine program.

1169   STARR, JEROLD MARTIN. <u>Cross-Cultural Encounter and Personality</u>
        <u>Change: Peace Corps Volunteers in the Philippines</u>. Ph.D.
        dissertation, Brandeis University, 1970.
            This dissertation in the field of social psychology focuses
        upon members of Peace Corps/Philippines. Its objective was to
        examine the degree (or absence) of personality change visible in
        these volunteers and to operationalize methods of systematically
        measuring and structuring such analysis within the overall field
        of personality research. Following an introductory chapter
        placing the research in a professional context within social
        psychological investigation, successive sections detail the compo-
        sition of the volunteer group their work situations in the Philip-
        pines and the contrasting cultural systems which affected them. A
        summary chapter reviews the findings of the interviews and obser-
        vations. Among these are that "the teaching of modern methods of
        mathematics and science instruction to elementary teachers is a
        waste of human and material resources" (p. 402), a conclusion
        substantiated by other analyses of the Peace Corps "co-teacher"
        program in the Philippines. The chief value of Starr's work is as
        an example of a total analysis of the matrix of social and psycho-
        logical forces impinging upon volunteers in a field setting, and
        the demonstration of ways in which many aspects of this array are
        purely behavioral and thus amenable to assessment for improvement
        of program evaluation and volunteer support. Appendixes provide
        full texts of the interview schedules used, analysis sheets and
        correspondence with the Peace Corps headquarters in Washington
        regarding various aspects of the study.

1170   SZANTON, DAVID L. "Cultural Confrontation in the Philippines".
        <u>The Cultural Frontiers of the Peace Corps</u>, Robert B. Textor,
        ed.   Cambridge: M. I. T. Press, 1966, 35-61.
            A member of Philippines Two, and an anthropologist, analyses
        the experiences of the first groups of volunteers in the
        Philippines in terms of confrontation between American and
        Filipino cultures, reasons affecting this situation (including
        resistance to statements made in training) and modes of coping
        which volunteers finally adopted. In training seven areas of
        marked difference were noted, ranging from the inappropriateness
        of American frankness to questions of deference and striving for
        power. Psychological reactions by the volunteers to this constant
        need to adapt took the form of hostility towards the Peace Corps
        itself, antagonism towards the Philippines, and general feelings
        of self-blame and inadequacy. Absence of support by staff members
        familiar with the nuances of Filipino culture and a highly
        unstructured job assignment were also contributing factors.

1171   U. S. Department of State. <u>Peace Corps. Bikol Lessons</u>.
        Washington, D.C.: 1967.
            This manual uses audio-aural methods of language instruction
        to present Bikol in a group of twelve lessons emphasizing drills,
        dialogues and phrases. No attempt is made to teach reading or
        writing skills. Full text of this document is available on the
        ERIC database as document ED 018 773.

1172   U. S. Department of State. <u>Peace Corps, Standard Bikol</u>. Jon
        Epstein. Washington, D.C.: 1967.
            The Bikol language of the Philippines is presented here,
        with "standard" Bikol taken to be the dialect used in the cities
        of Legazpi and Naga. Prior training in Bikol is assumed for users
        of this text. Full text is entered on the ERIC database as
        document ED 018 772.

1173   U. S. Department of State Peace Corps. <u>Peace Corps Primer for
        the Western Visayas</u>. David Zorc, et. al. Washington, D.C.:
        1967.
            Six dialects of the Panay and Romblon Islands region of the
        Philippines are covered in this manual. Following a brief intro-
        duction, each dialect--Aklanon, Kinaray-a, Capiznon, Ilongo,
        Loocnon, Odionganon and Romblonanon--is explored in a series of
        twelve short dialogues, grammatical notes and advice for Peace
        Corps volunteers faced with learning the languages in an unstruc-
        tured setting. The full text has been entered on the ERIC data-
        base as document ED 108 771.

1174   U. S. Department of State Peace Corps. <u>A Workbook for Learning
        Philippine Languages</u>. Washington, D.C.: 1967.
            This manual was prepared for the training program of Peace
        Corps/Philippines conducted in Lucena City in the summer of 1967
        and is intended to serve as a guide for volunteers learning
        languages similar to Tagalog on their own. Three sections
        present basic principles of linguistic analysis, basic structural
        points of grammar to orient the lessons, and daily expressions
        which may be translated from English as an aid in building vocabu-
        lary. Full text has been entered on the ERIC database under
        document ED 014 720.

1175   WATANABE, TOSHE. "The 'Non-American' Volunteer".
        S19.11/2:3/3. <u>Peace Corps Volunteer</u>, 3, n.3 (January 1965):
        5.
            A reprinted article from <u>Ang Boluntaryo</u>, newsletter of Peace
        Corps/Philippines, by a Japanese-American, on the problems
        minority membership can pose for host nationals who have a stereo-
        typed vision of the Peace Corps.

1176   WILSON, ANNE H. "An Experience to Declare". <u>Social Action</u>, 30
        (January 1964): 28-32.
            An account of her service in the town of Castilla in
        Sorsogon province in the Philippines by a member of Philippines I.
        The intensely personal aspects of Corps service comes through
        clearly, and offers a view of the experience of being one of the
        first volunteers in Asia from the inside.

1177   U. S. Department of State. <u>Rwanda. Peace Corps. Agreement</u>
        <u>Effected by Exchange of Notes Signed at Kigali December 20,</u>
        <u>1974</u>. United States Treaties and Other International Agree-
        ments Series, no. 7992, vol. 25, p. 3, Washington, D.C.:
        Government Printing Office, 1975, 3387-93. S9.12:25 Part 3.
             This document contains the complete French and English texts
        of notes given between Robert E. Fritts, ambassador of the United
        States, and His Excellency Lieutenant Colonel Aloys Nsekalije,
        minister of foreign affairs, setting out the legal basis upon
        which Peace Corps personnel would come to Rwanda.

1178   "PC Drought Efforts Expand". AA1.13:2/8. <u>InterACTION</u>, 2, n.8
        (May 1974): 1-2.
             Since the early 1960's, the Peace Corps has been involved
        with aid to the nations of the Sahelian region. Initial work in
        community development has shifted in recent years to more emphasis
        on irrigation, well-construction and reforestation, in addition to
        expanding present programs in health and nutrition. Examples of
        such projects are given from Senegal, Upper Volta, Niger, Mali,
        Ethiopia, Mauritania and Chad. Co-ordination with other aid
        groups such as Catholic Relief has also increased.

1179   U. S. Department of State. <u>Peace Corps: Agreement Between the</u>
        <u>United States of America and St. Kitts/Nevis Effective by</u>
        <u>Exchange of Letters Signed at Bridgetown and Basseterre May 15,</u>
        <u>1980 and January 13, 1981</u>. United States Treaties and Other
        International Acts Series, no. 6209, Washington, D.C.: Govern-
        ment Printing Office, 1982.
             The full texts of the notes exchanged between the Right
        Honorable Kennedy Symmonds, prime minister of St. Kitts/Nevis, and
        Sally Shelton, ambassador of the United States, which laid the
        foundation for Peace Corps Service in that nation. This agreement
        supersedes an earlier agreement dated December 19, 1966 and
        January 10, 1967.

1180   U.S. Department of State. <u>Nevis and Anguilla. Peace Corps.</u>
        <u>Agreement Effected by Exchange of Notes Signed at Bridgetown</u>
        <u>and St. Kitts December 19, 1966 and January 10, 1967</u>. United
        States Treaties and Other International Agreements Series, no.
        6209, vol. 18, p. 1, Washington, D.C.: Government Printing
        Office, 1968, 138-40. S9.12:18 Part 1.
             The complete texts of notes exchanged between George Dolgin
        American consul general, and His Honor Mr. Fred A. Phillips,
        administrator of St. Kitts-Nevis-Anguilla, setting out the basis
        upon which Peace Corps personnel would serve in that area.

1181   U. S. Department of State. St. Lucia, Peace Corps, Agreement
       Effected by Exchange of Notes Signed at Bridgetown, Barbados,
       October 19, 1965 and at Castries, St. Lucia, November 10, 1965.
       United States Treaties and Other International Agreements
       Series, no. 5902, vol. 16, p. 2, Washington, D.C.:   1753-5.
       S9.12:16 Part 2.
          This document consists of the complete texts of notes
       exchanged between Frank J. Walters, American consul, and His Honor
       Mr. G. J. Bryan, administrator of St. Lucia, in which the legal
       framework of Peace Corps service for that island nation is set
       forth.

1182   DUBOSE, MALINDA. "A Step In World Understanding". Journal of
       Home Economics. 56 (April 1964):   261-2.
          A thoughtful article written by a volunteer who served on
       the Caribbean island of St. Lucia considering both her fellow
       volunteers and their overall contribution to international under-
       standing. Projects mentioned include the areas of agriculture,
       fishing, poultry raising, and nursing. All these are related to
       the field of home economics, in which the author is a specialist.
       As she points out in her conclusion, "None are particularly
       dramatic, but their simplicity illustrates the job we tried to do,
       the types of rewards we have had" (p. 262).

1183   U. S. Department of State. St. Vincent. Peace Corps. Agree-
       ment Effected by Exchange of Notes Signed at Bridgetown
       December 16, 1966 and at St. Vincent January 18, 1967. United
       States Treaties and Other International Agreements Series, no.
       6211, vol. 18, p. 1, Washington, D.C.: Government Printing
       Office, 1968, 145-7. S9.12:18 Part 1.
          The complete texts of notes given between George Dolgin,
       American consul general, and His Honor Lt. Col. John L. Chapman,
       administrator of St. Vincent setting out the legal basis upon
       which Peace Corps service in that island would rest.

1184   U. S. Department of State. Peace Corps. Agreement Between the
       United States of America and St. Vincent and the Grenadines
       Effected by Exchange of Letters Signed at Bridgetown and St.
       Vincent May 15 and June 26, 1980. Treaties and Other Inter-
       national Acts Series, no. 10017, vol.   , p. 5, Washington,
       D.C.: Government Printing Office, 1981, 5815-21. S9.12:32
       Part 5.
          The full texts of notes exchanged between Hudson K. Tannis,
       minister of foreign affairs and tourism of St. Vincent and the
       Grenadines, and Sally Shelton, ambassador of the United States,
       creating the legal framework for that nation's Peace Corps
       program.

1185   U. S. Department of State. Senegal. Peace Corps Program.
        Agreement Effected by Exchange of Notes Signed at Dakar January
        10 and 17, 1963. United States Treaties and Other Inter-
        national Agreements, no. 5467, vol. 14, p. 2, (1963)
        Washington, D.C.:   1622-6. S9.12:14 Part 2.
            The complete texts, in both French and English, of notes
        exchanged between Philip M. Kaiser, ambassador of the United
        States, and His Excellency Doudou Thiam, minister for foreign
        affairs of the Republic of Senegal, which laid the legal founda-
        tion for the service of Peace Corps workers in that nation.

1186   CROSS, JAMES O. "Letter from Dakar". Modern Language Journal,
        47 (November 1963): 327-9.
            This letter was written by a volunteer serving as a swimming
        coach in the Senegal city of Dakar, and comments upon his efforts
        to continue his study of French while a volunteer. A description
        of the usages of the language laboratory tapes and exercises while
        in training, and some weaknesses which subsequently became appar-
        ent when in country, are given in detail. Close association of
        volunteers--with each other--sometimes occasioned by a housing
        shortage in a city such as Dakar, as well as the generally low
        usage of French as compared to Wolof in regions outside the urban
        sphere, forces volunteers to continue French study on their own.
        For some volunteers in Senegal, the nature of their work will
        determine what linguistic demands will be made of them. Of
        particular interest is Corss' comment that the Peace Corps train-
        ing manual used at the University of Massachusetts lacked many of
        the popular idioms of Senegal.

1187   GAYE, PAPE AMADOU. Practical Course in Wolof: An Audio-Aural
        Approach. Washington, D.C.: Peace Corps, December, 1980.
            This language manual for Wolof, the most widely spoken
        language of the Senegambian region, was produced under a contract
        from the Peace Crops Regional Training Resources Office in Lome,
        Togo. It is a revision and expansion of an earlier document
        developed for use at the Peace Corps training center in the Virgin
        Islands. Small classes with an instructor fluent in Wolof are
        seen as the prerequisite for successful use of these chapters. A
        glossary of 2,500 Wolof-English terms is appended, including the
        1,500 most used words, based on a survey carried out by the Centre
        de Linguistique Appliquee de Dakar. Orthography is based upon
        that officially adopted by the government of Senegal. The docu-
        ment can be located in the ERIC system as ED 226 616.

1188   HAPGOOD, DAVID. "Rural Animation in Senegal". Peace Corps
        Volunteer, 3, n.5 (March 1965): 5-7. S19.11/2:3/5.
            A summary article covering Senegal's program of animation
        rurale its origin, strategies and successes. Many of the volun-
        teers posted to Senegal have worked within this framework.

1189   "A Peace Corpsman Revisits An African Village". <u>Congressional</u>
       <u>Record</u>, 119, p.24, (22 September 1973): 30959-60.
       An article inserted into the <u>Record</u>, from <u>Parade</u> magazine
describing the return of Thomas Moore to the village of Cherif Lo
in Senegal where he served from 1968 to 1969 as an agricultural
worker. Finding that his project had been totally dismantled by a
government official, he vents his disillusionment with the effort,
saying "I don't think anyone pretends any longer that the Peace
Corps has even the remotest connection to real social and economic
development in the Third World" (p. 30960) Senator Fulbright, in
his prefatory remarks, noted that most of what was said about
Peace Corps and foreign aid originated in those agencies themselves, and that this article, by a participant in the field,
would serve as a correcion.

1190   "Senegal Trains Its Settlers". S19.11/2:2/3. <u>Peace Corps</u>
       <u>Volunteer</u>, 2, n.3 (January 1964):   5.
       As part of its development effort, the government of Senegal
planned three schools where village boys would receive training in
building skills and modern agricultural techniques. This article
describes one such camp near Dakar and the two volunteers posted
there. The background of the volunteers includes training and
work experience as masons, carpenters and repairing farm equipment. Special note is taken of the climate and agronomy of
Senegal and the problems they pose for the students' futures.

1191   TREADO, DOUGLAS. "Senegal's Sand Puts Athletes to Steep Test".
       <u>Peace Corps Volunteer</u>, 1, n.9 (July 1063): 21.
       The author arrived in Senegal in February, 1963, one of the
first group of Peace Corps athletic coaches to serve there.
Following his training of runners of Senegal's national track team
for the African Games (where they placed second), Treado moved to
the Isle of Goree, offshore from Dakar, and took up residence in a
stone fort overlooking the Atlantic. His Goreen projects were the
teaching of swimming and basketball.

1192   U. S. Department of State. <u>Seychelles. Peace Corps. Agree-</u>
       <u>ment Effected by Exchange of Notes Signed at Victoria May 31</u>
       <u>and June 9, 1978</u>. United States Treaties and Other Inter-
       national Agreements Series, no. 9300, vol. 30, p. 2,
       Washington, D.C.: Government Printing Office, 1980, 1916-24.
       S9.12:30. Part 2.
       The complete texts of notes given between Dr. Wilbert J.
LeMelle, ambassador to the Seychelles, and His Excellency Francis
Albert Rene, president of the Republic of the Seychelleis,
defining the legal basis for Peace Corps presence and service to
that island nation.

1193   U. S. Department of State. <u>Sierra Leone. Peace Corps Program.</u>
        <u>Agreement Effected by Exchange of Notes Signed at Freetown</u>
        <u>December 29, 1961</u>. United States Treaties and Other Inter-
        national Agreements Series, no. 4922, vol. 12, p. 3,
        Washington, D.C.: Government Printing Office, 1961, 3181-4.
        S9.12:12 Part 3.
              This document contains the full texts of notes exchanged
        between A. S. J. Carnahan, ambassador of the United States, and
        Dr. John Karefa-Smart, minister of external affairs, framing the
        legal basis for the entry of Peace Corps volunteers to Sierra
        Leone. This treaty has remained in force with no subsequent
        alternation of text.

1194   DORJAHN, VERNON R. "Transcultural Perceptions and
        Misperceptions in Sierra Leone". <u>The Cultural Frontiers of the</u>
        <u>Peace Corps</u>, Robert B. Textor, ed. Cambridge: M. I. T. Press,
        1966: 171-87.
              The author of this chapter is a noted Africanist who has
        taken part in the training of virtually every group of Peace Corps
        personnel bound for Sierra Leone, with the exceptions of two
        periods of extended fieldwork in that country. It was during one
        of the latter, in 1962-1963, that he was able to observe and
        evaluate the situations of the field and cultural perceptions
        which contributed to them. Background history on Sierra Leone is
        followed by a description of the split between the Creole and
        up-country sectors of the population, and the problems this
        occasions through reception of the volunteers. Difficulties
        encountered range from expatriate opposition to coping with role
        models uncomfortable to American sensibilities. Researchers
        should bear in mind that at the time this article was assembled,
        Corps had been in Sierra Leone for four years.

1195   "Great-Grandmother Joins Peace Corps". <u>Congressional Record</u>,
        129, n.158 (15 November 1983): E5535.
              An article reprinted from the Ravenna, Ohio <u>Record Courier</u>
        reporting on the acceptance for Peace Corps Sierra Leone of a
        seventy-year-old woman. Irene Steigerwald will be posted as an
        English, mathematics and shorthand teacher in the secondary
        schools of that nation. Her entry was sparked by a challenge from
        one of her family, who made her realize that "if Miss Lillian
        could do it, so could I." The reference is to Lillian Carter,
        mother of former President Carter, who served as a health
        volunteer in India.

1196   MILMOE, MEG. "New York's Peace Corps Teachers". <u>New York</u>
        <u>State Education</u>, 51 (November, 1963): 8-11.
              This essay examines the contribution certain members of
        Peace Corps/Sierra Leone are making to that nation's development.
        Their assignments were initially those of instructors in fields
        ranging from social studies to English, but other opportunities
        for service were also occupied as well. These latter include
        serving as the secretary of the Sierra Leone Museum, holding
        swimming classes for the Freetown police force, and assisting in
        the taking of the first national census.

1197   "PCV, Recovering in U.S. From Rare Fever, Raises Resources for
       Africa". AA1.13:5/1. InterACTION, 5, n.1 (October 1976): 1,
       14.
           While spending time in her Iowa home recuperating from a
       bout of lassa fever contracted in Mobai, Sierra Leone, Margaret
       Coe and her husband collected more than six tons of farming and
       medical equipment for their host community. Coe is interviewed
       and plans for the remainder of the two-year tour set forth.

1198   "PCV Teaches Science in Africa". AA1.13:2/2. InterACTION, 2,
       n.2 (November 1973): 10.
           An interview with Felicia Thacker of Peace Corps/Sierra
       Leone on her adaptation to teaching in an African school system
       and reacting to the challenges faced by being a black American
       returning to Africa. Her assignment is primarily to conduct
       workshops for science teachers as well as visiting some twenty
       primary schools on a regular basis.

1199   "Peace Corps in Sierra Leone". Congressional Record, 110, p.22
       (24 February 1964): A843-4.
           This entry is the text of an address given by the Honorable
       Ahmad Wuric, minister of Education of Sierra Leone, to a group of
       Peace Corps teachers. Note is made of the many non-academic
       subjects in which volunteers are contributing to Sierra Leone,
       among them creating bands and orchestras at their schools and
       instructing students in swimming, acting and other recreational
       activities. Thanks are returned and tribute is paid to the late
       President Kennedy.

1200   "President Stevens Honors Sierra Leone Volunteers". Peace
       Corps Times (July/August 1985): 4.
           President Siaka Stevens of Sierra Leone administered the
       oath of service to seventeen members of the Peace Corps at the
       training village of Gendembu. In a speech delivered at the
       occasion, he acknowledged the role played by volunteers in pro-
       moting agricultural development in that nation. Much of this has
       taken the form of extension activities with the rice crop, staple
       of the nations' diet. Performances by the military band and
       society "devils" also honored President Stevens' visit.

1201   SADOW, SUE. Into Africa with the Peace Corps. Westminster,
       Colo.: Beaumont Books, 1986.
           In 1961, Sue Sadow became part of the first Peace Corps
       contingent to be sent to Sierra Leone, and made history by shat-
       tering the myth that only young people could serve as volunteers.
       Beginning with her teaching days in Magburaka, Into Africa follows
       her collisions with the problems of a developing nation and the
       frank relish and humor that she used to respond to them. As the
       first senior citizen to serve in such a post, she enabled other
       older Americans to enter Peace Corps in subsequent years. Her
       travels across Africa upon completion of service are also
       recounted. For an interesting comparative study, researchers
       should consult Lillian Carter's Away From Home.

1202   SCHULZE, GARY. "Sierra Leone's Cultural Relics Find a Home of
        Their Own". S19.11/2:1/11. Peace Corps Volunteer, 1, n.11
        (September 1963): 4, 24.
            The story of the foundation and growth of the Sierra Leone
        Museum in Freetown by a member of the Peace Corps who served as
        assistant curator. Details of exhibit construction and arrange-
        ment and publicity campaigns are also included.

1203   SHUGARTS, DAVID. "Peace Corps: Who's the Alien in Africa?".
        Christian Science Monitor (26 August 1972): 9.
            "The Peace Corps volunteer is not allowed to forget that he
        is a rich man." With this reflection on the image of the white
        foreigner the author begins his examination of African expecta-
        tions and standards colliding with American realities in Peace
        Corps/Sierra Leone. Attitudes toward family, social obligations,
        and the informal network of village economics (including standards
        of dress) all pose difficulties for the volunteer attempting to
        bridge the cultures.

1204   "Sierra Leone". S19.11/2:3/5. Peace Corps Volunteer, 3, n.5
        (March 1965): 9-21.
            Donovan McClure, Director of Peace Corps/Sierra Leone, opens
        this collection of short articles with a consideration of the land
        and its history. His piece is followed by the voices of teachers,
        architects and mechanics, expressing in their own ways the life
        they share.

1205   "Sierra Leone Given Books". AA1.13:1/7. InterACTION, 1, n.7
        (April 1973): 2.
            The Peace Corps Teachers Resource Center in Sierra Leone has
        received a donation of twenty-five children's books from a
        publisher in Nashville, Tennessee. Copies of Magical Beasts and
        Palaver: Modern African Writings will be used in in-service
        training workshops at the center.

1206   "Sierra Leone President Salutes Peace Corps". AA1.13:5/5.
        InterACTION, 5, n.5 (February 1977): 5.
            In an address to a group of agriculture volunteers com-
        pleting training President Siaka Stevens of Sierra Leone commended
        the contributions of the Peace Corps to his nation. Particular
        emphasis was placed on the development of large regions for rice
        acreage through water control systems and new strains. Other
        fields in which volunteers have served Sierra Leone are education,
        health and rural development. A factor in the success of the
        program is seen to be the working partnership which the people
        have established with successive groups of volunteers over fifteen
        years.

1207   "Soules Join Peace Corps, Bound for Sierra Leone".
       Congressional Record, 117, p.29 (28 October 1971): 38118-9.
       An article from the Lexington Minute-Man of September 23,
       1971, reporting on the departure of Richard and Phoebe Soule for
       service in the Peace Corps in Sierra Leone. Training was to be
       conducted in-country. Their group consisted of water management
       specialists, engineers, architects and contractors. Soule had run
       a successful construction firm in the Lexington area and sold it
       prior to entering Corps.

1208   "They Couldn't Keep Him Out". Christian Science Monitor (27
       May 1964): 13.
       A story of Jeff Mareck, expelled on the last day of training
       for Sierra Leone, who travelled to the country on his own, walked
       into the Peace Corps office in Freetown, and offered his services.
       Volunteers in Sierra Leone are focusing their efforts on rural
       development projects such as school and bridge construction,
       digging wells and road surveying. A brief summary of the country
       projects is given. Mareck's chief contribution is a manual on
       jeep repair.

1209   THURBER, ALAN. "Volunteer Seeks Small Changes, Not Big Ones".
       Congressional Record, 132, n.137 (7 October 1986): S15530.
       An insertion in the Record by Senator DeConcini of Arizona,
       this article is one of a series examining the contribution of
       citizens of that state to the Peace Corps. Lori Buseck is serving
       as an agricultural worker in the village of Mansundu, some two
       hundred thirty miles up-country from the capital of Sierra Leone.
       Interviewed on site, she describes her life in the country by
       saying "when you are inside the photograph, it's not exotic." As
       part of her training she acquired facility in both Krio (the
       pidgin English widely spoken in Sierra Leone) and Kono, the
       regional language of Mansundu.

1210   U. S. Department of State. Peace Corps, Solomon Islands
       Pijin: Culture and Communications Handbook by Thom Huebner and
       Stephen Rex Horoi. Washington, D.C.: 1979.
       One of a set of volumes on the Pidgin of the Solomon Islands
       developed by the Experiment in International Living, this four-
       part text covers basic language for survival in the archipelago,
       travel, comprehending the cultural context of language and working
       situations. The full text of this manual has been entered on the
       ERIC database as document ED 205 042.

1211   U. S. Department of State. Solomon Islands Pijin: Grammar
       Handbook. Thom Huebner and Stephen Rex Horoi. Washington,
       D.C.: 1979.
       Created by the Experiment in International Living this
       volume is a basic grammar of the dialect of Pidgin spoken in the
       Solomon Islands. Following an introduction to the sound system,
       twenty four lessons provide descriptions and practical examples of
       the various parts of speech. The full text has been entered on
       the ERIC database as document ED 205 040.

1212   U. S. Department of State. <u>Peace Corps. Solomon Islands</u>
        <u>Pijin: Special Skills Handbook</u> by Thom Huebner. Washington,
        D.C.: 1979.
            Developed at the Experiment in International Living at
        Brattleboro, Vermont for the Peace Corps, this volume is meant to
        familiarize volunteers with the culture and geography of the
        Solomon Islands. It contains an atlas of pen-and-ink maps,
        customary stories in Pijin, posters, readings and a picture
        history. The full text is entered on the ERIC system as document
        ED 205 041.

1213   U. S. Department of State. <u>Peace Corps. Solomon Islands Pijin:</u>
        <u>Teacher's Handbook</u>. Raymond C. Clark and Thom Huebner.
        Washington, D.C.: 1979.
            A teacher's guide designed to accompany the series of texts
        on Solomon Islands Pijin developed for the Peace Corps by the
        Experiment in International Living. Topics covered include a
        description of the basic organization and purpose of the course,
        teaching techniques for various parts of the course and commentary
        and lesson notes for the handbooks on grammar and cultural commu-
        nication. The full text has been entered on the ERIC database as
        document ED 205 043.

1214   U. S. Department of State. <u>Somali Republic. Peace Corps</u>
        <u>Program. Agreement Effected by Exchange of Notes Sighed at</u>
        <u>Mogadiscio March 29 and April 17, 1962</u>. United States Treaties
        and Other International Agreements Series, no. 5016, vol. 13,
        p. 3, Washington, D.C.: Government Printing Office, 1962, 499-
        503. S9.12:13 Part 3.
            The complete texts of notes exchanged between Andrew G.
        Lynch, ambassador of the United States, and His Excellency
        Abdullahi Issa Mohamud, minister of foreign affairs, setting out
        the legal basis for the presence and service of Peace Crops volun-
        teers and staff in the Somali Republic. This agreement remained
        in force until the departure of Peace Corps from Somalia in 1970.

1215   "AID--Peace Corps Build Schools in Somalia". <u>School and</u>
        <u>Society</u>, 98 (October 1970): 338-40.
            Beginning in 1965, a joint effort of Peace Corps/Somalia and
        the Agency For International Development made possible the con-
        struction of one hundred seventy schools. A brief history of this
        effort after five years existence is provided, along with host
        country reactions.

1216   "A Letter from Somalia". <u>Congressional Record</u>, 109, p. 32 (1
        December 1963): A7393.
            This letter was sent to Rep. Wayne Aspinwall of Colorado by
        Thomas Ris, a volunteer serving as a teacher in the Somali
        Republic as part of an attempt to induce Peace Corps headquarters
        to send a full complement of personnel to replace the members of
        Somolia I upon their completion of service. The reception and
        activities of the volunteers in that nation are described.

1217   MAHONY, FRANK J. "Success in Somalia". Cultural Frontiers of
        The Peace Corps, Robert B. Textor, ed. Cambridge: M. I. T.
        Press, 1966, 125-39.
            This article, written by an applied anthropologist who
        witnessed the arrival of the Somalia I group of volunteers and
        traveled widely in the nation from 1960 to 1964 assisting AID
        projects, discusses the difficulties (both programmatic and
        political) which faced this group. Beginning with a brief consid-
        eration of the colonial history and rare linguistic and cultural
        unity of the Somali people, Mahony examines flaws in the overall
        Peace Corps effort in Somalia. Among these were insufficient and
        inaccurate cultural preparation, badly mismanaged in-country
        administration and support, and misperceptions of stereotypes
        among the Somali. Despite everything, twenty-seven of the first
        contingent of forty-five completed their tour, and paved the way
        for the more coherent success of Somalia II.

1218   PIA, J. J., P. D. BLACK and M. I. SAMATER. Beginning in
        Somali. Peace Corps, 1966.
            A manual prepared under Peace Corps contract by the Program
        of Eastern African Studies at Syracuse University. Its objective
        was to provide sufficient knowledge of Somali for a score of S2 on
        the Foreign Service Institute's language examination. One hundred
        "cycles" of topical lessons comprise the text. Full text is
        available as ERIC document ED 010 884.

1219   "Somalia". S19.11/2:8/3-4. Volunteer, 8, n.3-4 (March-April
        1970): 14-9.
            A photographic portfolio with accompanying text printed to
        mark the departure of Peace Corps from the nation of Somalia.
        Included is the full text of the statement from the Somali
        Ministry of Foreign Affairs. Political events in Somalia pre-
        ceding the expulsion are detailed. Corps workers first arrived in
        Somalia in 1962.

1220   U. S. Department of State. Swaziland. Peace Corps. Agreement
        Effected by Exchange of Notes Signed at Mbabane November 11,
        1970. United States Treaties and Other International Agree-
        ments Series, no. 6989, vol. 21, p. 3, Washington, D.C.:
        Government Printing Office, 1971, 2487-91. S9.12:21 Part 3.
            This document contains the complete texts of notes given
        between Robert W. Chase, ambassador of the United States, and His
        Excellency Prince Makhosini, prime minister and minister responsi-
        ble for foreign affairs. It was this set of understandings which
        opened the way for the entrance and service of Peace Crops person-
        nel to the Kingdom of Swaziland.

1221   NUSSBAUM, LOREN V. SANDLANE D. ZWANE and T. T. GININDZA.
        <u>Understanding and Speaking Siswati</u>. Washington, D.C.:   Peace
        Corps, 1969.
             This manual of instruction for the language of Swaziland is
        divided into two parts, one stressing comprehension of spoken si-
        Swati prior to attempting it, the other a more conventional course
        in dialogues, grammar and common usages. Appendixes cover special
        expressions and a siSwati-English vocabulary. Reading and writing
        siSwati are not addressed. The full text is preserved as ERIC
        document ED 045 976.

1222   U. S. Department of State. <u>Tanganyika. Peace Corps. Program.
        Agreement Effected by Exchange of Letters Signed at Dar-es-
        Salaam July 17 and 21, 1961</u>. United States Treaties and Other
        International Agreements, no. 4985, vol. 13, p. 1, Washington,
        D.C.: Government Printing Office, 1962, 336-8. S.9.12.13.
        Part 1.
             This document is the full text of letters exchanged between
        William R. Duggan, American consul general and the Honorable
        Julius K. Nyerere, prime minister of Tanganyika, forming the legal
        basis for the entry of the first contingent of volunteers to be
        invited to any nation. As such, it provides an historical marker
        in the development of the Peace Corps. Its brevity can be con-
        trasted with subsequent treaties and agreements of the same
        nature. Under this agreement, Peace Corps remained in Tanganyika
        until 1970, and returned to serve there in 1979 under a separate
        treaty.

1223   U. A. Department of State. <u>Tanzania. Peace Corps. Agreement
        Effected by Exchange of Letters Signed at Dar-es-Salaam January
        9, 1979</u>. United States Treaties and Other International Agree-
        ments Series, no. 9402, vol. 30, p. 3, Washington, D.C.:
        Government Printing Office, 1979, 3486-92. S9.12:30 Part 3.
             Under the terms of this agreement between Abel Mwanga,
        minister of manpower development and ambassador James W. Spain,
        the legal foundations for the return of Peace Corps workers to
        Tanzania were laid. Provisions for the place of volunteers under
        host country laws are stated with regard to such matters as duties
        and taxation.

1224   DYGERT, RUTH E. "Tanganyika". <u>National Geographic</u> (September
        1964):   320-3.
             One of the twenty-seven nurses of the Tanganyika II group
        vividly describes her experiences in a variety of linguistic and
        professional settings in a government hospital in the town of
        Tanga. Both love for the people and frustration at times with
        customs she chalks up, as her hosts often do, to <u>shauri la mungu</u>,
        "the will of God".

1225   FRIEDLAND, WILLIAM H. "Nurses in Tanganyika". The Cultural
       Frontiers of the Peace Corps, Robert B. Textor, ed. Cambridge:
       M. I. T. Press, 1966: 141-55.
       The second group of volunteers to serve in the east African
nation of Tanganyika/Tanzania was composed exclusively of nurses
and laboratory technicians, all female and most under thirty.
This article examines their training and problems of adjustment.
Among the latter were the fostering of inaccuracies regarding
Tanganyikan society by the training staff, lack of adequate
briefing on the different structure of nursing and hospital
practice in the British system in use in Dar-es-Salaam (where most
of the group was initially posted) and insufficient information on
the charged political situation following independence, especially
as it related to attitudes towards foreigners. The in-country
Representative also proved to be less effective than possible in
maintaining morale. This case provides an example of the sometimes painful lessons learned in the first few years of Corps work
about programming and overseas support.

1226   GILBERT, SCOTT. "Tanganyika and the Peace Corps: Unanswered
       Questions". Human Organization, 21 (Winter 1962-1963): 286-9.
       The preparation of Peace Corps volunteers for service over-
seas is seen to require information of a sort not readily available from scholarly sources in the fields of anthropology and
social science. This case is used as an example of what sort of
data would be necessary for anthropologists to play a wider role
in governmental programs and planning. The absence of information
is laid squarely on "the fact that gathering of data of this sort
would probably not be seen a meeting the qualifications of a
scholarly treatise" (p. 289). The bulk of this article is com-
prised of a list of questions regarding the culture and social
system of Tanganyika developed prior to a conference of experts on
the region intended to advise the Peace Corps in its planning.
Topics raised include general cultural concepts such as justice,
work situations, American behaviors which host country people
would find offensive, administrative structures, and mechanisms of
cultural change such as missionary influences. The panel of
experts on Tanganyika assembled to assist the volunteer training
program agreed that such information was not readily available but
was required. The list offers a useful illustration of the multiplicity of factors facing the volunteer in any posting.

1227   "Kinsey Acquitted of Murder Charge". S19.11/2:4/12. Peace
       Corps Volunteer, 4, n.12 (October 1966): 4.
       A court in Tanzania has found volunteer Bill Kinsey innocent
of murdering his wife while on a climbing trip. Cause of death
was ruled to be accidental.

1228   LEVITT, LEONARD.   An African Season.   New York: Simon and
        Schuster, 1967.
            Beginning with his arrival at Ndumulu School near Tukuyu in
        south-central Tanzania near Lake Malawi, Leonard Levitt takes the
        reader inside the course of a school year in that country's
        system.   Humorously reflective comments show the growth of cultur-
        al awareness and adaptation.   Of particular interest are the
        chapters discussing his holiday journey south to Cape Town and
        their descriptions of racial attitudes in Rhodesia and South
        Africa.

1229   HERT, RON.   "No Room for PC in Tanzania's Policy of Self-
        Reliance".   Peace Corps Volunteer, 7, n.10 (September 1969):
        2-8.   S19.11/2:7/10.
            A survey article detailing the slow erosion of the Peace
        Corps presence in Tanzania, both as regards U. S. foreign policy
        decisions and actions in Southeast Asia and Tanzania's reaction to
        them, and the development plans and philosophy adopted by Julius
        Nyerere.

1230   "Peace Corps Assistance to Tanganyika".   Congressional Record,
        107, p.5 (27 April 1961):   6816.
            An announcement that the Peace Corps has been contacted for
        its first pilot group of personnel, twenty-eight surveyors, geolo-
        gists and engineers for the nation of Tanganyika.   The project is
        the preliminary surveying and mapping work necessary for the
        construction of a network of feeder roads for improvement of the
        transportation system.   Training of local counterparts in survey-
        ing will also be a part of the effort.

1231   "Peace Corps Comeback".   Christian Science Monitor (20 February
        1979):   32.
            The request of President Julius Nyerere that Peace Corps
        return to Tanzania is used as a case study framing the consider-
        ation of basic issues regarding organizational priorities.   The
        Corps was originally expelled from Tanzania due to that govern-
        ment's objections to the U. S. role in Viet Nam and the American
        policy towards the South African regime.   Fifty volunteers will be
        assigned to projects in forestry and agriculture.

1232   "Peace Corps Criticized".   Christian Science Monitor (6 January
        1967):   3.
            A "lack of government progress towards socialism" is being
        criticized by Tanzania's only trade union, with the Peace Corps
        held partly to blame.   Union leaders presented a resolution that
        Corps teachers not be permitted in the primary schools because
        they "misdirect the minds of young people, making them hate
        socialism."

1233   "Peace Corps Shifts Teachers". Christian Science Monitor (28
       December 1966): 4.
          The government of Tanzania has issued a moratorium on the
       hiring of foreign primary-grade teachers. As a result of this
       announcement, ninety-five of one hundred fifty-five volunteers
       trained for Tanzanian service at Syracuse University are being
       reassigned to other African host nations. The decision does not
       affect the two hundred eighty-three volunteers already at work in
       Tranzania.

1234   "Political Conflicts Diminish U. S. Peace Corps in Tanzania".
       Christian Science Monitor (19 December 1968): 6.
          By January 1, 1969, Peace Corps/Tanzania had shrunk from a
       high of four hundred to merely eleven volunteers. Despite the
       early endorsements of their work by President Julius Nyerere,
       domestic political issues related to building socialism, as well
       as the United States policies towards South Africa and the war in
       Vietnam, had produced a climate radically cool to further work by
       the agency in that country.

1235   "Tanganyika (Tanzania) I". Peace Corps Times (March/April
       1986): 8-9.
          A review of the history of Peace Corps activity in Tanzania.
       The bulk of the article is composed of reflections by one of the
       members of the original team of surveyors sent to Tanganyika in
       1961 to lay out a system of roads. Richard Van Loenen's memories
       bring a vivid touch to the earliest days of Peace Corps in East
       Africa.

1236   "Tanganyika Ho!". Newsweek (1 May 1961): 35-6.
          The request of the government of Tanganyika for Peace Corps
       volunteers to serve as part of a project constructing a network of
       secondary feeder roads is presented. Some thirty civil engineers,
       geologist and surveyors will plan the roads in the dry season and
       instruct their host country counterparts during the rains. Prior
       to departure, volunteers are to receive some five to six months of
       indoctrination, with the final seven weeks of language study
       taking place in-country at a camp on the slopes of Mount
       Kilimanjaro. To promote further invitations, R. Sargent Shriver,
       Director of the Peace Corps, has recently left on a survey trip to
       India, Asia, Africa, Malaya and the Philippines. A probable
       second country for the Peace Corps will be Colombia, where
       community development work is planned.

1237   "Tanzania Cuts Peace Corps". Christian Science Monitor (27
       February 1969): 4.
          After eight years, the Peace Corps program in Tanzania is
       being scrapped by its host nation. Chief criticisms lie in the
       provision of too many teachers and too few technically experienced
       personnel. The last members of the Corps will leave by the end of
       1960.

1238   "Tanganyika Men on TV". S19.11/2:1/2. <u>Volunteer</u>, 1, n.2
        (February 1962): 3.
            A selection of newspaper reviews of the NBC television color
        special which aired December 15, 1961. Newspapers represented are
        the <u>Washington Post</u>, <u>New York Times</u> and the <u>Philadelphia
        Inquirer</u>.

1239   TRESCOTT, JACQUELINE. "Nyerere May Invite U. S. Peace Corps to
        Return to Tanzania". <u>Washington Post</u> (11 August 1977): A13.
            Before leaving the United States at the conclusion of a
        state visit, President Julius Nyerere of Tanzania met for half an
        hour with Sam Brown, Director of ACTION, regarding the possible
        reactivation of Corps work in that nation. Brown was invited to
        Dar-es-Salaam for further discussion. The Peace Corps left
        Tanzania in 1969 during a period of increased emphasis on self-
        sufficiency and sharp disagreement with the U. S. over its role in
        Viet Nam.

1240   YARBOROUGH, RALPH. "Peace Corps: Texas to Tanganyika".
        <u>Congressional Record</u>, 107, p.12 (14 August 1961): 15799.
            The full text of remarks made to the training volunteers of
        Tanganyika I at Texas Western College in El Paso, Texas on August
        12, 1961. This group of surveyors, geologists and engineers was
        intended to aid in the construction of a network of rural roads to
        improve that nation's transportation system.

1241   U. S. Department of State. <u>Peace Corps. Tanzanian Swahili:
        Communication and Culture Handbook</u>. Washington, D.C.: 1979.
            One of a set of volumes developed by the Experiment in
        International Living under Peace Corps contract, this manual
        presents lessons structured about social situations based on
        Tanzanian social norms, ranging from delivering apologies to
        social etiquette and myths. Stress is pl   ' on volunteers
        adapting to new social institutions. The .ll text is available
        on the ERIC database as document ED 206 169.

1242   U. S. Department of State. <u>Peace Corps. Tanzanian Swahili:
        Grammar Handbook</u>. Washington, D.C.: 1979.
            Thirty-six lessons developed by the Experiment in Inter-
        national Living under Peace Corps contract present basic points of
        Kiswahili grammar for volunteers posted to Tanzania. Full text is
        entered on the ERIC database as document ED 206 167.

1243   U. S. Department of State. <u>Peace Corps. Tanzanian Swahili:
        Special Skills Handbook</u>. Washington, D.C.: 1979.
            The "special skills" of the title are culture, health,
        agriculture and politics, with specialized vocabulary for each
        field presented. The format is of texts translated from Kiswahili
        to English. Developed by the Experiment for International Living,
        the text has been entered on the ERIC database as document ED 206
        168.

1244   U. S. Department of State. <u>Peace Corps. Tanzania Swahili:</u>
        <u>Teacher's Handbook</u>. Washington, D.C.: 1979.
            This volume was written to accompany the three classroom
        texts on Kiswahili as it is spoken in Tanzania used in Peace Corps
        training. Contents include an introduction to the format and
        scope of the complete Swahili course followed by a description of
        effective teaching techniques and lesson notes on the grammar and
        cultural communication textbooks. The full text of this handbook
        has been entered on the ERIC database as document ED 206 170.

1245   "Volunteer Held in Wife's Death". S19.11/2:4/7. <u>Peace Corps</u>
        <u>Volunteer</u>, 4, n.7 (May 1966): 3.
            Bill Kinsey, Peace Corps Tanzania, is being held in
        connection with the death of his wife during a climbing trip near
        their site of Maswa. Background on the case is given.

1246   WINGENBACH, CHARLES. "Training In Action--Project Tanganyika".
        <u>The Peace Corps</u>, Pauline Madow, ed. New York: Wilson, 1964,
        40-6.
            In this article, a detailed profile of the training struc-
        tures and programs designed for the first group of volunteers to
        serve in Tanganyika is presented. Beginning with the selection of
        Texas Western University as a training site, the trainees are
        followed through fitness and survival classes at Arecibo, Puerto
        Rico and the in-country training at the Natural Resources School
        at Tengeru near Kilimanjaro. Of particular interest are the
        objectives of each step in training.

1247   U. S. Department of State. <u>Thailand. Peace Corps Program.</u>
        <u>Agreement Effected by Exchange of Notes Signed at Bangkok</u>
        <u>November 20 and 28, 1961</u>. United States Treaties and Other
        International Agreements Series, no. 4929, vol. 12, p. 3,
        Washington, D.C.: Government Printing Office, 1961, 3225-8.
        S9.12:12 Part 3.
            This document contains the full texts of notes exchanged
        between Kenneth T. Young, ambassador of the United States, and
        Thanat Khoman, minister of foreign affairs of the Kingdom of
        Thailand, setting forth the legal framework for Peace Corps staff
        and volunteers to serve in that country. The treaty has remained
        in force since that time with no substantial alterations of the
        basic text.

1248   "Back to Earth Problems". <u>Los Angeles Times</u> (25 May 1972):
        2.
            A photograph of astronaut Donn Eisele and his wife after his
        swearing-in ceremony as the new country director of Peace
        Corps/Thailand. He will assume his post in June following train-
        ing with the Corps.

1249   COOPER, SARAH L. "The Parent Learns Too". S19.11/2:3/3.
        Peace Corps Volunteer, 3, n.3 (January 1965): 22-3.
            An account by the mother of a Peace Corps teacher of her
        visit to her daughter's site at Udon, Thailand, and her reactions
        to both the new culture and the change in her daughter. As her
        title indicates, both sides gain in such an event. Researchers
        may find it useful to compare Sarah Cooper's reactions with those
        chronicled in The Gringo Brought His Mother by Geneva Sanders.

1250   "Designing Thai Hospitals: A Two-Way Technology". AA1.13:3/8.
        InterACTION, 3, n.8 (May 1975): 12.
            In working with specialists and architects from the Thai
        Ministry of Health to design ten regional hospitals to relieve
        pressure on those of Bangkok, Robert Lawton has found the dual
        transfer of energy management technology to be effective. Lawton
        headed his own construction firm prior to serving. Details of the
        hospital and improvements are noted.

1251   FOISIE, JACK. "Ex-Astronaut Shakes Up Peace Corps in
        Thailand". Washington Post (20 January 1974): G1.
            The controversial career on Donn Eisele, former Apollo 7
        astronaut, as country director of Peace Corps/Thailand is
        examined. While acknowledged by the volunteers to be interested
        in the program and active in rebutting charges of CIA affiliation,
        Eisele has nevertheless lived in a style beyond the salary of the
        Director, kept contacts with volunteers infrequent and formal, and
        exhibited little inclination to learn Thai. Volunteers in
        Thailand are working chiefly as English teachers. Ambassador
        Leonard Unger having moved them out of rural development work to
        avoid possible incidents with insurgents.

1252   GORMAN, JOHN. "Americans Still Roam Globe to Sow Peace".
        Congressional Record, 130, n.59 (9 May 1984): S5492-3.
            A reprinted article from the Chicago Tribune of April 22,
        1984, inserted in the Record by Senator Percy of Illinois. The
        focus is upon work currently being done in Nepal and Thailand,
        with several volunteers discussing their work in teaching English
        to the blind, agricultural extension work with new varieties of
        seeds, agronomy and honeybees. Interviews with the country
        directors of Thailand and Nepal and host country ministers are
        also included. The author is himself an RPCV.

1253   GUSKIN, ALAN J. "Tradition and Change in a Thai University".
        The Cultural Frontiers of the Peace Corps, Robert B. Textor,
        ed. Cambridge: M.I.T. Press, 1966, 87-106.
            Alan Guskin was one of the first student leaders to press
        President Kennedy for the establishment of a Peace Corps, and with
        his wife served at a university in Bangkok as members of Thailand
        One from 1961 to 1964. In this chapter, he relates the challenges
        and difficulties encountered by volunteers adapting to the Thai

university system, with its unfamiliar role expectations, the image of rural service versus unacculturated realities, and coping with a status structure which de-emphasized innovation and change. As a window into a sphere different from the usual assignment given to volunteers in education, this essay is especially valuable.

1254 MACAULAY, BARBARA. "Speaking, Eating Thai Style". Christian Science Monitor (20 May 1971): 10.
An account by a member of a group of fifty volunteers of training for service in Thailand during a six week stay in Hawaii. Included in life in the model Thai village (staffed by Thai nationals and Peace Corps/Thailand veterans) are courses in Thai cooking, attendance at Buddhist services, together with an explanation of that religion, and language instruction. Following their six weeks at Honomu, the group will have another six weeks of practice teaching and living with host families prior to posting in Thailand.

1255 NEHER, CLARK. "Aspects of Westernization". S19.11/2:2/12. Peace Corps Volunteer, 2, n.12 (October 1964): 19-20.
A volunteer teaching political science at Chulalongkorn University in Bangkok relates his classroom experiences with traditional attitudes towards the authority of the teacher and the Western stress on individual thought and initiative.

1256 "PCV Aids Thais in Family Planning Project". AA1.13:3/6. InterACTION, 3, n.6 (March 1975): 6.
Using a computer intended to calculate odds and race payoffs at the Bangkok Turf Club, Corinne Dellenbaugh of Peace Corps/Thailand, is assisting the Ministry of Public Health in plotting the progress of the family planning effort. Statistics from all over Thailand are coded by Dellenbaugh and entered, permitting alterations in techniques of population management to be introduced while surveys and programs are still continuing.

1257 PAUL, GERALD. "A Trunked-Up Story". S19.11/2:2/3. Peace Corps Volunteer, 2, n.3 (January 1964): 8.
A story drawn from the newsletter of Peace Corps/Thailand about the request of a community of a volunteer to doctor a sick elephant.

1258 "Personal Efforts of Peace Corps Volunteers in Thailand". Congressional Record, 110, p.22 (2 March 1964): A1025-6.
Upon the third anniversary of the founding of the Peace Corps, Rep. Clement Zablocki of Wisconsin introduced an excerpt from a State Department report on activities of members of Peace Corps/Thailand. These range from preparing the first textbook in Thai in the field of animal husbandry, serving as community health resources in rural areas, writing and illustrating children's books, teaching courses in political science and economics, compiling a dictionary of the northern Thai language and editing a book on the hill tribes.

1259   RETKA, BOB and CAROL KIM. "Thailand". S19.11/2:7/6. Peace
        Corps Volunteer, 7, n.6 (May 1969): 11-23.
            A selection of photographs depicting the faces of Thailand
        as seen by a volunteer couple. Regions represented are the north-
        central plains and hill country, including the ancient capitals of
        Sukhothai and Ayuthaya.

1260   SJOSTROM, DON. "A Volunteer's Life in the Village of the Lion
        Forest". 19.11/2:1/12. Peace Corps Volunteer, 2, n.12
        (October 1964): 14-5.
            A teacher posted to the town of Yasothon describes his
        adjustments to the local culture and deep involvement with tradi-
        tional cultural patterns.

1261   "Thailand: Gentle Kingdom in the Eye of a Storm".
        S19.11/2:2/12. Peace Corps Volunteer, 2, n.12 (October 1964):
        8-21.
            Peace Corps/Thailand director John McCarthy introduces this
        collection of articles and impressions written by volunteers
        serving in many areas of Thai society. Included are the craft of
        bus riding in Thailand, community development, teaching in a
        border village near Laos, and coping with infuriating aspects of
        westernization at Chulalongkorn University. Illustrations are
        provided by drawings made by some of the volunteers.

1262   U. S. Department of State. Togo. Peace Corps Program. Agree-
        ment Effected by Exchange of Notes Dated at Lome August 1 and
        September 4, 1962. United States Treaties and Other Inter-
        national Agreements Series, no. 5191, vol. 13, p. 3,
        Washington, D.C.: Government Printing Office, 1962, 2251-6.
        S9.12:13 Part 3.
            The complete texts, in both French and English, of the notes
        exchanged between Leon B. Poullada, ambassador of the United
        States, and His Excellency Paulin J. Freitas, minister of state
        and foreign affairs of the Republic of Togo, which created a legal
        basis for the service of Peace Corps personnel in that nation.

1263   MCEVOY, MARGARET MICHELLE. "You Just Plunge In". R.N., 27
        (August 1964): 73-5, 92.
            A frank and vivid account of the work of a volunteer serving
        as a nurse in the clinic in Sokode, Togo. Among her experiences
        are adapting to local beliefs regarding parasitic diseases and
        coping with the problems of founding public health programs for
        the schools in the region, as well as the community. As she says,
        "doing a spinal tap by flashlight is an experience to remember."

1264   MAPEL, DANIEL. "Community Grain Banks". Peace Corps Times
        (May/June 1985): 21-2.
            A report on a project carried out in villages in the north-
        ern savannah lands of Togo for the formation of communal grain
        storage banks and improved harvest management techniques. Details
        of the effort are given and information on how to create such

groups is included. The system is highly adaptable to many climates in that it offers a way of stabilizing local food sup- plies in the slack season of the year while requiring little or no significant investment, and thus is a prime candidate for develop- ment assistance on a small scale.

1265 REISNER, GENA. "My African Father". S19.11/2:3/12. Peace Corps Volunteer, 3, n.12 (October 1965): 10.
A volunteer teaching in Woame, Togo recounts her abrupt adoption by the unofficial chief of the community and her lessons in Ewe, offering an example of cultural exchange initiated by the host culture.

1266 "Volunteers Help in Ferry Rescue in West Africa". S19.11/2:1/11. Peace Corps Volunteer, 1, n.11 (September 1963): 3.
A news note reporting on the roles played by two members of Peace Corps/Togo in rescuing a ferry-load of passengers and agri- cultural produce including manioc, bananas, eggs and chickens. The craft had become stranded in midstream and several passengers had been swept away trying to escape.

1267 U. S. Department of State. Peace Corps. Ewe Basic Course. Washington, D.C.: 1968.
Done under Peace Corps contract by the African Studies Program at Indiana University, this volume is a beginning course in the Ewe language of Togo for use with a teacher whose native tongue is Ewe. The text opens with a description of the tonal system of the language, followed by twenty-six lessons presenting grammatical structures of increasing complexity. A dictionary is also provided. The basic lesson format is one of dialogue and repetitive drills. Complete text is available from the ERIC database as document ED 028 444.

1268 U. S. Department of State. Peace Corps. Ewe (For Togo): Communication and Culture Handbook. Washington, D.C.: 1980.
Developed by the Experiment in International Living at Brattleboro, Vermont under the guidance of a returned volunteer from Togo, this text of thirty lessons presents situations drawn from daily life in Togolese society, preparing the volunteer for active participation in that culture. Full text has been entered on the ERIC system as document ED 203 708.

1269 U. S. Department of State. Peace Corps. Ewe (For Togo): Grammar Handbook. Washington, D.C.: 1980.
A handbook of basic grammar rules of the Ewe language of Togo, including analysis of the sound system, a glossary and a brief bibliography. The full text is available on the ERIC data- base as document ED 203 709.

1270 · SCHNEEBERG, NAN and PROSPER KPOTUFE. <u>Ewe Pronunciation</u>,
       Washington, D.C.: Peace Corps, 1966.
          A five-unit text and guide to proper pronunciation of the
       Ewe language of Togo prepared under Peace Corps contract at the
       Intensive Language Training Center at Indiana University. Each
       unit is arranged by a dialogue, vocabulary and grammatical drills.
       Full text is available as ERIC document ED 152 111.

1271   U. S. Department of State. <u>Peace Corps, Kabiye Communication</u>
       <u>and Culture Handbook</u>. Washington, D.C.: 1980.
          Using situations drawn from Togolese life, this volume
       presents useful vocabulary in a structured setting, including one
       lesson entitled "Explaining the Peace Corps." Familiarization
       with the basic institutions and patterns of Kabiye culture is
       emphasized. The full text is entered on the ERIC database as
       document ED 203 685.

1272   U. S. Department of State. <u>Peace Corps, Kabiye Grammar</u>
       <u>Handbook</u>. Washington, D.C.: 1980.
          A text of twenty lessons covering the phonology and grammar
       of the Kabiye language of Togo created by a team from the Experi-
       ment in International Living in conjunction with staff members of
       Peace Corps/Togo and members of that nation's educational communi-
       ty. Basic grammar points are presented in an illustrated format.
       Full text is available from the ERIC database as document ED 203
       684.

1273   U. S. Department of State. <u>Kabiye Special Skills Handbook</u>.
       Washington, D.C.: 1980.
          A text of six sections presenting the Kabiye language of
       Togo in folk tales, daily situations, a history of the Kabiye
       people, cultural institutions, samples from government literacy
       texts and newspaper articles. Format is facing page translations
       in either English or French. The full text has been entered on
       the ERIC database as document ED 203 686.

1274   U. S. Department of State. <u>Tonga, Peace Corps, Agreement</u>
       <u>Effected by Exchange of Notes Signed at Suva, Fiji and</u>
       <u>Nuku'alofa, Tonga, May 17 and 27, 1968</u>. United States Treaties
       and Other International Agreements Series, no. 6534, vol. 19,
       p. 5, Washington, D.C.: Government Printing Office, 1969,
       5486-90. S9.12:19 Part 5.
          The full texts of notes given between Louis J. Link,
       American Consul, and His Royal Highness Prince Tu'ipelehake,
       premier of Tonga, setting forth the legal foundations upon which
       Peace Corps presence in that island kingdom would be based.

1275   "Ask Not For Whom the Clock Tolls". AA1.13e:2/4. <u>InterACTION</u>,
       2, n.4 (January 1974): 13.
          The story of the restoration of a prized clock presented to
       the late Queen Salote of Tonga by Queen Elizabeth of England
       carried out by a member of Peace Corps/Tonga is related.
       Residents of Nuku'alofa are now complaining about the noise level
       of the bells.

1276   "An Endangered Species: Tonga's Sea Turtles". AA1.13:3/8.
        InterACTION, 3, n.8 (May 1975): 7.
             As part of the joint Peace Corps-Smithsonian Institution
        environmental program, marine biologist Richard Braley was
        assigned to the kingdom of Tonga. His project was assessing the
        impact of changing fishing technologies on the sea turtle popula-
        tion, a staple meat of the Tongan diet. In addition to prelimi-
        nary surveys defining the scope of the declining turtle colonies,
        alternative seafood sources of food, such as commercial oyster
        farming, are being investigated. The project began in 1973.

1277   "Peace Corps Volunteer from New Bedford Teaches Science, Math
        in Island Nation". Congressional Record, 121, p.15 (17 June
        1975): 19249.
             The teaching of general science, mathematics and chemistry
        at Tonga High School in Nuku'Alofa is being handled by Mervyn
        Hamer of Massachusetts. This article describes both his teaching
        and living conditions, as well as aspects of Tongan life. In
        1975, there were seventy-five volunteers serving in Tonga.

1278   SCHORR, JEFF. "Tonga". Peace Corps Times (May/June 1985):
        11-2.
             The climate and culture of the Kingdom of Tonga in western
        Polynesia, and the Peace Corps programs there, are profiled in
        this article. A problem for the country is the number of educated
        Tongans who emigrate rather than fill positions at home. Most of
        the volunteers are posted either in or around the capital city of
        Nuku'Alofa, on the regional center islands of Ha'apai and Vana'u
        and are working in fields ranging from education to development
        banking and fisheries. An aerobics class taken over by Tongans
        from two founding volunteers is profiled as an example of
        secondary projects.

1279   U. S. Department of State. Trinidad and Tobago. Peace Corps.
        Agreement Effected by Exchange of Notes Signed at Port of Spain
        July 11 and 21, 1969. United States Treaties and Other Inter-
        national Agreements Series, no. 6736, vol. 20, p.2, Washington,
        D.C.: Government Printing Office, 1970, 2729-33. S9.12:20
        Part 2.
             This document contains the complete texts of notes given
        between Robert B. Elwood, American charge d'affaires, and The
        Honorable A/N.R. Robinson, minister of external affairs, which
        created the legal framework within which Peace Corps would func-
        tion during its presence of this island nation.

1280   U. S. Department of State. Tunisia. Peace Corps Program.
        Agreement Effected by Exchange of Notes Dated at Tunis February
        7 and 13, 1962. United States Treaties and Other International
        Agreements Series, no. 4968, vol. 13, p. 3, Washington, D.C.:
        Government Printing Office, 1962, 249-53. S9.12:13 Part 3.
            The complete text, in both English and French, of notes
        given between Leo G. Cyr, charge d'affaires of the American
        embassy, and His Excellency Dr. Sadok Mokkadem, secretary of state
        for foreign affairs of Tunisia, setting out the legal basis and
        conditions under which Peace Corps workers would serve in that
        nation.

1281   BEN ABDELKADER, RACHED, et. al. Peace Corps English-Tunisian
        Arabic Dictionary. Washington, D.C.: Peace Corps, 1977.
            A supplement to the main text of the Peace Corps/Tunisia
        Arabic course. This text has a chart of all symbols used in the
        language, with nuances of meaning in Arabic not present in the
        English equivalent fully stressed. The full text is entered as
        ERIC document ED 183 017.

1282   BEN ADELKADER, RACHED and AZIZA NAWAR. Peace Corps Tunisia
        Course in Tunisian Arabic. Washington, D.C.: Peace Corps,
        1979.
            Thirty lessons of drills in the Tunisian variety of Arabic,
        based upon the dialect of the city of Tunis and created by Peace
        Corps Tunisia. Each unit stresses dialogues, questions, drills
        and communications activities, including acquisition of Arabic
        script. Full text has been entered as ERIC document ED 183 018.

1283   GALLAGHER, CHARLES F. "Programs and Potential in Tunisia and
        Morocco". The Cultural Frontiers of the Peace Corps, Robert B.
        Textor, ed. Cambridge: M. I. T. Press, 1966, 189-99.
            Terming the Peace Corps work in Tunisia and Morocco "a
        considerable but qualified success", the author, an expert on the
        culture and politics of the Middle East, reviews the host country
        needs and the places which the volunteers are filling there. Two
        general types of problems are visible, operational and procedural
        difficulties. The problems of coping with a host nation where an
        expatriate system is being defended by nationals in the Western
        language presents something of a different challenge. Researchers
        should bear in mind that the picture presented in this essay
        concerns the Corps in these nations as it had been functioning
        between 1962 and 1966.

1284   "Peace Corps Shift". Christian Science Monitor (8 September
        1965): 7.
            Speaking at Brown University in Providence, Rhode Island to
        a group of ninety-three volunteers completing eleven weeks of
        training for service in Tunisia, Franklin Williams, a former
        official of Corps, stated "you're not pioneers anymore." This and
        similar remarks in his address indicated the shift in overall
        perception of Peace Corps volunteers and their experiences by
        American society.

1285   RICE, JOHN ALDEN. "City Life: Seeking a Role Between Two
        Cultures". S19.11/2:5/2. Peace Corps Volunteer, 5, n.2
        (January 1967): 16-7.
            A teacher member of Peace Corps/Tunisia discusses the prob-
        lems posed for those volunteers stationed in an urban setting by
        lack of "traditional" Peace Corps deprivation and cities Tunisian
        examples of ways in which these barriers may be overcome.

1286   "Tunisia: Work Takes New Directions in Ancient Land".
        S19.11/2:2/7. Peace Corps Volunteer, 2, n.7 (May 1964): 8-
        18.
            A collection of short articles written by various members of
        Peace Corps/Tunisia. Among the jobs being done by the ninety
        members of the group are teaching English in Tunis, nursing at
        Hospital Habib Thameur, physical education instructor in Zaghouan
        and city planning and design. Specialists in the latter were the
        first group to arrive in Tunisia on August 15, 1962.

1287   U. S. Department of State. Turkey. Peace Corps Program.
        Agreement Effected by Exchange of Notes Signed at Ankara August
        27, 1962. United States Treaties and Other International
        Agreements Series, no. 5193, vol. 13, p. 3, Washington, D.C.:
        Government Printing Office, 1962, 2263-5. S9.12:13 Part 3.
            The complete text of notes exchanged between the vice presi-
        dent of the United States, Lyndon B. Johnson, and His Excellency
        Feridun Cemal Erkin, minister of foreign affairs, laying the
        foundations for the service of Peace Corps personnel in Turkey.

1288   BARTON, NAN and JAMES W. "Turkey". National Geographic
        (September 1964): 330-3.
            Two volunteers posted as public school teachers to the city
        of Antakya in southern Turkey share their experiences, which vary
        from killing a sheep in celebration of Kirban Bayrami, the
        Festival of Sacrifices, learning the etiquette of social visiting
        and coping with the Turkish system.

1289   BURKE, HOLLIS. "Festive Turks Aid Volunteer Wedding Rites".
        S19.11/2:4/10. Peace Corps Volunteer, 4, n.10 (August 1966):
        15.
            An account of the full participation of two villages in
        Turkey in the wedding of their resident volunteers.

1290   CALHOUN, SUSAN. "A Volunteer Wife as a Gelin". S19.11/2:4/8.
        Peace Corps Volunteer, 4, n.8 (June 1966): 20.
            A married volunteer in Turkey recounts her collisions with
        the traditional host culture concept of what is expected of a
        young bride, including her statement that "the Peace Corps forbids
        babies."

1291   COOLEY, JOHN K.   "Americans and Turks Join to Help Children".
        Christian Science Monitor (21 December 1968):   7.
            Of the two hundred thirty-eight volunteers in Turkey, most
        are involved in education and child care.   Examples are given of
        Corps personnel working in a home for street boys in Istanbul,
        teaching English, and assisting Maarif College with curriculum
        improvement and teacher training.   General reception of the volun-
        teers has been positive, despite criticisms in certain sectors of
        the Turkish press.

1292   PASLOV, EUGENE.   "Is it 'Peace Corps' in the City?".
        S19.11/2:2/9.   Peace Corps Volunteer, 2, n.9 (July 1964):   4.
            A member of Peace Corps/Turkey, stationed at the Middle East
        Technical University near Ankara, reflects on the "mud hut" image
        of the volunteer current in the press and concludes that "there is
        no one kind of job that a volunteer does."

1293   "Turkey".   S19.11/2:1/11.   Peace Corps Volunteer, 1, n.11
        (September 1963):   6-15.
            A collection of eight brief articles by members of Peace
        Corps/Turkey detailing their joys and adaptations to a land not
        really considered underdeveloped and with a substantial cultural
        tradition and pride.   Sites represented include Pendik, Ceyhan,
        Cankiri, Karabuk, Mersin, Kirikkale and Kastramanu.   Assignments
        included teaching English, working with heavy equipment and summer
        camp construction near the Black Sea.   The insights into one of
        the most unusual of Peace Corps host nations situations are
        striking.

1294   U. S. Department of State.   Peace Corps. Agreement Between the
        United States of America and the Turks and Caicos Islands
        Effected by Exchange of Letters Dated at Washington April 17
        and December 5, 1980.   Treaties and Other International Acts
        Series, no. 9945, Washington, D.C.:   Government Printing
        Office, 1981.   S9.10:9945.
            The full texts of the notes exchanged between Richard
        Celeste, Director of the Peace Corps, and Sir Nicholas Henderson
        of the Embassy of Great Britain, laying the legal framework with-
        in which the Peace Corps would function in the Turks and Caicos
        Islands.

1295   U. S. Department of State.   Tuvalu. Peace Corps. Agreement
        Effected by Exchange of Notes Signed at Suva and Funafuti
        August 25, 1977.   United States Treaties and Other Inter-
        national Agreements Series, no. 9119, vol. 29, p. 5,
        Washington, D.C.:   Government Printing Office, 1980, 5428-30.
        S9.12:29 Part 5.
            The complete texts of notes given between Robert L.
        Flanegin, American charge d'affaires, and T. H. Layng, Her
        Majesty's commissioner, Tuvalu, setting out the legal framework
        within which Peace Corps service to that nation would function.

1296   U. S. Department of State. <u>Uganda. Peace Corps. Agreement</u>
        <u>Effected by Exchange of Notes Signed at Kampala November 16,</u>
        <u>1964</u>. United States Treaties and Other International Agree-
        ments Series, no. 5735, vol. 15, p. 2, Washington, D.C.,
        Government Printing Office, 1964, 2433-6. S9.12:15 Part 2.
            The complete text of notes exchanged between Olcott H.
        Deming, United States ambassador to Uganda, and His Excellency S.
        N. Odaka, minister of state for foreign affairs, creating the
        legal foundation of Peace Corps service in that host nation. This
        document remained in force until the departure of Corps personnel
        from Uganda in 1971.

1297   KAMOGA, FREDERICK K. <u>Luganda Basic Course</u>. Washington, D.C.:
        Peace Corps, 1968.
            This document is not an outline of classroom instruction so
        much as a group of materials which can be used to prepare courses
        in Luganda. Ninety-four lessons comprise the text which is
        organized according to dialogues, followed by questions and pat-
        tern drills. A glossary and kinship charts of basic units in
        Baganda society are appended. The document has been entered into
        the ERIC database as ED 024 933.

1298   KAMOGA, FREDERICK K. <u>Lunyoro/Rutoro Instructions</u>. Washington,
        D.C.: Peace Corps, 1971.
            A textbook of thirty-two lessons for volunteers training to
        serve in the Lunyoro-speaking areas of Uganda. Format is struc-
        tured around key phrases, dialogues and basic vocabulary. Orga-
        nized by topics such as the weather, daily work and travel. A
        verb list follows the text. This document has been entered in the
        ERIC database as ED 148 157.

1299   KAMOGA, FREDERICK K. <u>Lwo Instructions</u>. Washington, D.C.:
        Peace Corps, 1971.
            A textbook of ninety-five lessons on Lwo, a group of
        dialects spoken in the northern regions of Uganda. Format
        includes pattern drills, grammar and usage and conversation.
        Eight model dialogues are interspersed throughout the text. A
        list of Lwo verbs and a Lwo-English vocabulary complete the
        manual. The full text is available as ERIC document ED 148 160.

1300   KAMOGA, FREDERICK K. <u>Madi Instructions</u>. Washington, D.C.:
        Peace Corps, 1971.
            Prepared for the 1971 training program of Peace Corps/Uganda
        by a faculty member of Makerere University in Kampala, this manual
        of thirty-two lessons covers introductions, common phrases,
        marketing and similar cultural situations and a listing of Madi
        verbs. The full text is available as ERIC document ED 148 161.

1301   MEISLER, STANLEY. "All Peace Corpsmen Pulling Out of Uganda".
       Los Angeles Times (6 October 1072): 5.
           Following upon the death of Louis Mailer, a Peace
       Corps/Uganda volunteer on September 17, 1972 at an army roadblock,
       the agency is quietly phasing out its program in that nation due
       to a general deterioration of security arrangements for the volun-
       teers. Each volunteer is said to have made a personal decision to
       request reassignment for various reasons. This low key approach
       is being taken out of fear of possible reprisals from General Idi
       Amin Dada. With most volunteers having to pass roadblocks to
       reach Kampala, tension has been high. Most Ugandan volunteers are
       travelling to Ethiopia for assignment to a new host nation or
       returning to the United States. Officials of the Ungandan govern-
       ment have tacitly approved the Corps tactics.

1302   "Peace Corps Hit". Christian Science Monitor (13 February
       1967): 5.
           Leaflets from an organization calling itself the "Freedom
       for Africa Movement" were circulated in Kampala, Uganda calling
       for the expulsion of all Peace Corps volunteers from African host
       nations. Uganda at this time had one hundred seventeen volun-
       teers, while Tunisia, where similar pamphlets also appeared on
       February 10 had two hundred twenty. The leaflets depicted a black
       fist striking a caricatured volunteer, who carries "a camera,
       transistor radio and whiskey bottle."

1303   SAIKOWSKI, CHARLOTTE. "Detention of Peace Corps Volunteers--
       Ugandan Ploy?". Christian Science Monitor (10 July 1973): 1.
           The seizure and subsequent release of one hundred twelve
       Peace Corpsmen travelling to postings in Zaire by order of
       President Idi Amin illustrates the difficulty of maintaining
       relations with that nation. No new ambassador to Kampala has been
       named, and the U. S. State Department notes that the removal of
       the one hundred fourteen members of Peace Corps/Uganda in the fall
       of 1972 occurred because they could no longer function
       effectively. The only Americans remaining in Uganda are some
       three hundred missionaries and embassy personnel.

1304   "Uganda Defends Peace Corps". Christian Science Monitor,
       (19 February 1967): 9.
           The Uganda Minister of Education, Joshua Zake, attacked
       recent anti-Peace Corps leaflets as being issued by "enemies of
       progress in Uganda" and called on the people to ignore them.
       Yellow mimeographed sheets calling for the expulsion of Corps
       appeared in Tunisia and Tanzania as well as on the streets of
       Kampala. Minister Zake stated his gratitude for the services
       being rendered by Corpsmen to Uganda.

1305   U. S. Department of State. <u>Peace Corps. Luganda Continuation.</u>
        Washington, D.C.: 1969.
        A secondary text of fifteen lessons aimed at improving the
        grammar of students and speaking ability in Luganda. Extracts
        from the newspapers of Uganda and a large vocabulary are also
        included. The full text is entered on the ERIC database as
        document ED 143 240.

1306   U. S. Department of State. <u>Peace Corps. Luganda Pretraining</u>
        <u>Program.</u> Washington, D.C.: 1970.
        Developed by the Foreign Service Institute of the State
        Department under Peace Corps contract, this is a self-teaching
        text for mastery of the tonal system of Luganda and is linked to
        an accompanying set of tape recordings. Topics discussed cover
        variations of pitch, verb forms and noun classes. The full text
        has been entered on the ERIC database as document ED 055 520.

1307   U. S. Department of State. <u>Upper Volta. Peace Corps. Agree-</u>
        <u>ment Signed at Ouagadougou February 6, 1973</u>. United States
        Treaties and Other International Agreements Series, no. 8183,
        vol. 26, p. 3, Washington, D.C.: Government Printing Office,
        1977, 2681-91. S9.12:26 Part 3.
        The complete French and English texts of the agreement
        between the Republic of Upper Volta establishing the legal basis
        upon which Peace Corps service to that nation would rest. Signa-
        tories are Pierre R. Graham, Ambassador of the United States, and
        S. Zerbo, minister of foreign affairs.

1308   "Ag Magazine Thrives". AA1.13:2/9. <u>InterACTION</u>, 2, n.9 (June
        1974): 7, 10.
        The history of the foundation and development of <u>Essor</u>
        <u>Rural</u>, a news bulletin for members of the agriculture ministry of
        Upper Volta, by two members of the Peace Corps assigned to that
        nation. As of 1974, eight issues had appeared.

1309   "Drought In Upper Volta: Crops Die in the Ground".
        AA1.13:2/12. <u>InterACTION</u>, 2, n.12 (September 1974): 1, 4.
        An overview of the work being done in Upper Volta by the
        sixty members of that nation's Peace Corps contingent coping
        with the six-year Sahel drought. The problem is seen as a combi-
        nation of natural and man-made disasters demanding an attack on
        several levels. Areas involved are health, nutrition education,
        well-digging and improvement and reforestation. Interviews with
        three volunteers in a garden/reforestation project are included.

1310   MILLER, JANET K. "Secondary Forest Products: Burkina Faso".
        <u>Peace Corps Times</u> (May/June 1985): 13-6.
        A member of Peace Corps serving in the West African nation
        of Burkina Faso (formerly known as Upper Volta) reports upon a
        survey of the uses of secondary plants and fruit resources avail-
        able in a section of forest carried out between March, 1984 and
        August, 1984. As part of this survey--intended as a guide to the
        management of forest lands and their optimum potential for the
        country--Miller visited regional markets and urban markets in her

area, making friends with the sellers of medicines and villagers, and learning from them, both by example and by accompanying them on collecting trips, seventy-seven species widely used in local culture. Among the uses documented were food items, craft woods, acidifiers, beverages, forage for domestic animals, fuel, religious resources and construction material. Such researches provide the type of information necessary for effective management of forest resources and serve as an alternative to the wholesale replacement of native forest with plantations of imported products which lack the secondary species.

1311   "Music, Folklore Documented". AA1.13:2/5. InterACTION, 2, n.5 (February 1974): 3, 33.
        In a period of service extending over six and one-half years, James Rosellini, a member of Peace Corps/Upper Volta, has established an archive of Voltan folklore and music. His efforts include traveling about the nation to record, photograph and film the dancers, minstrels and musicians in their traditional roles in market places, at celebrations and in the formal setting of the courts of chiefs. The project was originally proposed by Rossellini in 1969. The collection will be housed in the Volta Center for Scientific Research in Ouagadougou.

1312   "PCVs Cited for Starting Ag Magazine". AA1.13:2/2. InterACTION, 2, n.2 (November 1973): 9.
        The Minister of Agriculture of Upper Volta recently cited two members of the Peace Corps assigned to that nation for their role in launching a monthly magazine for rural development and agricultural extension agents. A typical issue of the publication, known as Essor Rural, covers subjects such as marketing cattle, organizing farm co-operatives and fighting locusts.

1313   "PCVs Help Upper Voltans Build Long-Lasting Wells". AA1.13:2/7. InterACTION, 2, n.7 (April 1974): 6-7.
        As part of the attempt of Upper Volta to cope with the six-year drought of the Sahel region, one of the programs in which Peace Corps personnel work is rural development. In this case, such activities as irrigation, construction of concrete-lined wells and land stabilization are included in this area. Examples of the involvement of volunteers in the digging and clearing of wells in northern Upper Volta are provided. On the average, two years of service will permit a volunteer to build some thirty wells. Photographs illustrating techniques of the construction projects are also included.

1314   "Upper Volta Gets Permanent Wells". AA1.13:1/6. InterACTION, 1, n.6 (March 1973): 1, 8.
        A profile of the work being done by volunteer Peter Persell as part of the Upper Voltan plan to expand the supply of safe water sources throughout the country. The program of replacing dirt wells with cement ones has proven extremely popular and presently has more requests than either teh Peace Corps or the government can fill. Background on the country is given, as is its response to the then-worsening Sahel drought.

1315   "Voltaic Arts Center Grows". AA1.13:2/9. InterACTION, 2, n.9
        (June 1974): 9.
            A brief account of the contributions made by various Peace
        Corps personnel to the establishment of the Voltaic Arts Center in
        Ouagadougou, capital of Upper Volta. These include the introduc-
        tion of batik techniques to wall hangings, teaching embroidery and
        keeping the books. The period covered is from 1969 to 1974.

1316   U. S. Department of State. Uruguay. Peace Corps Program.
        Agreement Effected by Exchange of Notes Signed at Montevideo
        March 19 and July 31, 1963. United States Treaties and Other
        International Agreements Series, no. 5443, vol. 14, p. 2,
        Washington, D.C.: Government Printing Office, 1964, 1455-8.
        S9.12:14 Part 2.
            This document contains the complete texts, in both Spanish
        and English, of notes exchanged between the United States
        ambassador to the Oriental Republic of Uruguay, Wymberley Coerr,
        and His Excellency, Alejandro Zorrilla de San Martin, minister of
        foreign affairs of Uruguay, creating the legal basis upon which
        all subsequent Peace Corps activities in that nation would be
        conducted.

1317   U. S. Department of State. Peace Corps Program. Agreement
        Effected by Exchange of Notes Signed at Caracas April 14 and
        May 28, 1962. United States Treaties and Other International
        Agreements Series, no. 5089, vol. 13, p. 3, Washington, D.C.:
        Government Printing Office, 1962, 1326-30. S9.12:13 Part 3.
            This document contains the complete Spanish and English
        texts of the notes given between the ambassador of the United
        States, C. Allan Stewart, and His Excellency Dr. Marcos Falcon
        Briceno, minister of foreign affairs of the Republic of Venezuela,
        which created a legal basis for the service of Peace Corps volun-
        teers in that nation. This agreement remained in force until the
        departure of Peace Corps from Venezuela in 1977.

1318   ARNOVE, ROBERT F. and JONATHAN SEELY. "Teaching English in
        Venezuela". Overseas, 3 (December 1963): 3-8.
            Two volunteers assigned to the newly-created University of
        Oriente in the eastern Venezuelan city of Ciudad Bolivar describe
        their involvement in both community projects and classroom
        instruction since their arrival in July, 1962. Detailed informa-
        tion on the construction and adaptation of American curricular
        approaches to Venezuelan needs is included.

1319   PCV's Help Artisans Receive Fair Prices". AA1.13:2/9.
        InterACTION, 2, n.9 (June 1974): 1, 8.
            An account of the work done in Venezuela by members of the
        Peace Corps to conduct a survey of the handicrafts industry. The
        data was requested by the Venezuelan Foundation for the Develop-
        ment of Socioeconomic Activities in an attempt to eliminate the
        middlemen, traditionally a source of inequity in the marketing of
        craftworks. Urban and foreign market surveys were also done.

1320   "Peace Corps Aide Slain in Venezuela". New York Times
        (21 February 1065): 1.
            A twenty-four-year old member of the staff of Peace Corps
        Venezuela, Joseph Rupley, was killed when a group of policemen in
        the Caracas suburb of San Bernardino mistook his party for a group
        of terrorists. The jeepload of people was returning from the
        airport after meeting a volunteer returning from compassionate
        leave in the United States. Earlier that day, the police station
        had been harassed by demonstrations protesting the killing of two
        students in a strike in the city of Merida. Dr. Ramon Salom,
        Minister of Justice, stated that all patrolmen attached to the
        station in question had been arrested.

1321   "Setting Up 'Kinders': The Do's and Don'ts". AA1.13:2/4.
        InterACTION, 2, n.4 (January 1974): 12.
            Practical advice on how to set up and run a preschool in the
        barrios of Venezuela is offered by two Peace Corps women, with
        problems illustrated from their own work. Recommendations include
        not excluding children who have no clothes and teaching basic
        motor skills before attempting to transmit the alphabet.

1322   "Texas Girl Teaches English". Congressional Record, 109, p.23
        (3 March 1963): A1273-4.
            This is a reprinted article from the San Antonio Light
        reporting on the activities of Graciela Ramirez, one of twelve
        volunteers serving as English instructors in eastern Venezuela.
        The program against illiteracy of the Venezuelan government has
        been unable to keep up with the demand for teachers. Volunteers
        make advanced training possible for host country teachers. The
        living conditions of Graciela and her two volunteer housemates in
        the coastal city of Cumana are described.

1323   "Venezuela". S19.11/2:2/8. Peace Corps Volunteer, 2, n.8
        (June 1964): 8-16.
            Introduced by a survey article from the Deputy Representa-
        tive, this group of four articles shares the challenges and
        rewards of service in the early groups of Corps personnel to enter
        Venezuela. Specialties covered include community development,
        swimming classes, cooking and chasing cockroaches. Communities
        represented are Maracaibo, Rubio, Valencia, and the upper Orinoco
        Valley.

1324   "Venezuela PCVs Promote Crafts". AA1.13:1/10. InterACTION, 1,
        n.10 (July 1973): 8.
            A report on the formation of a crafts store in Caracas,
        Venezuela, which specializes in the provision of a fair market for
        traditional local Indian handicraft items. The store, originally
        begun as a staff wife project, was assisted by two volunteers to
        gain the assistance of a Venezuelan government agency which will
        work to establish a country-wide plan for the development and
        preservation of Venezuela's cultural heritage in this area.

1325　WHITE, DIANE.　"P. C. Librarian".　KAT-LOG, 32 (Fall 1966):
　　　　15-8.
　　　　　　Having served as a librarian at the University of Zulia in
　　　　the city of Maracaibo, Venezuela from 1964 to 1966, Diane White
　　　　shares some of the technical problems she encountered in her
　　　　service.　Of particular note is the structure of the Latin
　　　　American university and the ways in which it contributes to the
　　　　work environment.　White concludes by stating that "the volunteer
　　　　whom I replaced described the job of P. C. librarian as an ideal
　　　　one.　I needed no convincing."

1326　U. S. Department of State.　Peace Corps. A Glossary of
　　　　Agricultural Terms, English-French, French-English.
　　　　Washington, D.C.:　1961.
　　　　　　Developed at the American Language Center of the American
　　　　University and adapted by Peace Corps as part of its reprint
　　　　series of specialized program support materials in 1967, this text
　　　　was used to train volunteers assigned to work in agricultural
　　　　extension projects in host nations in Francophone Africa.　The
　　　　full text has been entered on the ERIC database as document ED 148
　　　　159.

1327　KNEBEL, FLETCHER.　The Zinzin Road.　New York:　Doubleday,
　　　　1966.
　　　　　　This is one of the few novels set in the world of the Peace
　　　　Corps.　The story of how a volunteer in the mythical West African
　　　　nation of Kalya becomes involved with domestic political opposi-
　　　　tion, burning　cities, potholes, black mambas and President
　　　　Kennedy conveys the the atmosphere of the life of the Corps
　　　　vividly and accurately with regard to political restrictions and
　　　　regulations.　The most notable expression of the entire text, used
　　　　by the volunteers as a channel for frustration, is "wawa" standing
　　　　for "West Africa Wins Again."

1328　U. S. Department of State.　Western Samoa. Peace Corps.
　　　　Agreement Effected by Exchange of Notes Signed at Wellington
　　　　October 1, 1970.　United States Treaties and Other Inter-
　　　　national Agreements Series, no. 6967, vol. 21, p. 3,
　　　　Washington, D.C.:　Government Printing Office, 1971, 2186-90.
　　　　S9.12:21 Part 3.
　　　　　　The complete texts of documents given between Kenneth
　　　　Franzheim, ambassador of the United States, and the Honorable
　　　　Tupua Tamasese Lealofi IV, prime minister of Western Samoa.　These
　　　　notes form the legal basis for the entrance and service of Peace
　　　　Corps personnel to the Western Samoan archipelago.

1329   MEYER, JOHN F. <u>Samoan Language: A Manual for the Study and</u>
        <u>Teaching of The Samoan Language As Taught by Peace</u>
        <u>Corps/Western Soma</u>. Washington, D.C.: Peace Corps, 1975.
            Designed for use by both teachers and students, this manual
        stresses total immersion in Samoan. Eight units of lessons
        cover nominatives, numbers, pronouns, verb tenses, adverbs and
        adjectives, idioms, conjunctives, miscellaneous and dialogues and
        stories. Appendixes provide a Samoan grammar and glossaries on
        both languages. Full text is available as ERIC document ED 233
        587.

1330   "PCVs Help Samoans Start School for Blind". AA1.13:5/8-9.
        <u>InterACTION</u>, 5, n.8-9 (May 1977): 7.
            A profile of the work being done with the Western Samoan
        Association for the Blind by volunteers Deanna and Curtis Noriega.
        Their tasks have included advising on the construction of the
        Alafamua School, the first school for the blind in Samoa, devel-
        oping curriculum and attempting to modify public and traditional
        attitudes towards blind persons.

1331   "PCV Organizes Teacher Training". AA1.13:2/12. <u>InterACTION</u>,
        2, n.12 (September 1974): 12.
            In recognition of her contributions to improving the Teacher
        Training College at Apia, Western Samoa, Elsie Bach, a veteran of
        four and one half years service, was awarded the title of <u>matai</u>, a
        chiefly rank, by the family of one of her student teachers. She
        is also believed to be the first white woman to receive the full
        Samoan woman's tattoo, or <u>malu</u>, which extends from the feet to the
        knees.

1332   U. S. Department of State. <u>Yemen Arab Republic. Peace Corps.</u>
        <u>Agreement Effected by Exchange of Notes Dated at San'a</u>
        <u>September 30, 1972 and January 29, 1973</u>. United States
        Treaties and Other International Agreements Series, no. 7588,
        vol. 24, p. 1, Washington, D.C.: Government Printing Office,
        1974, 853-7. S9.12:24 Part 1.
            The complete Arabic and English texts of documents exchanged
        between Robert A. Stein, American charge d'affaires, and His
        Excellency Muhsin al-Aini, prime minister of the Yemen Arab
        Republic, creating a legal framework for the service of Peace
        Corps personnel to that nation.

1333   SHIM, K. SHERROD. "Peace Corps Takes High Tech to Yemen".
        <u>Sunworld</u>, 9, n.2 (1985): 46-7, 55.
            A report of a pilot application of solar photovoltaic tech-
        nology to the construction of a water pumping station in the town
        of Hodeidah in coastal Yemen. The history of the project and
        similar projects underway by Peace Corps workers in Yemen is
        recounted, with accent on this type of assistance as an unusual
        form of appropriate technology.

1334   "Amin Screams 'Bring Them All Back'". Chicago Tribune, 9 July
        1973, Section 1: 13.
            Ugandan officials who requested anonymity reported that
        President Amin had been at the Entebbe airport on July 8, 1973.
        Upon learning that a departing plane was carrying Peace Corps
        volunteers, he screamed that they should all be brought back
        immediately. Instructions to return or be shot down by two
        Ugandan Air Force jets circling over Entebbe were then relayed to
        the flight. The spontaneity of this decision was a great shock to
        most of the witnesses.

1335   "Boosting Food Production In Zaire". AA1.13:3/10.
        InterACTION, 3, n.10 (July 1975): 7-9.
            A profile of the types of projects in which volunteers
        assigned to the Ministry of Agriculture in the central African
        nation of Zaire are participating. Objectives are to increase
        overall crop yields and introduce appropriate technologies to
        achieve this. Several volunteers of Peace Corps/Zaire are inter-
        viewed and the history of their work recounted.

1336   "Mom Asks God's Help for Daughter". Chicago Tribune, 9 July
        1973, Section 1: 12.
            An interview with Constance Saville of Lake Forest,
        Illinois. Her daughter Nancy was among the one hundred twelve
        volunteers being held under order of President Amin at the Entebbe
        airport. Upon hearing of the fear that the group might be merce-
        naries, she commented "there's nothing less ominous . . . than a
        bunch of Peace Corps Volunteers."

1337   "111 Americans Resting in Zaire After Detention". Chicago
        Tribune, 11 July 1973, Section 1C: 2.
            The group of volunteers intercepted by President Amin of
        Uganda were reported recovering quickly from the experience in
        Kinshasa, Zaire. The sixty-three men and forty-eight women
        reported no physical harm from the ordeal.

1338   "111 Peace Corps Volunteers Freed by Uganda Chief". Chicago
        Tribune, 10 July 1973, Section 1A: 9.
            After some fifty-one hours of detention, one hundred eleven
        Peace Corps volunteers were permitted to continue their journey to
        Zaire by Uganda's President Idi Amin Dada. Their release followed
        assurances by President Mobutu Sese Seko of Zaire that "the volun-
        teers were welcome in his country and were neither mercenaries nor
        Israeli agents". The majority of them will be posted as teachers
        in the eastern highland of Zaire. A special chartered aircraft
        was sent by President Mobutu to bring the group to Kinshasa.

1339   "PCVs' Behavior 'Commendable'". AA1.13:1/12. InterACTION, 1,
        n.12 (September 1973): 2.
            An editorial remarking upon the way in which the one hundred
        eleven volunteers held by General Idi Amin responded to their
        situation with suitable restraint, and the positive publicity
        gained for the agency as a result of the affair.

1340   "Peace Corps Volunteers Seized in Uganda". Christian Science
        Monitor, 1 July 1973: 6.
             One hundred twelve volunteers en route to service and train-
        ing in Zaire were removed from their chartered East African Air-
        ways jet at Entebbe airport and interned in the Lake Victoria
        Hotel. No reasons for this action were given by the government of
        President Idi Amin Dada.

1341   "Uganda Detains Planeload of 112 Peace Corpsmen". Chicago
        Tribune, 8 July 1973, Section 1: 27.
             An East African Airways flight transporting 112 volunteers
        to Bujumbura enroute to service in Zaire was ordered back to the
        airport at Entebbe, Uganda almost immediately after taking off
        from a refueling stop, on July 7, 1973. No reason was given for
        the detention by officials of the government of President Idi
        Amin. Relations between the United States and Uganda had worsened
        in recent months, although State Department officials indicated
        that "the responsibility for the incident seemed to rest with teh
        head of state."

1342   "Uganda Holds 112 Americans". Chicago Tribune, 9 July 1973,
        Section 1: 1, 13.
             Charging that "these could be mercenaries trying to enter
        Rwanda through Burundi", President Idi Amin ordered the detention
        of one hundred twelve Peace Corps volunteers enroute to the train-
        ing camp at Bukavu, Zaire. Their flight had barely cleared the
        field at Entebbe when it was ordered to return or be shot down.
        Upon landing, the plane was surrounded by one hundred troops of
        the Ugandan Army. Passengers were removed and held in the airport
        transit lounge. In Washington, State Department officials
        referred to a sharp exchange of notes between Amin and President
        Nixon which ordered America to "stop meddling in the affairs of
        other nations."

1343   RADFORD, JEFF. "Uganda Releases 112 in Peace Corps".
        Christian Science Monitor, 10 July 1973: 3.
             The planeload of volunteers bound for Zaire seized at
        Entebbe were released to continue their interrupted journey to
        Burundi. They were interned in a local hotel "until some accept-
        able entity--excluding the U. S. Government--could vouch for their
        identity". Their credentials were supported in a formal message
        from President Mobutu Sese Seko of Zaire to Amin.

1344   "Uganda Silent on Anti-U.S. Move". Christian Science Monitor
        11 July 1972: 2.
             The detention of one hundred twelve volunteers in Uganda is
        placed in the recent political history of that portion of Africa,
        with a military coup in Rwanda, massacres in Burundi and a failed
        invasion attempt by Uganda exiles based in Tanzania all contrib-
        uting to an atmosphere of nerves and suspicion. The episode gave
        these volunteers "a more insightful introduction to African
        realities than any training course could have."

Returned Volunteers

1345   "ACTION Staff One-Fifth PC/VISTA Volunteers". AA1.13:4/5.
InterACTION, 4, n.5 (March 1976): 1, 4.
    As of March, 1976, some three hundred eighty-one veterans of
Peace Corps and the VISTA program were working in various capacities on the ACTION staff. This figure represented twenty-one percent of all positions in the agency, with appointments often at a
high level. Statistical data for the 1975 fiscal year are
provided.

1346   "Afghan Refugees". AA1.16:2/2. Reconnection, 2, n.2
(September 1979): 3.
    American Friends of Afghanistan, an organization founded by
returned Peace Corps volunteers, requests assistance in aiding the
estimated 135,000 refugees now living in border camps in Iran and
the Northwest Frontier Province of Pakistan.

1347   "'Alumni' Busy In Training, Staff Posts". S19.11/2:2/1. Peace
Corps Volunteer, 2, n.1 (November 1963): 5.
    As of November, 1963, sixty-six Peace Corps veterans were
working for the agency in various training and staff roles. A
list of these persons and their country of service is provided.

1348   AMIDEI, NANCY. "Magic From Below: Anniversary for an Ideal".
Commonweal, 113, n.17 (10 October 1986): 517-8.
    A spirited account of the twenty-fifth anniversary reunion
held for returned volunteers and staff in a great white tent on
the Mall in Washington, D.C., on September 18, 1986. Featured
speakers included Her Excellency Madame Corazon Aquino, President
of the Philippines, Loret Ruppe, current Director of the Peace
Corps, and Sargent Shriver. A memorial march and service to honor
the one hundred ninety-eight volunteers killed in service since
the beginning of Corps and embassy receptions were also part of
the event. The author is a returned volunteer from Peace Corps/
Nigeria in the 1960's.

1349   "Arab/Islamic Group in the Works". AA1.16:2/2. <u>Reconnection</u>,
        2, n.2 (September 1979): 9.
            The response to a request for contact by returned volunteers
        who served in host nations in the Islamic world has been encourag-
        ing. Fields represented include journalism, Islamic studies,
        international business and the media. A call is issued for the
        possible formation of a national network of volunteers from this
        part of the world.

1350   AUGUSTIN, CHARLES. "Square Roots In Africa". <u>Christian
        Science Monitor</u> (29 December 1986): 13.
            A letter from a veteran of Peace Corps/Zaire addressing the
        need for mathematical proficiency as part of the basis of African
        development. With more than three hundred volunteers in the field
        now as mathematics teachers, and twenty-five years of experience
        the Corps is able to answer this all well as other skills needed
        by the developing of nations of Africa and elsewhere.

1351   "Beyond War Award Ceremony". <u>Peace Corps Times</u> (December
        1987): 3.
            Excerpts from the speech given by Loret Miller Ruppe, Direc-
        tor of the Peace Corps, on Sunday, December 6, 1987 at a ceremony
        honoring all present and former Peace Corps volunteers in San
        Francisco, California. By decision of the Beyond War Foundation,
        their annual award, a column of Steuben crystal engraved with the
        continents of the Earth on three sides, was presented to represen-
        tatives of both returned and currently serving volunteers.

1352   "Boat People". AA1.16:2/2. <u>Reconnection</u>, 2, n.2 (September
        1979): p.2.
            A summary article detailing the efforts of former volunteers
        working with Southeast Asian refugees, some 400,000 of whom are
        presently in camps in Thailand, Malaysia and the Philippines.
        Speaking at an International Refugee Conference in Geneva,
        Switzerland held July 20-21, 1979, Vice-President Walter Mondale
        stated the willingness of the United States to assign qualified
        Peace Corps personnel to these camps. The proposal has been made
        to the United Nations High Commission for Refugees (UNHCR) and
        discussions are planned.

1353   BOWSER, HALLOWELL. "Rattling Good History". <u>Saturday Review</u>
        (3 April 1965): 26.
            A conference of returned Peace Corps volunteers held in
        Washington, D.C. in March, 1965 is described in detail. Most of
        the panel discussions dealt with re-entry and coping with American
        employment opportunities. Also raised was what the purpose of
        RPCV's should be in their own country and what they could possi-
        bly contribute to the United States. Of note is the vote taken on
        creating an organization of returned volunteers--the proposal was
        turned down. The title is taken from a comment made by President
        Lyndon Johnson that "the Peace Corps has made the pursuit of peace
        rattling good history."

1354   "Breakfast for RPCV's Proved a Capitol Idea". AA1.13:4/9-10.
        InterACTION, 4, n.9-10 (June-July 1976): 1, 7.
            An informal breakfast meeting was held on May 11, 1976 at
        the U. S. Capitol for some forty former Peace Corps members, now
        serving as Congressional staff members and Congress members them-
        selves. Rep. Chris Dodd of Connecticut and Paul Tsongas of
        Massachusetts hosted the event, at which ACTION Director Michael
        Balzano briefed the audience--most veterans from the 1960's--on
        current agency work and Peace Corps Director John Dellenback
        addressed current priorities.

1355   BROWN, PAT. "Do RPCV's Really Make a Difference?".
        S19.11/2:5/4. Peace Corps Volunteer, 5, n.4 (February 1967):
        2-5.
            This article considers the role played by returned volun-
        teers in the functioning of the agency, finding them to be solidly
        represented on staff but ineffectual as regards most decisions of
        policy.

1356   BUHLER, FRANCHOT. "Lessons from the Peace Corps". Harpers,
        246 (February 1973): 7.
            In this letter, the writer details her observations of
        returning volunteers and the ways in which they cope with being
        "strangers in their own land." Problems include readjustment to
        professional life, networking with other returned volunteers for
        support, and "a healthy case of reverse culture shock."

1357   CALVERT, ROBERT. "The Returning Peace Corps Volunteer--What
        Happens To Him". Journal of College Placement, 26 (April-May
        1966): 55-64.
            This overview of the Career Information Service of the Peace
        Corps, written by its founder and director, provides detailed
        information on the methods used to counsel the returning Corps
        members. Information packets are distributed to volunteers on-
        site in their last year of service, and arrangements made to
        obtain career data. In addition, many of them are referred to
        established sources such as college placement offices and profes-
        sional societies. CIS also studies the career plans of returning
        personnel, which often change significantly as a result of their
        time abroad. The fields of continuing education, teaching, gov-
        ernment work and business attract the majority of the groups.
        Executive Order 11103 providing for non-competitive hiring of
        volunteers for federal employment, is also mentioned.

1358   CALVERT, ROBERT. "The Returning Volunteer". Annals of the
        American Academy of Political and Social Science, 365 (1966):
        105-18.
            Calvert, Director of the Career Information Service of the
        Peace Corps since September, 1963, describes the problems and
        challenges faced by returning volunteers. After five years, some
        seven thousand volunteers had completed their service and re-
        entered American life with varying degrees of success. Details of
        the operations of the Career Information Service, the re-entry
        period experienced by volunteers (made more sudden by jet speeds

of return), effects of Peace Corps experiences upon career choice-
-often a spur to graduate training (or entry into government
service in other capacities) business and industry--and reactions
of the returned volunteer make this an extremely valuable account
of the Peace Corps in its first five years of existence.

1359   CALVERT, ROBERT. "Two-Way Street: Peace Corps and N.Y. State
         Teachers". New York State Education, 54 (October 1966): 15- 7.
              This article examines both the contribution made by Peace
         Corps Teachers to foreign education systems, with Ethiopia,
         Nigeria and Ecuador specifically cited, and looks at the ways in
         which their expertise can be used in the United States. New York
         State Commissioner of Education James Allen's work at making
         possible the maximum number of places and internships for
         returning volunteers through accreditation and reduced teaching
         loads is also detailed.

1360   CALVERT, ROBERT and PADRAIC KENNEDY. "Career Assistance for
         Returning Peace Corps Volunteers". Personnel and Guidance
         Journal, 43 (January 1965): 447-50.
              "There is no career in the Peace Corps". Beginning with
         this statement, an outline of the services offered to the
         returning volunteer through the Career Information Service is
         presented. Three goals are listed for the CIS: to publicize
         educational and employment opportunities for volunteers, answering
         individual queries, and serving as liaison to established place-
         ment institutions.

1361   CHAMBERS, ANDREA. "After the Peace Corps--What?". Christian
         Science Monitor (30 June 1972): 14.
              The difficulties faced by returning volunteers in the early
         1970's are examined in this short essay. Changes in political
         climate (both in the United States and host nations, due to
         involvement in Viet Nam and overall American foreign policy) have
         resulted in protest letters to the press and a disillusionment on
         the part of many volunteers with Peace Corps goals. Host country
         demands for skilled workers has proven to be a factor in the
         reduction of Corps numbers. While a Harris poll of one thousand
         five hundred eighty-two returnees showed ninety-one percent to
         believe that the experience had been of personal value, seventy-
         four percent also believed their time had been of little benefit
         to their host nation. Returned Peace Corps volunteers in the job
         market usually affiliate with social service agencies. A marked
         decline of interest in hiring volunteers is noted from the 1960's.
         An official of the agency observed that "as Peace Corps loses its
         luster through time, the number of organizations who want Peace
         Corps volunteers diminishes."

1363   Citizen in a Time of Change: The Returned Peace Corps
        Volunteer. Report of the Conference, Washington, D.C., March
        5-7, 1965. Washington, D.C., 1965.
            In January, 1965, Vice President Hubert Humphrey was
        appointed Chairman of the Peace Corps National Advisory Council by
        President Lyndon Johnson. Among his charges was the calling of a
        conference of returned Peace Corps volunteers as soon as possible.
        Citizen In A Time Of Change is the report issued by that confer-
        ence, held at the Department of State in Washington in March,
        1965. The three-day sessions addressed a wide array of topics:
        twenty-four separate workshops were held, each issuing its own
        reports and recommendations, which are printed in full in this
        volume. Subjects debated were local community involvement, read-
        justment to American society, need for a network of returned
        volunteers, primary and secondary education, foreign students,
        government and contemporary social ferment, colleges and
        universities, international service and the potential of returned
        volunteers, involvement in revitalizing the labor movement, train-
        ing programs and objectives, business, programming and the draft.
        An abridged transcript drawn from the full recordings made at the
        plenary sessions forms the bulk of the work. Speakers at these
        sessions ranged from Sargent Shriver, Chief Justice Earl Warren
        and Secretary of Defense Robert McNamara to returned volunteers
        then active in education, business and political work. An
        appendix of "afterthoughts" presents excerpts from letters written
        to Shriver following the meetings, as well as newspaper coverage
        of the conference. As the first effort at establishing a
        consensus of the problems facing returning volunteers, their
        perceptions of the value of Peace Corps in their lives and
        organizing their suggestions for change, this document is invalu-
        able to the historian of Peace Corps activity. One noteworthy
        recommendation was the rejection of the one thousand attending of
        the formation of a national organization to represent them.

1363   CLEARY, PATRICIA K. "Back to the Land Via the Peace Corps".
        Mother Earth News, 50 (1979): 69-70.
            A volunteer with service in Yemen and Barbados reports on
        how her life and her husband's were reoriented through the Third
        World living experience of Peace Corps to the rural life movement
        in the United States. Details of both their lives in the field
        are included, as well as the utility of certain sources on back-
        to-the land information.

1364   CUBAN, LARRY. "Cardozo Project In Urban Teaching". Education,
        88 (February 1968): 216-20.
            The Cardozo, Peace Corps Pilot Project in Urban Teaching
        began in May, 1963, funded by the President's Committee On
        Juvenile Delinquency. Its goals were twofold: to improve the
        quality of education in the urban schools of America through
        "reconstructing what happens between 9 A.M. and 5 P.M." (p. 220)
        and to train returned Peace Corps volunteers as history,
        mathematics, science and English teachers. A detailed outline of
        the project structure of paired interns and master teachers,

development of curricular materials, and after-school contact with
students is provided. While admitting that, after three years,
"no systematic evaluation of the project has been undertaken",
general impressions of both trained teachers and students are
positive. A reworking of the American urban educational structure
is called for using Cardozo as a model.

1365   "Culture Shock". Newsweek, 65 (15 March 1963): 30-3.
        A conference of one thousand returned volunteers held in
Washington, D.C. in March, 1965 is used as a focus for the discussion of problems of re-entry encountered in some professions and
ways to deal with them. Two volunteers from Belize and West
Pakistan are interviewed. Difficulties raised include employers
who regard service in the Peace Corps as a liability on work
histories and questions of how best to apply the overseas
experience for the benefit of American society.

1366   DARLING, LYNN. "Coming Home: Peace Corps--20 Years of Its
        Messages". Washington Post Section B (20 June 1981): 4, 6.
        On June 19-20, 1981, two thousand returned Peace Corps
volunteers gathered on the campus of Howard University in
Washington, D.C. to celebrate the twentieth anniversary year of
the organization's existence and to discuss ways of applying their
overseas heritage to American society. Speakers at the conference
included His Excellency Edward Seaga, prime minister of Jamaica,
Sargent Shriver, and Loret Ruppe. Program cuts due to budget
reductions were met with loud protests. Interviews with RPCV's
from Lesotho and Turkey illustrate the shifting orientation of
Corps programming from generalists in the 1960's to more specialized personnel such as librarians and woodworking instructors in
the 1970's.

1367   "East-West Center Puts PC Overseas Experience to Work".
        AA1.13:4/12. InterACTION, 4, n.2 (September 1976): 5.
        An account by Dennis Olkowski, Peace Corps/Fiji, of the
opportunities for Peace Corps veterans at the East-West Center in
Honolulu. Three returned volunteers working at the center are
interviewed.

1368   "Ex-PCVs to Serve in Emergencies". AA1.13:2/10. InterACTION,
        2, n.10 (July 1974): 3.
        In a joint announcement with the Peace Corps director, Mayor
Tom Bradley of Los Angeles, noted that over one hundred former
Peace Corps volunteers have offered their experiences to form a
"skills bank" for community problems in the Los Angeles area.
Subjects covered by the group include education, management,
business and social services.

1369   "Ex-Peace Corps Aide Starts 'Summer '64 Tutor Corps'".
       S19.11/2:2/11. Peace Corps Volunteer, 2, n.11 (September
       1964): 2.
            A reprinted piece from Time magazine of the work done by
       Robert Binswanger, a former training officer for volunteers
       assigned to West Africa, in creating a tutoring program for five
       hundred thirty-five students in the Greater Cleveland, Ohio area.
       A history of the program structure and function is given.

1370   "Eye Care, Inc., Serving People of Haiti". Congressional
       Record, 129, n.75 (1 June 1983): E2622-3.
            A summary of the origins and activities of Rye Care, Inc.,
       founded by RPCV Timothy Carroll. Working as part of the host
       country medical establishment, its efforts at training Haitian
       ophthalmologists and expanding medical care for the populations
       surrounding its five clinics, this organization is an illustration
       of what well planned foreign aid can do in the private sector. It
       stands as one returned volunteer's dream made real. Carroll
       stated that Eye Care came out of a visit made to Haiti with a
       friend in 1977, but that a lot of the background to the effort
       "was all in the Peace Corps experience."

1371   "Former PC/VISTA Volunteers Rechanneled". AA1.13:2/7.
       InterACTION, 2, n.7 (April 1974): 2.
            Returning Peace Corps volunteers and VISTA members may
       continue to serve in voluntary action projects organized through
       if (the Independent Foundation), a group dedicated to social
       change. Created by alumni of the two programs in 1969, activities
       such as community networking in Los Angeles and health care in
       Washington, D.C. are examples of the type of involvement offered.
       A profile of the organization is given and regional offices
       indicated.

1372   "Former PCVs, VISTAs Keep Commitment Through if". AA1.13:4/12.
       InterACTION, 4, n.12 (September 1976): 9-10.
            The Independent Foundation (if), an organization of some
       fifteen hundred Returned Peace Corps volunteers and VISTA members,
       is reviewed as a way of maintaining participation in voluntarism
       following completion of formal service. Ten local chapters were
       in existence in 1976.

1373   "Former Volunteer Directs Community Center". S19.11/2:2/12.
       Peace Corps Volunteer, 1, n.12 (October 1964): 4.
            A veteran of Peace Corps/Philippines, Lila Ballendorf, has
       been appointed the first full-time director of Hollyday House, a
       community neighborhood center in Washington, D.C. Her husband,
       Dirk, is teaching in the Cardozo High School project in the same
       area of the city. Details of the project are included.

1375   "Former Volunteer Aid in Refugee Resettlement". National
        Council of Returned Peace Corps Volunteers Newsletter, 1, n.1
        (July 1980): 1.
            A news item reporting on the involvement of returned Peace
        Corps volunteer organizations in the massive effort to resettle
        the 208,000 Indochinese refugees applying to the United States.
        Four test sites are planned to develop possible long-range plans
        for involvement in New Jersey, Colorado, California and North '
        Carolina. The proposal was endorsed by the National RPCV Council
        in October, 1979.

1375   FUCHS, LAWRENCE H. "The Peace Corps and American
        Institutions". The Task of Universities in a Changing World,
        Stephen D. Kertesz, ed. London: University of Notre Dame
        Press, 1971, 174-97.
            Fuchs begins his examination of the impact of returning
        volunteers on American institutions and their involvement in
        training and recruitment by stating "virtually no hard research
        has been authorized by the Peace Corps on the subject" (p. 175).
        Institutions viewed from the perspective of Peace Corps impact are
        the Foreign Service, the university community, and private organi-
        zations. Among the latter are the civil rights groups and many
        organizations such as the Teacher Corps. The bulk of the article
        is concerned with Peace Corps and the universities. Returned
        volunteers have also been very active in political action
        campaigns, ranging from the support by the Madison Committee of
        Returned Volunteers of Sen. Eugene McCarthy to the vocal criti-
        cisms of the U. S. involvement in Vietnam of the Committee of
        Returned Peace Corps Volunteers of New York. The extremist views
        of the National Committee of Returned Volunteers, calling for the
        abolition of the organization itself as a tool of American imperi-
        alism are also noted. Basic change in institutions is seen as
        occurring through the changing perceptions of individuals through
        overseas service.

1376   "Grad Opportunity for Agriculture RPCV's". Peace Corps Times
        (December 1985): 9.
            A discussion of the International Agricultural Development
        program of the California Polytechnic. Returned Peace Corps
        volunteers comprise almost ninety percent of the students in this
        program, using their services as the first two years of overseas
        experience requirement. Emphasis is upon a multidisciplinary
        hands-on approach fitting students with the ability to manage
        situations and factors encountered in designing and implementing
        projects in rural development and agriculture.

1377   HARTLEY, RAYMOND. "The Peace Corps Volunteers Return: What
        Are They Doing Now?". Seventeen, 24 (May 1965): 20-2.
            By March, 1965, there were four thousand returned Peace
        Corps volunteers. To accommodate their needs for reentry to
        American society, the Career Information Service has been estab-
        lished. While emphasizing that it is not a placement agency, it
        provides data on scholarships and other opportunities to volun-
        teers completing their tours of duty. A study done on the first

two thousand returnees by the Peace Corps reveals that the majority have pursued further education on the graduate level, with the fields of engineering, mathematics, teaching and social sciences well represented. Employed volunteers represent some forty-one percent of the sample and have centered their work on the federal government, with state governments and international organizations well aware of their potential. The remainder were either traveling or had not yet made a new career choice. A detailed table of percentages is also included.

1378   HELMING, DENNIS. "Return of the Peace Corpsmen". Catholic Digest, 30, n.9 (July 1966): 137-40.
        An overview of the 7,000 returned volunteers in the United States as of mid-1966 and their reactions to American culture and institutions. While the cultural and political views of all had changed significantly, and many were pursuing careers in government or further study, none had gone into the religious life. Reentry crises were seen as proportional to the degree of success and tangible results enjoyed overseas. As a mirror of the first major impact of Peace Corps on American society, this contribution is very valuable.

1379   HIMELSTEIN, MARK. "Returnees Help Foreign Students". S19.11/2:4/2. Peace Corps Volunteer, 4, n.2 (December 1965): 23.
        Following the 1965 Washington conference of returned volunteers, Hugh Jenkins, Director of the Foreign Student Service Council, created an international student community program. In this design, foreign students are matched with Americans who are able to communicate easily and are knowledgeable about the students' home nations. Many veterans have thus far participated, with the number of students accommodated presently set at sixty.

1380   "Information For Returning Peace Corps Volunteers". AA1.10:1/11. Transition, 1, n.1 (December 1972): 19-20.
        The procedures for application to the federal government for non-competitive appointment to Federal service jobs extended as part of the benefits of Peace Corps work are explained for those volunteers wishing to take advantage of the privilege.

1381   JENNINGS, FRANK G. "Are They Asking Too Much?". Saturday Review (15 May 1965): 65-6.
        Addressing the question of whether returned Peace Corps volunteers were asking too much to be allowed to be useful in their own country, this editorial explores what has happened to many of them. Of all the fields reviewed, education is seen to have been the most hospitable to these people. The contrast between assumed maturity in overseas assignments and work considered suitable for beginning professionals in the United States is noted in sharp relief. An insert offers examples of cases in which service in the Peace Corps was discounted by employers as invalid or insufficient.

1382   "Join Peace Corps and Be A Success". <u>Chicago Tribune</u>, 24
        January 1988, Section 6: 1.
            A summary article reporting on the completion of a study
        analyzing the professional lives of former Peace Corps volunteers.
        The results, presented at the 1987 convention of the American
        Psychological Association by Drs. Joseph and Mary O'Donoghue,
        indicate that Corps veterans "are consistently outperforming their
        fellow workers in terms of salary gains and upward career
        mobility." The title of the report is <u>The Peace Corps Experience:</u>
        <u>Its Lifetime Impact On U. S. Volunteers</u>. Three RPCVs in the
        business world of Chicago and New York City are interviewed. Six
        thousand Fulbright alumni were compared with one thousand RPCVs.

1383   KNOWLES, JERRY, TOM PIETRAS and TED URICH. "Peace Corps
        Veterans: An Approach to Urban Education". <u>Contemporary</u>
        <u>Education</u>, 42, n.1 (1970): 35-8.
            A general review of the possibilities of utilizing the
        potentials of returning Peace Corps teachers in the inner city and
        urban schools of America. The bulk of this article is a detailed
        consideration of how a program to certify and reintegrate such
        personnel into the present system would have to be structured.
        The authors are on the education faculty at Purdue University.

1384   KOHNFELDER, EARL. "Peace Corps 'Vets' Draw On 25 Years of
        Helping". <u>Pittsburgh Press</u> (2 March 1986):
            An interview with Representative Tom Murphy of Pittsburgh,
        containing information about his time as a volunteer in Paraguay
        and the subsequent involvement with political matters at home.
        His wife also a volunteer, shares her memories of the time. The
        involvement of returned volunteers in the Greater Pittsburgh area
        in forming an organization is also noted.

1385   KOZOLL, CHARLES E. "The Ex-Peace Corps Volunteer: Asset Or
        Liability In Teaching?". <u>New York State Education</u>, 55 (April
        1968): 28-9.
            Written by a consultant to the New York State Education
        Department, this opinion piece examines the record established in
        that state by returned volunteers who have been recruited for
        teaching positions. While successes have been reported, chiefly
        from districts which have a flexible outlook and have been
        aggressive in obtaining and keeping volunteers, cases of
        mediocrity are noted. Realizing that the Peace Corps itself
        cannot accept the responsibility of determining in what ways these
        returning volunteers can fit into the American educational system,
        a call is issued for the system itself" to ask serious questions
        about . . . specific ways of exploiting these capabilities" (p.
        29).

1386   KREMER, NICK. "What Did You Do for the Third World Today?".
       AA1.10:1/10. <u>Transition</u>, 1, n.10 (November 1972): 7-10.
            A returned volunteer from St. Lucia and Somalia describes
       the work of World Neighbors, an organization involved in the
       promotion of the study of development in American secondary
       schools and colleges. Such groups are offered as a way for the
       volunteer to remain involved in Third World-related activity
       following the completion of Corps service.

1387   "L. A. Conference". AA1.16:2/1. <u>Reconnection</u>, 2, n.1 (May
       1979): 20.
            A conference of former volunteers entitled "The Peace Corps
       Comes Home: A Public Policy for the 1980's "was scheduled for Los
       Angeles on June 23, 1979. The theme of the conference was to be
       the types of work being done by RPCV's with ethnic communities
       within the state of California. Sponsors were the Community
       Volunteers of Southern California and the Southern California
       Peace Corps Service Council.

1388   "Let's Help PC Veterans Teach". <u>Michigan Education Journal</u>, 42
       (May 1965): 21.
            At their conference in Washington, D.C. from April 5-7,
       1965, the National Commission on Teacher Education and
       Professional Standards recommended that school systems put forth
       effort to actively recruit and retain returning volunteer
       teachers. Key elements in such a plan were seen to be clearly
       specified criteria for judging equivalency, involvement of experi-
       enced classroom teachers, individual assessment, and the use of
       academic departments of teacher training.

1389   LONGSWORTH, SAM. "The Returned Volunteer: A Perspective".
       AA1.10:1/2. <u>Transition</u>, 1, n.2 (December 1971): 11-7.
            A four-part questionnaire was mailed out to all returned
       volunteers in 1971, with three thousand five hundred responses, or
       approximately ten percent of the total, being returned. This
       article explores what was considered to be an area to which little
       attention had been paid, the contribution of returned volunteers
       to American culture. While emphasizing that the results of this
       survey are at best preliminary, the data offer a picture of what
       returning volunteers perceived to be their roles and opportunities
       in the early 1970's. The author, a volunteer and staff member
       with service in Guinea, Togo and Dahomey, states in his conclu-
       sions that "it is extremely hard . . . to isolate them for study.
       There are forty thousand of them strung out all over the globe
       doing every imaginable thing . . . They are intellectuals who have
       been to the marketplace . . . idealists who have tried their
       principles in action and they have kept the faith" (p. 17).

1390   MAY, CLIFFORD D. "A Village In the Gambia: 'Welcome to the
       Real World". <u>Christian Science Monitor</u> (15 April 1987): 12.
            An article on the small West African nation of the Gambia,
       with an interview of Evelyn Phillips, a volunteer serving as a
       medical and community development worker in the village of Keneba.
       A brief historical background to the country is also provided.

1391   MCDANIEL, CAROL. "Infant Formula Abuse: Congressional Leaders
        Back ACTION Role". AA1.16:2/2. Reconnection, 2, n.2
        (September 1979): 3, 15.
             The efforts of American firms such as Nestle and Bristol-
        Meyers to persuade Third World mothers that their prepared
        formulas are better than mother's milk for their infants, and the
        problems this poses in light of an increased infant mortality
        rate, are explored in this article. A letter signed by forty-five
        members of Congress sent to President Carter suggested that Peace
        Corps should develop an educational program for all volunteers to
        stop the misuse of formula. Congressman Christopher Dodd,
        RPCV/Dominican Republic has endorsed the letter and a portion of
        this article is an interview with him. Two health volunteers from
        Liberia and Malaysia have called attention to the problem prior to
        this time. With their influence in the community, volunteers are
        in a position to influence the spread of industrial propaganda,
        although the hiring of host country nationals as promoters is seen
        to be difficult to counter.

1392   MCDANIEL, CAROL. "PV's Play Key Role In Women's Political
        Caucus". AA1.16:2/2. Reconnection, 2, n.2 (September 1979):
        7.
             At the biennial convention of the National Women's Political
        Caucus in Cincinnati on July 13-15, 1979, a large number of
        returned Peace Corps volunteers and staff were conspicuous in
        both committee posts and as speakers. The panel entitled
        "Breaking The Barriers: Women In Non-traditional Jobs" featured
        Julia Chang Bloch, Deputy Director for Africa with AID, Eileen
        Mattei (PC-Cameroon) who used her experiences in-country to start
        her own fish farm, and Donna Shalala, Assistant Secretary for
        Policy Development and Research at HUD. A workshop on delegate
        selection and political activities was also held. Former Peace
        Corps Director Carolyn Payton participated in a panel and workshop
        on the International Year of the Child. On August 8, 1979, Debbie
        Harding, former member of the Peace Corps staff, was named as
        executive director of the NWPC.

1393   MCHUGH, PAMELA N. "Returned Peace Corps Volunteers As Resource
        Individuals". Social Education, 34 (January 1970): 87-9.
             The advantages of using returned Peace Corps volunteers as
        speakers in social studies classrooms is explored and advocated.
        More than thirty thousand RPCVs had completed service at the time
        this article was written. The urgency of expanding student aware-
        ness of and appreciation for other nations and cultures is under-
        scored by reference to an item in the New York Times of July 20,
        1969. In this essay, which reported the results of a survey done
        among college-bound students, twenty-eight percent admitted having
        had little or no substantive instruction on Africa, Asia and Latin
        America. The author, a public affairs official of Corps for the
        Midwestern region, notes that Africa, like many other continents
        and countries, "is the 'Dark Continent' only in our knowledge of
        it" (p. 89). The Peace Corps School Partnership Program is also
        discussed.

1394   "MIA Lauds African Leader". AA1.16:2/2. Reconnection, 2, n.2
        (September 1979): 9.
            Minorities In ACTION (MIA), the national organization for
        minority former VISTA and Peace Corps volunteers sponsored a
        reception on June 8, 1979, for Chief Masupha Tseiso of Lesotho,
        representing the Ministry of the Interior. The former president
        of MIA, Dennis Bethea, is a Peace Corps Fellow who has assumed the
        post of Associate Director in Lesotho's Peace Corps program.

1395   "The Middle-Class Revolutionaries Are Home--Peace Corps
        Returnees Are Putting Into Practice Here What They Learned
        Overseas". Congressional Record, 114, p.5 (7 March 1968):
        5689-92.
            A reprinted article from Mademoiselle magazine examining the
        role and impact of returning volunteers upon the professions,
        social service agencies, educational and government institutions
        of America. Problems addressed in this series of interviews are
        locating attractive jobs, coping with culture shock, translating
        Corps experiences into frameworks comprehensible to the employment
        market, and changes in careers. American reaction to the RPCV has
        ranged from academic credits for overseas time and work histories
        to encouraging volunteer application for the Foreign Service. One
        volunteer summed up the experience by stating that "you don't
        change the world--you change yourself" (p. 5692).

1396   "Miz Lillian Honored By Ohio RPCV's". AA1.16:2/2.
        Reconnection, 2, n.2 (September 1979): 8.
            The Association of Returned Peace Corps volunteers at Ohio
        University at Athens, Ohio, recently held a breakfast to honor
        Lillian Carter "for her continued commitment to world peace
        through understanding." The group is composed of both graduate
        students and faculty and is headed by Michael Walker, who served
        with Miss Lillian in India.

1397   "New Cleveland Program". S19.11/2:3/5. Peace Corps Volunteer,
        3, n.5 (March 1965): 22.
            The public school system of Cleveland, Ohio has drawn up a
        plan to utilize fifty returned volunteers in elementary education.
        Beginning with the 1965-1966 school year, a dozen elementary
        schools in the greater Cleveland area will provide openings for
        volunteers who are qualifying for certification. Full details of
        the program and application procedures are provided.

1398   "Peace Corps". Christian Science Monitor (12 May 1986): 17.
            A letter from Diane Botnick of the National Council of
        Returned Peace Corps Volunteers replying to an earlier editorial
        discussing how Americans can know "what's going on overseas." The
        resources information and insights of returned volunteers with
        more than sixty local groups available for community education and
        contribution are noted. The frustration often lies in trying to
        find appropriate channels for communicating this information.

1399   "Peace Corps 1985: Meeting The Challenge. Report Of the Task
        Force On Peace Corps Recommendations-December, 1984".
        Congressional Record, 113, n.1 (3 January 1985): E77-8.
            Following the presidential elections of 1984, the Returned
        Peace Corps Volunteers of Washington, D.C. appointed a task force
        to develop recommendations to President Reagan regarding actions
        deemed necessary for the improvement of Corps. The complete text
        of the resulting report was inserted in the Congressional Record
        by Rep. Tony P. Hall of Ohio, an RPCV from Thailand. Five
        specific points are stated in the report: that Peace Corps should
        set a goal of having ten thousand volunteers in the field in 1985,
        and explore the possibility of re-entering nations from which it
        had departed or to which it had never been invited; that Goal III
        of the Peace Corps Act, the education of the American people as to
        the realities of the Third World, be made a central part of
        programming; that the appointment of in-country directors of Peace
        Corps programs be removed from the ranks of those positions which
        are seen to be political appointments; that, following the tenure
        of the present Director, Loret Miller Ruppe, a suitably qualified
        returned volunteer be appointed to the position, with concomitant
        advantages in recruiting and experience; and that a special
        committee of volunteers be set up to advise the Peace Corps
        Director on operational improvements.

1400   "Peace Corps Policy". Christian Science Monitor (11 November
        1969): 18.
            The acceptance and success of the Peace Corps in its host
        nations has rested in large part on its strenuous efforts to
        remain apolitical. This position is being challenged by members
        of the Committee of Returned Volunteers. The CRV would rather see
        volunteers working to change the political structures of their
        host nations, noting that "real development is often impossible
        without a revolution which carries out an equitable redistribu-
        tion of economic and political power." Such a view is regarded as
        antithetical to the basic idea of Corps service.

1401   "Peace Corps Veterans to Teach and Study In Inner Cities". Phi
        Delta Kappan, 66 (April 1986): 586.
            The Peace Corps, the Teacher's College of Columbia
        University and Xerox Corporation announced an educational partner-
        ship for graduate education in mathematics and science to returned
        Peace Corps volunteers wishing to pursue an M.A. and teacher's
        certificate at Columbia. While participating in the program,
        volunteers would also be teaching in the inner city schools of New
        York City. The goal of the plan was both to use the potential of
        Peace Corps veterans and to expand the supply of teachers avail-
        able for New York and similar urban areas.

1402   PEARSON, DAVID. "The Peace Corps Volunteer Returns". <u>Saturday</u>
        <u>Review</u>, v.   (17 October 1964):   54-6, 74.
            Returning Peace Corps volunteers and their problems are
        discussed from employment and psychological perspectives. Agree-
        ment on the maturational aspects of service was widespread in the
        data drawn from completion of service conference data. Whether
        the volunteer will take up new challenges in American society is
        seen as the next and most vital question facing the organization.

1403   "Peace Corps Volunteers Come Home to Involvement".
        <u>Congressional Record</u>, 117, p.20 (19 July 1971):   25999-26000.
            An insert in the <u>Record</u> of an article originally printed in
        the <u>Louisville Courier-Journal</u> examining what happens to returning
        volunteers and how they adapt to American society again.   Ten
        RPCV's were interviewed in the Louisville area. Most were working
        in education, law and city government. All were unanimous as to
        the value of their Corps experiences, declaring "you are never the
        same."

1404   PIXLER, REBECCA. "Personally Rewarding, But . . . ACTION Can
        be Hazardous to Your Career". <u>American Libraries</u>, 9 (November
        1978):   610-12.
            A personal memoir by a former volunteer librarian in VISTA
        examining the general attitude of the library profession to
        service in the Peace Corps. Misinformation and a tendency to
        dismiss the work out of hand or to undervalue it are seen as
        widespread in the professional community, so much so that volun-
        teers overseas are driven to wonder if they have permanently
        damaged their futures through Peace Corps service. This situa-
        tions is viewed as stemming from librarians' obsessions with
        voluntarism and nonprofessionalism. The author encountered more
        than a year of difficulty in locating a position. A call is
        issued for a serious change in attitudes within the library
        community of the United States on this matter.

1405   POLLOCK, FRANCIS. "Peace Corps Returnees: the New World They
        See". <u>Nation</u>, 205 (3 July 1967):   15-7.
            Written by a returned volunteer, this article looks at the
        political involvement of this group, beginning with early efforts
        at constructing a national organization at the 1965 conference
        "Citizen In a Time of Change". While proposals for a national
        group were voted down at that time, the scene appeared to be
        changing. New York volunteers have created the Committee of
        Returned Volunteers and many of the more than twelve thousand
        returnees are affiliated with one of the eighty local councils.
        Opposition to the war in Viet Nam was one of the main foci of
        these groups' political work. A letter signed by eight hundred
        RPCV's and sent to President Johnson is noted, as is the silence
        from the White House. Created by the Former Peace Corpsmen's
        Committee For Peace, this protest is seen as only the beginning of
        involvement by returned personnel in politics. Developments in
        this area are described as "the most important story yet to be
        written about the Peace Corps and its Volunteers" (p. 17).

1406   Reconnection: The Newspaper for Former VISTA and Peace Corps
        Volunteers. AA1.16:1/1. Washington, D.C.: ACTION, 1978 to
        date.
            This publication serves as an information source for
        returned Peace Corps volunteers (RPCVS) on the continuing work
        being done in their countries of service, the challenges posed by
        changing world conditions, and the manners and response which
        Peace Corps has taken to cope with them. Selected articles from
        the journal have been annotated under the appropriate headings in
        the present bibliography.

1407   ROVERE, RICHARD. "Letter from Washington". New Yorker, 41
        (20 March 1965): 182-6.
            In this general discussion of recent events in Washington,
        space is given over to the conference called by the Peace Corps to
        celebrate four years of existence. With the theme "Returned Peace
        Corps Volunteer--Citizen In A Time of Change", some eight hundred
        and seventy-two veterans attended. A questionnaire sent out to
        all returned volunteers in advance of this conference obtained
        some twenty-three hundred responses. Patterns evident in these
        responses showed discontent with American society and significant
        career orientation as a result of the Corps service. The
        potential impact of growing numbers of veterans upon the institu-
        tions of American society is also speculated upon, with the author
        anticipating many changes for the better.

1408   ROWE, JONATHAN. "Peace Corps Fellows Bring Teaching Skills
        Home to U.S.". Christian Science Monitor (21 November 1986):
        27-30.
            The Peace Corps fellows program worked out by the Teachers
        College of Columbia University and the Hebrew Technical Institute
        is reviewed. Under its aegis returned volunteers teach science
        and mathematics for two years at $20,000 and complete the course
        work for their M.S. at Columbia in night school. The goal has
        been to fill a deep need for math and science teachers in New York
        City Schools. Interviews with volunteers teaching at two schools,
        veterans of Zaire, Tunisia, the Central African Republic and
        Malawi are included. The success of the program has sparked calls
        for its expansion.

1409   "RPCV Is First Black Woman Judge". AA1.13:3/10. InterACTION,
        3, n.10 (July 1975): 5.
            Joan Tarpley of Dallas, Texas served as an instructor at a
        teacher training college in northern Nigeria from 1962 to 1964.
        Following her completion of service, she returned to the United
        States, married and obtained certification as a practicing
        attorney in the state of Texas. Her appointment makes her the
        first and only woman barrister in the city of Dallas.

1410   "RPCVs Hold Reunion in Southern California". AA1.13:5/6.
        InterACTION, 5, n.6 (March 1977):   11.
            In celebration of the fifteenth anniversary of the arrival
        of the first group of volunteers overseas, more than one hundred
        returned Peace Corps veterans attended a reunion dinner in Los
        Angeles, California in December, 1976. This was the first such
        gathering in the ten-year history of the Los Angeles Peace Corps
        Service Council, the nation's largest organization of returned
        volunteers. The event also signaled the beginning of a new
        recruitment drive in the southern California area.

1411   "RPCVs Make Outstanding Contributions to Business, Government
        and Education". AA1.13:4/12. InterACTION, 4, n.12 (September
        1976): 8, 12.
            A survey article examining the contributions made by some of
        the sixty-three thousand RPCVs who were working in the United
        States in 1976. Among their roles were the first black woman
        judge in Texas, city controller of Houston, congressional aides
        and educators. Interviews with several individuals are included.

1412   "RPCV's Organize In Cleveland". AA1.16:2/2. Reconnection, 2,
        n.2 (September 1979): 9.
            Following a social event on July 4, 1979, an alumni group of
        former Peace Corps volunteers is being organized in the greater
        Cleveland area. Contact information is provided.

1413   "RPCVs Tackle Pacific Media Lag". AA1.13:4/5. InterACTION, 4,
        n.5 (February 1976): 3.
            A mass communications study aimed at setting up effective
        media for several island nations of the Pacific is underway
        through the East-West Center Communications Institute in Honolulu.
        Participating are several individuals with service experience
        in the region. One of them, Dennis Olkowski, is interviewed and
        the case of Fiji offered as illustration of the types of problems
        facing the host nations. Media deficiency has proven to be a
        severe handicap to the effective use of national development
        information and its distribution.

1414   "RPCV's To Convene In Omaha". AA1.16:2/2. Reconnection, 2,
        n.2 (September 1979): 9.
            The convention of the Nebraska Area Returned Peace Corps
        Volunteers will be held October 24-27 at the Omaha Hilton in
        conjunction with the University of Nebraska. The convention is
        expected to draw up formal recommendations on Corps for forwarding
        to Director Richard Celeste and to examine the possibility of a
        charter for a national group of returned volunteers.

1415   "Second RPCV Convention Held". National Council of Returned
        Peace Corps Volunteers Newsletter, 1, n.1 (July 1980): 1.
            A news report covering the second convention of returned
        volunteers, held in Omaha, Nebraska on October 24-27, 1979. The
        eighty-two RPCV's in attendance adopted by-laws for the council,
        elected a Board of Directors, and passed resolutions supporting
        RPCV group involvement in aiding the resettlement of Indochinese
        refugees.

1416   SHRIVER, SARGENT. "Free Human Services". Vital Speeches, 47
        (1 September 1981): 760-4.
            This is the full text of the address given by R. Sargent
        Shriver, first Director of the Peace Corps, to the Second National
        Conference of Former Peace Corps Volunteers and Staff at Howard
        University, Washington, D.C., on June 20, 1981. In it, he calls
        for a recommitment to the ideals of peace and caring in finding
        solutions to America's domestic problems and a resumption of
        engagement by former volunteers in debates affecting national
        security and cultural issues. Speaking of the power of caring,
        Shriver stated that "No free market can ever replace free human
        services rendered by one free human being to another human being"
        (p. 703).

1417   SHRIVER, ROBERT SARGENT. "When Peace Corps Teachers Return".
        NEA Journal, 52 (March 1963): 13-4, 75.
            Written by the Director of Peace Corps upon the imminent
        return to the United States of the first groups of volunteers,
        this essay raises the question of how best to utilize and reinte-
        grate this new potential into productive channels in the United
        States. Examples of overseas work in education are given from
        Ghana and the Philippines. Granting academic credit for Corps
        service and waiving practice teaching for certification require-
        ments have been some of the possibilities offered by American
        education and school systems.

1418   SINICK, DANIEL. "The Impact of Returning Peace Corps
        Volunteers". Vocational Guidance Quarterly, 14, n.4 (Summer
        1966): 241-3.
            The twofold impact of the returning volunteers can be seen
        as affecting their society and themselves. Describing the
        phenomenon of reaction to America as "reverse culture shock", the
        author focuses on the generally dim view of volunteers taken by
        the average person. Comments by columnists and speakers such as
        Eric Sevareid that "nothing whatever is owed to the returning
        Corpsmen" (p. 242) have done little to improve the situation.
        Employers appear to pay only lip service to utilizing the skills
        of the returnees. On a personal level, the re-entry period can be
        used to channel the energies of disillusionment towards effecting
        needed changes in American society. This can be done either
        through pursuing careers which offer such opportunities or working
        to educate their countrymen cross-culturally.

1419   STOLLEY, RICHARD B. "The Re-entry Crisis". Life, 58 (19 March
        1965): 98-110.
            Using the occasion of a three-day conference of returned
        volunteers and staff as the pretext, this article delineates and
        explores the psychological and emotional reactions volunteers
        suffer upon re-entering American culture after service abroad.
        Psychological testing indicates two periods of adjustment: the
        first four months of the return and one year later. Problems
        encountered are provincial attitudes, ignorance of other

countries, devaluing of Corps experiences by business and industry, and general incomprehension of how such personnel can fit into the American structure of education and industrial offices. Many of the returning volunteers report a career change, and Peace Corps headquarters has set up a small and rather ineffectual career counseling service. The major flaw in it lies in the fact that it is limited to assisting RPCV's for only one year after their completion of service. Recent Corps information supplied to volunteers in the field has been changed to stress the problems of returning in an effort to minimize re-entry shock. Examples are given of several volunteers and the ways in which they coped with their own crises. The author notes that "in the long haul, the dissatisfaction of returnees with things as they are . . . may be the best thing to come out of the Peace Corps" (p. 110).

1420   STUART, PETER C.   "Peace Corps Returnees In 'Postgraduate' Work".   Christian Science Monitor (18 September 1968):   4.
      A brief historical piece on the Council of Returned Volunteers, a political action group whose membership contains many former Corpsmen. Its activities range from opposition to the United States presence in Vietnam to sharp criticisms of the role and plans of Peace Corps itself. John McAuliff and Aubrey Brown, chairs of the group, are interviewed. Peace Corps has been neutral regarding the actions of this group.

1421   "Support Given to Peace Corps by Two Alumni Serving in Congress".   AA1.13:3/10.   InterACTION, 3, n.10 (July 1975):   1-2.
      A profile of newly-elected Congressmen Christopher Dodd of Connecticut and Paul Tsongas of Massachusetts, veterans of service in the Dominican Republic and Ethiopia respectively. The bulk of the article is their views on both the value of their service to the host nation and its effect on their decisions to enter political life in the United States.

1422   "They Like Peace Corps Grads".   Business Week (22 March 1976):   160-2.
      A review article describing the various ways in which returned volunteers have entered the world of international business, specifically in the areas of banking and multinational corporations. Examples are given from Brazil, Colombia and North Africa. Language training, familiarity with the culture of a specific region and having "already conquered the adjustment problem" are seen as major qualities making returned volunteers attractive to corporations.

1423   "This Is Your Award".   RPCVoice, 8, n.3 (Spring, 1988):   1,4.
      A news summary of the Beyond War Award Ceremony held in San Francisco's Masonic Auditorium on December 6, 1987. At that occasion, the foundation's annual recognition award, a shaft of crystal engraved with the outlines of the continents, was given to all present and former members of the Peace Corps. Accepting for the Peace Corps were Director Loret Miller Ruppe, Katy Hansen, President of the National Council of Returned Peace Corps Volunteers and newly-sworn volunteers.

1424   THURSTON, JUANITA. "Valuable Job of Volunteer". Christian
        Science Monitor (16 June 1971): 12.
            An interview with Franzine Jones, one of nine hundred eighty
        black veterans of the Peace Corps, who is presently working as a
        minority recruiter for the agency. 1971 is the first year Corps
        has made a major effort to recruit black Americans. Jones'
        posting as a volunteer was in the city of Suva, Fiji. The advan-
        tages of service in the Peace Corps for blacks are set out,
        including increased self-confidence and determination to succeed.

1425   TIGNER, BROOKS. "Big Money Jobs: the Peace Corps Link".
        Management Review, 74 (February 1985): 12-4.
            The impact of the large numbers of returned volunteers who
        have found their way into the financial services field is
        reviewed, with emphasis placed upon those institution doing a
        great deal of business with the Third World. Volunteers are seen
        to bring an increased sensitivity, knowledge of culture and
        customs, and a willingness to negotiate in host country terms
        which is a decided advantage to their parent companies. The focus
        of the article is an interview with Peter White, of the Equator
        Bank of Hartford, Connecticut, and his relation of the experiences
        encountered in dealing with various West African governments.

1426   TODD, TRUDY. "On Coming Home". AA1.16:2/3. Reconnection, 2,
        n.2 (December 1979): 9.
            A returned member of Peace Corps/Thailand comments upon the
        ecological insensitivity of the majority of Americans and
        expresses her sorrow and determination to work for change.

1427   WALSH, JOHN. "Peace Corps Physicians: Reflections On the
        Future". Science, 169 (25 September 1970): 1293-6.
            On September 12-13, 1970, a group of more than two hundred
        returned Peace Corps physicians met in a conference near
        Washington, D.C. to discuss the health care crisis of both the
        United States and the Third World. Historically, until 1967,
        service as a physician to the Peace Corps fulfilled the military
        obligation. With the amendment of draft legislation in that year,
        doctors already in practice became the chief source of physicians.
        Although many of the physicians attending were in research or
        administrative capacities, the major theme was the inadequacy of
        care being provided to low income and minority groups. Lincoln
        Hospital in New York City was offered as an example. While
        discussion was heated, no coherent agenda resulted.

1428   WARREN, PAUL B. "The Peace Corps Returnee--Teacher?". Phi
        Delta Kappan, 48, n.10 (June 1967): 520-2.
            The work being done by the experimental National Teacher
        Corps personnel in the Five Boroughs of New York City is profiled.
        This program offers returning Peace Corps teachers a method of
        putting their skills to work in problem areas of the United
        States. Due to the lack of appropriations from Congress, the
        program will not be continued.

1429   WASHINGTON, BENNETTA B. "Growth and Cultural Conflict: An
       Approach to the School's Role in Cultural Enrichment".
       Vocational Guidance Quarterly, 12 (Spring 1964): 153-8.
       The problem of defining cultural enrichment and providing
       programs which convey it to students in a classroom setting is
       discussed by the principal of Cardozo High School in Washington,
       D.C. Issues of promoting a unique self-image in the individual
       student and questions of cultural integrity, inferiority--and the
       school's role in promoting it--and the contribution which can be
       made to American teaching by veterans of the Peace Corps are
       presented. Cardozo High School was at that time the site of an
       experimental project using returned Peace Corps teachers in the
       inner city schools.

1430   "When PCV's Come Home". Newsweek, 73 (17 March 1969): 106- 11.
       The application of the experiences and skills of returned
       volunteers to the American school system through the granting of
       professional credit to veterans for Corps work, and the place of
       such a development within an inward-turning American world view,
       are presented and considered. The foundation of Teachers, Inc.,
       by Roger Landrum, a returned volunteer from Nigeria, is also
       noted. Criticism of this new angle to the Peace Corps experience
       charges that it drains energy away from the main objective of
       Corps in assisting developing nations. Among the most vocal
       critics is the radical Council of Returned Volunteers.

1431   WILSON, JACK A. "Reverse Culture Shock in Cleveland".
       S19.11/2:4/7. Peace Corps Volunteer, 4, n.7 (May 1966): 20- 1.
       A descriptive account of the participation of twenty-eight
       returned volunteers in a program jointly sponsored by the Cleve-
       land Board of Education and Western Reserve University. Under
       this project, the applicants would work in the Cleveland inner-
       city schools for 21 months, while gaining their master's certifi-
       cation. The idea for this effort came from Robert B. Binswanger,
       a former Corps staffer and president of the PACE Association.
       This last is a non-profit organization dedicated to the improve-
       ment of education in the greater Cleveland region.

1432   WOFFORD, HARRIS. "The Peace Corps at 25: The New Work Begins
       At Home". Nation, 241 (30 November 1985): 577-9.
       The roles and activities of the returned Peace Corps volun-
       teers within the American political system have been varied and
       catalytic. Charges that the CIA has attempted to employ or enlist
       volunteers have never been substantiated. Despite continued
       criticisms from both the conservative and liberal elements of
       society, groups such as the National Council of Returned Peace
       Corps Volunteers, and leaders such as Reagan's Director of Corps,
       Loret Miller Ruppe, have been instrumental in keeping the program
       alive and vitally relevant. Properly organized, the one hundred
       twenty thousand returned volunteers can be an effective force for
       change in the United States as they were in their host country
       postings.

Appendix I
Directors of the Peace Corps, 1961-1986

Shriver, R. Sargent Jr.   3/22/61-2/28/66
  Director of the Peace Corps

Vaughn, Jack H.   3/1/66-4/30/69
  Director of the Peace Corps

Blatchford, Joseph H.   5/1/69-7/1/71
  Director of the Peace Corps

O'Donnell, Kevin   7/1/71-4/30/72
  Acting Director for International Operations, ACTION
             7/1/71-1/4/72
  Assoc. Director for International Operations, ACTION
             1/4/72-4/30/72

Hess, Donald K.   8/11/72-9/30/73
  Assoc. Director for International Operations, ACTION

Craw, Nicholas W.   9/2/73-9/1/74
  Assoc. Director for International Operation, ACTION

Dellenback, John R.   4/28/75-5/13/77
  Assoc. Director for International Operations, ACTION

Payton, Carolyn R.   10/11/77-12/18/78
  Assoc. Director for International Operations, ACTION
  and Director of Peace Corps

Celeste, Richard F.   4/27/79-1/20/81
  Assoc. Director for International Operations, ACTION
  and Director of the Peace Corps
             4/27/79-5/16/79
  Director of the Peace Corps
             5/16/79-1/20/81

Ruppe, Loret M.   5/5/81-
  Director of Peace Corps

Appendix II
Periodicals of the Peace Corps

Belize
    Belize. Newsletter
    Belize R.A.P.
    Rice and Beans

Benin
    Benin. Newsletter

Botswana
    Kagiso Kalahari

Cameroon
    Huskayn Nyus

Central African Republic
    Kete Mbeti ti Kota Bule
    Na be ti Afrika

Chad
    Aryal

Chile
    El Trapo

Colombia
    Cloaca
    Home Economics Review

Costa Rica
    La Cadena

Dominican Republic
    Gringo Grita
    Peace Corps Dominican Republic
    VAC Newsletter

Eastern Caribbean
    Eastern Caribbean Newsletter

Ecuador
        Newsletter (title changes each month)

El Salvador
        Newsletter

Gabon
        Gabon Gab

Gambia
        The Bantaba

Ghana
        Talking Drums

Guatemala
        ID

Honduras
        Newsletter--Aiti No Mas

Ivory Coast
        The Jungle Line
        On Dit Ke

Jamaica
        The Kisko News

Kenya
        Habari za Peace Corps: Newsletter of Peace Corps Kenya
                Nairobi, Kenya:

Korea
        Jam Pong

Lesotho
        Pieces

Liberia
        Kuman Ju
        Newsletter

Malaysia
        Pokok pokok
                Kuala Lumpur, Malaysia: Peace Corps Malaysia, 1970-
                (Text in English)

Malawi
        Ujeni

Mali
    Mirage

Micronesia
    Micro Wave

Morocco
    All-vol Newsletter
    Peaceworks
    TEFL Newsletter

Nepal
    Fisheries Bulletin
    Iskool Days
    Machha Samachar
    Village Voice East
    THe Volunteer's Gazette

Niger
    Camel Express
    Newsletter

Papua New Guinea
    Garamut

Paraguay
    Erehwon News

Philippines
    Ang Boluntaryo
    Back to the Islands
    Peace Corps Philippines
    Salaysayan

Senegal
    Newsletter/Teranga
    Sahealth
        Dakar, Senegal: Peace Corps Senegal, v.1, January,
        1980

Seychelles
    Sey What

Sierra Leone
    Di News De

Solomon Islands
      Enikaen Nius

Swaziland
      Incwadzi Yetindzaba/Asisitane/Yetfu

Thailand
      The Aggie Newsletter
      Engineer's Newsletter
      Hey You/Engineer's newsletter
      KLONG
      Sticky Rice

Togo
      PCV Newsletter

Tonga
      Taimi Totonu
      Times

Tunisia
      Newsletter

Western Samoa
      Peace Corps News: Western Samoa

Zaire
      Newsletter

Index

ACTION, 2-13, 45, 77, 105, 116,
136, 150, 164, 193, 206, 211,
243, 314, 323, 338, 341, 383,
400, 415, 455, 481, 1345,
1394, 1404

Afghanistan, 137, 274, 295, 298,
310, 334, 353, 364, 441, 448,
531, 546

Africa, 37, 178, 360, 401

African Food Systems Initiative,
17, 86, 114, 202, 300, 360,
372, 408, 413, 419, 430, 453,
528

Aged See Senior volunteers

Agency for International
Development, 65, 305, 309,
1022, 1215

Agricultural Extension See
Agriculture

Agriculture 17, 20-21, 23, 103,
105, 112, 114, 212, 215, 252,
288, 300, 312, 318, 325, 328,
357, 360, 372, 453, 471, 495,
518, 538, 565, 581, 586, 622-
3, 649, 674, 678, 706-7, 710,
716, 721, 723, 725, 763, 794,
827-8, 835-6, 838, 842, 855,
883, 892, 908, 919, 983,
1000, 1027, 1099, 1105, 1139,
1142, 1148, 1162-3, 1190,
1197, 1200, 1206, 1209, 1212,
1264, 1308, 1309, 1312, 1326,
1335, 1376

AID See Agency for International
Development

Aklanon, 1143, 1173

Alphabets, 703

American Friends of Afghanistan,
1346

American University, 232, 530

Amharic, 737, 740

Anguilla, 546

Animal Husbandry and Livestock,
249, 318, 343, 372, 658,
838,1163-4, 1258

Animation rurale See Rural
Development

Annual Reports, 2-10, 173, 292-
301, 398

Anthropology, 96, 207, 287, 426,
466, 476, 576, 584, 611, 768,
775, 878, 935, 982, 1008,
1051, 1081, 1116-7, 1152,
1170, 1217, 1226, 1254, 1289,
1311

Appropriate Technology, 8, 90,
289, 590, 710, 988, 1006,
1020, 1031, 1333.

Aquino, Corazon. President, 49,
1348

Arabic, 620, 675, 1281-2

Archaeology, 654, 813

Architects, 364, 402, 806, 854,
857-8, 861, 1010, 1029, 1204,
1207, 1250